Drug Metabolism Reviews

Volume 1

Drug Metabolism Reviews

Edited by **FREDERICK J. DI CARLO**

Warner-Lambert Research Institute
Morris Plains, New Jersey

Volume 1

1973

MARCEL DEKKER, INC., New York

MARCEL DEKKER, INC.
305 East 45 Street, New York, New York 10017

LIBRARY OF CONGRESS CATALOG CARD NUMBER: 72-76719

ISBN: 0-8247-1142-4

Current printing (last digit):
10 9 8 7 6 5 4 3 2

Printed in the United States of America

Editorial Board

Preface

Numerous factors have acted synergistically during the last two decades to produce explosive expansion of drug metabolism research. The basic reason is that drug metabolism shares interfaces with so many vital and exciting areas of study. As a consequence, scientists in many fields are interested in drug metabolism, and drug metabolism scientists are interdisciplinary.

At this point in time we toil still to explore the boundaries of the familiar paradigm set forth in less than two pages by Bernard B. Brodie, Julius Axelrod, Jack R. Cooper, Leo E. Gaudette, Bert N. La Du, Choco Mitoma, and Sidney Udenfriend in *Science 121*, 603 (1955). The inevitable result is research which reveals similar vistas from different vantage points. Our reviews reflect this reality.

Drug metabolism has today gained public attention in terms of concern for our environment. It is realized that foreign bodies are being absorbed in quantities which may exceed the capacity of detoxication mechanisms in living systems. *Drug Metabolism Reviews* is addressed to covering this area.

It is now evident that many of the hazards of drug interactions stem from modifications of drug biotransformation. It is clear also that a drug interaction may result after administering a single compound because the interaction may be due to the drug and one of its metabolites or indeed only to metabolites. Enzymology is a major consideration of *Drug Metabolism Reviews*.

There may be a drug lag, but there is no slackening of the pace of performing drug metabolism studies in animals to determine the clinical relevence of toxicological findings and in man to learn about bioavailability, excretion, and all the rest. These endeavors are essential to the drug discovery process and are well within the purvey of *Drug Metabolism Reviews*.

It was one of those rainy and windy days which only Atlantic City bestows so regularly upon convening scientists when Mr. Marcel Dekker and I first met in April of 1970. We talked about developing a communication system to meet the needs of the spectrum of scientists interested in drug metabolism, and we agreed to attempt to summarize and to evaluate critically the rapid flow of drug metabolism information. During the next several weeks, Mr. Dekker and I exchanged ideas, usually by telephone. We also met with Dr. Maurits Dekker, Marcel's father, who pioneered scientific publishing in this country. And in June of 1970, *Drug Metabolism Reviews* was created. Then an international Editorial Board was formed by inviting a small number of distinguished and energetic scientists with germane, but diversified interests. It is a pleasure to have this opportunity to thank all of these people for their counsel, cooperation, and enthusiasm. The outstanding contributions made by the authors of the reviews published in this volume will be evident to all readers. The readers will decide whether *Drug Metabolism Reviews* has succeeded. We shall continue to try.

Frederick J. DiCarlo

Morris Plains, New Jersey
January 1973

Contributors to Volume 1

L. B. BRATTSTEN, *Department of Entomology, Cornell University, Ithaca, New York*

FRANCIS J. BULLOCK, *Life Sciences Division, Arthur D. Little, Inc., Cambridge, Massachusetts*

MILTON T. BUSH, *Department of Pharmacology, Vanderbilt University School of Medicine, Nashville, Tennessee*

JOHN J. COFFEY, *Life Sciences Division, Arthur D. Little, Inc., Cambridge, Massachusetts*

T. R. FUKUTO, *Department of Entomology and Department of Chemistry, University of California, Riverside, California*

S. GARATTINI, *Istituto di Ricerche Farmacologiche "Mario Negri," Milan, Italy*

CORWIN HANSCH, *Department of Chemistry, Pomona College, Claremont, California*

A. HORITA, *Department of Pharmacology, School of Medicine, University of Washington, Seattle, Washington*

M. R. JUCHAU, *Department of Pharmacology, School of Medicine, University of Washington, Seattle, Washington*

STANLEY A. KAPLAN, *Department of Biochemistry and Drug Metabolism, Hoffmann-La Roche Inc., Nutley, New Jersey*

JOSEPH J. MC PHILLIPS, *Department of Pharmacology, West Virginia University Medical Center, Morgantown, West Virginia*

F. MARCUCCI, *Istituto de Ricerche Farmacologiche "Mario Negri," Milan, Italy*

E. MUSSINI, *Istituto de Ricerche Farmacologiche "Mario Negri," Milan, Italy*

ERIC C. SCHREIBER, *Department of Drug Metabolism, The Squibb Institute for Medical Research, New Brunswick, New Jersey*

JAMES T. STEVENS,* *Department of Pharmacology, West Virginia University Medical Center, Morgantown, West Virginia*

*Present address: *Department of Pharmacology, Hershey Medical Center, Hershey, Pennsylvania.*

ROBERT E. STITZEL, *Department of Pharmacology, West Virginia University Medical Center, Morgantown, West Virginia*

WILLIAM L. WELLER, *Department of Pharmacology, Vanderbilt University School of Medicine, Nashville, Tennessee*

C. F. WILKINSON, *Department of Entomology, Cornell University, Ithaca, New York*

KEITH K. WONG, *Department of Drug Metabolism, The Squibb Institute for Medical Research, New Brunswick, New Jersey*

DAVID W. YESAIR, *Life Sciences Division, Arthur D. Little, Inc., Cambridge, Massachusetts*

Contents of Volume 1

Drug Metabolism Reviews

Volume 1

Quantitative Relationships Between Lipophilic Character and Drug Metabolism

CORWIN HANSCH
Department of Chemistry
Pomona College
Claremont, California 91711

INTRODUCTION

In this report we are primarily concerned with metabolism of organic compounds by microsomes. These organelles are the site of a complex set of enzymes which display a remarkable ability to produce many kinds of changes in organic molecules. A number of these enzymes show a particular affinity for lipophilic molecules. The selectivity of the enzymes appears to be much more associated with the relative hydrophobic character of their substrates than the stereoelectronic nature of the carbon-hydrogen bonds which they have such an amazing ability to oxidize.

A problem which has become less mysterious since the pioneering work of Brodie and his collaborators [1] is how the multitude of organic compounds necessary for living processes of animals resists being randomly modified by the numerous microsomal enzyme systems. Gaudette and Brodie showed [2] that for a wide variety of organic compounds, microsomes demethylated only those molecules which were quite lipophilic as judged by their chloroform-buffer (pH 7.4) partition coefficients. A most interesting aspect of their study was the nonspecificity of action displayed by the microsomal enzymes. The electronic and steric structural features of the mole-

1

cules undergoing demethylation appeared to play a minor role in setting the rate of metabolism.

In a later follow-up study Mazel and Henderson [3] came to the conclusion that there was no relationship between the partition coefficients of drugs and their rates of demethylation. However, McMahon [4, 5] obtained results which supported the view of Brodie and Gaudette.

DRUG-MICROSOMAL INTERACTIONS AS MEASURED BY NADPH DISAPPEARANCE

The problem of metabolism by microsomal enzymes is complicated by two features: first, drugs must penetrate to and be bound to the metabolic enzymes; second, a chemical reaction must be brought about, followed by desorption of the product(s). Different structural features appear to govern the rates of the two different processes. For the clearest understanding of the structure-activity relationships, the two processes must be studied independently.

Such a study has recently been carried out using rat liver microsomes in vitro [6]. The data from this work (Table 1) were obtained by following the rate of disappearance of NADPH spectrophotometrically. A most interesting aspect of this study is that despite the wide variation in chemical structure of the compounds in Table 1, there is a small range in the values of V_{max}. In fact, it is only five-fold. Leaving out the one rather active molecule (ephedrine), the variation is little more than threefold. In contrast to this, K_m has a 1000-fold range. Thus a most important fact of microsomal activity is the binding of drug to enzyme. Once this is accomplished, oxidative enzymes attack many kinds of structures in a surprisingly indiscriminate manner. It is difficult to see much relationship between V_{max} and chemical structure. On the other hand, K_m is correlated [6] with partition coefficients as indicated by Eqs. (1) and (2). In these equa-

$$\log 1/K_m = 0.82(\pm 0.58) \log P + 2.46(\pm 0.29) \quad \begin{matrix} n \\ 14 \end{matrix} \quad \begin{matrix} r \\ 0.874 \end{matrix} \quad \begin{matrix} s \\ 0.508 \end{matrix} \quad (1)$$

$$\log 1/K_{m(corr)} = 0.69(\pm 0.19) \log P + 2.90(\pm 0.38) \quad 14 \quad 0.920 \quad 0.330 \quad (2)$$

tions P is the octanol/water partition coefficient of the *neutral* form of the drug, n is the number of data points used in formulating the equation, r is the correlation coefficient, and s is the standard deviation. The figures in parentheses are the 95% confidence intervals. In Eq. (2), corrected K_m values are employed. The corrected K_m rep-

Table 1

Michaelis Constant and V_{max} for Substrates of Microsomal NADPH Oxidase

Compound	log P[a]	$-\log K_m$ Obs[b]	$-\log K_m$ Calc[c]	$|\Delta - \log K_m|$	V_{max} (mμM/min/mg protein)
N,N-Dimethyl-β-naphthylamine	3.55	5.63	5.36	0.27	172
3-Chloro-N,N-dimethylaniline	3.29	4.94	5.18	0.24	109
3-Methyl-N,N-dimethylaniline	2.81	4.73	4.85	0.12	220
4-Methyl-N,N-dimethylaniline	2.80	4.70	4.84	0.14	177
Pentobarbital	2.07*	4.67	4.33	0.34	185
Hexobarbital	1.49*	4.35	3.93	0.42	311
N,N-Dimethylaniline	2.31*	4.19	4.50	0.31	195
Codeine	1.41	4.02	3.88	0.14	376
4-Amino-N,N-dimethylaniline	1.08	3.87	3.65	0.22	151
3-Amino-N,N-dimethylaniline	1.08	3.85	3.65	0.20	136
Ephedrine	0.93*	3.78	3.54	0.24	569
Barbital	0.65*	3.00	3.35	0.35	161
Physostigmine	1.05*	2.94	3.63	0.69	251
Caffeine	-0.07*	2.86	2.85	0.01	298

[a] Values marked by * are experimental values; others are calculated via additivity principles.
[b] From Ref. 6.
[c] Calculated using Eq. (2).

resents the concentration of the neutral form of the molecule present at half-maximal velocity. Since a much better correlation is obtained in Eq. (2), it appears that the ionized forms of the molecules must be attacked relatively little by the microsomes. There is a very large difference in the partition coefficient of the neutral and ionized forms of acids and bases. For example, log P for $C_5H_{11}COOH$ is 1.90 and the apparent log P for $C_5H_{11}COO^-Na^+$ is -2.20. There is a 10,000-fold difference in the tendency between the ionic and neutral forms to enter the fatty phase (octanol). In the case of amines (RNH_2 vs $RNH_3^+Cl^-$), there is 3 orders of magnitude difference in the partition coefficients [7]. Comparatively speaking, there is so little tendency for the ionized form of acids and bases to partition into the fatty phase that, unless the process is aided by the charge on the ion, one can consider the ionized forms "safe" from metabolic change. Equation (2) helps one to understand why many of the biochemically important molecules such as the amino acids, sugars, anions, and other very polar molecules are not indiscriminately and rapidly metabolized by the liver microsomes.

The range of structures in Table 1 is rather wide so that quite a variety of bonds in the substrates are being attacked by the oxidative microsomal system. Nevertheless, electronic and steric factors play a small role relative to that of hydrophobic character operationally defined by log P.

DRUG-MICROSOMAL INTERACTION AS MEASURED BY CYTOCHROME P-450 → P-420 CONVERSION

The work of Ichikawa and Yamano [8, 9] makes an interesting comparison with that embodied in Eqs. (1) and (2). These authors studied the concentration of phenols and anilines necessary to convert microsomal cytochrome P-450 to P-420. As seen from Eqs. (3) and (4), the parameter of importance in this process is the hydrophobic character of the organic molecules. For practical purposes, the slopes and intercepts of Eqs. (3) and (4) are about the same. We

$$\text{Phenols: } pC = 0.57(\pm 0.08)\log P + 0.36(\pm 0.19) \quad \begin{array}{ccc} n & r & s \\ 13 & 0.979 & 0.132 \end{array} \quad (3)$$

$$\text{Anilines: } pC = 0.67(\pm 0.14)\log P + 0.34(\pm 0.21) \quad \begin{array}{ccc} n & r & s \\ 7 & 0.984 & 0.079 \end{array} \quad (4)$$

($pC = \log 1/C$. C = molar concentration.)

have employed log P rather than π employed by the Japanese workers so that a comparison could be made. Actually, the results could be included in a single equation. The intercept of about 0.3 is the same as that observed for many nonspecific processes involving the perturbation of macromolecules by organic compounds [7, 10]. The slopes of these equations are the same (within experimental error) as Eq. (2). Equations (3) and (4), taken with many others of a similar nature [7, 10], indicate that simply partitioning the small molecules onto the macromolecule brings about the conformational change. The dependency of this partitioning on the hydrophobic character (log P) of the organic compound is the same as for metabolic attack (Eq. 2).

MICROSOMAL DEMETHYLATION

Equations (2) - (4) are all simple linear equations. One can expect such results as long as structural changes in a set of congeners are not large. When large changes are made, more complex equations are needed to rationalize the data. Such a complex set comes from the study of McMahon [4, 5]. Table 2 lists a set of N-methylamines whose log P values differ by almost 4 log units and whose pK_a values differ by 4.8 log units. With such large variation in both electronic and lipophilic character, one finds a nonlinear dependence of activity on ΔpK_a. The best equation correlating the relative demethylation rates of the compounds of Table 2 is:

$$\log RBR = 0.33(\pm 0.10) \log P - 0.08(\pm 0.04)(\Delta pK_a)^2$$

$$- 0.15(\pm 0.04)\Delta pK_a - 0.44(\pm 0.32) \qquad \begin{array}{ccc} n & r & s \\ 22 & 0.900 & 0.163 \end{array}$$

$$(5)$$

In obtaining the data upon which Eq. (5) is based, a fixed amount of amine was employed and the amount of formaldehyde produced measured. We have observed that this procedure does not give as good results as determining the concentration which yields a standard response. Of course, ideally one should also factor the demethylation process into at least two steps (K_m and V_{max}). However, even with these limitations in the data, Eq. (5) does illustrate the very important role of lipophilic character in the demethylation reaction and confirms Brodie's early and most important insight into the lipophilic dependence of metabolic processes. It also illustrates that an optimum electron density on nitrogen is necessary for the maximum rate of demethylation. Equation (5) is slightly different than our previously published analysis [11]; at that time we did not have experimental log P values upon which to base our analysis.

Table 2

Microsomal Demethylation of N-Methylamines

Compounds	log P^a	ΔpK_a^b	log RBR Obs^c	Calc^d	$\lvert\Delta$ RBR$\rvert$
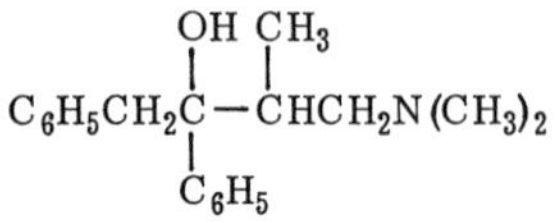 $\underset{\underset{C_6H_5}{\vert}}{C_6H_5CH_2\overset{\overset{OH}{\vert}}{C}}-\overset{\overset{CH_3}{\vert}}{C}HCH_2N(CH_3)_2$	3.83*	−0.10	0.90	0.82	0.08
$(C_5H_{11})_2NCH_3$	4.20	0.90	0.86	0.72	0.14
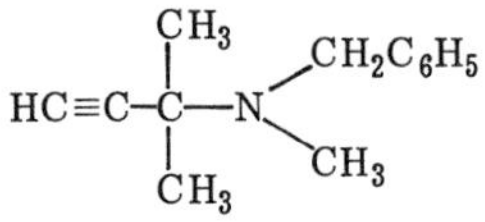 $HC{\equiv}C-\overset{\overset{CH_3}{\vert}}{\underset{\underset{CH_3}{\vert}}{C}}-N\overset{CH_2C_6H_5}{\underset{CH_3}{\big\langle}}$	3.63	−2.40	0.81	0.64	0.17
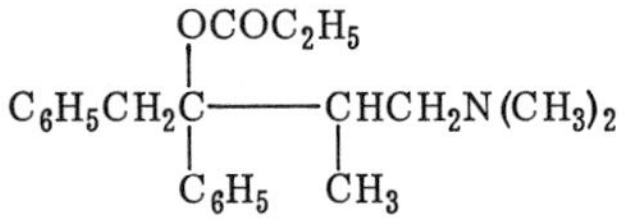 $\underset{\underset{C_6H_5}{\vert}}{C_6H_5CH_2\overset{\overset{OCOC_2H_5}{\vert}}{C}}-\underset{\underset{CH_3}{\vert}}{C}HCH_2N(CH_3)_2$	4.18*	−0.60	0.73	0.98	0.25
$(C_5H_{11})C_4H_9NCH_3$	3.70	0.90	0.68	0.56	0.12
$4{-}ClC_6H_4(CH_2)_3N(CH_3)_2$	3.44	0.10	0.65	0.66	0.01
$C_6H_5(CH_2)_3N(CH_3)_2$	2.73*	0.00	0.63	0.45	0.18
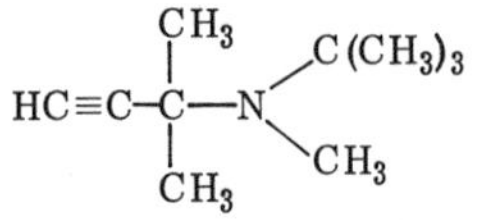 $HC{\equiv}C-\overset{\overset{CH_3}{\vert}}{\underset{\underset{CH_3}{\vert}}{C}}-N\overset{C(CH_3)_3}{\underset{CH_3}{\big\langle}}$	2.53*	−0.20	0.61	0.41	0.20
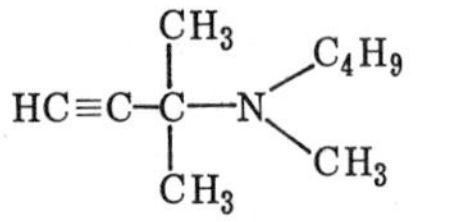 $HC{\equiv}C-\overset{\overset{CH_3}{\vert}}{\underset{\underset{CH_3}{\vert}}{C}}-N\overset{C_4H_9}{\underset{CH_3}{\big\langle}}$	3.00	−1.30	0.59	0.60	0.01
$C_6H_5CH_2CH_2N(CH_3)_2$	2.21*	−0.20	0.46	0.30	0.16
$C_6H_5CH_2N(CH_3)_2$	1.75*	−0.60	0.46	0.19	0.27
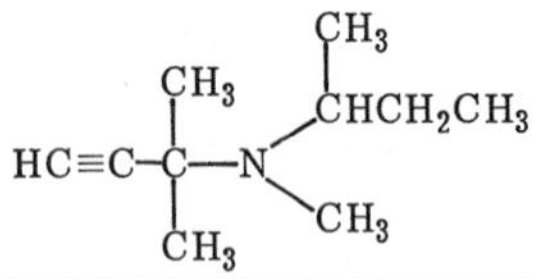 $HC{\equiv}C-\overset{\overset{CH_3}{\vert}}{\underset{\underset{CH_3}{\vert}}{C}}-N\overset{\overset{CH_3}{\vert}}{\underset{CH_3}{\big\langle}}\!\!CHCH_2CH_3$	2.80	−0.70	0.41	0.54	0.13

(continued)

TABLE 2 (continued)

Compounds	log P[a]	ΔpK_a[b]	log RBR Obs[c]	log RBR Calc[d]	$\|\Delta RBR\|$
$HC{\equiv}C{-}\overset{\underset{\displaystyle CH_3}{\vert}}{\underset{\displaystyle CH_3}{C}}{-}N\overset{\displaystyle CH(CH_3)_2}{\underset{\displaystyle CH_3}{}}$	2.30	−0.80	0.36	0.38	0.02
$HC{\equiv}C{-}\overset{\underset{\displaystyle CH_3}{\vert}}{\underset{\displaystyle CH_3}{C}}{-}N\overset{\displaystyle C_3H_7}{\underset{\displaystyle CH_3}{}}$	2.50	−1.30	0.35	0.43	0.08
$(C_4H_9)_2NCH_3$	3.20	1.00	0.31	0.37	0.06
$(C_4H_9)C_3H_7NCH_3$	3.20	0.90	0.24	0.40	0.16
$[(CH_3)_2CHCH_2]_2NCH_3$	2.80	0.60	0.19	0.35	0.16
$HC{\equiv}C{-}\overset{\underset{\displaystyle CH_3}{\vert}}{\underset{\displaystyle CH_3}{C}}{-}N\overset{\displaystyle C_2H_5}{\underset{\displaystyle CH_3}{}}$	2.00	−1.30	0.04	0.27	0.23
$HC{\equiv}C{-}\overset{\underset{\displaystyle CH_3}{\vert}}{\underset{\displaystyle CH_3}{C}}{-}N(CH_3)_2$	1.50	−1.60	−0.02	0.08	0.10
$CH_3CH_2\overset{\underset{\displaystyle CH_3}{\vert}}{\underset{\displaystyle CH_3}{C}}{-}N\overset{\displaystyle CH(CH_3)_2}{\underset{\displaystyle CH_3}{}}$	2.53	1.70	−0.13	−0.11	0.02
$(CH_3CH_2\overset{\underset{\displaystyle CH_3}{\vert}}{CH})_2NCH_3$	2.80	1.60	−0.15	0.02	0.17
$t{-}Amyl{-}N\overset{\displaystyle C(CH_3)_3}{\underset{\displaystyle CH_3}{}}$	2.78	2.40	−0.30	−0.37	0.07
$(C_3H_7)_2NCH_3$	2.20	0.90	−0.62[e]	0.07	0.69

[a]Values marked by * are experimental; others are calculated.
[b]$\Delta pK_a = pK_a - 9.5$.
[c]From Refs. 4 and 5.
[d]Calculated using Eq. (5)
[e]This data point not used in the formulation of Eq. (5).

MICROSOMAL HYDROXYLATION

As Ichikawa et al. have pointed out, not all microsomal enzymatic reactions are heavily dependent on log P; this can be illustrated with their data [12] in Table 3. Considering first the 2-substituted anilines (compounds 1-8), we have derived Eqs. (6) - (8):

$$\log RBR = 0.11(\pm 0.49) \log P + 1.73(\pm 0.80) \qquad \begin{array}{ccc} n & r & s \\ 7 & 0.253 & 0.209 \end{array} \quad (6)$$

$$\log RBR = -1.16(\pm 0.50)\Re + 1.76(\pm 0.10) \qquad \begin{array}{ccc} 7 & 0.936 & 0.076 \end{array} \quad (7)$$

$$\log RBR = 0.13(\pm 0.11) \log P - 1.17(\pm 0.31)\Re$$
$$+ 1.55(\pm 0.19) \qquad \begin{array}{ccc} 7 & 0.984 & 0.044 \end{array} \quad (8)$$

The above equations indicate that lipophilic character plays a small role in the 4-hydroxylation of anilines. The role is significant, however. Comparing Eqs. (7) and (8), we find $F_{1,4}$ to be 24.8 while $F_{1,4\alpha.01}$ is 21.2. In addition to log P and $\Re$ employed in Eq. (8), the parameters E_s, E_R, $\mathfrak{F}$, σ_R, and σ_I were also considered singly and in all reasonable combinations. Nothing superior to Eq. (8) was uncovered.

Considering now the 3-substituted anilines, we have formulated the following equations:

$$\begin{array}{ccc} & n & r & s \end{array}$$
$$\log RBR = 0.39(\pm 0.34) \log P + 1.00(\pm 0.68) \qquad \begin{array}{ccc} 11 & 0.653 & 0.313 \end{array} \quad (9)$$

$$\log RBR = 0.41(\pm 0.17)E_s + 1.52(\pm 0.16) \qquad \begin{array}{ccc} 11 & 0.877 & 0.199 \end{array} \quad (10)$$

$$\log RBR = 0.27(\pm 0.09) \log P + 0.36(\pm 0.07)E_s$$
$$+ 1.03(\pm 0.18) \qquad \begin{array}{ccc} 11 & 0.982 & 0.082 \end{array} \quad (11)$$

Again, in this larger set of congeners a small role is seen for log P. The best single-variable equation is that in E_s. The best equation, considering all of the above-mentioned parameters, is that involving log P and E_s. Adding a term in $\Re$ or other electronic parameters does not improve the correlation.

Before considering the implications of Eqs. (8) and (11), one must consider the mechanism of hydroxylation. Evidence is conclusive now that this reaction goes through an epoxide intermediate [13]. Correlating substituent effects on this reaction sequence presents a most difficult problem; not only must the steric, electronic, and hydrophobic effects of substituents on the formation of enzyme-sub-

Table 3

Microsomal 4-Hydroxylation of Anilines

	Compound	log P[a]	ℜ[b]	E_s[c]	log RBR Obs[d]	log RBR Calc[e]	| Δ log RBR|
1.	2–I	2.09	−0.20	−0.16	2.11	2.06	0.05
2.	2–F	1.15	−0.34	0.78	2.07	2.10	0.03
3.	2–Cl	1.90*	−0.16	0.27	2.00	1.99	0.01
4.	2–Br	1.79	−0.18	0.08	1.99	2.00	0.01
5.	2–CH$_3$	1.32*	−0.14	0.00	1.87	1.89	0.02
6.	Unsub	0.90*	0.00	1.24	1.72	1.67	0.05
7.	2–NO$_2$	1.83*	0.16	−1.28	1.57	1.61	0.04
8.	2–OCH$_3$	0.95	−0.50	0.69	0.34[f]	2.26	1.92
9.	N–Bu	3.16	0.00	1.24	2.31	2.33	0.02
10.	N–Pr	2.66	0.00	1.24	2.21	2.20	0.01
11.	N–Et	2.16	0.00	1.24	2.14	2.06	0.08
12.	N–CH$_3$	1.66*	0.00	1.24	1.76	1.93	0.17
13.	3–Cl	1.88*	−0.16	0.27	1.71	1.64	0.07
14.	3–F	1.30*	−0.34	0.78	1.69	1.66	0.03
15.	3–Br	2.07	−0.18	0.08	1.64	1.62	0.02
16.	3–I	2.37	−0.20	−0.16	1.58	1.62	0.04
17.	3–CH$_3$	1.40*	−0.14	0.00	1.50	1.41	0.09
18.	3–NO$_2$	1.37*	0.16	−1.28	0.88	0.94	0.06
19.	3–OCH$_3$	0.93*	−0.50	0.69	0.57[f]	1.53	0.96

[a]Values marked by * are experimental; others are calculated.

[b]From C. G. Swain and E. C. Lupton, *J. Amer. Chem. Soc.*, **90**, 4328 (1968).

[c]From E. Kutter and C. Hansch, *J. Med. Chem.*, **12**, 647 (1969).

[d]From Ref. 12.

[e]Calculated using Eqs. (8) and (11).

[f]These points not used in formulating Eqs. (6) − (11).

strate complex be considered, but in addition there are the three chemical reactions of epoxide formation, nucleophilic attack by water and, finally, elimination.

The variance in the data correlated by Eqs. (6) - (8) is not large and only 7 data points are available, so the results should be taken as suggestive. The most important factor appears to be electron release via resonance by the 2-substituent. This result is probably largely determined by the 2-NO_2 function and would indicate that electron withdrawal by this function is the main reason for the low activity of this derivative. There are a number of points in the hydroxylation reaction where this effect might play a role. One which seems particularly interesting is the destabilization of the intermediate in the dehydration step (Scheme I). Resonance of the type indicated between A and B would hinder the formation of a carbonium ion intermediate.

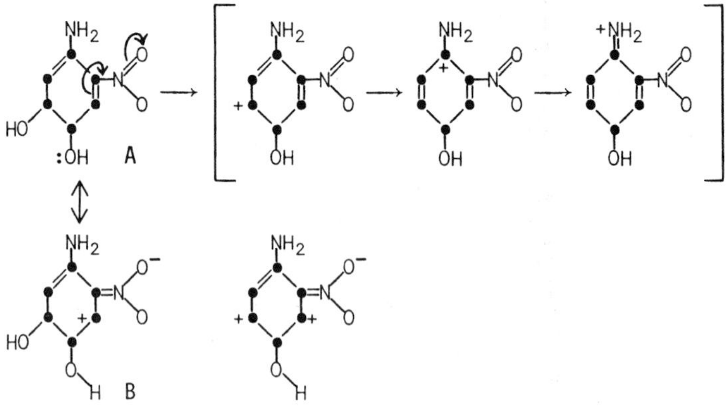

Scheme I

In the case of the 3-substituted anilines (compounds 9-19, Table 3), no role is found for $\mathcal{R}$. Instead, a significant role is found for E_s, indicating a steric effect by the 3-substituent. This relatively small steric inhibition might occur in the epoxidation reaction or in the nucleophilic attack of water on the epoxide or in both of these steps.

The over-all hydroxylation reaction shows a small but significant dependence on the hydrophobic character of the substituents. If the reaction sequence were studied in a stepwise manner, it might be found that hydrophobic character is more important in the binding of the substrate but that this advantage is offset in the desorption of reactant from the enzyme [14].

The above conclusions on the role of substituents in the 4-hydroxyl-
ation are tentative. While it is clear that the relative lipophilic character is not the only important factor, the set of substituents studied
does not contain the ideal kind of variation necessary to more sharply
delineate electronic and steric effects. In deriving Eqs. (6) - (11),
both the 2-OCH$_3$ and 3-OCH$_3$ data points were excluded. Both of these
derivatives are quite poorly hydroxylated and both are poorly predicted by Eqs. (8) and (11). Since the methoxy function itself is
rapidly attacked by microsomal enzymes, it is felt that involvement
of this function in the demethylation reaction might be the cause of
the slow rate of 4-hydroxylation. In any event, the results embodied
in Eqs. (8) and (11) will be of help in designing a better set of derivatives to study para-hydroxylation.

IN VIVO METABOLISM

Good in vivo data to compare directly with Eqs. (2) - (4) are lacking. However, an example from the work of Dorfman and Goldbaum
[15] is worth considering. They measured the percent barbiturate
metabolized in mice by grinding up the whole mouse and measuring
spectrophotometrically the amount of barbiturate unchanged. Using
their data and partition coefficients from Ref. 16, Eq. (12) was formulated. Since Eq. (12) is based on only 3 data points, it must be accepted with great reservation. While the statistics for this equation
mean little or nothing, it is of interest that the slope is in good
agreement with those of Eqs. (2) - (4).

$$\log \% \text{ metabolized} = 0.63 \log P + 0.60 \qquad \begin{array}{ccc} n & r & s \\ 3 & 0.999 & 0.026 \end{array} \qquad (12)$$

Another way of viewing metabolism in relation to lipophilic character is from the duration of action of a set of drugs. Equation (13)
has been derived from the data of Cope and Hancock [17] in Table 4.

$$\log T = -0.63(\pm\ 0.18) \log P + 0.79(\pm\ 0.35) \qquad \begin{array}{ccc} n & r & s \\ 13 & 0.918 & 0.138 \end{array} \qquad (13)$$

In Eq. (13), T represents duration of action in hours. The correlation
is reasonable both from the point of view of r and s. The slope of
Eq. (13) is exactly what we would expect from Eqs. (2) - (5); that is,
the negative of that observed for metabolism. The more lipophilic
the drug, the faster the molecule is metabolized and, hence, the
shorter its duration of action.

Table 4

Duration of Action of 5,5-Barbiturates
Given I.P. to Mice

			log T		
Substituents		log P[a]	Obs[b]	Calc	|Δ log T|
Me	EtCH=C (Me) −	1.15	0.00	0.06	0.06
Et	EtCH=C (Me) −	1.65	−0.40	−0.25	0.15
Pr	EtCH=C (Me) −	2.15	−0.52	−0.57	0.05
I−Pr	EtCH=C (Me) −	1.95	−0.52	−0.44	0.08
Me	MeCH=C (Et) −	1.15	0.00	0.06	0.06
Et	MeCH=C (Et) −	1.65	−0.15	−0.25	0.10
Pr	MeCH=C (Et) −	2.15	−0.40	−0.57	0.17
I−Pr	MeCH=C (Et) −	1.95	−0.52	−0.44	0.08
Me	PrCH=C (Me) −	1.65	0.00	−0.25	0.25
Et	PrCH=C (Me) −	2.15	0.08[c]	−0.57[c]	0.65
Me	I−PrCH=C (Me) −	1.45	−0.22	−0.13	0.09
Me	BuCH=C (Me) −	2.15	−0.40	−0.57	0.17
Et	BuCH=C (Me) −	2.65	−1.00	−0.88	0.12
Et	EtCH=C (Pr) −	2.65	−1.00	−0.88	0.12

[a]All of the log P values employed are calculated based on $\pi = -1.35$

found for (structure) C=O. For example, log P for the first molecule in

the table was calculated as follows:

$$\log P = -1.35 + 0.50 + 1.00 + 0.70 + 0.30 = 1.15$$

The value of 0.5 is for the 5−Me group, π for Et = 1.00, π for CH=CH = 0.7,
and π for a branched Me = 0.30.
[b]From Ref. 17.
[c]This molecule not used in the derivation of Eq. (13).

Although the results are fragmentary, Eqs. (2) - (13) do indicate
that the modification of organic compounds by the microsomal enzymes can be understood in terms of physicochemical constants in
a quantitative fashion. As more complete and more precise studies
are made, we should reach the position where the relative effects

of substituents on the metabolism of drugs can be estimated in advance. Such information will be of the utmost value to the drug designer.

References

[1] B. B. Brodie, J. R. Gillette and B. N. LaDu, *Ann. Rev. Biochem.*, **27**, 427 (1958).

[2] L. E. Gaudette and B. B. Brodie, *Biochem. Pharmacol.*, **2**, 89 (1959).

[3] P. Mazel and J. Henderson, *Biochem. Pharmacol.*, **14**, 92 (1965).

[4] R. E. McMahon, *J. Med. Chem.*, **4**, 67 (1961).

[5] R. E. McMahon and N. R. Easton, *J. Med. Chem.*, **4**, 437 (1961).

[6] Y. C. Martin and C. Hansch, *J. Med. Chem.*, **14**, 777 (1971).

[7] C. Hansch and W. R. Glave, *Mol. Pharmacol.*, **7**, 337 (1971).

[8] Y. Ichikawa and T. Yamano, *Biochim. Biophys. Acta*, **147**, 518 (1967).

[9] Y. Ichikawa and T. Yamano, *Biochim. Biophys. Acta*, **200**, 220 (1970).

[10] C. Hansch and W. J. Dunn III, *J. Pharm. Sci.*, **61**, 1 (1972).

[11] C. Hansch, A. R. Steward, and J. Iwasa, *J. Med. Chem.*, **8**, 868 (1965).

[12] Y. Ichikawa, T. Yamano, and H. Fujishima, *Biochim. Biophys. Acta*, **171**, 32 (1969).

[13] D. M. Jerina, J. W. Daly, B. Witkop, P. Zaltman-Nirenberg, and S. Udenfriend, *Biochemistry*, **9**, 147 (1970).

[14] C. Hansch, E. W. Deutsch, and R. N. Smith, *J. Amer. Chem. Soc.*, **87**, 2738 (1965).

[15] A. Dorfman and L. R. Goldbaum, *J. Pharmacol. Exp. Ther.*, **90**, 330 (1947).

[16] C. Hansch, A. R. Steward, S. M. Anderson, and D. Bentley, *J. Med. Chem.*, **11**, 1 (1968).

[17] A. C. Cope and E. M. Hancock, *J. Amer. Chem. Soc.*, **61**, 776 (1939).

Biopharmaceutical Considerations in Drug Formulation Design and Evaluation

STANLEY A. KAPLAN
Department of Biochemistry and Drug Metabolism
Hoffmann-La Roche Inc.
Nutley, New Jersey 07110

INTRODUCTION

A particularly important problem facing many drug metabolism research groups is the determination of bioavailability, i.e., the actual amount of drug available to the body after the administration of a given dose of the drug in a pharmaceutical dosage form. There is substantial evidence to suggest that a significant number of compounds may be largely unavailable after oral administration because of certain properties of the drug itself and/or its dosage form.

The biological availability of a drug is the result of many processes. Factors such as low solubility, slow dissolution or release rate, poor permeability, gastrointestinal degradation, and rapid biotransformation may all contribute to poor availability. Experience has shown that these factors can be studied individually and that many possible problems can be anticipated before the drug reaches the clinic.

The relationship between the physicochemical properties of a drug in a dosage form and the biological response (including bioavailability) observed following its administration is the subject of an area of drug research known as biopharmaceutics. Several years

15

ago a biopharmaceutical program was established within our drug
metabolism group with two major goals: 1) to anticipate potential
clinical problems arising from poor absorption of a candidate drug,
and 2) to optimize bioavailability of newly developed compounds.
The establishment of a biopharmaceutical program within a drug
metabolism group appeared to be eminently reasonable since the
primary research efforts of such groups is the physiological disposition of drugs. As such, a drug metabolism group would have the
tools, such as analytical methodology, instrumentation, and animal
facilities needed to perform biopharmaceutical studies; and perhaps
more importantly would interface with other research groups, such
as clinical pharmacology, pharmaceutical research and development,
and analytical research and development that are essential to carry
the studies from the laboratory to the clinical environment.

The essential elements of the biopharmaceutical program that
has been developed is the focus of this review. The points to be
covered include 1) those studies done to decide the physicochemical
nature of the drug to be used, e.g., salt, particle size; 2) the timing
of these studies in relation to the preclinical studies with the drug;
3) the evaluation of drug absorption and physiological disposition
studies; and 4) the design and evaluation of the final drug formulation. The execution of preliminary studies on a drug in the sequence
listed below enables the making of crucial decisions based on in vivo
and in vitro biopharmaceutical data prior to the commencement of
time consuming and costly animal tolerance and clinical trials.

1) Evaluation of physicochemical and acute toxicity data.

2) Standardization of the physicochemical properties of the drug.

3) Development of a method for measurement of the drug in biological fluids.

4) Determination of the solubility and dissolution characteristics
as a function of pH.

5) Determination of the permeability characteristics of the drug.

6) Studies of the in vivo absorption and physiological disposition
of the drug, usually in the dog, using the intravenous and oral routes
of administration.

7) Determination of adjuvants for use with the drug.

These points will be discussed, and data obtained from such
studies will be presented and interpreted in relation to spotting potential problems. If an absorption problem exists, the nature of the
problem should be defined to allow for meaningful interpretation of
subsequent tolerance and efficacy studies. An incompletely absorbed

drug can still be clinically effective and worthwhile if the right information regarding this problem is known at an early stage in the
drug's development.

IN VITRO CONSIDERATIONS

Essentially, the evaluation of absorbability as a function of the
physicochemical properties of the drug substance would determine
whether any changes in the physical and/or chemical properties of
the substance could enhance the absorbability of the drug. Therefore, if such is indicated, an alternative physical form or chemical
analog of the substance may be substituted and evaluated in the early
stages of drug development. This will ensure that the drug substance
used in all subsequent studies will have the maximum potential for
absorbability. Even prior to the first biopharmaceutical studies one
indication of the absorbability of a drug substance can be obtained
based on solubility, pK_a, and acute toxicity (intravenous and oral LD_{50})
data.

Biopharmaceutical studies on a potential drug substance should
be carried out with a pure chemical compound which has been stan-
dardized as to its physicochemical properties by analytical quality
control. This is necessary since different lots of a chemical with
different physical properties, e.g., crystalline state, may result in
different absorption profiles for what appears to be the same compound. Different absorption profiles were observed recently with a
compound when administered in two polymorphic forms, photomicro-
graphs of which are shown in Fig. 1. Identical oral doses of this
basic compound with a pK_a of 2.3, from two different lots, were administered in gelatin capsules to the same dog two weeks apart and
resulted in the blood level curves shown in Fig. 2. Aside from the
differences in crystal structure, the two lots of compound could not
be distinguished, yet the resulting absorption profiles as determined
via the blood level curves were markedly different. The blood level
peak after administration of drug from Lot B was three times greater
and the area under the curve six times greater than that observed
with drug from Lot A.

In order for an orally administered solid chemical to be absorbed
it must first dissolve in the aqueous environment of the gastrointestinal tract and once in solution permeate across the lipoidal gastrointestinal mucosa into the bloodstream. Therefore, the potential absorbability of a chemical substance must be ascertained in terms of
two basic parameters: dissolution and permeability. A screening
program has been established to define these parameters.

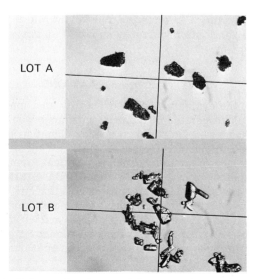

Fig. 1. Polymorphic forms of the same chemical compound.

An *aqueous solubility* of less than 1% in solution at 37° over a pH range of 1 to 7 suggests potential problems in the absorption of the chemical substance. In addition, if the solubility decreases with an increase in pH, there may be a potential for incomplete absorption if dissolution is not attained rapidly in the more acidic environment. Studies on the dissolution rate of a drug over the above pH range can predict problems in the absorption of the compound. The dissolution rate procedure used is the rotating disc method [1] which maintains a constant surface area.

By utilizing this apparatus, the intrinsic dissolution rate is determined in units of milligrams per minute per centimeter square. Experience with this apparatus and utilizing 500 ml of dissolution media over a pH range of 1-7 at 37°C and stirring at 50 rpm indicates that compounds with intrinsic dissolution rate above 1 mg/min/cm^2 are usually not prone to dissolution rate limited absorption. Compounds with intrinsic dissolution rates below 0.1 mg/min/cm^2 are suspect and usually exhibit problems of dissolution rate limited absorption. Compounds with intrinsic dissolution rates between 0.1 and 1.0 mg/min/cm^2 are considered borderline and additional information would be required to ascertain the effect of dissolution on the absorption rate.

An effective in vitro *permeability screen* has been developed [2] to assess the permeability characteristics of new drug substances. This procedure is an adaptation of the Crane and Wilson [3] everted

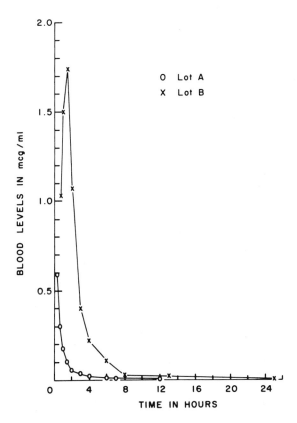

Fig. 2. Blood levels in a dog following the oral administration of an identical dose of polymorphic forms of the same chemical compound.

sac system. In essence a cannulated everted intestinal rat sac is placed in a drug solution buffered at pH 7.4 and incubated in a shaker bath at 37°C under carbon dioxide and oxygen. Since the drug is first placed in solution, permeability is the absorbability parameter being studied. Serial specimens of serosal fluid (from within the sac) are obtained with time up to 90 min and analyzed for drug content. Graphs of cumulative amount transferred per unit concentration of drug with time are plotted, and the linear segment extrapolated to the abscissa as shown in Fig. 3. The intercept with the abscissa is the "Lag Time" in minutes, and the cumulative amount transferred in 60 min per unit concentration of drug in mucosal solution is the "Clearance" in milliliters per minute. The "Lag Time" of all the compounds

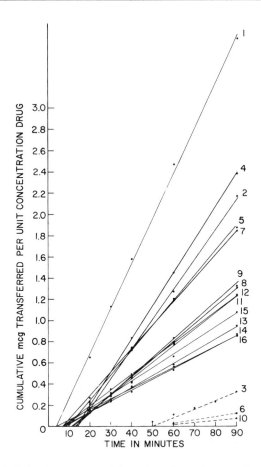

Fig. 3. Cumulative micrograms of drug transferred per unit concentration of drug across the everted sac preparation with time for several experimental compounds.

except Nos. 3, 6, and 10 in Fig. 3 ranged from 3 to 18 min and the "Clearance" ranged from 0.01 to 0.04 ml/min. All of these compounds exhibited absorption profiles in the dog which were consistent with good permeability. The curves in Fig. 3 indicate there was no transport of compounds Nos. 3, 6, and 10 during the first hour, and the observed low levels may simply be an artifact due to breakdown of the epithelial barrier. Compounds Nos. 3 and 10 exhibited dissolution characteristics consistent with good absorbability yet were poorly absorbed in vivo. Although compound No. 6 exhibited poor dissolution characteristics as well, it was poorly absorbed in vivo even when administered in solution. It is interesting to note that the rate of transfer or "Clearance" has been shown to relate directly to the degree of undissociation of the compound in the pH 7.4 in vitro system. Compound No. 1 was neutral and exhibited the fastest rate. Compounds Nos. 2, 4, 5, and 7 were weak bases undissociated at the pH of the system and transferred more rapidly than compounds Nos. 8, 9, and 11 through 16 which were weak acids and highly ionized. If the permeability characteristics are found to be inconsistent with good absorbability, this problem may be overcome by selecting an active analog with different chemical properties such as an analog with a different pK_a, or an ester with a greater lipid solubility.

The results presented above indicate that simple in vitro techniques can provide information as to the potential absorbability of a chemical compound. The chemist sometimes chooses a compound for pharmacological testing because of its ease of synthesis, percent yield, or the purity of the crystalline form. Since chemical derivatives with a potential for better absorption may have been previously synthesized and available for further screening, this would be the time to pursue related compounds and subject them to the in vitro screening procedure.

IN VIVO AND CLINICAL STUDIES

In the preliminary screening program the drug concentrations determined can be sufficiently high to allow the use of relatively insensitive analytical procedures. However, in order to analyze biological specimens in subsequent studies, a sensitive and specific assay is required. The assay may utilize chemical techniques or radioactive drug.

Biological availability is assessed as a function of the blood and/or urinary excretion profiles following intravenous and oral administration of the drug. Therefore, one must be aware of the factors that may influence or alter these profiles. Although dissolution and permeability are essential parameters of biological availability, other factors must also be considered. These include stability, biodegradation, and biotransformation, particularly during the "first pass" of the drug through the liver. It is possible to separate out and determine those factors affecting the absorption and availability of a drug, i.e., 1) the rate and extent of absorption of the dose, and 2) the percent of absorbed dose available as intact drug. This will

establish a standard for evaluating the physiological availability of
a drug from its dosage formulation. A drug may be completely absorbed yet only partially available to the peripheral circulation as
intact drug. In order to circumvent such problems the nature of a
blood level profile obtained with the drug substance of choice must
be understood.

Comparison of the areas under an intravenous and oral blood level
curve provides a measure of the availability of the drug following
oral administration. If the comparison of areas under a blood level
curve was the only interest, a rectilinear plot of the data would be
sufficient. However, additional pharmacokinetic information pertaining to a drug can be obtained by evaluating a semilogarithmic
plot of the data, and assuming first-order transfer processes. In
this case the shape of the oral blood level curve as compared with
that of the intravenous blood level curve will provide an index of the
rate and extent of absorption. If the oral blood level peak, as shown
in curve No. 2 of Fig. 4, is sharp and coincides in time and magnitude
with that of the start of the linear (elimination) segment of the intravenous blood level curve, curve No. 1, one may assume rapid and complete absorption of the administered dose, and complete availability
as intact drug.

Curves Nos. 3 and 4 in Fig. 4 indicate the blood levels of the drug
when administered in two different formulations which should be compared with blood level curves No. 1 or 2 to assess physiological
availability. It should be noted that the slower the absorption rate,
the lower the blood level peak and the later in time it will occur. In
curve No. 4 absorption is proceeding slowly, resulting in a broad
blood level plateau. Drug absorption is essentially complete when
the linear portion of the semilogarithmic blood level curve is parallel with that following intravenous administration. With curve No. 3
this occurred at 4 to 5 hr post administration while with curve No. 4
this did not occur within the 24-hr experimental period. The prolonged absorption phase in curve No. 4 suggests that the drug is
being absorbed all along the gastrointestinal tract. Although the
blood level peak in curve No. 4 was one-third that seen in curve
No. 2, the same amount of drug may be excreted in the total urine
collection. Therefore, both the rate and extent of absorption must
be determined. It is not uncommon to see biological availability
studies in which only total urinary excretion levels are compared
and equivalence is assumed.

The most commonly encountered absorption problems involve
drugs which are poorly water soluble and dissolve slowly in the
gastrointestinal tract. In one study the solubility of a base with pK_a

BLOOD LEVELS OF INTACT DRUG

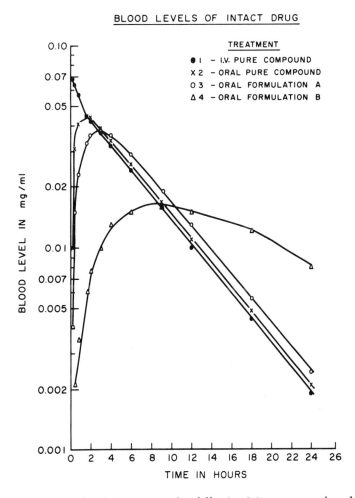

Fig. 4. Typical blood level curves in a dog following intravenous and oral administration of a drug, and oral blood level curves of formulations A and B.

values of 1.5 and 10.5 exhibited its maximum solubility of 75 mcg/ml in an acidic environment. The dissolution rate was too slow to be measured. The in vivo absorption characteristics were determined following administration of identical doses of the drug intravenously, orally as the solid and orally as a solution in propylene glycol. The blood levels versus time data are shown in Fig. 5. The results clearly

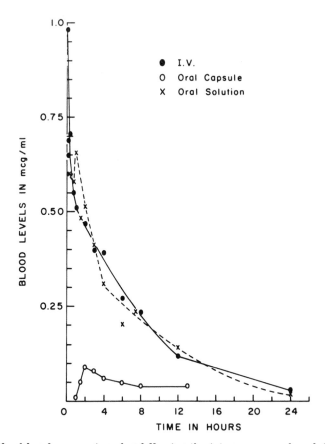

Fig. 5. Blood level curves in a dog following the intravenous and oral (solid and solution) administrations of a poorly soluble compound.

indicate a dissolution rate limited absorption of the drug. The drug was rapidly and completely absorbed when administered orally in solution, whereas only about 2% of the dose was absorbed following oral administration of the solid chemical compound.

In another study the solubility of an acidic compound with pK_a values of 7.4 and 12.3 was found to be 430 mcg/ml at pH 1. The dissolution rate of the sodium salt was twice that observed for the free acid at pH 1 and 29-fold greater at pH 5.3. The results following intravenous and oral administration of the free acid and oral administration of the sodium salt, at identical doses, indicate rapid and complete absorption of the drug when administered as the sodium salt with a blood level peak of 12 mcg/ml 2 hr post administration as seen in Fig. 6. Evaluation of the area under the blood level curve following oral administration of the free acid indicates slow but complete absorption. In this case a blood level maximum of 6 mcg/ml was observed 8 to 12 hr post administration. The blood level maximum was only one-half that achieved with the more rapidly absorbed

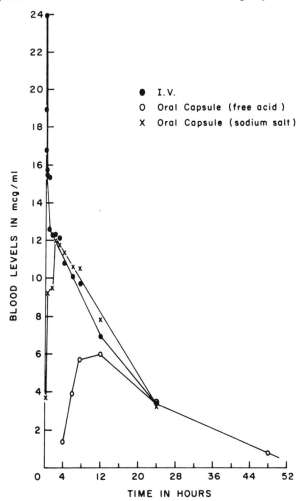

Fig. 6. Blood level curves in a dog following the intravenous administration of the free acid and oral administration of the free acid and sodium salt.

sodium salt. The data in Fig. 6 emphasizes an important point in evaluating drug absorption data, in terms of the rate and extent of absorption. In this study the extent of absorption was approximately the same with both the free acid and its sodium salt. Had the extent of absorption been considered merely by comparing blood level areas or total urinary excretion and the rate of absorption ignored, biological equivalence would have been assumed. In addition, slowly absorbed drugs tend to be absorbed in a much more variable fashion from administration to administration. Therefore, in striving for optimum availability, the rate of absorption may be a meaningful parameter.

Figure 7 presents the blood level curves of an acidic compound with pK_a values of −2.05 and 4.77. The drug was found to have poor

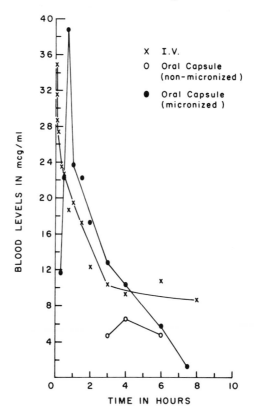

Fig. 7. Blood level curves in a dog following intravenous and oral (micronized and nonmicronized) drug administration.

solubility properties which indicated a potential dissolution rate limited absorption. However, the permeability characteristics were consistent with good absorbability. The curves in Fig. 7 indicate that administration of nonmicronized drug in a capsule resulted in poor absorption with a low blood level peak of 6.5 mcg/ml 4 hr post administration. The micronized drug in a capsule was completely absorbed with a blood level peak approximately sixfold greater 45 min post absorption when compared with the blood level peak observed with the nonmicronized drug which occurred considerably later in time.

The in vitro studies with a basic compound with pK_a values of 1.5 and 10.5 suggested dissolution rate limited absorption characteristics but good permeability characteristics. However, in this case the projected therapeutic dose was low, under 5 mg. Again using the intravenous curve as a standard, the curves in Fig. 8 indicate that both the micronized and nonmicronized tablet preparations were well absorbed. This example indicates the need to be aware of the intended dose of the drug. The drug exhibited definite dissolution rate limiting characteristics. However, since the dose was extremely small, very little drug had to go into solution, so that the slow dissolution rate was not critical in the absorption process.

If it is found that the solubility and dissolution characteristics of a drug are inconsistent with good absorbability, these problems may be overcome by micronization, altering the crystalline structure, or substituting a salt form for the free acid or base. Another factor pertaining to the potential dissolution rate limited absorption of a drug would be the projected therapeutic dose. If the therapeutic dose was very low, the slow dissolution rate could be counterbalanced by the small amount of drug required to go into solution.

The blood level curves in Fig. 9 represent those obtained after administration of identical doses of a base with a pK_a of 9.5. Although its solubility characteristics were consistent with good absorbability, its permeability characteristics were not, i.e., delayed onset in transfer across the everted intestinal sac preparation. The resulting oral blood level curve indicated slow, erratic, and incomplete absorption using the intravenous curve as the standard.

The blood level curves in Fig. 10 were obtained following intravenous and oral solution administrations of an identical dose of an amphoteric compound with pK_a values of 4.9 and 5.8 for the acidic and basic functions, respectively. This compound exhibited in vitro solubility and permeability limitations to absorption. In vivo only 4% of the orally administered dose in solution was absorbed. This finding would substantiate the in vitro prediction of a permeability limited absorption process.

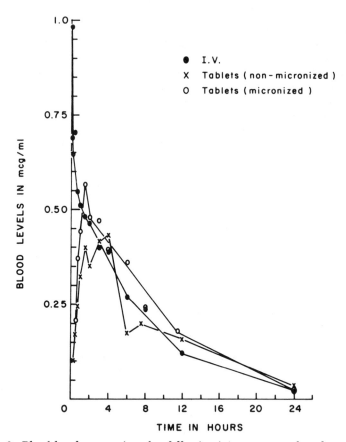

Fig. 8. Blood level curves in a dog following intravenous and oral (micronized and nonmicronized) drug administration.

An antibiotic compound was found to be poorly absorbed. Various formulations prepared with different types of excipients and complexing agents were evaluated. The curves in Fig. 11 indicate that approximately 15% of the administered dose was absorbed. This absorption pattern was consistent in a group of subjects. Although complete absorption of the drug could not be realized, the physiological availability had been defined and was reproducible. Therefore, in the subsequent evaluation of the clinical data the extent of absorption could be considered. This indicates that although a drug may not be completely absorbed, the extent and reproducibility of absorption should be defined.

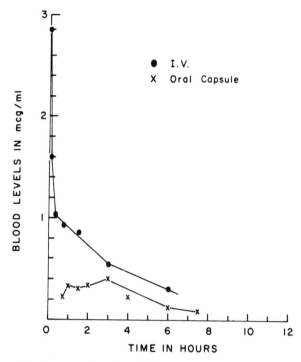

Fig. 9. Blood level curves in a dog following intravenous and oral administration of a drug exhibiting poor permeability characteristics.

Interpretation of blood level data may not always be as straight-
forward as indicated above. Although dissolution and permeability
are essential parameters of biological availability, other factors
must be considered. Biodegradation of the drug in the gastrointestinal tract with subsequent absorption of the breakdown products
and/or substantial biotransformation of the drug during its "first
pass" through the liver, after oral administration, may reduce the
availability of the parent drug relative to its availability observed
after intravenous dosing. The administered dose may have been completely absorbed but incompletely available to the peripheral circulation as intact drug. This might lead to the erroneous conclusion
that the dose was incompletely absorbed. This effect is seen in the
example presented in Fig. 12. Comparison of the total ^{14}C plasma
levels and areas under the curves following intravenous and oral administration indicate complete absorption of the administered dose.
However, when one examines merely the corresponding intact drug levels

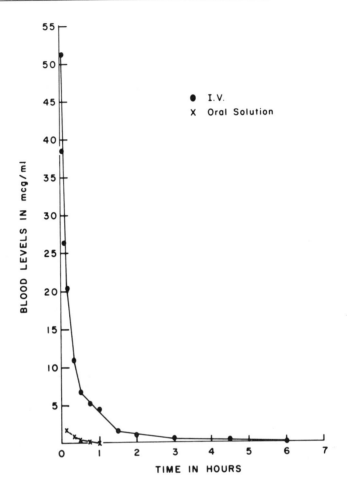

Fig. 10. Blood level curves in a dog following intravenous and oral solution administrations of a drug exhibiting poor solubility and permeability characteristics.

and areas, it would be concluded that only 30% of the administered dose was absorbed. Therefore, with this type of compound reduced physiological availability resulted from metabolic and not formulation or absorption factors. Lack of information on the nature of the absorption and the availability limiting factors may result in unnecessary and prolonged formulation studies in an attempt to in-

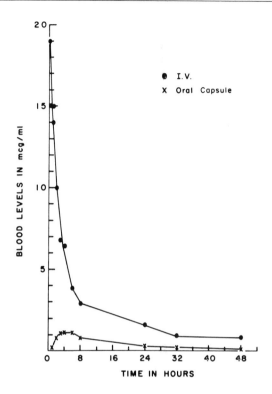

Fig. 11. Serum level curves in man following intravenous and oral administration of an antibiotic compound.

crease the availability of the drug. If, in fact, the poor availability is known to be due to metabolic factors, then formulation studies would not be needed.

A first indication of poor availability of intact drug would be lack of correlation of in vivo and in vitro findings. If the dissolution and permeability data observed in vitro are consistent with good absorbability, poor availability as indicated by low plasma levels may be the result of metabolic and not absorption factors. In this case, the shape of the blood level curve may be that of a well-absorbed compound, i.e., and early and sharp peak with a linear elimination segment on a semilogarithmic plot. However, the area under the oral blood level curve would be lower than that anticipated for complete absorption.

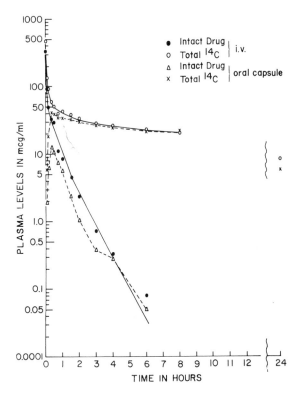

Fig. 12. Plasma level curves of intact drug and total radioactivity in the dog following intravenous and oral administration.

CONCLUSIONS

All of the above examples were chosen to show the need for a biological end point in defining the physiological availability of a drug as well as for evaluating the physiological availability of a drug from its formulation.

Concomitant with the biopharmaceutical studies program, the pharmacy research and development group screen the drug substance and possible excipients in terms of their stability and incompatibilities so that potential problems in this area may also be considered in determining the preferred physical and chemical nature of the drug for further development. Thereafter, when chronic animal tolerance studies begin with the drug substance of choice, the drug formulating department can design and evaluate drug formulations based on the biopharmaceutical studies described above. Once in vivo data become available, an appropriate in vitro system could then be developed to evaluate new production batches. When clinical studies begin on the physiological disposition of the drug, additional information will be available to substantiate the initial conclusions regarding the bioavailability of the drug. In conclusion, therefore, in the development of a new drug, a sequentially designed biological availability study does not begin with a drug formulation, it results in a drug formulation.

References

[1] J. H. Wood, J. Syarto, and H. Letterman, *J. Pharm. Sci.*, **54**, 1068 (1965).
[2] S. A. Kaplan and S. Cotler, *Abstracts of the 31st International Congress of Pharmaceutical Sciences*, Washington, D.C., September 7-12, 1971.
[3] R. K. Crane and T. H. Wilson, *J. Appl. Physiol.*, **12**, 145 (1958).

The Pharmacodynamics of Drug Interaction

DAVID W. YESAIR, FRANCIS J. BULLOCK and JOHN J. COFFEY
Life Sciences Division
Arthur D. Little, Inc.
Cambridge, Massachusetts 02140

INTRODUCTION

Domino Theory of Therapeutics

Increasing recent awareness of the problem of drug interactions must be viewed in the context of other trends which have developed during the last three decades of medical progress. First, the great number of new drug products—approximately 3,700 during the period 1938-1970—provides by itself much opportunity for therapeutic mishap due to drugs used in combination. Even if one considers only the 195 new single entity drugs introduced in the 10-year period 1961-1970 [1], there are about 15,000 theoretically possible combinations of two different drugs! Then, very efficient communication of information regarding adverse drug effects in general has resulted in greater awareness by all in the health professions. The thalidomide disaster without doubt contributed greatly to the establishment of worldwide systems for monitoring adverse drug reactions. The operation of the U.S. Food and Drug Agency's drug monitoring program and the American Medical Association's Registry on Adverse Drug Reactions have been described [2, 3]. Other sources of contemporary information on adverse drug effects are described in the preface to Moser's recent book [4].

Of great consequence in bringing attention to drug interactions were a number of still-continuing efforts to obtain reliable epidemiological data on the over-all incidence of adverse drug effects [5-9]. Active surveillance of hospitalized patients for adverse drug effects has revealed very high incidence rates—up to 18% in the Johns Hopkins study [7] and 10.2% in a study in Belfast [9]. Other studies where surveillance was not carried out by a special team but relied on reports from hospital resident staff showed a lower rate of incidence, 1-3% [6, 8, 10]. Hospital admissions due to adverse drug effects ranged from 2.9% [11] to 5% [7] of the total admissions. In the Hopkins study [7] it was found that an average of 14 different drugs were employed during an average patient's hospital stay. In at least two studies [11,17] a direct relationship between the number of drugs used and the probability of adverse reaction emerged. Without doubt, drugs are used to treat unrecognized reactions to other drugs. Moser [12] has used the phrase "the domino theory of therapeutics" to describe this situation.

Statistical data such as those above do not distinguish whether the increased incidence of adverse drug effects is due to real drug interactions or results from the mathematically increased probability of an adverse effect with increasing number of drugs. Nevertheless, the potential hazard has been made clear by these studies, and articles and books with disquieting titles such as "The Diseases Drugs Cause" [13], "Ill-Health Due to Drugs" [14], and *Diseases of Medical Progress* [4] are now widely cited.

Fixed Drug Combinations

In retrospect, the U.S. Food and Drug Administration's toughening posture on fixed-combination multiple drug products also seems, at least in part, a culmination of increased awareness during the past 10 years of possible adverse effects from multiple drug use. Five years ago, in an article, "Problems of Drug Interaction" [15], it was concluded, "The problem of fixed drug combinations must be considered in the problem of drug interaction." In the National Academy of Sciences drug efficacy review [16] it was concluded, regarding certain fixed dose combinations of drugs, "Risks of adverse drug reactions (from combinations) should not be multiplied unless there is overriding benefit."

Thus the problem of potential adverse effects from drug interactions has come to have, by indirect means, the potential for profound economic consequences to the pharmaceutical industry as well as to have a general impact on the practice of medicine.

Scope of the Review

In preparing this article we have not attempted to present an encyclopedic compilation of all known drug interactions. Such reviews have been prepared by others [18-21]. We have attempted here to review in a critical way mechanisms by which drug interactions can occur, giving particular emphasis to recent work. The bibliography is, we believe, adequate to permit further background reading in the several areas we have considered. We use generic names throughout this chapter. Trade names may be located in several standard works [22, 23]. No attempt has been made to consider interaction between drugs and alcohol, as a review has recently appeared [24].

Although the interference of drugs with clinical laboratory determinations is not without consequence and may be considered within the purview of drug interactions, we have excluded this subject from our review. The reader interested in this topic is referred to the work of Cross et al. [25].

PHARMACODYNAMICS

Protein Binding

Binding of drugs to plasma proteins is commonly believed to play an important role in drug interactions, especially those involving tightly bound substances. A great deal of emphasis has been laid on the possibility of adverse drug reactions arising from competition for plasma protein binding sites. Classes of compounds for which protein binding is considered significant include the penicillins [26], sulfonamides [27], anticoagulants [28, 29], nonsteroid anti-inflammatory agents [30], several compounds of interest in cancer chemotherapy [31, 32], and certain endogenous hormones such as thyroxine [33] and the corticosteroids [34]. Brodie [35] has called attention to several cases of drug toxicity where changes in binding may be implicated. Particular emphasis in this review will be placed on the interactions of warfarin and several sulfonamides with phenylbutazone [28, 29, 36] and the observation of sulfonamide-related kernicterus in the newborn [37-40].

In qualitative terms, the role of plasma protein binding competition in drug interactions may be explained quite simply by considering a simple two-compartment pharmacokinetic model, as illustrated in Fig. 1. Drug introduced into the plasma compartment (of volume V_1) will exist partially as bound drug and partially as free drug, the proportion depending on the total concentration of binding sites and

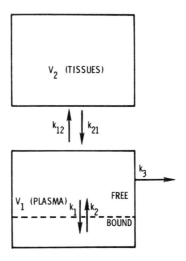

Fig. 1. Schematic diagram of a two-compartment pharmacokinetic model, including drug binding to plasma proteins.

the binding and unbinding rate constants k_1 and k_2. Only the free portion of the drug, however, will be available for equilibration with tissues, here represented simply as an equilibration with a single "tissue" compartment of V_2 with forward and backward rate constants k_{12} and k_{21}, and for elimination, represented as a single rate constant k_3 which is the sum of all excretion and metabolic rate constants for the drug.

It is fairly apparent that the amount of drug in the tissue compartment will depend strongly on the proportion of free drug in the plasma compartment—i.e., on the amount of drug that is available for exchange with tissues. Particularly in the case of highly bound drugs, small changes in binding would be expected to cause relatively large changes in the concentration of free drug, which will result in more rapid elimination, and a rise in drug concentration in tissues. A decrease in the proportion of bound drug from 90 to 80%, for example, doubles the plasma concentration of free drug. Such shifts in binding of a drug could easily be brought about by the introduction of a second drug, which competed for the same plasma protein binding sites. By increasing tissue levels of drugs, binding competitors would be expected to potentiate drug action.

It is important in evaluating potential drug interactions arising from binding competition to consider the nature of the protein responsible for drug binding. Numerous plasma proteins have been

implicated in the binding of small molecules: specific transport proteins such as those which bind thyroxine [33] and corticosteroids [34];
lipoproteins, which bind Δ^9-tetrahydrocannabinol [41] and may bind
other hydrophobic compounds; and serum albumin, whose drug-binding properties appear to be a special case of its binding capacity
for anions, hydrophobic compounds, and even some cations [42]. Because of the large number and variety of the substances which it
binds, serum albumin is the most likely to be involved in this type
of drug interaction. The best-documented cases seem, in fact, to
involve competition at the anion-binding sites of serum albumin, the
sites of binding of warfarin [28], the anti-inflammatory drugs [43],
the penicillins [44], and the sulfonamides [36], as well as fatty acids
[42]. There appear to be a large but variable number of these sites,
depending somewhat on the size of the ion involved, ranging from 10
strongly binding sites for chloride or thiocyanate to 5 for p-(2-hy-
droxy-5-methylphenylazo)benzoate [42], and one for warfarin [28].
It may be that a large number of positively charged areas on the
serum albumin molecule represent potential binding sites, the availability of which is subject to steric restrictions, local hydrophobicity,
etc.

The quantitative effects of binding competition on pharmacokinetics have recently been investigated in this laboratory, using numerical techniques to solve the nonlinear differential equations generated
by the model of Fig. 1 [45]. The magnitude of competition effects may
be illustrated by considering the use of a hypothetical drug of molecular weight 150, administered at a dose of 10 mg/kg. The plasma
volume is assumed to be 50 ml/kg and the tissue distribution volume
600 ml/kg, a reasonable approximation of total body water. Figure 2
presents the remaining assumptions necessary to calculate plasma
and tissue concentrations, and shows the effect on the plasma concentration-time curve of reducing protein binding of the drug from
90 to 80%, and to 9%, representing a small and a relatively large
competitive effect, respectively. The weaker binding competition
causes very little change in the plasma concentration-time curve,
while, as might be expected, the effect of the stronger competition
is far more dramatic. More interesting, however, is the effect on
tissue levels of the drug, shown in Fig. 3. Despite the doubling of
free drug concentration caused by the shift from 90 to 80% bound,
there is almost no change in tissue levels of drug. Even the change
to 9% bound causes less than a doubling of drug concentration in tissues, except at very early times. Thus, if a drug is redistributed
into body water, it seems unlikely that binding competition, no matter
how effective, could cause large increases in tissue concentration,
at least after a single dose of drug.

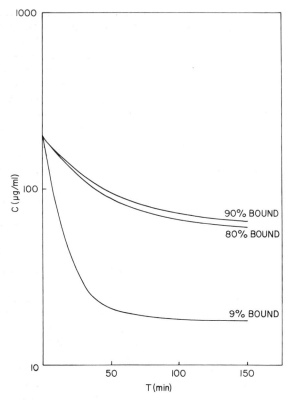

Fig. 2. Calculated concentration-time curves in plasma of a 10 mg/kg dose of a hypothetical drug of molecular weight 150 in a two-compartment system with protein binding. The inner distribution volume is 50 ml/kg; the outer is 600 ml/kg. The drug is bound to serum albumin (molecular weight = 67,000). which is present at a concentration of 4.4% and has 10 drug-binding sites per molecule. The percentage of bound drug indicated with each curve refers to the behavior of the system at low drug concentrations, where binding is approximately linear. Reprinted from Ref. 45 by permission of the American Pharmaceutical Association.

The crucial variable is the ratio of tissue distribution volume to plasma volume—in the notation used for the two-compartment case, V_2/V_1. If V_2/V_1 is large, the total amount of drug liberated from plasma proteins, even with relatively large shifts in binding, is insufficient to cause a large concentration change in the tissue volume into which it is diluted.

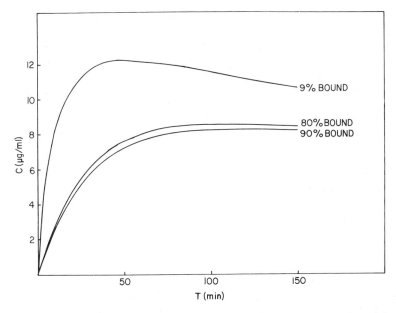

Fig. 3. Calculated concentration-time curves in the tissue compartment for a 10 mg/kg dose of a hypothetical drug of molecular weight 150, corresponding to the plasma curve of Fig. 2. Reprinted from Ref. 45 by permission of the American Pharmaceutical Association.

However, even though the binding competition effect may be limited to a few special cases, there are several examples in the literature where this effect is thought to be of major importance. It is not always possible to evaluate these cases in a quantitative fashion; the kinetics, or more often the binding parameters, of the compounds in question are often reported in an incomplete or contradictory fashion. In the case of the sulfonamide-bilirubin interaction, for example, Josephson and Furst [40] report that bilirubin appears to be more tightly bound to serum albumin than sulfamethoxypyridazine or sulfamethoxazole; yet, the sulfa drugs appear to displace bilirubin in competitive binding experiments while bilirubin will not displace the sulfa drugs. This apparent contradiction may be due, in part, to the difficulty of measuring bilirubin binding. In other cases the simple qualitative observation of binding competition in vitro has been accepted as evidence that competition in vivo is responsible for drug interaction, with no quantitative consideration whether the competition can account for the observed effects.

This latter approach was taken by O'Reilly and Levy [29] in the case of the warfarin-phenylbutazone interaction, despite the availability of extensive binding data for both compounds. They have shown that the effect of phenylbutazone is on the relationship between the synthesis of prothrombin complex activity and total concentration of warfarin in plasma, and conclude that phenylbutazone increases the proportion of free warfarin in plasma, making it more available to its pharmacologic receptor site. Now that methods are available to calculate predicted kinetic curves from binding data [45], it is no longer necessary to make qualitative predictions. Accordingly, we have used the kinetic and binding data of Aggeler et al. [28] to generate predicted concentration-time curves for a 1.5-mg/kg dose of warfarin in the presence and absence of a dose of phenylbutazone sufficient to produce a blood level of 100 µg/ml.

Figure 4, taken from Aggeler et al. [28], illustrates the time course of warfarin disappearance from plasma. Extrapolation to

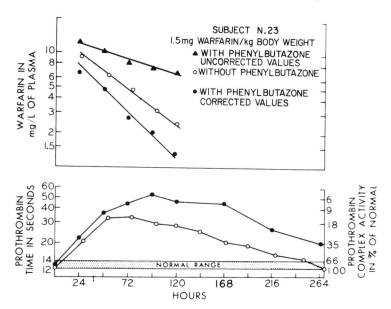

Fig. 4. Effect of administration of phenylbutazone on the prothrombic response and on the plasma level and disappearance rate of warfarin in a normal subject. Phenylbutazone, 600 mg/day, was given by mouth for 14 days before and 11 days after administration of a standard dose of warfarin, 1.5 mg/kg orally. Reprinted from Ref. 28 by permission of the Massachusetts Medical Society.

zero time yields an estimated total distribution volume of only
100 ml/kg. In the rat, dog, and monkey, where more extensive
studies have been carried out, total distribution volumes of 120-
150 ml/kg were observed [46]. If one assumes that warfarin can be
fitted to a two-compartment model with inner and outer compartment volumes both equal to 50 ml/kg, it becomes apparent that the
dilution factor due to V_2/V_1 will be quite small. The effect of phenylbutazone at 100 μg/ml on the protein binding of warfarin is shown
in Fig. 5, from Aggeler et al. [28]. The warfarin-protein association
constant is decreased from 6.7×10^4 to 7.0×10^3. The effect of
this binding competition, and of the small dilution factor, is apparent
in Fig. 6, which illustrates the predicted concentrations of warfarin
in the tissue compartment of the two-compartment model. In this
case, the competitive binding effect of phenylbutazone is sufficient

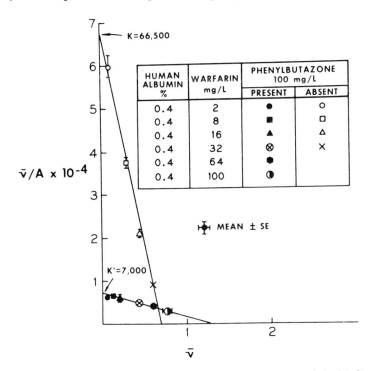

Fig. 5. Scatchard plot of data in equilibrium-dialysis studies of the binding
of ^{14}C-warfarin sodium and albumin in the presence and absence of phenylbutazone. Reprinted from Ref. 28 by permission of the Massachusetts Medical Society.

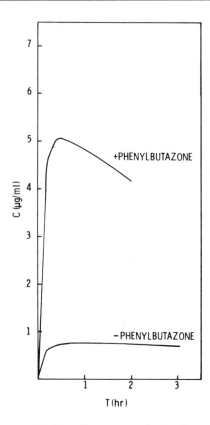

Fig. 6. Calculated concentration-time curves in the tissue compartment of warfarin in the presence and absence of phenylbutazone. Reprinted from Ref. 45 by permission of the American Pharmaceutical Association.

to cause a more than fivefold increase in the maximum level of warfarin in the tissue compartment. Because V_2/V_1 is small, the competitive binding mechanism is sufficient to produce a severe interaction.

However, the fact that the magnitude of the expected binding competition effect is sufficient to account for the warfarin-phenylbutazone interaction does not, of course, establish that this effect is in fact responsible for the observed clinical symptoms. To begin with, the assumptions involved in the calculation of the competition effect are, in some cases, rather arbitrary. In particular, in the absence of data on plasma phenylbutazone concentrations during the combined

drug administration, the magnitude of its competitive effect on warfarin binding may only be estimated. Furthermore, the predicted
effects can only be calculated over a period of a few hours [45],
while the first observations on warfarin concentrations in clinical
patients were made 24 hr after administering the drug [28]. It would
be of considerable interest to observe the changes in warfarin concentration over the first few hours after a single large dose of phenylbutazone, during the time period that redistribution of newly-released
free drug would presumably be taking place.

It is also worth noting that other factors are known to influence
the fate of warfarin: barbiturates, for example, increase the rate of
warfarin metabolism and may decrease its absorption from the gastrointestinal tract [47]. The importance of these effects will be discussed further in a later section.

Other special cases, in which binding competition is of great importance but V_2/V_1 is large, may arise from other circumstances.
The sulfonamide-related kernicterus of the newborn [37-40] appears
to be due to binding competition between sulfonamides and endogenous
bilirubin. Even if bilirubin is distributed in body water [48], and
V_2/V_1 is quite large, the continuous endogenous synthesis of the compound could still give rise to a large increase in tissue bilirubin concentration by titrating the patient, so to speak, up to a new steady-
state level. This titration effect, which would not be possible with a
single dose of an exogenous drug, may be responsible for the severity
of the sulfonamide-bilirubin interaction, and for some of the interactions seen after multiple drug doses.

Drug interactions arising from effects on protein binding need
not, of course, be confined to competitive effects; many cases are
known in which the binding of a ligand to a protein molecule will
increase the binding constant for a second type of ligand. A plausible
mechanism for this type of interaction, based on conformational
transitions in the protein, has been advanced by Monod, Wyman, and
Changeux [49]. An increase in protein binding may be responsible
for the unusual interaction between chlorothiazide and the antihypertensive pempidine (1,2,2,6,6-pentamethylpiperidine), observed by
Dollery et al. [50]. Chlorothiazide treatment of patients receiving
pempidine results in approximately a threefold increase in plasma
pempidine concentration, with no corresponding increase in hypotensive effect. The speculation that this increase might represent
pempidine bound to plasma protein has been supported by the recent
observations of Breckenridge and Rosen [51]. Ultrafiltration of
pempidine added to plasma from human subjects showed that 4% of
the drug was bound in control subjects, while with plasma from

patients given chlorothiazide, 40% of the pempidine was bound. However, the mechanism of this effect remains obscure. No binding of pempidine to human serum albumin was observed in vitro, in either the presence or the absence of chlorothiazide. Furthermore, pempidine was without effect on the observed binding of chlorothiazide. It seems likely, then, that other proteins than serum albumin are involved in pempidine binding; serum albumin would, in any case, be an unlikely candidate for positive binding interactions since these have not been observed with a large variety of ligands.

With the numerical techniques presently available, it is both feasible and desirable to investigate the quantitative basis of suspected drug interactions resulting from effects on protein binding. In general, it appears that for single doses of exogenous compounds, this mechanism will be of small importance unless the total distribution volume of the drug is not much greater than the plasma volume.

Biotransformation

One of the most common mechanisms of drug interaction involves the effects of one drug on the metabolism of another. A given metabolic pathway may be either stimulated or inhibited, affecting either the detoxication or activation of a drug. Some such interactions, like those involved in binding competition, may be reciprocal, especially if both drugs are metabolized by the same enzyme system with similar affinity constants; however, for the sake of clarity in the discussion to follow, the compound whose metabolism is altered will be referred to as the drug, while the compound affecting the metabolic pathway will be referred to as the agent. In some cases—e.g., phenobarbital—the drug and the agent may be one and the same, but these are not, in the strict sense, cases of drug interaction.

Agents can exert their effects through any of a number of mechanisms. They may induce the formation of drug-metabolizing enzymes, increasing the rate of metabolism, or compete for substrates or enzymes needed for drug metabolism, decreasing the rate. In some cases the structure of the agent may lead to a reasonable prediction of its effects on the metabolism of other compounds: allopurinol, an example which will be discussed in detail presently, was designed as a purine analog for the explicit purpose of inhibiting xanthine oxidase. In other cases, however, effects on drug metabolism are fortuitous and unforeseen, and lead to unexpected drug interactions. The nature, and particularly the severity, of the interaction may depend in part on the mechanism of the metabolic effect. In particular, irreversible inhibitors, such as those used to block monoamine oxidase, cause intense and long-lasting effects.

The metabolic pathways affected may be responsible either for detoxication or activation of drugs; hence, either a stimulating or an inhibitory effect may result in either antagonism or potentiation of pharmacologic actions. In general, detoxication mechanisms are involved, so that enzyme induction leads to antagonism while inhibition leads to potentiation. The specificity of the effect may be either broad or narrow, involving, for example, either the liver microsomal enzyme system, which is responsible for the metabolism of numerous drugs, or specific enzymes whose action is limited to a single compound or class of compounds.

One of the most common mechanisms of metabolically mediated drug interactions, the induction of the liver microsomal enzyme system, will not be discussed in this review, since the large volume of literature on this topic has been adequately summarized elsewhere [52]. The present review will discuss a limited number of cases of inhibition, with a view to exploring the mechanisms involved and their consequences in some detail, rather than developing a comprehensive catalog of proven and potential interactions. For the most part, the interactions discussed will be those which, whether or not foreseeable, were not desired effects of the drug combination—however, examples will be presented of competitive metabolic interactions deliberately exploited for therapeutic purposes.

Conceptually, perhaps the simplest case of metabolic inhibition is that of competition for substrates, a case of which has been studied by Levy and Yamada [53]. Both acetaminophen and salicylamide are excreted in the urine chiefly as the glucuronide and sulfate conjugates. The formation of acetaminophen sulfate appears to be capacity-limited: the peak excretion rate of the sulfate is substantially less than doubled in human subjects when the acetaminophen dose is raised from 1 to 2 g. Furthermore, in some subjects, a plateau in plots of excretion rate vs time was seen at high doses, indicating that a maximum rate had been reached.

Concomitant dosing with acetaminophen and salicylamide led to a mutual decrease in the amount of acetaminophen and salicylamide sulfates excreted. The limitation on sulfate formation suggests that the two drugs competed for some part of the metabolic mechanism. The nature of the competition became clear when it was observed that a dose of 2 g L-cysteine every hour from 1.5 hr before the acetaminophen dose to 2.5 hr afterward, prevented the mutual inhibition of sulfate formation by acetaminophen and salicylamide. The effect of this sulfur source would suggest that the limiting substance for which the drugs compete is sulfate. A similar limitation of sulfate in the metabolism of phenols by the rabbit was noted earlier by Bray and co-workers [54, 55].

The behavior of the glucuronide conjugates, however, is rather less simple. Salicylamide decreased the excretion of acetaminophen—thus less acetaminophen (including metabolites) was excreted after salicylamide treatment. Particularly in the absence of data on drug concentrations in blood, it is difficult to say whether this effect was on metabolism or directly upon excretion. The excretion of total salicylamide (plus metabolites) is unaffected by acetaminophen; however, the decrease in sulfate formation is accompanied by a roughly compensating increase in glucuronide formation. Apparently, then, acetaminophen is without direct effect on the conjugation of salicylamide with UDP-glucuronic acid.

The sulfate effect seems to be one of simple competition for endogenous substrate: it is reciprocal and can be reversed with an excess of the limiting substrate. The glucuronide competition, on the other hand, is one in which reciprocity is not seen and which might involve excretory mechanisms in addition to a metabolic effect.

At least under some experimental conditions, glutathione may also be a limiting substrate. If hepatic glutathione is depleted in rats by pretreatment with iodomethane, biliary excretion of sulfobromophthalein is decreased and a larger proportion of the excreted material is unaltered drug rather than the glutathione conjugate [56]. It is unclear whether the presence of more than one drug which was conjugated in this manner would sufficiently deplete the glutathione supply, but the possibility of this type of interaction should be considered.

Not infrequently, an agent will directly inhibit the enzymatic mechanisms of drug metabolism, even though it was not designed as an enzyme inhibitor. Antitubercular drugs, like isoniazid, for example, have been observed to potentiate the effects of diphenylhydantoin in clinical patients [57]. Over a period of several weeks on combined therapy with the two drugs, patients showed a gradually increasing blood concentration of diphenylhydantoin. The formation of the metabolite, 5-phenyl-5'-parahydroxyphenylhydantoin, was decreased, suggesting that isoniazid inhibited the metabolic detoxication of diphenylhydantoin.

Subsequent studies in vitro with cell-free systems from rat liver [58] showed that isoniazid is an inhibitor of the diphenylhydantoin-hydroxylating enzyme system, comparable in potency to SKF-525A. Inhibition is noncompetitive and is not reversed upon addition of excess co-factors. It appears, then, that isoniazid acts directly on the microsomal drug-hydroxylating system, inhibiting the detoxication of diphenylhydantoin. One might predict, from this apparent mechanism, that isoniazid would also potentiate the effects of other drugs which were detoxified by this pathway.

In some cases enzyme inhibition is itself a desired property of a drug. Nonetheless, unforeseen interactions may arise because of the participation by the enzyme in reactions of diverse physiological or pharmacological significance. Inhibitors of monoamine oxidase (MAO), for instance, have been used widely in psychopharmacology. The MAO inhibitors are irreversible and recovery must await the synthesis of new enzyme; hence, untoward reactions involving this system tend to be severe and long-lasting. In particular, potentiation of the hypertensive effects of dopamine and tyramine [59, 60] has been known to produce fatalities. Furthermore, amine precursors such as 5-hydroxytryptophan, DOPA, and tyrosine can give rise to interactions. These amino acids, which pass the blood-brain barrier, can cause a central accumulation of the corresponding amines in experimental animals treated with MAO inhibitors [61].

Monoamine oxidase inhibitors give rise to interactions not only with drugs, but also with amines normally present in foodstuffs. The tyramine content of several cheeses, innocuous in a normal subject, may cause serious hypertension and even death in patients incapable of detoxifying the amine [59, 60].

The inhibition of MAO is responsible for a number of important interactions with drugs which are not themselves metabolized by this enzyme. Sjöqvist has reviewed these interactions extensively [61]. It is important to note that an excessively narrow conception of the mechanism of action of an inhibitor can lead one to overlook indirect interactions which may be of great clinical importance.

The effect of allopurinol (4-hydroxypyrazolopyrimidine) on drug metabolism may serve as an illustration of the complications that can be encountered in unraveling the mechanism of action of what seems to be a simple metabolic inhibitor. Allopurinol was synthesized as a specific inhibitor of xanthine oxidase, to be used in treating the hyperuricemia associated with gout. The compound is quite effective against xanthine oxidase in vitro and has a binding constant to the enzyme of about 5×10^{-7} M [62]. The effect in man appears to be what might be expected from inhibition of xanthine oxidase: serum uric acid levels drop, and urinary excretion of uric acid is greatly diminished. These metabolic changes are associated with relief of symptoms of gout in clinical patients [63-65].

Leukemia patients, particularly those in chemotherapy, frequently have high blood concentrations of uric acid. As in the classic case of gout, hyperuricemia may lead to serious clinical consequences and must frequently be controlled as a part of leukemia therapy. Allopurinol has proven effective as an adjunct to leukemia therapy [63-65] and is often employed for this purpose.

There exists, however, the possibility of a serious interaction with one of the drugs commonly employed as an antileukemic agent. The purine analog 6-mercaptopurine (6-MP) is detoxified, at least in part, by oxidation to 6-thiouric acid (6-TU) by xanthine oxidase [63-65]. It has also been observed that allopurinol has little inhibitory effect on inosinic acid pyrophosphorylase (binding constant about 10^{-3} M), the enzyme which converts 6-MP to its presumed active metabolite 6-thioinosinic acid (6-TIMP) [62]. Thus it has been suggested by Elion and co-workers [63-65] that allopurinol would potentiate the action of 6-MP by inhibiting its metabolism. They have, in fact, observed a drastic decrease in the excretion of 6-TU by allopurinol-treated patients and report a potentiation by allopurinol of the chemotherapeutic effect of 6-MP against adenocarcinoma 755 in mice [63].

However, a detailed study of the excretion of ^{14}C-labeled 6-MP and its metabolites in tumor-bearing mice has shown that the decrease in 6-TU excretion is compensated for by an increase in labeled dethiolated purines. It appears that there is an alternative pathway available to maintain the over-all rate of 6-MP detoxication [66]. In view of the fact that up to half the ^{35}S-labeled 6-MP administered to human subjects appeared in the urine as sulfate [67], it would appear that this alternative pathway may operate in the same fashion in man. An increase in dethiolation of 6-MP when xanthine oxidase is inhibited would explain the lack of effect of allopurinol on the plasma half-life of high i.v. doses of 6-MP in cancer patients [68] and on the clinical response to 6-MP in childhood acute leukemia [69].

If allopurinol were to potentiate the action of 6-MP, it would presumably lead to an increase in the tissue levels of 6-TIMP. This is clearly not the case in solid L1210 tumors growing in mice, where the concentration of 6-TIMP in the tumor is decreased by 80% in allopurinol-treated animals. Furthermore, despite this decrease in the presumed active metabolite, allopurinol is without effect on the chemotherapeutic activity of 6-MP against L1210 [66].

The pharmacodynamics of the allopurinol-6-MP interaction may differ in different tissues. In adenocarcinoma 755, in which a therapeutic potentiation was observed [63], allopurinol has no effect on 6-TIMP levels after 6-MP treatment. On the other hand, in the liver of L1210-bearing animals, the level of 6-TIMP was increased [66].

Not only is there considerable uncertainty about the mechanisms and consequences of the actions of allopurinol directly related to xanthine oxidase inhibition, but it appears that there may also be allopurinol effects of a more general nature. Vesell et al. [70] have observed an increase in the plasma half-life of antipyrine in subjects dosed chronically with allopurinol, and conclude that the compound may be a general inhibitor of drug metabolism, at least when given chronically. It may, in fact, turn out that the most significant drug interactions with allopurinol, from a clinical point of view, will be those unrelated to its primary action as a specific enzyme inhibitor.

Not all the interactions due to metabolic inhibition are to be considered clinically adverse reactions. The potentiation of drug action may, in fact, be utilized to convert an agent of marginal utility to one of considerable effectiveness. The antileukemic agent 1-β-D-arabino-furanosylcytosine (ara-C) is rapidly converted by a pyrimidine nucleoside deaminase to a biologically inactive product, 1-β-D arabino-furanosyl uracil (ara-U). This enzyme is found in human plasma and appears to be responsible for the limited effectiveness of the drug, particularly by the oral route, in man [71]. Tetrahydrouridine (THU) is a potent inhibitor of pyrimidine nucleoside deaminase, both in vitro and in vivo [72, 73]. Thus Neil and co-workers [74] have attempted to produce a potentiation of ara-C activity by THU treatment of tumor-bearing mice. Ordinarily, three to ten times as much ara-C must be administered orally as parenterally to mice to achieve the same chemotherapeutic effect. After THU treatment, however, oral doses equal or exceed the effect of the same dose given intraperitoneally despite the lack of antitumor activity of THU alone.

Plasma levels of ara-C after an oral dose are increased three-to fivefold by THU treatment. Although these levels are still only about 20% of those seen after intraperitoneal administration, there is also an increase in ara-C half-life, leading to a still greater increase in over-all exposure. Considering the total exposure to drug as the area under the concentration-time curve, it appears that, over the 4-hr course of the experiment, the exposure to ara-C after an oral dose with THU is considerably less than that after an intraperitoneal dose without THU. However, over the last hour of the experiment, blood levels in the THU-treated, orally-dosed animals exceeded those in the intraperitoneally-dosed animals, and the total exposures may eventually become equal if exposure at long time intervals is of importance. The relative role of THU treatment in the chemotherapy and toxicity of ara-C may well depend on the tissue levels and distribution of pyrimidine nucleoside deaminase in various species.

In conclusion, the effects of metabolic inhibitors on drug interactions—even in the cases where the inhibitors appear to have a specific effect on a single enzyme—may be complex and indirect. Secondary effects due to accumulation of metabolites from blocked normal pathways in tissues, or even effects unrelated to the primary site of inhibitor action, may occur and may, in fact, be of greater pharmacological and clinical significance than the presumed primary effect. Detailed consideration of the mechanism of even the simplest metabolic interaction appears to uncover unforeseen complications, and it is never safe to assume that an interaction has been adequately explained on the basis of an inhibition experiment in vitro.

Urinary Excretion

To facilitate understanding of the alterations in drug kinetics which may occur in certain drug combinations, some knowledge of renal mechanisms is important. The factors determining the rate of urinary drug excretion are glomerular filtration, tubular reabsorption, and tubular secretion. Alterations of tubular processes rather than glomerular filtration rate are involved in drug interactions at the level of the kidney.

It is by now well recognized [75] that a urinary acidifying agent such as ammonium chloride decreases tubular reabsorption of basic drugs and thereby increases their rate of elimination. Increased rates of excretion of pseudoephedrine [76] and amphetamine [77] in humans by urinary acidification are recent examples. Conversely, urinary alkalinizing agents such as bicarbonate accelerate excretion of acidic drugs such as salicylate by decreasing tubular reabsorption.

Tubular secretion, being an active process, may be decreased by metabolic inhibitors or by competition for transport systems. There are several examples of drug interactions resulting from interference with renal tubular processes.

Best known for its inhibition of renal tubular transport of organic acids is probenecid. It effectively blocks renal tubular transport of penicillin [78], resulting in prolonged plasma half-life of antibiotic. A recent, detailed pharmacokinetic study of this combination in humans [79] suggests that this mechanism alone is inadequate to quantitatively account for the decrease in rate of excretion of penicillin. The action of probenecid appears additionally to result in a decrease in the volume of distribution of penicillin.

The potent uricosuric agent, sulfinpyrazine, also reduced renal tubular secretion of other organic acids such as salicylate [80]. The drug in addition interacts with sulfonamides, decreasing their renal clearance probably by inhibition of a tubular secretion mechanism [81].

High blood levels of the antidiabetic agent chlorpropamide, and correspondingly lower levels of blood glucose, have been observed in humans when salicylate is used [82]. Interference with tubular secretion by salicylate was thought responsible.

The potentiation of the antidiabetic action of acetohexamide by phenylbutazone observed in humans [83] illustrates another point. The plasma half-life of acetohexamide was unchanged by phenylbutazone, but the plasma half-life of its active metabolite, hydroxyacetohexamide, increased from 5.3 ± 0.9 hr in controls to 22.1 ± 3.2 hr. Phenylbutazone appears to inhibit renal excretion of the active metabolite.

Inhibition of renal tubular transport of catecholamines by cocaine has recently been studied in the chicken [84]. The technique used is based on infusion of the test substance into renal portal circulation of one kidney of an unanesthetized hen followed by independent collection of urines from control and infused kidneys. Rate of excretion of ^{14}C-labeled norepinephrine, epinephrine, and tyramine was decreased by cocaine. Cocaine appears to compete for the organic base (cation) transport system in the kidney. It was also observed that tricyclic antidepressants such as imipramine compete for norepinephrine transport sites in the kidney. Aspirin has recently been reported [85] to reduce the renal clearance of ^{125}I-diatrizoate in humans. The mechanism is unknown.

Clearly patients with renal disease will show impaired renal clearance of drugs and drug combinations. Drug dosage must be reduced and practical guides for alterations of dosage schedules have been published [86, 87]. Of interest, however, is the report of a statistically reduced incidence of adverse drug effects in hospitalized patients with diagnosed renal disease [10]. This undoubtedly reflects the great care exercised with these patients since, in general, renal disease appears to be a predisposing factor toward adverse drug reactions [6].

There is some evidence in the rabbit that p-aminohippurate and penicillin enhance the maturation of renal transport mechanisms for organic acids in the newborn [88]. This study in vitro was based on the ability of renal cortical slices to accumulate p-aminohippurate. Twice daily administration of drug for 3 to 7 days significantly increased uptake. These results support the hypothesis that treatment of young animals with organic anions can lead to selective stimulation of mechanisms responsible for renal organic acid transport in the newborn. The resulting increased efficiency of drug excretion could be a mechanism for drug interaction in the newborn but the issue is unexplored.

Gastrointestinal Absorption and Biliary Excretion

The process of drug absorption has been the subject of a recent review [89]. Several interactions due to effects of complexation on drug absorption are known. Interference with absorption of tetracyclines by calcium salts is an example and is due to formation of a calcium chelate. A recent report [90] shows that iron salts administered for treatment of iron deficiency anemias also interfere with absorption of tetracyclines in man. Cholestyramine, a basic ion exchange resin used to treat hypercholesteremia, binds organic acids, including drugs, preventing their absorption. Absorption of chlorothiazide, phenylbutazone, phenobarbital, and tetracycline is inhibited. The resin also interferes with absorption of thyroxine [91]. Intraperitoneal administration of desipramine interferes with oral absorption of phenylbutazine in the rat [92]. The cholinergic blocking properties of the dibenzazepine class of antidepressants are distinct [93], and it seems possible that a decrease in intestinal motility produced by desipramine results in decreased oral absorption of phenylbutazone.

The effect of surfactants and bile salts on the rates of drug absorption may also be profound [94]. It should be recognized that bile flow in man is appreciable, up to 2-3 liters being produced daily. Several grams of bile salts may be secreted into the small intestine and recirculated 2-3 times during a meal by an enterohepatic pathway. Enhanced bile flow favors absorption of sulfadiazine [95]. When bile salts are administered to remedy deficiencies in endogenous bile salts, the rate of absorption of other drugs may be modified. Below we review several additional examples of drug interactions where absorption and/or biliary effects may play a role.

Indomethacin/Aspirin/Probenecid. Aspirin and indomethacin, common anti-inflammatory drugs, interact in patients with rheumatoid arthritis [96]. Salicylic acid also markedly influences the pharmacokinetics of indomethacin in the rat [97], causing a significant decrease in plasma indomethacin levels. In the rat the interaction is observed in all possible combinations of oral and intravenous administration of both agents.

Acetate and chlorogenic acid, the principal organic acid in coffee, are without influence on indomethacin levels, as is phenylbutazone. In contrast, probenecid significantly increases indomethacin plasma levels in the rat [97] and in man [98]. Salicylate in the rat and probenecid in man decreased urinary excretion of indomethacin and/or metabolites, presumably by inhibition of their secretion by the renal tubules.

As the urinary route of excretion is a minor one for indomethacin, it seems certain that an effect on the rate of biliary excretion and/or intestinal reabsorption of indomethacin and its metabolites is involved in the interaction of this drug with aspirin.

Displacement of endogenous plasma-protein-bound steroids has been suggested as a mode of action of indomethacin and other non-

steroidal anti-inflammatory agents [99], although several attempts
to demonstrate displacements of steroids by indomethacin at therapeutic levels in vivo have failed [100-102]. These results, together
with the results of Winter [103] which also failed to implicate endogenous anti-inflammatory steroids in the action of indomethacin,
suggest this mechanism cannot now be supported. At therapeutic
levels, salicylate is without effect on the free/bound ratio of indomethacin in vitro and in vivo [103]. It therefore seems unlikely that
displacement of plasma bound indomethacin is involved in the interaction between these drugs.

Salicylate and indomethacin are both metabolized to glucuronides
[104, 105]. Competition for glucuronide synthesizing enzymes and/or
transport sites for these conjugates nevertheless seems improbable
as an explanation of the interaction. Acetaminophen, also conjugated
and excreted largely as glucuronide and sulfate, is much less efficient in influencing the kinetics of indomethacin than is salicylate
[106]. Using a molar dose of acetaminophen 80% greater than used
with salicylate or aspirin, the effect was less than half (Fig. 7). Competition for sulfate or sulfate synthesizing enzyme seems in general
more probable than competition for UDP-glucuronic acid.

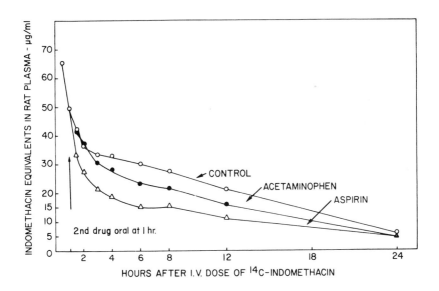

Fig. 7. Effect of oral administration of acetaminophen and aspirin on plasma
levels of indomethacin injected in vivo in rats. Indomethacin was administered
at 10 mg/kg, aspirin at 138 mg/kg, and acetaminophen at 200 mg/kg.

It may be that the metabolically derived sulfate ester of acetaminophen is responsible for the effects of the parent drug or indomethacin. This might explain the quantitative difference between salicylate and acetaminophen. It has already been shown, for example, that administration of acetaminophen influences the extent of conjugation of salicylamide with sulfate as has been noted previously [53]. The matter might be resolved by preparation and separate evaluation of acetaminophen sulfate.

The decreased plasma levels of indomethacin in rats administered salicylate are accounted for by the increased fecal excretion of drug and metabolites. As salicylate inhibits transport of many substances across the intestinal wall [107, 108], it seems possible that salicylate inhibits intestinal reabsorption of indomethacin. Salicylate is observed to be secreted in bile in amounts equivalent on a molar basis to the secreted indomethacin-derived radioactivity. Accordingly, interruption of the reabsorption phase of the enterohepatic cycle of indomethacin by salicylate may account for the decreased plasma levels.

The following seems pertinent with respect to the indomethacin-probenecid interaction. Although probenecid is well known to inhibit tubular secretion of organic acids [78], it also inhibits biliary excretion of a number of carboxylic and sulfonic acids [109]. Biliary excretion of chlorothiazide, not a carboxylic or sulfonic acid, is also markedly depressed by probenecid in the rat [110]. It therefore seems reasonable to postulate that probenecid interferes with the biliary secretion of indomethacin.

Another example of an effect involving alterations in biliary excretion is the depression of biliary p-aminohippuric acid excretion by chlorothiazide in the rat [110].

Coumarin/Heptabarbital. The effect of barbiturates on clinical use of coumarin anticoagulants appears definitely to result in part from the induction of liver drug metabolizing enzymes by barbiturate. Nevertheless, recent studies suggest an effect on the oral absorption or biliary excretion of anticoagulant.

It has been reported [111] that heptabarbital reduces the prothrombinogenic effect and plasma levels of orally administered coumarin anticoagulants but not intravenously administered drug. In another study [47], it was shown that pretreatment with heptabarbital significantly decreased plasma half-time and prothrombin levels in humans receiving bishydroxycoumarin either by mouth or intravenously. However, effects were greater in subjects given anticoagulant orally. In subjects receiving both drugs orally, the lowered plasma level was accompanied by an increase in the fecal excretion of anticoagulant. In those given barbiturate by mouth and anticoagulant intravenously, increased fecal excretion of only the metabolite of bishydroxycoumarin was found.

Griseofulvin/Phenobarbital. Phenobarbital is known to stimulate the flow of bile in the rat [112] and it may be that increased bile flow from barbiturates can play a role in accelerating clearance of drugs excreted in bile. Unless care is exercised in the experimental design, it may be difficult to quantitatively differentiate the role of stimulated drug metabolism by barbiturate from enhanced biliary excretion and decreased absorption in a particular drug interaction. Another case where a mechanism involving influence on oral absorption or biliary excretion seems involved is the griseofulvin/phenobarbital combination.

It has been reported that phenobarbital decreased blood levels of griseofulvin in the rabbit [113]. The effect of orally administered phenobarbital on the pharmacokinetics of griseofulvin has been studied in man [114]. The kinetics of elimination of orally or intravenously administered griseofulvin were identical whether or not phenobarbital was administered. However, oral phenobarbital did decrease absorption of orally administered griseofulvin. It was suggested in this case that decreased absorption due to phenobarbital may have resulted from stimulation of bile flow which stimulated peristalsis. This possibility might be evaluated in the rat. Griseofulvin is extensively metabolized in the rat and the metabolites are rapidly secreted into bile and reabsorbed from the intestine [115].

Other Factors

In addition to the well-identified mechanisms described previously, there are a number of other factors which seem relevant to the overall problem of drug interactions. Clinical reports require critical scrutiny. At least one study [116] points up the ease with which "adverse non-drug effects" may be elicited from subjects and notes the need to determine the incidence of "symptoms" before drug treatment. Increased incidence of drug "side effects" after placebo has been demonstrated [117].

In at least two recent cases, careful clinical re-evaluation of earlier reports of drug interactions failed to confirm the original finding. It was found [118] that chloral hydrate does not interact with warfarin in patients on long-term warfarin therapy, at least under the condition of dosage studied. Also, methylphenidate and a similar drug available only in Europe, prolindane, were observed not to influence the metabolism of ethyl biscoumacetate in a follow-up study, although interaction between these drugs had earlier been reported [119].

The effect of old age and gender on incidence of drug interactions has not yet been carefully studied, although these factors have clearly been related to the over-all incidence of adverse drug effects. In one study [120], women showed a greater incidence of adverse drug reactions than men, the relative incidence rates being 14.2 to 7.3%. In a study of efficacy and toxicity of heparin [121], the rate of incidence of adverse effects in women over age 60 was 50% while that of men over 60 was 19%. Age was also a clearly predisposing factor in the incidence of adverse drug effects in the Belfast study [120], even when incidents due to digitalis, commonly used in these elderly patients, were excluded. Alterations in drug activity in the elderly have been reviewed elsewhere [122-124]. In general it appears that decreased absorption, possibly related to decreased intestinal motility and decreased rates of drug biotransformation, occurs in the elderly. Declining activity in accomplishing oxidative drug metabolism in vitro has been observed with the liver microsomes of 600-day old rats [125].

Sex differences in response to various drugs are also common in experimental animals and in many cases have been related to differences in rates of drug metabolism [126, 127]. Of particular interest in the context of drug interactions is the possible effect of use of the oral contraceptive steroids on the action of other drugs. Smaller amounts of metabolites of meperidine and promazine were excreted in urine when these drugs were given to women taking oral contraceptives than occurred when these drugs were given to a control group of women [128]. It has also been reported [129] that the hypoprothrombic response to coumarin anticoagulants is decreased by the oral contraceptives. The mechanism is not clear, but it should be noted that pregnancy also results in a decreased responsiveness to oral anticoagulant drugs [130].

High doses of ethynodrel decrease the metabolism in vivo of hexobarbital and zoxazolamine in the rat [131]. Norethynodrel also results in prolongation of pentobarbital-induced sleeping time in the mouse [132]. It appears that the estrogenic component (ethynylestradiol or mestranol) of the oral contraceptive results in inhibition of metabolism and prolongation of barbiturate activity, while the progestogen (norethynodrel, megestrol acetate, or norethindrone acetate) results in increased rates of metabolism and shortened activity [133]. In this latter study, carried out in the mouse, neither estrogen nor progestin pretreatment altered the effect produced by the largely unmetabolized drug, barbital. Since pretreatment with estrogen or progestin produced large effects with the extensively metabolized barbiturates, pentobarbital and hexobarbital, it was concluded that effects on hepatic metabolism must be at least partly responsible for the results observed. Estrogen pretreatment also appears to decrease the rate of metabolism of chlorpromazine in male rats [134].

Other hormones and related substances can interact with drugs. There has been a report of a 30% increase in plasma levels of oxyphenbutazone when the drug is used with anobolic steroids in humans [135]. The rate of decline of plasma levels of oxyphenbutazone was unchanged in these experiments as the increased plasma levels appear to reflect a change in the volume of distribution of drug rather than a change in rate of metabolism. The mechanism of this change is unknown.

Thyroidal hormones and the status of the thyroid can also influence drug action. Hyperthyroidism results in potentiation of the pharmacological effects of catecholamines. The locomotor activity of d-amphetamine and its toxicity are both potentiated by d-thyroxine in the rat. Toxicity of caffeine is also increased in the hyperthyroid rat [136]. Administration of d-thyroxine (2 mg/kg) in the rat results in great increases in hexobarbital-induced sleeping times. A decreased rate of metabolic transformation of hexobarbital is probably involved in the latter result since administration of thyroxine to male rats results in a decreased rate of hydroxylation of hexobarbital in vitro by liver microsomes [137]. N-Demethylation of aminopyrine by liver microsomes was also found to be decreased. On the other hand, increased metabolism of these drugs is produced by thyroxine in the female rat.

Thyroxine prolongs the prothrombin time in patients on dicumarol [138]. Decreased metabolism of anticoagulant produced by thyroxine is thought to be the mechanism of this effect. It must be noted, however, that increased catabolism of vitamin K-dependent clotting factors in hypermetabolic states such as hyperthyroidism is also thought to be involved in increased responsiveness to oral anticoagulant drugs [139].

One further example of an interaction involving thyroxine is of interest. An intravenous administration of 2 g of sodium salicylate increased the early rate of disappearance of injected ^{131}I-thyroxine from plasma in humans [140]. Unbound thyroxine was unchanged and scanning of the liver showed no increase of radioactivity in this tissue. The amount of thyroxine entering nonhepatic tissue must have been increased. Accordingly, intravenous salicylate appeared to have resulted in a change of the volume of distribution of injected thyroxine.

The role which genetic variation can play in influencing individual response to drugs and possibly drug combinations also merits refer-

ence here. The general topic of pharmacogenetics has already been
the subject of several reviews [140-143]. Of interest here is the fact
that genetic factors can change the pharmacokinetics of drugs. For
example, large individual differences have been observed in steady-
state blood levels and mean plasma half-life of psychotropic drugs
[144, 145]. In view of the fact that only small individual differences
are ordinarily found in plasma binding, absorption, and urinary excretion, differences in individual rates of metabolism or possibly
rates of biliary excretion are implied. This conclusion has been
reached in several studies with different drugs [146-148].

Plasma levels of dicumarol have recently been studied in identical
and fraternal twins by Vesell and Page [148]. Large differences were
found in pairs of fraternal twins while plasma levels of drug in identical twins were always similar. The differences found are believed to
result from genetic differences. Although caffeine and nicotine are
known to induce hepatic drug metabolizing enzymes [149, 150], no
correlation between variation in rates of dicumarol metabolism and
coffee drinking or smoking habits could be demonstrated.

A similar study with fraternal and identical twins has been carried
out using nortriptyline [151]. Results were analogous to those noted
above in the study of dicumarol. Interestingly, however, the intrapair
similarity of identical twins was not found in pairs of twins if other
drugs were taken during the study. Pairs taking barbiturate-contain-
ing drugs always showed lower steady-state blood levels than un-
treated twins. In one monozygotic pair both individuals were being
treated with barbiturate. As expected, the steady-state blood levels
of nortriptyline for this pair were low when compared with the mean
for the entire group under study. However, they continued to show a
remarkable intrapair similarity. An important over-all conclusion
of the Alexanderson study was that concomitant drug exposure, in
addition to genetic factors, played a role in determining the steady-
state blood levels of nortriptyline.

PREDICTABILITY OF EXPERIMENTAL MODELS

Animal experimentation has been one of the chief methods of predicting drug toxicity in man, at least since the beginning of the nine-
teenth century. As interest in the toxicology and pharmacology of
drug combinations, as well as individual drugs, has increased, animal
models for the investigation of drug interactions have been developed
in ever-increasing numbers.

Many of the problems that have been encountered in using animal
models to predict drug toxicity are relevant as well to the prediction

of drug interactions. As Koppanyi and Avery [152] have pointed out, the crucial variable in the toxicology or pharmacology of a drug is not the dose—even when normalized to some function of body size— but rather the effective concentration of drug at some receptor site. Thus interspecies differences in the pharmacodynamics of a drug may seriously complicate attempts to predict drug effects in man.

These differences may involve any of the pharmacodynamic mechanisms previously discussed, although most commonly, metabolic differences are involved. Comparative drug metabolism has been the subject of a recent review [153]. A case in point here is phenylbutazone, which is metabolized slowly in man (15% per day) but which in most animal species, including the dog, disappears in a few hours [154, 155]. In considering the pharmacokinetics of interaction between phenylbutazone and warfarin in man and in dogs, man received 200 mg of phenylbutazone orally 2-3 times a day and warfarin by mouth at 1.5 mg/kg, whereas dogs were dosed by mouth twice daily with 50 mg/kg of phenylbutazone and once daily with bishydroxy-coumarin at 1 mg/kg. This difference in total dose of phenylbutazone— 5-10 mg/kg for man and 100 mg/kg for dog—probably counters the difference in the rate of its metabolism by man and dogs. Yet, in spite of this difference in rate of metabolism, phenylbutazone at appropriate doses can effect a decrease in the plasma concentration of the anticoagulant and prothrombin clotting times in both dogs and men.

The pharmacokinetics of indomethacin differ greatly among animal species and man [156]. In rats, the plasma half-life is about 6 hr, yet in man the half-life is less than 1 hr. Although, as has been pointed out, one sees marked differences in the metabolism of indomethacin between man and rat, both respond similarly to the effect of administered salicylates or probenecid. Assuming that the pharmacokinetics of aspirin and probenecid are similar in man and rats, both of these interacting drugs are probably affecting the enterohepatic cycle of indomethacin which, in turn, affects the plasma concentration of indomethacin in man and rats.

In considering these two types of interaction, phenylbutazone and warfarin, and salicylates/probenecid and indomethacin, the pharmacokinetics of both interacting drugs were important in demonstrating the interaction in both animals and man. Therefore, in evaluating potential drug interaction in animals that might apply to man, one needs to know the pharmacokinetics of both drugs. With this information, meaningful experiments can be undertaken in animals which should predict the pharmacokinetics of such drug interaction in man as well as suggest alternatives to the drug combination. For example, animal studies with indomethacin and acetaminophen [104] indicate that substituting acetaminophen for aspirin may not affect the pharmacokinetics of indomethacin in man.

In the absence of interspecies differences in metabolism, however, some useful generalizations may be drawn. Dedrick et al. [157] have observed that the plasma concentration curves of methotrexate in mouse, rat, dog, monkey, and man are superimposable if the dose per body weight is normalized to the fourth root of body weight. This relationship appears to be due to the fact that the predominant mode of elimination of methotrexate is renal excretion and, in many species, renal inulin clearance per unit body weight varies inversely as the fourth root of body weight. Thus this approximation should be useful in many cases in which unaltered drug is excreted by the kidneys.

The approximate relationship stated above may underlie the observation of Freireich et al. [158] that, in mouse, rat, hamster, dog, monkey, and man, the toxicities of a number of anticancer agents were best compared if doses were equalized on the basis of body surface area rather than body weight. According to the model of Dedrick et al., the area under the drug concentration-time curve in plasma should vary as the 3/4 power of body weight. Body surface area should be roughly proportional to the 2/3 power of body weight, and these values may be indistinguishable in practice.

In practice there is frequently no alternative to using animal systems to predict drug toxicity or interaction in man. However, this should be done with a clear understanding of the limitations inherent in such extrapolations. In particular it is important to be aware of any differences in metabolic or excretory rates and pathways between man and the experimental species.

THERAPEUTIC INCOMPATIBILITY

The results of drug interactions such as those discussed previously can frequently be overcome by adjustment of dosage. Our intent in using the term therapeutic incompatibility is to indicate that there are certain drug combinations which are dangerous or ineffective when used together in any dosage combination. These interactions usually result directly from the pharmacological or physiological changes produced by the drugs rather than secondarily from changes in rates of metabolism or excretion. An example is the interaction between reserpine and the monoamine oxidase inhibitors. Most of the pharmacological effects of reserpine have been attributed to its ability to deplete stores of catecholamines and 5-hydroxytryptamine in many organs such as brain, heart, and blood vessels [159]. Phar-

macological effects of the released catecholamine are minimal unless MAO has been inhibited. Depletion of tissue catecholamines by
reserpine is antagonized by MAO inhibitors.

Therapeutic incompatibilities with digitalis are also of concern.
Deaths have occurred after injection of calcium salts into digitalized
patients [160]. Calcium ion is synergistic with digitalis and can pre-
cipitate arrhythmias and ventricular fibrillation.

Drugs such as isoproterenol are useful in the treatment of a
variety of conditions requiring relief of bronchospasm. The action
of these drugs involves predominantly β-adrenoreceptor stimulation
[161]. Use of a β-adrenergic blocking agent such as propranolol in
combination with such drugs is another example of therapeutic incompatibility.

The toxicity of monoamine oxidase inhibitors is greatly increased
by thyroid feeding to the rat [162]. Thyroid extract and monoamine
oxidase inhibitors are considered to be therapeutically incompatible
in humans [163].

The activity of levodopa in the treatment of parkinsonism is completely reversed by administration of pyridoxine [164]. The mechanism of this reversal is unknown. One possibility is that codecar-
boxylase activity results in extensive conversion of levodopa to
dopamine in tissue and that no amino acid is left to cross the blood-
brain barrier.

Thorough knowledge of the pharmacology of the drugs involved
usually permits anticipation of therapeutic incompatibilities.

FUTURE TRENDS IN THE STUDY OF DRUG INTERACTIONS

Because of the large and still increasing interest in the problem
of drug interactions, and in no small part because of the present-day
popularity of multiple drug use, the frequency of reports of adverse
drug interactions, from both clinical and experimental groups, is
likely to continue its dramatic increase for some time to come. If
these reports are to be useful to the clinician who wishes to plan
optimum therapy for his patients, it will be necessary to evolve considerable sophistication in evaluating them and in applying them to
specific cases at hand. In particular, it would be desirable to lay
more emphasis upon the pharmacodynamics of a reported interaction.

The simple occurrence of a drug interaction in animals is, of
course, no guarantee that it will present a clinical problem. What
is needed is a rational method for screening the cases most likely
to be clinically relevant. A detailed study of its mechanism may provide valuable clues as to its probable occurrence and severity in man.

Generally, if the mechanism of the interaction suggests that the effect in man will be measurable, the supposed interaction must be considered in the light of other factors which could affect the pharmacodynamics of the agent in question. Vesell and Page [148], for example, have shown that the plasma half-life of dicumarol in pairs of identical twins ranges from a high of 70-75 hr to a low of 25 hr. One might well wonder, in the light of this presumably environmental effect, whether the other interactions affecting the half-life of warfarin to a lesser extent will be significant in the clinic.

The existence of an adverse interaction, even if it is clinically significant, is, of course, not always a sufficient indication to discontinue therapy. Especially when the beneficial effects of the drugs involved are truly necessary to the life and well-being of the patient, it may be possible to look to the pharmacodynamics of the interaction to suggest means of making it manageable. Suitable adjustments in dosage scheduling or choice of drugs may improve the situation.

A highly desirable innovation might involve determination of blood levels of drug in individual patients where drug interaction has been observed. This could provide insight regarding the pharmacodynamics of the combination in the individual patient. Such an increase in sophistication would permit more ready critical evaluation of large numbers of reports of adverse interactions; and it seems realistic to expect that these reports will increase in frequency in the future.

It must be admitted that the prospect of being able to carry out well-controlled studies of all drug combinations which might be encountered in medical practice is remote. We must accept the fact that retrospective studies will probably continue to provide important clinical information on drug interactions. The prospects for carrying on comprehensive drug surveillance for hospitalized patients is good. Various experiments for accomplishing drug surveillance with paramedical personnel have been described [165, 166] and acceptance by hospital resident staff has been good.

Less promising are the possibilities for carrying on drug use surveillance in the general community. The tremendous use of over-the-counter preparations, likely along with prescription items, will frustrate attempts at comprehensive drug surveillance. The patient, already becoming testy about the cost of drugs, is unlikely to willingly bear the additional cost of this service.

Finally, it must be recognized by all in the health professions that the reporting of adverse effects from drugs or drug combinations has definite medico-legal implications. This point has also been emphasized by others [167], and it is clear that careful scientific investigation of drug interactions must replace the mere reporting of cursory observations.

References

[1] This estimate is made from the data presented in a recent survey. See P. de Haen, *Drug Intell. Clin. Pharm.*, **5**, 148 (1971).

[2] G. L. Saiger, *Pharmakotherapia*, 2, 124 (1965).

[3] N. de Nosaquo, *J. Amer. Pharm. Assoc.*, 6, 66 (1966).

[4] R. H. Moser (ed.), *Diseases of Medical Progress*: *A Study of Iatrogenic Disease*, 3rd ed., Thomas, Springfield, Illinois, 1969.

[5] L. G. Seidl, G. F. Thornton, and L. E. Cluff, *Amer. J. Public Health*, **55**, 1170 (1965).

[6] L. G. Seidl, D. Friend, and J. Sadusk, *J. Amer. Med. Assoc.*, **196**, 421 (1966).

[7] L. G. Seidl, G. F. Thornton, J. W. Smith, and L. E. Cluff, *Bull. Johns Hopkins Hosp.*, **119**, 299 (1966).

[8] R. I. Ogilvie and J. Ruedy, *Can. Med. Assoc. J.*, **97**, 1450 (1967).

[9] N. Hurwitz and O. L. Wade, *Brit. Med. J.*, **1**, 531 (1970).

[10] M. G. MacDonald and B. R. MacKay, *J. Amer. Med. Assoc.*, **190**, 1071, (1964).

[11] N. Hurwitz, *Brit. Med. J.*, **1**, 539 (1969).

[12] R. H. Moser, *Mil. Med.*, **135**, 619 (1970).

[13] L. Lasagna, *Perspect. Biol. Med.*, **7**, 457 (1964).

[14] G. M. Wilson, *Brit. Med. J.*, **1**, 1065 (1966).

[15] M. J. Ellenhorn and F. A. Sternad, *J. Amer. Pharm. Assoc.*, **6**, 62 (1966).

[16] *Drug Efficacy Study*: *Report to Commissioner of Food and Drugs*, National Academy of Sciences, Washington, D.C., 1969, discussed in *J. Amer. Med. Assoc.*, **13**, 1172 (1970).

[17] J. W. Smith, L. G. Seidl, and L. E. Cluff, *Ann. Int. Med.*, **65**, 629 (1966).

[18] E. A. Hartshorn, in *Handbook of Drug Interactions* (D. E. Francke, ed.), Francke, Cincinnati, 1970.

[19] N. J. Sawyer, C. M. King, Jr., and B. A. Hellmus, *Amer. J. Hosp. Pharm.*, **27**, 986 (1970).

[20] G. Swidler, *Handbook of Drug Interactions*, Wiley (Interscience), New York, 1971.

[21] D. A. Hussar, *Amer. J. Pharm.*, **141**, 109 (1969).

[22] *Modern Drug Encyclopedia and Therapeutic Index* (A. J. Lewis, ed.), 11th ed., Donnelly, New York, 1970.

[23] *Physicians' Desk Reference*, 25th ed., Medical Economics, Inc., Oradell, New Jersey, 1971.

[24] W. J. Parker, *J. Amer. Pharm. Assoc.*, **10**, 664 (1970).

[25] F. C. Cross, A. T. Canada, Jr., and N. M. Davis, *Amer. J. Hosp. Pharm.*, **23**, 235 (1966).

[26] C. M. Kunin, *Clin. Pharmacol. Ther.*, **7**, 166 (1966).

[27] E. Krüeger-Thiemer, W. Diller, L. Dettli, P. Bünger, and J. Seydel, *Antibiot. Chemother. Advan.*, **12**, 171 (1964).

[28] P. M. Aggeler, R. A. O'Reilly, L. Leong, and P. E. Kowitz, *New Eng. J. J. Med.*, **276**, 496 (1967).

[29] R. A. O'Reilly and G. Levy, *J. Pharm Sci.*, **59**, 1258 (1970).

[30] J. J. Burns, R. K. Case, T. Chenkin, A. Goldman, A. Schulert, and B. B. Brodie, *J. Pharmacol. Exp. Ther.*, **109**, 346 (1953).

[31] R. L. Dixon, E. S. Henderson, and D. P. Rall, *Fed. Proc.*, **24**, 454 (1965).

[32] J. J. Coffey, P. E. Palm, E. P. Denine, P. E. Baronowsky, and C. J. Kensler, *Cancer Res.*, **31**, 1908 (1971).

[33] G. Salvatore, M. Andreoli, and J. Roche, *Transport Function of Plasma Proteins* (P. Desgrez and P. M. De Traverse, eds.), Elsevier, Amsterdam, 1966, p. 57.

[34] P. Desgrez, *ibid.*, p. 87.

[35] B. B. Brodie, *ibid.*, p. 137.

[36] A. H. Anton, *J. Pharmacol. Exp. Ther.*, **129**, 282 (1960).

[37] G. B. Odell, *J. Clin. Invest.*, **38**, 823 (1959).

[38] G. B. Odell, *J. Pediat.*, **55**, 268 (1959).

[39] M. Fulop, J. Sandson, and P. Brezeau, *J. Clin. Invest.*, **44**, 666 (1965).

[40] B. Josephson and P. Furst, *Scand. J. Clin. Lab. Invest.*, **18**, 51 (1966).

[41] M. Wahlquist, I. M. Nilsson, F. Sandberg, and S. Agurell, *Biochem. Pharmacol.*, **19**, 2579 (1970).

[42] I. M. Klotz, in *The Proteins* (H. Neurath and K. Bailey, eds.), Part B, Vol. 1, Academic, New York, 1953, p. 727.

[43] I. F. Skidmore and M. W. Whitehouse, *J. Pharm. Pharmacol.*, **17**, 671 (1965).

[44] I. M. Klotz, J. M. Urquhart, and W. W. Weber, *Arch. Biochem.*, **26**, 420 (1950).

[45] J. J. Coffey, F. J. Bullock, and P. T. Schoenemann, *J. Pharm. Sci.*, **60**, 1623 (1971).

[46] R. Nagashima and G. Levy, *J. Pharm. Sci.*, **58**, 845 (1969).

[47] P. M. Aggeler and R. A. O'Reilly, *J. Lab. Clin. Med.*, **74**, 229, (1969).

[48] A. K. Brown, W. W. Zeulzer, and A. R. Robinson, *Amer. Med. Assoc. J. Dis. Child*, **93**, 274 (1957).

[49] J. Monod, J. Wyman, and J. P. Changeux, *J. Mol. Biol.*, **12**, 88 (1965).

[50] C. T. Dollery, D. Emslie-Smith, and D. F. Muggleton, *Brit. J. Pharmacol.*, **17**, 488 (1961).

[51] A. Breckenridge and A. Rosen, *Biochim. Biophys. Acta*, **229**, 610 (1971).

[52] S. P. Sher, *Toxicol. Appl. Pharmacol.*, **18**, 780 (1971).

[53] G. Levy and H. Yamada, *J. Pharm. Sci.*, **60**, 215 (1971).

[54] H. G. Bray, B. G. Humphris, W. V. Thorpe, K. White, and P. B. Wood, *Biochem. J.*, **52**, 412 (1952).

[55] H. G. Bray, B. G. Humphris, W. V. Thorpe, K. White, and P. B. Wood, *Biochem. J.*, **52**, 416 (1952).

[56] B. G. Priestly and G. L. Plaa, *J. Pharmacol. Exp. Ther.*, **174**, 221 (1970).

[57] H. Kutt, W. Winters, and F. H. McDowell, *Neurology*, **16**, 594 (1966).
[58] H. Kutt, K. Verebely, and F. McDowell, *Neurology*, **18**, 706 (1968).
[59] D. Horwitz, L. H. Goldberg, and A. Sjoerdsma, *J. Lab. Clin. Med.*, 56, 747 (1960).
[60] D. Horwitz, W. Lovenberg, K. Engelman, and A. Sjoerdsma, *J. Amer. Med. Assoc.*, 188, 1108 (1964).
[61] F. Sjöqvist, *Proc. Roy. Soc. Med.*, **58**, (Suppl.), 967 (1965).
[62] G. H. Hitchings, *Cancer Res.*, **29**, 1895 (1969).
[63] G. B. Elion, S. Callahan, H. Nathan, S. Bieber, R. W. Rundles, and G. H. Hitchings, *Biochem. Pharmacol.*, **12**, 85 (1963).
[64] R. W. Rundles, J. B. Wyngaarden, G. H. Hitchings, G. B. Elion, and H. R. Silberman, *Trans. Assoc. Amer. Phys.*, 76, 126 (1963).
[65] G. B. Elion, F. M. Benezra, I. Canellas, L. O. Carrington, and G. H. Hitchings, *Israel J. Chem.*, **6**, 787 (1968).
[66] J. J. Coffey, C. A. White, M. L. Meloni, and W. I. Rogers, *Proc. Amer. Assoc. Cancer Res.*, **12**, 45 (1971).
[67] L. Hamilton and G. B. Elion, *Ann. N.Y. Acad. Sci.*, **60**, 304 (1954).
[68] J. J. Coffey, C. A. White, A. B. Lesk, W. I. Rogers, and A. A. Serpick, *Cancer Res.*, submitted for publication.
[69] A. S. Levine, H. L. Sharp, J. Mitchell, W. Krivit, and M. E. Nesbit, *Cancer Chemother. Rep.*, **53**, 53 (1969).
[70] E. S. Vesell, T. Passananti, and F. E. Greene, *New Eng. J. Med.*, **283**, 1484 (1970).
[71] G. W. Camiener and C. G. Smith, *Biochem. Pharmacol.*, **14**, 1405 (1965).
[72] G. W. Camiener, *Biochem. Pharmacol.*, **17**, 1981 (1968).
[73] L. T. Mulligan, Jr., and L. B. Mellett, *Pharmacologist*, **10**, 167 (1968).
[74] G. L. Neil, T. E. Moxley, and R. C. Manak, *Cancer Res.*, **30**, 2166 (1970).
[75] B. B. Brodie and C. A. M. Hogben, *J. Pharm. Pharmacol.*, **9**, 345 (1957).
[76] R. G. Kuntzman, I. Tsai, L. Brand, and L. C. Mard, *Clin. Pharm. Ther.*, **12**, 62 (1971).
[77] A. H. Beckett and M. Rowland, *J. Pharm. Pharmacol.*, **17**, 628 (1965).
[78] P. Brazeau, in *Pharmacological Basis of Therapeutics* (L. S. Goodman and A. Gilman, eds.) 4th ed., Macmillan, New York, 1970, p. 888.
[79] M. Gibaldi and M. A. Schwartz, *Clin. Pharmacol. Ther.*, **9**, 345 (1968).
[80] T. F. Yü, P. G. Dayton, and A. B. Gutman, *J. Clin. Invest.*, **42**, 1330 (1963).
[81] A. H. Anton, *J. Pharmacol. Exp. Ther.*, **134**, 291 (1961).
[82] J. M. Stowers, L. W. Constable, and R. B. Hunter, *Ann. N.Y. Acad. Sci.*, **74**, 689 (1959).
[83] J. B. Field, M. Ohta, C. Boyle, and A. Remer, *New Eng. J. Med.*, **277**, 889 (1967).
[84] A. Quebbemann and B. Rennick, *J. Pharmacol. Exp. Ther.*, **175**, 248 (1970).
[85] L. Beeley and M. J. Kendall, *Brit. Med. J.*, **1**, 707 (1971).

[86] W. M. Bennett, I. Singer, and C. H. Coggins, *J. Amer. Med. Assoc.*, **214**, 1468 (1970).

[87] M. M. Reidensberg, *Renal Function and Drug Action*, Saunders, Philadelphia, London, 1971.

[88] G. H. Hirsch and J. B. Hook, *J. Pharmacol. Exp. Ther.*, **171**, 103 (1970).

[89] L. Ther and D. Winne, *Ann. Rev. Pharmacol.*, **11**, 57 (1971).

[90] P. J. Neuvonen, G. Gothoni, R. Hackman, and K. af Björksten, *Brit. Med. J.*, **4**, 532, 1970.

[91] H. A. Eder, in *Pharmacological Basis of Therapeutics* (L. S. Goodman and A. Gilman, eds.), 4th ed., Macmillan, New York, 1970, p. 769.

[92] S. Consolo, *J. Pharm. Pharmacol.*, **20**, 574 (1968).

[93] M. E. Jarvik, in *Pharmacological Basis of Therapeutics* (L. S. Goodman and A. Gilman, eds.), 4th ed., Macmillan, New York, 1970, p. 187.

[94] M. Gibaldi and S. Feldman, *J. Pharm. Sci.*, **59**, 579 (1970).

[95] C. H. Nightingale, J. E. Axelson, and M. Gibaldi, *J. Pharm. Sci.*, **60**, 145 (1971).

[96] R. Jeremy and J. Towson, *Med. J. Aust.*, **2**, 127 (1970).

[97] D. W. Yesair, L. Remington, M. Callahan, and C. J. Kensler, *Biochem. Pharmacol.*, **19**, 1591 (1970).

[98] M. D. Skeith, P. A. Simkin, and L. A. Healey, *Clin. Pharmacol. Ther.*, **9**, 89 (1968).

[99] B. B. Brodie, *Proc. Roy. Soc. Med.*, **58** (Suppl.), 946 (1965).

[100] J. B. Stenlake, A. G. Davidson, M. K. Jasani, and W. D. Williams, *J. Pharm. Pharmacol.*, **20**, 248S (1968).

[101] J. B. Stenlake, W. D. Williams, A. G. Davidson, and W. W. Downie, *J. Pharm. Pharmacol.*, **23**, 145 (1971).

[102] E. Hvidberg, J. Schou, and J. A. Jansen, *Eur. J. Clin. Pharmacol.*, **3**, 102 (1971).

[103] C. A. Winter, E. A. Risley, and R. H. Silber, *Fed. Proc.*, **26**, 620 (1967).

[104] R. E. Harman, M. A. P. Meisinger, G. E. Davis, and F. A. Kuehl, Jr., *J. Pharm. Exp. Ther.*, **143**, 215 (1963).

[105] D. Schachter, D. J. Kass, and T. J. Lannon, *J. Biol. Chem.*, **234**, 201 (1959).

[106] D. W. Yesair, unpublished observation.

[107] M. J. Smith, *Amer. J. Physiol.*, **193**, 29 (1958).

[108] G. Levy, N. J. Angelino, and T. Matsuzawa, *J. Pharm. Sci.*, **56**, 681 (1967).

[109] S. L. Stone, in *Liver Function* (R. W. Braver, ed.), American Institute of Biological Science, Washington, D.C., 1958, p. 298.

[110] L. G. Hart and L. S. Shanker, *Amer. J. Physiol.*, **211**, 643, 1966.

[111] P. G. Dayton, Y. Tarcan, T. Chenkin, and M. Weiner, *J. Clin. Invest.*, **40**, 1797 (1961).

[112] C. D. Klassen, *J. Pharmacol. Exp. Ther.*, **175**, 289 (1970).

[113] D. Busfield, K. J. Child, and E. C. Tomich, *Brit. J. Pharmacol.*, **22**, 137 (1964).

[114] S. Riegelman, M. Rowland, and W. L. Epstein, *J. Amer. Med. Assoc.*, **213**, 426 (1970).

[115] S. Symchowitz, M. S. Staub, and K. K. Wong, *Biochem. Pharmacol.*, **16**, 2405 (1967).

[116] M. M. Reidenberg and D. T. Lowenthal, *New Eng. J. Med.*, **279**, 678 (1968).

[117] D. M. Green, *Ann. Intern. Med.*, **60**, 255 (1964).

[118] P. F. Griner, L. G. Raisz, F. R. Rickles, P. J. Wiesner, and C. L. Odoroff, *Ann. Intern. Med.*, **74**, 540 (1971).

[119] D. E. Hague, M. E. Smith, J. R. Ryan, and F. G. McMahon, *Clin. Pharmacol. Ther.*, **12**, 259 (1971).

[120] N. Hurwitz, *Brit. Med. J.*, **1**, 539 (1969).

[121] H. Jick, D. Slone, and I. T. Borda, *New Eng. J. Med.*, **279**, 284 (1968).

[122] A. D. Bender, *J. Am. Geriat. Soc.* **16**, 1331 (1968).

[123] A. D. Bender, *J. Amer. Geriat. Soc.*, **12**, 114 (1964).

[124] A. D. Bender, *J. Pharm. Sci.*, **54**, 1225 (1965).

[125] R. Kato, P. Vassanelli, G. Frontino, and E. Chiesara, *Biochem. Pharmacol.*, **13**, 1037 (1964).

[126] R. Kato, E. Chiesara, and G. Frontino, *Biochem. Pharmacol.*, **11**, 221 (1962).

[127] A. H. Conney and J. J. Burns, *Adv. Pharmacol.*, **1**, 45 (1962).

[128] J. S. Crawford and S. Rudofsky, *Brit. J. Anaesth.*, **38**, 446 (1966).

[129] J. J. Schrogie, H. M. Solomon, and P. D. Zieve, *Clin. Pharmacol. Ther.*, **8**, 670 (1967).

[130] Cf. R. A. O'Reilly and P. M. Aggeler, *Pharmacol. Rev.*, **22**, 35 (1970).

[131] M. R. Juchau and J. R. Fouts, *Biochem. Pharmacol.*, **15**, 891 (1966).

[132] A. Jori, A. Bianchetti, and P. E. Prestini, *Eur. J. Pharmacol.*, **7**, 196 (1969).

[133] A. Blackham and P. S. J. Spencer, *Brit. J. Pharmacol.*, **37**, 129 (1969).

[134] H. P. Fletcher, T. S. Miya, and W. F. Bousquet, *J. Pharm. Sci.*, **54**, 1007 (1965).

[135] M. Weiner, A. A. Siddiqui, R. Shakani, and P. G. Dayton, *Proc. Soc. Exp. Biol. Med.*, **124**, 1170 (1967).

[136] Cf. P. F. Covolle and J. M. Telford, *Brit. J. Pharmacol.*, **36**, 189P (1969).

[137] R. Kato and A. Takahashi, *Mol. Pharmacol.*, **4**, 109 (1968).

[138] J. J. Schrogie and H. M. Solomon, *Clin. Pharmacol. Ther.*, **8**, 70 (1967).

[139] H. Wollman and R. D. Dripps, in *Pharmacological Basis of Therapeutics*, (L. S. Goodman and A. Gilman, eds.), 4th ed., Macmillan, New York, 1970, p. 56.

[140] B. U. Musa, R. S. Kumar, and J. T. Dowling, *J. Clin. Endocrinol Metab.*, **28**, 1461 (1968).

[141] W. Kalow, *Pharmacogenetics: Heredity and the Response to Drugs*, Saunders, Philadelphia, London, 1962.

[142] W. Kalow, *Ann. Rev. Pharmacol.*, **5**, 9 (1965).

[143] A. G. Motulsky, *Ann. N.Y. Acad. Sci.*, **123**, 167 (1965).

[144] W. Hammer, and F. Sjöquist, *Life Sci.*, 6, 1895 (1967).

[145] F. Sjöqvist, in *Toxicity and Side Effects of Psychotropic Drugs* (S. B. deC. Baker, J. R. Bosia, and W. Koll, eds.), Excerpta Medica, Amsterdam, 1970, p. 246.

[146] E. S. Vesell and J. G. Page, *Science*, 159, 1479 (1968).

[147] E. S. Vesell and J. G. Page, *Ibid.*, 161, 72 (1968).

[148] E. S. Vesell and J. G. Page, *J. Clin. Invest.*, 47, 2657 (1968).

[149] D. G. Wenzel and L. L. Broadie, *Toxicol. Appl. Pharmacol.*, 8, 455 (1966).

[150] C. Mitoma, T. J. Sorich, and S. E. Neubauer, *Life Sci.*, 7, 145 (1968).

[151] B. Alexanderson, D. A. P. Evans, and F. Sjöqvist, *Brit. Med. J.*, 4, 764 (1969).

[152] T. Koppanyi and M. A. Avery, *Clin. Pharmacol. Ther.*, 7, 250 (1966).

[153] L. B. Mellett, *Forsch. Arzneimittelforsch.*, 13, 136 (1969).

[154] J. J. Burns, R. K. Rose, T. Chenkin, A. Goldman, A. Schulert, and B. B. Brodie, *J. Pharmacol. Exp. Ther.*, 109, 346 (1953).

[155] J. J. Burns, *Ann. N.Y. Acad. Sci.*, 151, 959 (1968).

[156] D. W. Yesair, M. Callahan, L. Remington, and C. J. Kensler, *Biochem. Pharmacol.*, 19, 1579 (1970).

[157] R. L. Dedrick, K. B. Bischoff, and D. S. Zaharko, *Cancer Chemother. Rep.*, 54, 95 (1971).

[158] E. J. Freireich, E. A. Gehan, D. P. Rall, L. H. Schmidt, and H. G. Skipper, *Cancer Chemother. Rep.*, 50, 219 (1966).

[159] M. Nickerson, in *Pharmacological Basis of Therapeutics* (L. S. Goodman and A. Gilman, eds.), 4th ed., Macmillan, New York, 1970, p. 575.

[160] J. O. Bower and H. A. K. Mengle, *J. Amer. Med. Assoc.*, 106, 1151 (1936).

[161] I. R. Innes and M. Nickerson, in *Pharmacological Basis of Therapeutics*, (L. S. Goodman and A. Gilman, eds.), 4th ed., Macmillan, New York, 1970, p. 516.

[162] S. d'A. Bailey, L. Bucci, E. Gosline, N. Kline, I. H. Park, D. Rochlin, J. C. Saunders, and M. Vaisberg, *Ann. N.Y. Acad. Sci.*, 80, 652 (1952).

[163] N. S. Kline, *J. Neuropsychiat.*, 2 (Suppl. 1), 15 (1961).

[164] D. B. Calne, *Clin. Pharmacol. Ther.*, 11, 789 (1970).

[165] P. Gardner and L. Watson, *Clin. Pharmacol. Ther.*, 11, 802 (1970).

[166] D. Slone, H. Jick, I. Borda, T. C. Chalmers, M. Beinleib, H. Muench, L. Lipworth, C. Belfoti, and B. Gilman, *Lancet*, 2, 901 (1966).

[167] C. H. Roth and M. E. Trout, *Hosp. Formulary Management*, 5, 13 (1970).

Metabolism of Hydrazine Derivatives of Pharmacologic Interest

M. R. JUCHAU and A. HORITA
Department of Pharmacology
School of Medicine
University of Washington
Seattle, Washington 98195

INTRODUCTION

General Considerations

Hydrazine, substituted hydrazine derivatives, hydrazides, hydra-zones, and related compounds currently are receiving increasing attention from a large number of biological scientists, including pharmacologists, toxicologists, biochemists, aerospace biologists, and ecologists. The high chemical reactivity of many compounds of this class imparts a wide spectrum of biological activities, some of which have found application in therapeutics. Other effects are to be regarded as distinct hazards both from medical and ecological viewpoints. Current interest in such compounds has increased largely as a result of three primary factors: 1) A rapid increase in the use of hydrazine and its methyl derivatives in the aerospace industry as high energy fuels (e.g., rocket propellents): 2) extensive use in practical and experimental therapeutics as antidepressive agents (monoamine oxidase inhibitors), compounds useful in tuber-culosis therapy, antihypertensive agents, antianginal agents, cancer chemotherapeutic and immunosuppressive compounds, tranquillizers,

71

antiviral substances, antimicrobials, antihistamines, coccidiostats, and antiasthmatics; 3) recognition of many undesirable or toxic biological effects, including methemoglobinemias, hypotensive episodes, mutagenic, carcinogenic, and teratogenic potential, extensive liver damage (particularly fatty infiltration and jaundice), convulsive and other central nervous system disorders, hypoglycemias, contact dermatitis and allergic manifestations, and a wide range of other, somewhat less serious, toxicities.

Because of their diverse chemical reactivity, such as basicity, reducing power, and bifunctionality, hydrazine and its derivatives are utilized in a broad spectrum of practical and commercial applications. In agriculture, maleic hydrazide and aminotriazole are employed as plant growth regulators and herbicides. Numerous hydrazine-based polymers have been prepared and converted to films, fibers, and resins. Hydrazine and derivatives are used widely in the petroleum industry as antioxidants, mercaptan and carbon dioxide scavengers, corrosion inhibitors, and in the recovery of platinum catalysts. Metal industries employ these compounds in a number of processes such as metal plating of glass and plastics, in the processing of radioactive metals, as antitarnish agents, and in copper soldering flux. In chemical processing they are utilized as chlorine scavengers in the preparation of hydrochloric acid and as polymerization inhibitors in hydrocarbon processing. They are used as antioxidants in soaps and detergents, in photographic processing and, in addition to their use as energy sources in rocket fuels, they are used commonly as primers in ammunition, in fuel cells, and in boiler feedwater treatment in electric power generating plants.

As is the case with all chemicals or drugs, when used intelligently they can be of great benefit to mankind; when used unwisely they may be detrimental to the extent of catastrophe causation. Knowledge of the chemistry, pharmacology, and toxicology of the chemicals involved provides one of our most important deterrents against misuse of this important group of substances.

In view of the wide application and ubiquitous presence of such chemicals in our environment, it becomes imperative to understand their effects on biological systems. One of the more important aspects of such understanding is the elucidation of chemical species which arise following their introduction into biological systems, i.e., the metabolism of hydrazine and its derivatives.

Scope of Review

Several recent reviews of hydrazines and hydrazides have appeared in the literature. Of particular pertinence is the review by

Colvin [1] in which several aspects of the metabolic fate of hydrazine derivatives are discussed.

In this review some of the basic aspects of the chemistry of hydrazine and its derivatives will be presented, particularly as they
may apply to their biotransformation. The pharmacology and toxicology of some of the more common compounds will be briefly reviewed. Recent developments regarding the metabolism of hydrazine and its derivatives, biological and environmental factors which
regulate rates of biotransformation through various metabolic sequences, and biologic consequences of altered rates of metabolite
formation will be discussed. Specific attention will be given to the
role of biotransformation as it affects monoamine oxidase inhibition
by hydrazine derivatives, and attempts to correlate structure to
monoamine oxidase inhibiting properties will be made. Literature
through January 1971 is included in this review.

Chemistry

Nomenclature. Hydrazine (H_2N-NH_2) is one of a homologous
series of chemical compounds known as the hydronitrogens. It was
first identified by Fischer in 1875, in the form of organic derivatives,
and first isolated by Curtius in 1887. It was first synthesized in 1907
by Raschig and practically all commercial hydrazine is produced by
the Raschig process.

One of the best known organic reactions of hydrazine is its reac-
tion with carbonyl compounds to yield either hydrazones $\left(R-\overset{\overset{\displaystyle H}{\mid}}{C}=N-NH_2 \right)$
or azines $\left(R-\overset{\overset{\displaystyle H}{\mid}}{C}=N-N=\overset{\overset{\displaystyle H}{\mid}}{C}-R', R_2C=N-N=CR_2 \right)$. Reactions with
organic acids, acid anhydrides, acid chlorides, esters, thioesters,
and amides form the corresponding hydrazides $\left(R-\overset{\overset{\displaystyle O}{\parallel}}{C}-\overset{\overset{\displaystyle H}{\mid}}{N}-NH_2 \right)$.
With acids such as maleic and phthalic, cyclic hydrazides are pro-
duced. Hydrazine derivatives vary widely in chemical properties
and have been subdivided into six groups for purposes of discussion
and referral: 1) the parent compound (hydrazine); 2) N-substituted
and N,N-disubstituted compounds which are characterized by one
amino group; 3) N,N'-substituted derivatives which have one available hydrogen on each of the nitrogen atoms (hydrazo compounds
are symmetrical N,N'-substituted derivatives); 4) N,N,N'-trisubsti-
tuted and N,N,N',N'-tetrasubstituted derivatives which have one or
no nitrogen bond hydrogen atoms; 5) N,N'-disubstituted derivatives

of the hydrazone $\left(\begin{array}{cc} H & H \\ | & | \\ R-C=N-N-R' \end{array}\right)$ and dihydrazone $\left(\begin{array}{cc} H & H \\ | & | \\ R-C=N-N=C-R' \end{array}\right)$ (azine) types; and 6) N-substituted derivatives of the hydrazide $\left(\begin{array}{cc} O & H \\ || & | \\ R-C-N-NH_2 \end{array}\right)$ and hydrazine $\left(\begin{array}{c} N-NH_2 \\ || \\ R-C \\ | \\ NH_2 \end{array}\right)$ types.

Chemical Properties. Hydrazine is a hygroscopic, water-white liquid with an ammonia-like odor. It fumes in air, reacting with both the oxygen and the carbon dioxide present in the atmosphere. It has a boiling point of 113.5°C and a freezing point of 2°C. It forms a monohydrate $(N_2H_4 \cdot H_2O)$, bp 120.1°C, freezing point -51°C. Hydrazine decomposes thermally to yield ammonia, nitrogen, and hydrogen. At sufficiently high temperatures, nitrogen and hydrogen are the only products.

Hydrazine, hydroxylamine, and ammonia are electron pair donors and basic compounds of comparable strength. It is informative to compare the ammonium ion (NH_4^+), the hydrazinium ion $(H_2N-NH_3^+)$, and the hydroxylammonium ion (H_3N-OH^+) since the latter two may be considered as substituted ammonium ions. In the hydroxylammonium ion the highly electronegative hydroxy group has replaced a hydrogen and thus the hydroxylammonium ion is a stronger acid than the ammonium ion. The hydrazinium ion is an ammonium ion in which a hydrogen has been replaced by an amino group which is less electronegative than the hydroxy group but more electronegative than a hydrogen. Thus the hydrazinium ion is more acidic than the ammonium ion but is less acidic than the hydroxylammonium ion.

Hydrazine is capable of forming salts with both organic and inorganic acids. It can also react with certain metal salts to form hydrazinates $(MeX \cdot N_2H_4)$, double salts $(MeX \cdot N_2H_4 \cdot HX)$ and complexes $[Me(N_2H_4)_nX]$. In these metal complexes the hydrazine forms a bridge between two metal atoms. Hydrazine is a strong reducing agent, however, and will reduce certain heavy metal oxides and metallic salts to the free metal. It is also capable of reducing aromatic nitro groups to amines.

Like the hydrogen peroxide molecule, the hydrazine molecule contains two different kinds of bonds. The N—N bond is a nonpolar covalent bond, whereas the four N—H bonds are polar covalent bonds. The assignment of a partial ionic charge implies adjacent negative charge centers:

$$\begin{array}{ccc}
\overset{\delta^+}{H} & & \overset{\delta^+}{H} \\
\diagdown & \overset{\delta^-}{N}\text{---}\overset{\delta^-}{N} & \diagup \\
\diagup & & \diagdown \\
\underset{\delta^+}{H} & & \underset{\delta^+}{H}
\end{array}$$

In addition, the very high bond energy for the N≡N triple bond suggests that the triple bond is preferred over the N—N single bond. All of this indicates that hydrazine is an unstable, reactive compound. This is particularly true in the presence of air or oxidizing agents. Its derivatives show varying degrees of stability, depending on the arrangement, number, and type of substituents. The instability is attributed to their tendency to dissociate into free radicals of short life.

The alkylhydrazines are strong bases and vigorous reducing agents. They are normally oxidized to nitrogen and the corresponding hydrocarbon. Aryl hydrazines likewise are reducing agents. Phenylhydrazine and N,N-diphenylhydrazine, for example, are both active antioxidants. The chemistry of the quaternized hydrazine compounds is similar in many ways to the quaternary ammonium salts, as would be expected. A review of this subject has been presented by Sisler et al. [2].

In view of the above considerations it is not surprising that hydrazine and derivatives thereof would react with a wide variety of biological materials. Hydrazines and hydrazides are both capable of reacting with various natural aldehydes and ketones—thus serving as carbonyl trapping agents. Both hydrazines and hydrazides can react rapidly and nonenzymically with pyridoxal phosphate. Such compounds would be expected to inhibit all pyridoxal-dependent transaminases, decarboxylases, and other enzymes, e.g., serine dehydrase and certain racemases [3]. Phenylhydrazine and other substituted hydrazines react with the monosaccharides and other carbohydrates containing a free sugar group to form hydrazones and osazones. The reaction of D-glucose with phenylhydrazine is illustrative:

$$\begin{array}{lcl}
H\text{---}C\text{=}O & & H\text{---}C\text{=}N\text{---}NH\text{---}C_6H_5 \\
| & & | \\
H\text{---}C\text{---}OH & & H\text{---}C\text{---}OH \\
| & & | \\
HO\text{---}C\text{---}H & +\ H_2N\text{---}NH\text{---}C_6H_5 \longrightarrow H_2O\ + & HO\text{---}C\text{---}H \\
| & & | \\
H\text{---}C\text{---}OH & & H\text{---}C\text{---}OH \\
| & & | \\
H\text{---}C\text{---}OH & & H\text{---}C\text{---}OH \\
| & & | \\
CH_2OH & & CH_2OH
\end{array}$$

D-Glucose   D-Glucose phenylhydrazone

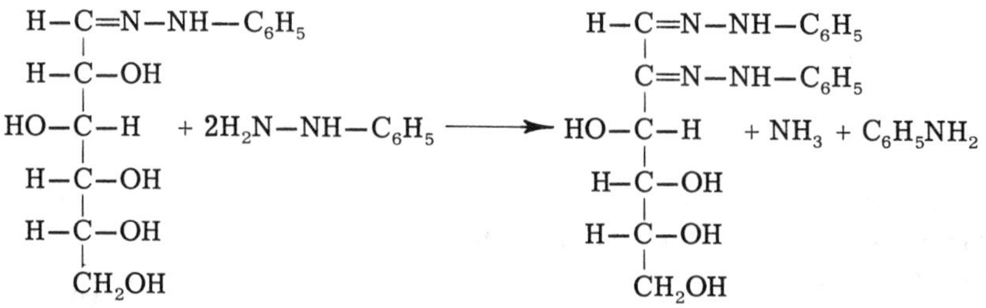

$$H-C=N-NH-C_6H_5$$
$$H-C-OH$$
$$HO-C-H \quad + 2H_2N-NH-C_6H_5 \longrightarrow$$
$$H-C-OH$$
$$H-C-OH$$
$$CH_2OH$$

D-Glucose phenylhydrazone

$$H-C=N-NH-C_6H_5$$
$$C=N-NH-C_6H_5$$
$$HO-C-H \quad + NH_3 + C_6H_5NH_2$$
$$H-C-OH$$
$$H-C-OH$$
$$CH_2OH$$

D-Glucose phenylosazone

Ketonic steroids react with hydrazides to yield the corresponding hydrazone derivatives. This principle has been employed in steroid extraction procedures utilizing the hydrazide of betaine chloride (Girard's reagent) to produce water-soluble salts of the resultant substituted hydrazones. Its importance in biological systems has not been explored.

When a peptide is treated with hydrazine, all the peptide groups are split and the carbonyl component is converted to the corresponding hydrazide:

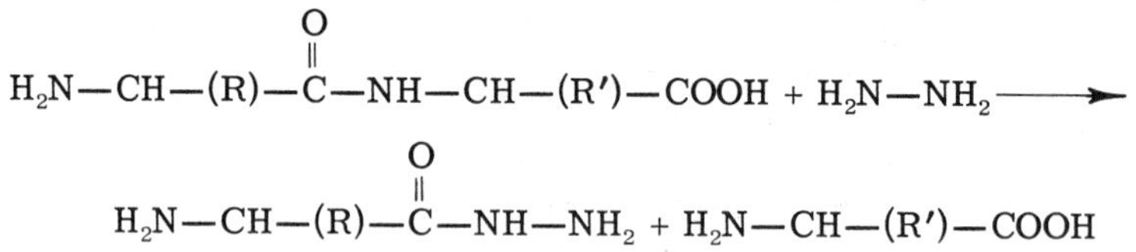

$$H_2N-CH-(R)-\overset{\overset{\text{O}}{\|}}{C}-NH-CH-(R')-COOH + H_2N-NH_2 \longrightarrow$$

$$H_2N-CH-(R)-\overset{\overset{\text{O}}{\|}}{C}-NH-NH_2 + H_2N-CH-(R')-COOH$$

The final amino acid (COOH terminal or C-terminal) has a free carboxyl group which does not undergo hydrazide formation. The principle of this reaction has been utilized in the determination of C-terminal amino acids. Its significance with respect to pharmacological and toxicological effects likewise has not been assessed.

In addition, it has been shown that treatment of deoxyribonucleic acid with hydrazine results in the formation of apyrimidinic acids [4]. It is to be expected that hydrazine and its derivatives would react with a host of other biologic substances, thus accounting, in part at least, for the wide spectrum of pharmacologic and toxicologic effects which they produce.

Pharmacologic and Toxicologic Aspects

Therapeutic Applications. As medicinal agents, hydrazine derivatives have found a wide variety of applications. Iproniazid and two of the drugs still suggested for use as antidepressive agents are hydrazides (nialamid, Niamid; and isocarboxazid, Marplan) while another antidepressive monoamine oxidase inhibitor, phenelzine (Nardil) is a hydrazine. The relationships between monoamine oxidase inhibition, treatment of depressed states, and structure of the hydrazine derivatives are dealt with extensively in a subsequent section. It should be noted only that several hydrazine derivative monoamine oxidase inhibitors once employed in the therapy of depression have been removed from the market as the result of a comparatively high incidence of serious toxicities, most notable of which is hepatocellular damage. Diffuse cellular necrosis and inflammatory changes comparable to those observed in infectious hepatitis are commonly observed effects, even in those still marketed. Other common effects of these drugs are usually manifest in varying degrees of central nervous system stimulation and/or a variety of effects on the autonomic nervous system.

Isoniazid, a hydrazide, is still the most active tuberculostatic drug available. In spite of extensive studies, the mechanism by which this compound inhibits the tubercle bacillus is unknown. It apparently is capable of selectively binding to an enzyme which is peculiar to susceptible strains of the bacillus. Administration of large doses of pyridoxine to patients receiving isoniazid does not antagonize its tuberculostatic action. Although iproniazid is a much more powerful inhibitor of monoamine oxidase than isoniazid, it is much less effective as a tuberculostatic agent.

Hydralazine (Apresoline) has often been regarded as the drug of choice in the management of hypertensive crises associated with toxemias of pregnancy (eclampsia) or acute glomerulonephritis. The extent of its use, however, has diminished since the advent of α-methyl dopa (Aldomet). Present evidence indicates that the major mechanism by which hydralazine exerts its hypotensive effect is through a direct action on the vascular smooth muscle. Headache, palpitation, anorexia, nausea, vomiting, and diarrhea are common untoward effects.

Procarbazine (Natulan) and similar compounds have been employed as carcinostatic agents and immunosuppresive compounds. As expected, then, such compounds also have potential to produce teratogenesis, carcinogenesis, and mutagenesis, and have been shown to do so experimentally [5-7]. In cell-free systems, methylhydrazine is autooxidized with the formation of hydrogen peroxide and oxygen-hydrogen radicals which are capable of degrading DNA. It is thought that procarbazine may exert its effects by this mechanism. Chromosome breaks and mitotic inhibition have been observed following administration of the compound to experimental animals. Its greatest value appears to be in the treatment of advanced Hodgkins disease.

It is not cross resistant with alkylating agents or vinblastine. It inhibits monoamine oxidase but, interestingly, a common side effect is mental depression.

Methisazone (Marboran), an antiviral thiosemicarbazone marketed in Europe, appears to inhibit virus replication by interfering with the synthesis of a specific ("late") structural protein. This compound can block replication of smallpox (variola) virus in man if administered to contacts within 1-2 days after exposure and gives striking prophylactic protection against clinical smallpox, as shown in controlled trials [8]. Vomiting appears to be the most frequently reported adverse reaction.

A number of furan compounds also may be considered as hydrazine derivatives. Nitrofurantoin (Furadantin), nitrofurazone (Furacin), and furazolidone (Furoxone) are representative of this category. The antibacterial activity of such compounds, however, does not appear to depend on the —N—N— moiety. More critical is the nitro group on the 5 position of the furan ring [9].

Although reputed to give excellent prophylactic protection against the pain of angina, serious hypotensive and hepatic reactions have resulted in the virtual abandonment of hydrazine derivatives for anginal therapy. Many other hydrazine derivatives have been and are currently being used for therapeutic purposes and still many others are being tested for such. Space limitations, however, do not allow their consideration in this review.

Mechanisms of Adverse Reactions. The variety and incidence of adverse reactions to hydrazine and its derivatives have received a large share of the attention given to these compounds over the past few years. Several reviews of this subject very recently have appeared in the literature [10-13]. Although a tendency still remains to attribute pharmacologic and toxicologic effects to interactions of hydrazine and derivatives with pyridoxal or monoamine oxidase, it is becoming increasingly apparent that these compounds can produce alterations in biologic function not only by such interactions but also via a host of other separate mechanisms. Considerations of their chemistry leads to the expectation that, if the compound can be distributed to the site in sufficient amounts, many functionally important electron-deficient regions would be susceptible to nucleophilic attack by the hydrazine moiety. A recent example of such has been shown by Hidaka and Udenfriend [14] who demonstrated that iproniazid and other hydrazines would combine covalently with the nonheme portion of horseradish peroxide and markedly inhibit enzymic activity. Evidence indicated that the electron-deficient site was a carbonyl (or unusual thiol) moiety on a carbohydrate portion of the enzyme near the active site. Other investigations [15] have demonstrated inhibition of thyroid iodide peroxidase by iproniazid, perhaps by a similar mechanism. In this regard it is interesting to note that ^{14}C-iproniazid has been shown to yield ^{14}C-isopropyl hydrazine or possibly an oxidation product thereof which then interacts with a putative carbonyl function in monoamine oxidase [16].

Procarbazine inhibits DNA [17], RNA [18], and protein [19] synthesis and is capable of decreasing DNA methylation in the 7-position of guanine [20]. Such effects likewise might be explained on the basis of the reducing power of the hydrazine compound.

Extreme caution, however, must be exercised in stating generalizations concerning toxic effects of derivatives of hydrazine. Marked differences between various derivatives exist and in some cases opposite effects may be observed [11]. Also profound differences in the toxic effects of the same compound can be observed when various species of animals are compared. It is to be expected that many of these described differences would result from differences in absorption, distribution, biotransformation, and excretion of the compounds in question. Thus one of the most important aspects in the development of understanding of the biological effects of hydrazine and its derivatives is the study of those parameters of drug disposition.

BIOTRANSFORMATION CATALYSIS

Nonenzymic Mechanisms

A wide variety of substances with —NH_2 groups, including hydrazine derivatives, will condense with carbonyl compounds to give C=N— compounds and water. These types of reactions, however, usually require acid catalysts. Whether many of these are also catalyzed by enzymes in biological systems is not known at the present time. However, pyruvic acid isonicotinyl hydrazine and α-ketoglutaric acid isonicotinyl hydrazone appear in the urine of rats, humans, and monkeys after isoniazid administration [1]. Typical reaction products with ammonia, alkyl, or aryl amines as reactants are imines (Schiff's bases); with hydrazine, a hydrazone or azine compound; with substituted aryl or alkyl hydrazines, substituted hydrazones are commonly formed. In such systems the dependence of the rates of these condensations on acid concentration is revealing with respect to the reaction mechanism. Typically the reaction rate goes through a maximum with pH, the position of the maximum depending principally on the nature of the R group of R—NH_2. Consideration of the possible equilibria involving R—NH_2

and the carbonyl compounds provides an explanation of the pH maximum:

$$R-NH_2 + H^{\oplus} \rightleftharpoons R-NH_3^{\oplus}$$
$$(CH_3)_2-C=O + H^{\oplus} \rightleftharpoons (CH_3)_2-C^{\oplus}=OH$$

If the unshared pair on the nitrogen of $R-NH_2$ is protonated, it cannot then attack the carbon of the carbonyl group. On the other hand, protonation of the carbonyl group should enhance its reactivity toward nucleophilic agents. The favorable combination of reactants is then

If this is the slow step in the reaction, the maximum rate will be found when the product of the concentrations $[(CH_3)_2-C\overset{\oplus}{=}OH][R-NH_2]$ is a maximum. These concentrations, of course, are oppositely affected by pH. Thus the optimum pH falls in the region where not all of the $R-NH_2$ is converted to $R-NH_3^{\oplus}$ and there is a sufficient concentration of the conjugate acid of the carbonyl compound to give a reasonable reaction rate. (The rest of the steps for formation of

$>C=N-R$ usually proceed more rapidly.) Such considerations are of obvious importance in discussions of conjugations of hydrazine derivatives with acetyl Co A, pyridoxal, pyruvate, α-ketoglutarate, and other endogenous carbonyl-containing compounds.

Hydrazine undergoes autooxidation when exposed to oxygen. The nonenzymic reaction is catalyzed by traces of copper (Cu^{2+}), certain metal oxides, and activated carbon. The autooxidation reaction produces water and a diimide which is the active agent in the hydrogenation of certain unsaturated centers such as carbon-carbon and nitrogen-nitrogen double bonds.

The alkylhydrazines, as strong bases and vigorous reducing agents, are normally oxidized to nitrogen and the corresponding hydrocarbon. A dilute aqueous solution of monomethylhydrazine, for example, yields methane, nitrogen, and a small quantity of carbon monoxide when allowed to come in contact with a dilute solution of sodium hypochlorite [21]. The nonenzymic formation of methane from monomethylhydrazine also has been reported to occur in vivo [22].

isoniazid in which N-methylation of the ring nitrogen has been shown
to occur in dogs [35]. Other investigators [36], however, were unable
to demonstrate N-methylation of isoniazid, an observation that may
indicate species differences in this pathway.

Although acetylation of hydrazine derivatives via acetyl coenzyme
A represents a true detoxication mechanism, conjugation with other
endogenous compounds appears to increase toxicity in some instances.
Dubnick et al. [37] found that the pyridoxal hydrazones of β-phenethyl
hydrazine and phenylisopropyl hydrazine were more toxic than the
parent compounds.

Hydrolase Reactions

The C—N bond of hydrazides is particularly labile and susceptible
to hydrolytic attack. Cleavage of this bond constitutes the second primary mechanism for metabolism of hydrazides. The reaction also
assumes importance because of the consequent release of highly reactive free hydrazine which has been implicated frequently in the
toxic effects of hydrazine derivatives. For certain species, such as
the dog, which appears to be deficient in its capacity to acetylate
such compounds, hydrolysis represents a degradative pathway of
major significance. (It is noteworthy that hydrazine compounds exhibit increased toxicity in this species.) Although the reaction presumably is catalyzed by a hydrolase or hydrolases, specific enzymes
involved have not been identified or characterized and most data
concerning hydrazide hydrolyses are derived from studies on urinary
metabolites. It is conceivable that certain peptidases or amidases
might catalyze the hydrolytic reactions. It would seem important to
determine the various sites of hydrolytic degradation and the nature
of possible enzyme involvement.

The N—N bond of hydrazides appears to be comparatively unsus-
ceptible to hydrolytic cleavage as the formation of amides from hydrazides has not been demonstrated as urinary metabolites [36, 38].
The alkyl hydrazine bond is more stable than the hydrazide bond in
the biological systems studied, and compounds containing this structure (phenelzine, unsymmetrical dimethylhydrazine, monomethylhydrazine) are preferentially acetylated rather than hydrolyzed. However, according to Dost et al. [22] the formation of methane from
monomethylhydrazine is a quantitatively significant pathway. Also,
the fate of the hydrazine nitrogens of alkyl hydrazines, such as
phenelzine, is not well known, and in fact, only a portion of hydrazine itself is accounted for as acetylated or unchanged base [26].
Therefore, a significant portion of the hydrazine nitrogen may be
converted to N_2 or NH_3 in such cases.

The third important aspect of hydrolysis of hydrazine derivatives relates to the hydrolytic cleavage of bonds formed as a result of conjugation reactions in vivo. Deacetylation of acetylated hydrazine derivatives, however, is not a frequently observed metabolic pathway. The carbonyl to nitrogen bond formed as a result of conjugation with acetyl coenzyme A is apparently more stable in vivo than the bond between the aryl carbonyl carbon and the hydrazino nitrogen.

Although not shown specifically for hydrazine derivatives, deacetylation would be expected to occur at significant rates in species in which high deacetylation activity has been demonstrated utilizing other acetylated substrates. The dog, fox, and chicken have high levels of aromatic deacylase in liver or kidneys, and it still has not been determined whether the low levels of acetylated products excreted by such species are due to low levels of acetyl transferase, the presence of a specific inhibitor of arylamine acetyl transferase that is present in dog liver and kidney [35], or high deacetylating capacity which could overwhelm acetylation mechanisms.

Other hydrolytic reactions appear to be of relatively minor significance in the studies which have been conducted. β-Glucuronidases and arylsulfatases conceivably could hydrolyze glucuronidated and sulfated derivatives of aryl hydrazines, although, to our knowledge, sulfation of such compounds has never been reported. Two hydrazone derivatives of isoniazid (pyruvate and α-ketoglutarate conjugates) appear to be hydrolyzed in the gastrointestinal tract [39]. It is to be expected that other conjugates would be hydrolyzed in the gastrointestinal tract or in other tissues.

Oxidoreductase Reactions

Oxidation-reduction reactions are particularly important for methylated hydrazine derivatives and for aryl hydrazine compounds. Evidence for the reductive cleavage of —N—N bonds of hydrazo compounds and of the —N=N— bonds of azo compounds is abundant in the literature. Such bonds can be reduced nonenzymically by NADH or NADPH to form the resultant amines and in such cases the rate of the reaction is dependent upon the activity of enzymes which function in the generation of the nucleotide electron donors [40], particularly glucose-6-phosphate dehydrogenase and 6-phosphogluconolactone dehydrogenase. In hepatic microsomes, the reactions proceed at a much more rapid rate, catalyzed by microsomal NADPH cytochrome C reductase [41] and apparently other microsomal components (including P-450 dependent mechanisms) as well. In experiments in vivo, Schwartz [42] reported that rats given methyl amine excreted it unchanged; but when monomethylhydrazine or 1-methyl-

2-p-(isopropylcarbonyl) benzene hydrazide was administered, methylamine was also excreted, demonstrating that reductive cleavage of N—N bonds of alkyl or aryl hydrazines would occur in vivo. Other reduction reactions involving hydrazine derivatives have not been reported but would be expected to depend upon the nature of the R group of R—N—N compounds.

In view of the reducing capacity of hydrazine and its derivatives, it is not surprising that many of the metabolites formed are oxidation products. As previously mentioned, hydrazine, in the presence of oxygen, is converted to water and a diimide. At elevated temperatures only water and molecular nitrogen are formed. Such reactions would proceed spontaneously in vivo, but it is not known whether enzymes may also catalyze them. However, it has been reported [38, 43] that the conversion of hydrazine to ammonia in vivo is catalyzed by an oxidase enzyme.

Some of the most significant recent findings regarding the metabolism of hydrazine derivatives have come from the laboratory of Reed and his co-workers [24, 44-46]. Long recognized as inhibitors of amine oxidases, various hydrazines were found to act as substrates for plasma amine oxidase, with a high affinity for the active site of the enzyme. Although the reaction products were not identified, they were found not to be effective inhibitors of the plasma amine oxidase [40].

Equally interesting is the finding that several hydrazine derivatives were oxidized via enzyme systems present in liver microsomes. Two modes of oxidative enzyme catalysis were reported, both of which were found to be dependent upon molecular oxygen and NADPH. The conversion of alkylhydrazines to the corresponding alkanes was not influenced by pretreatment of rats with phenobarbital or 3-methylcholanthrene and did not appear to be dependent upon cytochrome P-450. By contrast, catalysis of the formation of formaldehyde from the N-methyl group of N-methylhydrazine derivatives was increased by phenobarbital pretreatment, and the induced activity of this system was inhibited by carbon monoxide, indicating that P-450 was functioning in the demethylation reaction. Their data also indicated that microsomal cytochrome b_5 was not a participant in either reaction.

Kreis [47] has reported that the N-methyl group of 1-methyl-2-(p-isopropylcarbamyl) benzylhydrazine hydrochloride is partially oxidized to CO_2, and partially utilized in the methylation of RNA when injected into mice bearing P-815 ascites tumor cells.

Sometimes overlooked in considerations of pharmacologic-toxicologic potency of such compounds are biotransformation reactions occurring in the nonhydrazine portion of hydrazine derivative molecules. Aromatic hydroxylation via hepatic mixed-function oxidase systems followed by glucuronidation would tend to terminate biologic effects of aryl hydrazine compounds and is a common reaction. Other redox mechanisms would depend upon the nature of the nonhydrazine portion of the molecules involved.

III. HYDRAZINE-HYDRAZIDE METABOLISM AND MONOAMINE OXIDASE (MAO) INHIBITION

The surge of interest in the 1950s and early 1960s in the hydrazine compounds as possible therapeutic agents was generated by the finding that the antidepressant and anti-MAO activities of iproniazid (Marsilid) were related. This compound, chemically designated as 1-isopropyl-2-isonicotinylhydrazide (I), was employed as an antitubercular and as an antidepressant agent for a brief period of time

Iproniazid (I)

but, after undergoing a stormy therapeutic history, was reduced to the role of an experimental inhibitor of MAO. Nevertheless, iproniazid served as the springboard for the synthesis and clinical testing of a number of hydrazine compounds as possible antidepressants. From these evaluations several therapeutically active MAO inhibitors emerged, some of which are still in clinical use. The historical development and pharmacology of the inhibitors of MAO have been adequately reviewed [48-53].

Though limiting our discussion to hydrazines and MAO inhibition, we do want to distinguish this property from the ability of many of these compounds to inhibit diamine oxidase (DAO). While both are oxido-reductase enzymes and are inhibited by various hydrazine compounds, the structure-activity relationship of inhibitors for each of these enzymes is quite different. For example, iproniazid possesses considerable anti-MAO and anti-DAO activity, but isoniazid (isonicotinylhydrazide, III) acts only on DAO. DAO is dependent on pyridoxal phosphate as a prosthetic group and, typical of such enzymes, is inhibited by the various carbonyl trapping agents. MAO, on the other hand, appears not to require pyridoxal, and inhibition is produced by some other mechanism. The structure-activity relationships of MAO- and DAO-inhibiting hydrazines have been discussed previously [54-56].

Iproniazid Metabolism

A discussion of the metabolism of iproniazid and related compounds necessitates a consideration of their mechanism of anti-MAO activity. From early studies of this compound investigators have constantly referred to a possible biotransformation product as the active component in MAO inhibition, and that the rate of transformation determined the onset and extent of its inhibitory action. Thus Davison [53] suggested the possible conversion of iproniazid into isopropylhydrazine, a much more potent and rapid-acting inhibitor of MAO, although he considered this to be unlikely. However, this view received further support by Seiden and Westley [57] who demonstrated by a polarographic technique the liberation of isonicotinic acid upon incubating iproniazid with a partially purified MAO preparation. From these results the authors concluded that iproniazid was first hydrolyzed by MAO to form isonicotinic acid and isopropylhydrazine. The latter metabolite then combined with MAO to yield the inactivated enzyme.

Whether the conversion of iproniazid to isopropylhydrazine and isonicotinic acid requires MAO is a point of conjecture. Several workers have demonstrated the nonenzymatic conversion of iproniazid to isopropylhydrazine or a similar volatile compound [58, 59]. This conversion was oxygen-dependent, enhanced by cyanide and boiled tissue extracts, and the product was trapped by 1,2-naphthoquinone-4-sulfonate (NQS). These studies were of interest especially because the inhibition of MAO via the volatile compound occurred when the enzyme was physically separate from the iproniazid, which was placed in the side arm of a Warburg flask. The enhancement of the formation of the volatile MAO inhibitor by cyanide also should be emphasized, for it may explain the potentiation of the anti-MAO activity observed by Davison [53].

The authors who described these phenomena suggest that possibly the formation of a volatile product by a nonenzymic mechanism may precede the irreversible inhibition of MAO by iproniazid and related hydrazine derivatives. In order to determine whether the anti-MAO potency of hydrazine compounds might be related to their abilities to volatilize into active compounds, similar studies were done with several other hydrazides in our laboratory (Horita, unpublished results). The compounds were assayed both for the formation of the "volatile" inhibitor and their in vitro anti-MAO activities. The structures of these compounds and the results of the experiments are shown in Table 1. It is evident that while iproniazid exhibits the greatest volatile inhibitor formation, other related hydrazides which possess greater anti-MAO activity in vitro do not appear to undergo appreciable volatilization to yield the active product. Compounds as closely related to iproniazid as shown in Table 1 (Ia-c), while possessing varying anti-MAO activities in vitro, did not share the property of volatilizing into active inhibitors. These results indicate that such a volatile product need not be a prerequisite for the anti-MAO activity of the hydrazide compounds. However, these results do not preclude the possibility of the formation of some nonvolatile inhibitor under similar experimental conditions.

The metabolism in vivo of iproniazid presents an even more complex picture. Employing a dose of 5 mg/kg of ^{14}C-iproniazid (labeled at the isopropyl carbon), Koechlin and Iliev [60] observed tissue levels of radioactivity peaking at 4 hr, then rapidly falling to a plateau level which persisted beyond 24 hr. Of significance was the finding that at least 60% of the ^{14}C administered was given off as labeled ^{14}CO$_2$ in the expired air. The rate of ^{14}CO$_2$ release varied with the species of animals and even within the same species. The formation of ^{14}CO$_2$ resulted from cleavage and oxidation of the N$_2$-attached isopropyl side chain (isopropylhydrazine, IV), with acetone as an intermediate of this reaction. By various methods the authors were also able to detect isonicotinic acid (II), isoniazid (III), and their metabolites, and proposed the scheme shown for the in vivo metabolism of iproniazid. In man a similar pathway of metabolism for iproniazid was proposed when it was found that some 50-60% of the radioactive dose was eliminated as ^{14}CO$_2$ within 24 hr [61].

Hess et al. [62] also have demonstrated the appearance of isonicotinic acid after pretreatment of rats with large doses (195 mg/kg) of iproniazid. With this dosage, maximum tissue levels of iproniazid occurred within 20 min, and fell progressively within the following 24 hr. Isonicotinic acid was found primarily in plasma and liver, and levels of this compound were minimal or nil within 7 hr. MAO inhibition, on the other hand, extended far beyond the duration of detectable levels of the drug or metabolites. Employing ^{14}C-iproniazid labeled on the C=O group and at a dose of 25 mg/kg, Nair [63] essentially confirmed the previous authors' work. In addition he supported the view that the isopropylhydrazine, which is hydrolyzed from iproniazid in brain (and other tissues), is responsible for the irreversible inhibition of MAO as well as some of the toxic effects of iproniazid.

Since the chemical nature of the active constituent of iproniazid was not known, Horita [64] assayed the anti-MAO activity of brain supernatant fractions biologically at varying times after the administration of 100 mg/kg of iproniazid to rats. The assays were performed by adding aliquots of the supernatant fraction to isolated liver mitochondrial preparations and measuring the extent of MAO inhibition. These studies showed that measurable quantities of the active form of iproniazid persisted in brain tissue for more than 18 hr; during that time it is presumed that the active form is progressively increasing the inhibition of MAO in vivo. Therefore, if the doses of iproniazid are large, total inhibition will take place sooner. With smaller doses it would appear that a progressively increasing inhibition of MAO would occur as long as the active form of iproniazid is present in tissue. Thus the extent of inhibition produced by iproniazid in vivo would be a function not only of dose but also of the time of sacrifice of the animal after its administration. It should be emphasized that this property of persisting tissue levels of active inhibitor is not a general property of all hydrazine-type inhibitors of MAO. As we shall see in a later section, other compounds are only fleetingly present in an active form.

Table 1

A Comparison of Several Hydrazine Compounds in Inhibiting
Liver Homogenate MAO and in Liberating a "Volatile" Inhibitor[a]

Compound	Percent inhibition of MAO[b]		
	Inhibitor (10^{-5} M) incubated with homogenate	Inhibitor in side arm	
		10^{-2} M	10^{-1} M
(I) — pyridine-4-C(=O)–NHNHCHCH$_3$ with CH$_3$	47 (25–78)	50 (36–88)	96 (89–100)
(Ia) — pyridine-4-C(=O)–NHNHCH$_2$CH(CH$_3$)(phenyl)	89 (74–100)	5 (0–15)	3 (0–7)
(Ib) — pyridine-3-C(=O)–NHNHCH$_2$CH(CH$_3$)(phenyl)	34 (25–51)	2 (0–12)	9 (0–16)

		83 (70–97)	3 (0–12)	4 (0–19)
(Ic)	pyridine-C(=O)-NHNHCH$_2$CH(CH$_3$)-C$_6$H$_5$			
(VII)	H$_2$NNHCH$_2$CH(CH$_3$)-C$_6$H$_5$	91 (82–100)	12 (0–25)	97 (91–100)

[a]See Ref. 8 for details of the procedure for generating volatile inhibitor.
[b]Figures represent mean values from 4–12 determinations. Range of results are enclosed in parentheses.

Conclusion. From all of the diverse results reported in the literature regarding iproniazid, its metabolism, and its mode of anti-MAO
activity, the following conclusions could be made: 1) The inhibition
of MAO produced by iproniazid persists far beyond its presence or
that of its metabolites; and 2) The hydrolysis of iproniazid to release
isonicotinic acid + isopropylhydrazine is an essential step for MAO
inhibition, but this process may or may not be enzymatically catalyzed; in either case, this step is not dependent on contact between
iproniazid and MAO.

Isocarboxazid Metabolism

One of the few MAO inhibitors which has survived the scourge of
hydrazine compounds from clinical practice is isocarboxazid (Marplan), 1-benzyl-2-(5-methyl-3-isoxazolyl carbonyl)-hydrazine (V).
When this compound was incubated in liver homogenates for 2 hr,

Isocarboxazid (V)

about 90% was destroyed. The degradation of isocarboxazid was
catalyzed to the same extent under either aerobic or anaerobic conditions. Analyses of the intermediates of metabolism by liver homogenates led to the interpretation that benzyl hydrazine and 5-methyl-
3-isoxazolyl carboxylic acid are the major metabolites [65].

In the intact rat the administration of ^{14}C-benzyl labeled isocarboxazid (1 mg/kg) resulted in peak radioactivity in all tissues examined within the first 15 min, with the highest concentrations in
the kidney and liver. The urinary excretion data for the radioactivity
gave a 2-component curve, an initial fast rate with a half-life of
45 min, and a slower one of 8 hr. Unlike iproniazid, the pathway of
isocarboxazid metabolism yielded no labeled CO_2. However, approximately 75% of the labeled benzyl moiety was excreted as urinary
hippurate, indicating that isocarboxazid gave rise to benzylhydrazine,
which was converted to benzoic acid and then to benzoyl CoA before
conjugation with glycine to form the urinary hippuric acid. These
results, as well as others, have led Schwartz [66, 67] to postulate
that "isocarboxazid exerts its MAO inhibitory effects by being hy-

drolyzed to benzylhydrazine which is the actual enzyme inhibitor."
Similar conclusions have been reached by Koechlin et al. [61] in
their studies on the metabolism of isocarboxazid in man.

Metabolism of Phenethylhydrazines

The compounds phenelzine (Nardil, 2-phenethylhydrazine, VI) and
pheniprazine (Catron, 2-phenylisopropylhydrazine, VII) both received
initial praise as antidepressant agents, but with the appearance of

$$\text{—CH}_2\text{CH}_2\text{NHNH}_2 \qquad\qquad \text{—CH}_2\underset{\underset{\text{CH}_3}{|}}{\text{CH}}\text{NHNH}_2$$

Phenelzine (VI)   Pheniprazine (VII)

serious side effects pheniprazine was withdrawn from clinical application. Phenelzine, however, has not been plagued with the same extent of untoward actions, and is still used therapeutically.

The distribution and metabolic fate of phenelzine have been defined more extensively than that of pheniprazine. In mice ^{14}C-
phenelzine (81 mg/kg) reaches peak tissue levels within 5 min after
its in vivo administration. These levels disappeared rapidly, and
were barely detectable in 2 hr. It was concluded that phenelzine dis-
tributes freely, is metabolized rapidly, and less than 5% of the total
dose remains in tissues after 20 hr [68]. Studies on the biotransformation products of phenelzine indicated that most of the products
were extractable by ether from acidified urine, and that less than
2% of the radioactive biotransformation product could be found in a
neutral or alkalinized urine. Analysis of the acidic derivative indicated that phenaceturic acid was the primary metabolite [69].

Incubation of phenelzine with rat liver homogenates resulted in a
rapid inactivation of its anti-MAO activity [70]. This process was
seen to be O_2-dependent, not blocked by SKF-525A, but inhibited when
boiled tissue was used in place of fresh tissue. Moreover, it was inhibited by a variety of irreversible MAO inhibitors. These results,
and the attenuation of the rapid disappearance of anti-MAO activity
of phenelzine in vivo in animals pretreated with MAO inhibitors, led
the author to conclude that phenelzine was degraded by MAO or a
MAO-like enzyme system in vitro and in vivo. This conclusion was
subsequently confirmed when the incubation of phenelzine-1-^{14}C with
rat liver mitochondria resulted in the recovery of carboxy labeled

[14]C-phenylacetic acid. The formation of phenylacetic acid, however, was inhibited by preincubation of the mitochondrial preparation with other MAO inhibitors [71]. Similar results were seen in the urinary excretion of ^{14}C-phenylacetic acid after intraperitoneal administration of ^{14}C-phenelzine to the intact rat [72]. It is apparent from these studies that one of the major routes of phenelzine inactivation is via the MAO pathway. This presents an interesting aspect of the biochemistry of phenelzine in that it acts not only as an irreversible inhibitor of MAO but also as its substrate. However, the substrate property is self-limiting, for after producing total MAO inhibition phenelzine no longer can act as a substrate of MAO. The hypothetical relationship between phenelzine and MAO has been proposed [73] as

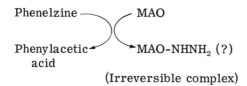

Phenelzine   MAO

Phenylacetic   MAO-NHNH$_2$ (?)
    acid

(Irreversible complex)

The reaction of MAO with phenethylhydrazine was further investigated by Tipton [74] who employed kinetic and physicochemical methods. His results suggest that the oxidation of phenelzine by MAO and the inhibition of the enzyme may be interdependent phenomena. They also are in accord with the idea of the formation of an enzyme-hydrazone complex which is resistant to hydrolysis.

The metabolic pathway of pheniprazine is less well understood. Although the degradation products of pheniprazine have not been determined, ample evidence indicates that this potent anti-MAO compound reacts with a variety of biological substances and becomes inactivated. Thus incubation with fresh or boiled brain homogenates leads to a rapid appearance of anti-MAO activity in brain tissue, but excess free and active inhibitor levels drop rapidly, indicating a short sojourn of the active inhibitor in tissues in vivo [64]. However, the inhibition of MAO is irreversible and prolonged. The sojourn of the active inhibitor in any given tissue or organ appears to determine the extent of over-all MAO inhibition.

Nialamide Metabolism

The compound nialamide (1-(2-[benzylcarbamyl])-ethyl-2-isonicotinylhydrazine, Niamid, VIII), also employed as an antidepressant, appears to undergo a multiple metabolic breakdown process [75] as shown.

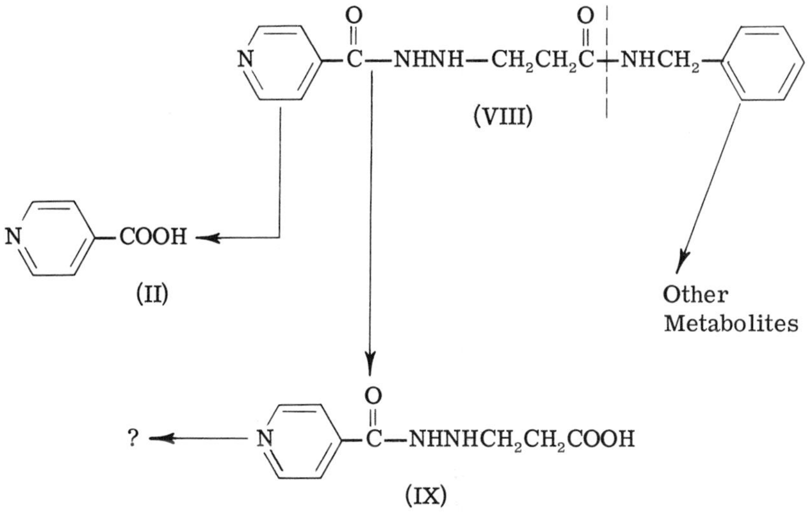

For the most part the initial step of degradation appears to be at the carboxamide group of the parent compound. The extent of iso-nicotinic acid excretion is reported to be minor—far less than that for iproniazid. Furthermore, a major excretion product is the un-changed compound itself. However, it has not been established whether nialamide, the 1-isonicotinyl-2-carboxyethylhydrazine (IX), or a further breakdown product is responsible for the ultimate in-hibition of MAO.

Other Hydrazine-Type Inhibitors of MAO

The metabolism of other hydrazine-type MAO inhibitors has not been studied extensively. A novel pathway of metabolism of yielding a hydrazine-type MAO inhibitor has been described with the nitro-furan derivatives. These compounds, especially furazolidone (X), were found to be relatively potent inhibitors of MAO which resembled other hydrazine-type inhibitors [76-78]. The pathway for the biotrans-formation of furazolidone which has been proposed is shown here.

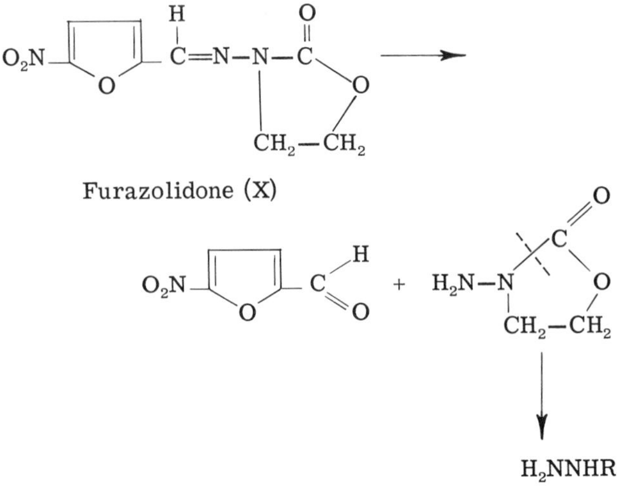

Furazolidone (X)

H$_2$NNHR

N-alkylhydrazine (XI)

In investigating a series of related nitrofurans, only those containing a hydrazine moiety could be converted to MAO inhibitors. Thus the authors concluded that a hydrazine derivative with a free NH$_2$-group (XI) was responsible for the anti-MAO activity in vivo.

Interactions of Hydrazine-Type MAO Inhibitors with Biological Components

In addition to metabolic processes influencing their anti-MAO activities, these highly reactive hydrazine compounds are capable of interacting with a variety of chemical and biochemical substances to become inactivated as MAO inhibitors. Roewer and Werle [79] first observed in vitro the antagonism of the anti-MAO activity of high concentrations of iproniazid in the presence of blood or red blood cells. Horita [80] confirmed and extended these observations by showing that not only red cells but also hemoglobin and hemin were effective in inactivating pheniprazine but not iproniazid. The mechanism of the antagonism of pheniprazine and iproniazid by red blood cells appears to be quite different. Whereas the former compound is chemically inactivated by red cells, it is the transformation of iproniazid into an active MAO inhibitor which is prevented.

The interaction of hydrazines with pyridoxal phosphate is well known. Generally, the pyridoxal compounds are considered as antidotes to hydrazine or semicarbazide toxicity. Dubnick et al. [37] observed the opposite effect, i.e., an increase in the toxicity of several hydrazine compounds, including MAO inhibitors, upon coadministration with pyridoxal. The explanation for this unexpected result is based on the interaction of the hydrazine compounds with pyridoxal to form pyridoxal hydrazones, which possess greater toxicity than the parent hydrazine compound. Similar conclusions were reached for the inhibitory action of several hydrazine compounds on pyridoxal phosphokinase. The pyridoxal hydrazone, rather than the hydrazine, was active in inhibiting the enzyme.

Other substances known to interact with hydrazine-type inhibitors of MAO include sodium pyruvate and other aldehydes or ketones [82, 83], copper ions [84, 85], and 1,2-naphthoquinone-4-sulfonate [67].

Conclusion. The highly reactive nature of the hydrazine inhibitors of MAO is responsible for the varied enzymic and nonenzymic reactions that they undergo. From a review of the literature the following conclusions may be reached: 1) The inhibition of MAO by the hydrazines or hydrazides appears to require the structure, $R-CH_2NHNH_2$, in which R may be a variety of substituents the chemistry of which will affect the potency of the compound as an inhibitor; 2) N,N'-disubstituted hydrazides appear to undergo enzymic or nonenzymic cleavage to yield a primary hydrazine which acts as the inhibitor; and 3) The rate of conversion to the active form determines the rate of peak onset of MAO inhibition, and the rate of inactivation or removal of the activated agent determines the duration of presence of the active agent.

SUMMARY

Hydrazine and its derivatives represent a group of highly reactive chemicals which are utilized extensively for many varied purposes. They are capable of producing a wide spectrum of biological effects, some of which are useful therapeutically, others of which are definitely harmful. The manner and rate of biotransformation of these compounds play a major role in determining the nature of the observed effects. Acetylation appears to be the most important mode of biotransformation with respect to inactivation of such compounds, whereas hydrolysis, oxidation, and reduction frequently result in the formation of metabolites with potent biological effects. Biotransformation appears to be essential to the capacity of many of these compounds to inhibit monoamine oxidase. Conversion to substances which contain a free $-NH_2$ group is frequently requisite to inhibition of this important enzyme system. Other biotransformation reactions tend to terminate the inhibitory effect on monoamine oxidase but may result in the formation of compounds which inhibit other biochemical systems.

References

[1] L. B. Colvin, *J. Pharm. Sci.*, **58**, 1433 (1969).
[2] H. H. Sisler, G. M. Omietanski, and B. Rudner, *Chem. Rev.*, **57**, 1021 (1957).
[3] S. Shifrin, B. N. Ames, and G. FerroLuzzi-Ames, *J. Biol. Chem.*, **241**, 3424 (1966).
[4] V. Habermann, *Biochim. Biophys. Acta*, **55**, 999 (1962).
[5] W. Kreis, *Cancer Res.*, **30**, 82 (1970).
[6] V. T. von Kreybig, R. Preussmann, and I. v. Kreybig, *Arzneim.-Forsch.*, **20**, 363 (1970).
[7] A. K. Gupta and N. S. Grover, *Mutation Res.*, **10**, 519 (1970).
[8] D. J. Bauer, *Ann. N.Y. Acad. Sci.*, **130**, 110 (1965).
[9] M. C. Dodd and W. B. Stillman, *J. Pharmacol. Exp. Ther.* **82**, 11 (1944).
[10] K. C. Back, *Fed. Proc.*, **29**, 2000 (1970).
[11] K. C. Back and A. A. Thomas, *Ann. Rev. Pharmacol.*, **10**, 395 (1970).
[12] Cited in *Food Cosmet. Toxicol.*, **7**, 662 (1969).
[13] E. Marley and B. Blackwell, *Adv. Pharmacol. Chemother.*, **8**, 185 (1970).
[14] H. Hidaka and S. Udenfriend, *Arch. Biochem. Biophys.*, **140**, 174 (1970).
[15] H. Hidaka, S. Udenfriend, A. Nagasaka, and L. J. DeGroot, *Fed. Proc.*, **29**, 3030 (1970).
[16] T. E. Smith, H. Weissbach, and S. Udenfriend, *Biochemistry*, **2**, 746 (1963).
[17] G. Weitzel, F. Schneider, D. Kummer, and H. Ochs, *Z. Krebsforsch.*, **70**, 354 (1968).
[18] G. Weitzel, F. Schneider, W. Herschmann, W. Durst, J. Thauer, H. Ochs, and D. Kummer, *Hoppe-Seyler's Z. Physiol. Chem.* **348**, 443 (1967).
[19] H. Koblet and H. Diggelmann, *Eur. J. Cancer*, **4**, 55 (1968).
[20] W. Kreis, S. B. Piepho, and H. V. Bernhard, *Experientia*, **22**, 431 (1966).
[21] E. W. Neumann and J. G. Nadeau, *Anal. Chem.*, **36**, 640 (1964).
[22] F. N. Dost, D. J. Reed and C. H. Wang, *Biochem. Pharmacol.*, **15**, 1325 (1966).
[23] G. H. Beaven and J. C. White, *Nature*, **173**, 389 (1954).
[24] R. A. Prough, J. A. Wittkop, and D. J. Reed, *Arch. Biochem. Biophys.*, **131**, 369 (1969).
[25] H. McKennis, Jr., A. S. Yard, E. J. Adair, and J. H. Weatherby, *J. Pharmacol. Exp. Ther.*, **131**, 152 (1961).
[26] H. McKennis, Jr., A. S. Yard, J. H. Weatherby, and J. A. Hagy, *J. Pharmacol. Exp. Ther.*, **126**, 109 (1959).
[27] M. J. Mattila, *Humangenetik*, **9**, 212 (1970).
[28] W. C. Govier, *J. Pharmacol. Exp. Ther.*, **150**, 305 (1965).
[29] H. M. Perry, Jr., A. Sakamoto, and E. M. Tan, *Proc. Central Soc. Clin. Res.*, **40**, 81 (1967).
[30] W. Schloot and H. W. Goedde, *Humangenetik*, **9**, 208 (1970).
[31] H. W. Goedde, W. Schloot, and A. Valesky, *Biochem. Pharmacol.*, **16**, 1793 (1967).

[32] W. W. Weber, *Ann. N.Y. Acad. Sci.*, **151**, 734 (1968).

[33] S. N. Cohen, *Mol. Pharmacol.*, **3**, 266 (1967).

[34] T. A. White, J. W. Jenne, and D. A. P. Evans, *Biochem. J.*, **113**, 721 (1969).

[35] D. V. Parke in *The Biochemistry of Foreign Compounds* (H. H. V. Arnstein, P. N. Campbell, S. P. Datta, and L. L. Engel, eds.), Pergamon, New York, 1968, Chap. 10.

[36] J. M. Kelly, R. B. Poet, and R. M. Chesner, Abstracts, 122nd National Meeting of the American Chemical Society, September 1952, p. 3c.

[37] B. Dubnick, G. A. Leeson, and C. C. Scott, *Toxicol. Appl. Pharmacol.*, **2**, 403 (1960).

[38] I. Toida, *Amer. Rev. Respirat. Diseases*, **85**, 720 (1962).

[39] J. H. Peters and V. E. Hayes, *Arch. Intern. Pharmacodyn.*, **159**, 328 (1966).

[40] M. R. Juchau, J. Krasner, and S. J. Yaffe, *Biochem. Pharmacol.*, **17**, 1969 (1968).

[41] P. H. Hernandez, P. Mazel, and J. R. Gillette, *Biochem. Pharmacol.*, **16**, 1877 (1967).

[42] D. E. Schwartz, *Experientia*, **22**, 212 (1966).

[43] G. Procellanti and P. Preziosi, *Enzymologia*, **17**, 47 (1954).

[44] J. E. Hucko-Haas and D. J. Reed, *Biochem. Biophys. Res. Commun.*, **39**, 396 (1970).

[45] R. A. Prough, J. A. Wittkop, and D. J. Reed, *Arch. Biochem. Biophys.*, **140**, 450 (1970).

[46] J. A. Wittkop, R. A. Prough, and D. J. Reed, *Arch. Biochem. Biophys.*, **134**, 308 (1969).

[47] W. Kreis, *Cancer Res.*, **30**, 82 (1970).

[48] Conference on "New Reflections on Monoamine Oxidase Inhibition," *Ann. N.Y. Acad. Sci.*, **107**, 809 (1963).

[49] Conference on "Amine Oxidase Inhibitors," *Ann. N.Y. Acad. Sci.*, **80**, 551 (1959).

[50] I. H. Biel, A. Horita, and A. E. Drukker, in *Psychopharmacological Agents* (M. Gordon, ed.), Vol. 1, Academic, New York, 1964, pp. 359-443.

[51] G. R. Pscheidt, *Int. Rev. Neurobiol.*, **7**, 191 (1964).

[52] A. Pletscher, K. F. Gey, and N. P. Burkard, in *Handbook of Experimental Pharmacology* (O. Eichler and A. Farah, eds.), Vol. 19, Springer, New York, 1966, pp. 593-743.

[53] A. N. Davison, *Biochem. J.*, **67**, 316 (1957).

[54] P. A. Shore and V. H. Cohn, *Biochem. Pharmacol.*, **5**, 91 (1960).

[55] W. P. Burkhard, K. F. Gey and A. Pletscher, *Biochem. Pharmacol.*, **11**, 177 (1962).

[56] E. A. Zeller, in *Metabolic Inhibitors* (R. M. Hochster and J. H. Quastel, eds.), Vol. 2, Academic, New York, 1963, pp. 53-78.

[57] L. S. Seiden and J. Westley, *Arch. Int. Pharmacodyn.*, **146**, 145 (1963).

[58] T. E. Smith, H. Weissbach, and S. Udenfriend, *Biochemistry*, **2**, 746 (1963).

[59]   M. Kori and E. Mingioli, *Biochem. Pharmacol.*, 18, 577 (1964).

[60]   B. Koechlin and V. Iliev, *Ann. N.Y. Acad. Sci.*, 80, 864 (1959).

[61]   B. A. Koechlin, M. A. Schwartz, and W. E. Oberhaensli, *J. Pharmacol. Exp. Ther.*, 138, 11 (1962).

[62]   S. Hess, H. Weissbach, B. G. Redfield, and S. Udenfriend, *J. Pharmacol. Exp. Ther.*, 124, 189 (1958).

[63]   V. Nair, *Biochem. Pharmacol.*, 3, 78 (1959).

[64]   A. Horita, *J. Pharmacol. Exp. Ther.*, 142, 141 (1963).

[65]   M. A. Schwartz, *Proc. Soc. Exp. Biol. Med.*, 107, 613 (1961).

[66]   M. A. Schwartz, *J. Pharmacol. Exp. Ther.*, 130, 157 (1960).

[67]   M. A. Schwartz, *J. Pharmacol. Exp. Ther.*, 135, 1 (1962).

[68]   G. A. Leeson, R. Leverett, and B. Dubnick, Abstracts, 138th Meeting, American Chemical Society, Sept. 1960, p. 65c.

[69]   R. Leverett, G. A. Leeson, and B. Dubnick, Abstracts, 138th Meeting, American Chemical Society, Sept. 1960, p. 65c.

[70]   A. Horita, *Brit. J. Pharmacol. Chemother.*, 24, 245 (1965).

[71]   B. V. Clineschmidt and A. Horita, *Biochem. Pharmacol.*, 18, 1011 (1969).

[72]   B. V. Clineschmidt and A. Horita, *Biochem. Pharmacol.*, 18, 1021 (1969).

[73]   A. Horita, B. V. Clineschmidt, and J. J. McMonigle, in *Excerpta Med. Int. Congr. Ser.*, 180, 4 (1968).

[74]   K. F. Tipton, *Biochem. J.*, 121, 33P (1971).

[75]   J. A. Schneider, B. M. Bloom, C. Delahunt, K. F. Finger, M. Finkelstein, R. P. Rowe, R. Stebbins, and A. Weissman, *J. Soc. Das Ciencias Med. DeLisboa, Suppl.*, 123, 43 (1959).

[76]   D. Palm, U. Magnus, H. Grobecker, and J. Jonsson, *N. Schmied. Arch. Pharm. Exp. Path.*, 256, 281 (1967).

[77]   D. Palm and U. Magnus, *Klin. Wochenschr.*, 46, 720 (1968).

[78]   K. Quiring and D. Palm, *N. Schmied. Arch. Pharm. Exp. Path.*, 265, 397 (1970).

[79]   F. Roewer and E. Werle, *Arch. Exp. Path Pharmak.*, 230, 552 (1957).

[80]   A. Horita, *Toxicol. Appl. Pharmacol.*, 7, 97 (1965).

[81]   D. B. McCormick and E. E. Snell, *Proc. Nat. Acad. Sci.*, 45, 1371 (1959).

[82]   A. Horita and C. Matsumoto, *Life Sci.*, 10, 491 (1962).

[83]   A. Horita, *Ann. N.Y. Acad. Sci.*, 107, 951 (1963).

[84]   L. E. Eberson and K. Persson, *J. Med. Pharm. Chem.*, 5, 738 (1962).

[85]   A. L. Green, *Biochem. Pharmacol.*, 13, 249 (1963).

Recent Developments in Beta Adrenergic Blocking Drugs

KEITH K. WONG and ERIC C. SCHREIBER
Department of Drug Metabolism
The Squibb Institute for Medical Research
New Brunswick, New Jersey 08903

INTRODUCTION

The sympathetic nervous system exerts its effects through nor-epinephrine, a chemical transmitter secreted at the endings of the adrenergic post-ganglionic fibers. The response which is evoked in the tissue is elicited by the action of the chemical transmitter on the tissue receptor. In addition to the response brought about by release of norepinephrine at the post-ganglionic fiber-tissue junction, responses can also be induced by the administration of exogenous catecholamines. The effects seen in the tissue may be of a stimulatory or an inhibitory nature. The concept of the adrenergic receptor site is due to the fundamental contributions of Langley and Dale. On the basis of the diverse responses seen in tissues when subjected to nervous stimulation, Langley [1] concluded that two types of tissue receptors must be present, excitatory or inhibitory, and that the observed tissue response reflected which of these receptor sites was dominant in that tissue. Dale [2] may be credited with the discovery of the first adrenergic blocking agent, when he conclusively demonstrated that the pressor effect of epinephrine could be prevented by pretreatment with the ergot alkaloids.

Ahlquist [3] studied the order of potency of five sympathomimetic amines: d,l-norepinephrine (NE); epinephrine (E); d,l- and l-α-

101

methylnorepinephrine (MeNE); α-methylepinephrine (MeE); and isoproterenol (ISO) on a variety of tissue responses both in isolated
organs and intact animals. According to the order of potency for
stimulation, two series of responses were observed; one was
E > NE > MeNE > MeE > ISO, and the other was ISO > E > MeE
> MeNE > NE. These response patterns were subsequently sug-
gested to be the reflection of two types of receptors, designated as
alpha and beta. In general, stimulation of alpha receptors produces
an excitatory response, and of beta receptors an inhibitory response.
Cardiac excitation is classified as a beta receptor response due to
the fact that the cardiac inotropic and chronotropic effects of epinephrine and isoproterenol can be reversed by the action of beta,
but not alpha, adrenergic blocking drugs [4, 5]. Thus adrenergic
blockers have been recognized as a useful tool for the study of the
specificity of adrenergic receptors as well as for clinical applications.

Dale [2] demonstrated the alpha blocking effect of ergot alkaloids.
In addition, phentholamine [6] and phenoxybenzamine [7] have become
widely used alpha adrenergic blockers. The first synthetic beta adrenergic blocker, dichloroisoproterenol (DCI), was described by
Powell and Slater [8] in 1957. Intensive efforts have been devoted
since then to the development of other beta adrenergic blockers.
Their pharmacological actions and structure-activity relationships
have been reviewed by Ariens [9], Ahlquist [10], and more recently
by Dollery et al. [11]. It is our purpose not only to summarize the
structure-activity relationship of the commonly used beta adrenergic
blockers, but to discuss, in depth, their metabolism.

STRUCTURE-ACTIVITY RELATIONSHIP

Since the introduction of DCI, more than 20 beta adrenergic
blockers have been reported. Figure 1 shows the chemical structures of beta-blockers along with the most potent beta adrenergic
agonist, isoproterenol. The term "beta-agonist" applies to those
chemical agents which stimulate beta receptors to produce specific
biologic responses. When such activity occurs in a beta adrenergic
blocker, it is described as intrinsic activity. On the other hand, the
term "beta-antagonist" refers to the chemical agents which compete
with beta-agonists for the beta receptor; some are devoid of the intrinsic activity. Another criterion of beta adrenergic blockade is
specificity. Its action in preventing the response of beta adrenergic
receptor to a beta adrenergic drug does not necessarily affect the
response of other types of receptors.

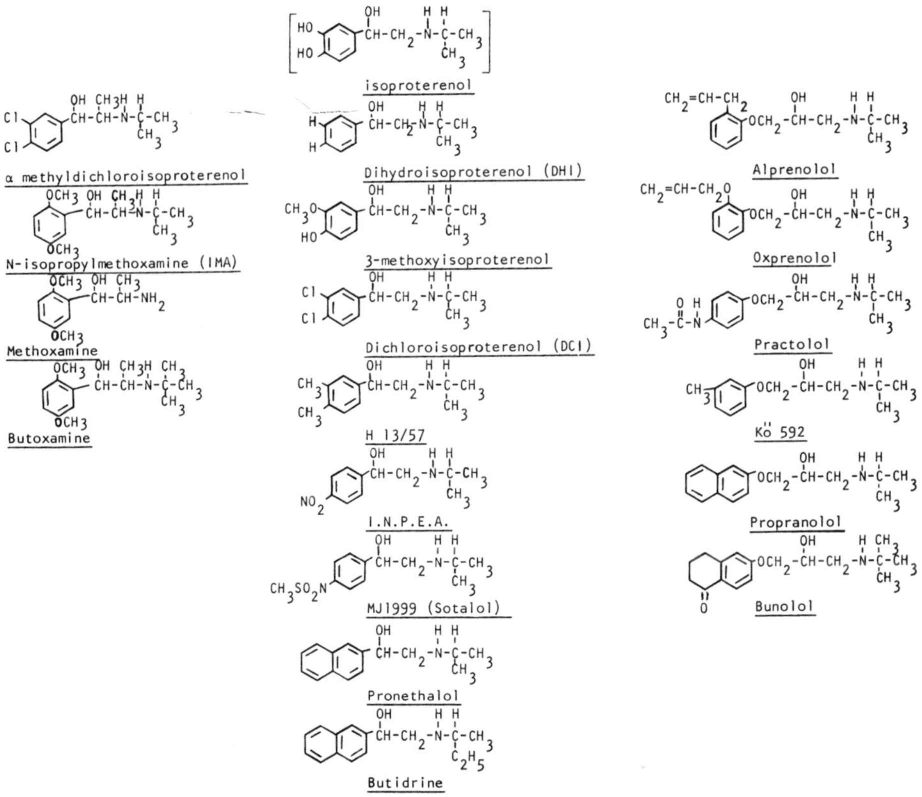

Fig. 1. Chemical structure of beta adrenergic blocking drugs.

The chemical structures of beta adrenergic blockers are closely related to each other and also to the beta adrenergic agonists. Thus the same structure-activity relationship can be applied to both agonists and antagonists. In fact, studies showed that some beta-blockers, such as DCI, exhibit intrinsic activity by increasing the rate of heartbeat in both intact animals and atrial preparations. However, it is their specific blocking activity in reversing the beta adrenergic stimulation that makes the beta-blockers a unique series of drugs.

Beta adrenergic blockers can be considered as derivatives of phenylethylamine, where substitution has been made on the aromatic ring, the alpha and beta carbon atoms, and the terminal amino group.

Thus, the structure can be represented as

$$m \underset{p}{\overset{}{\bigcirc}} \overset{OH}{\underset{|}{C}} - \overset{R}{\underset{|}{C}} - \overset{H}{\underset{|}{N}} - R'$$

The activity of beta-blockers is affected by the substituents at the positions designated R, R', m, and p. Two general features are apparent; affinity for the receptor site is associated with the amine end of the molecule, whereas the intrinsic activity of drugs depends on the aromatic ring and the distance between the aromatic ring and the amino group.

The function of N-alkylation in beta adrenergic blockers has been studied by Ariens [9] and others [12-16]. The affinity for beta receptors is greater in branched alkyl groups, such as isopropyl and tertiary butyl, than it is in the straight-chain alkyl functions. The N-isopropyl moiety becomes an important feature in the structural requirements of beta adrenergic blockers. As shown in Fig. 1, methoxamine is the only compound which contains a primary amino group. This feature, combined with its α-methyl group, is thought to be the reason for the absence of cardiac blocking effect of this agent.

Introduction of alkyl substituents on the alpha carbon atom results in an alteration of beta-blocking activity [17]. α-Methyl substitution, such as in N-isopropylmethoxamine (IMA) and butoxamine, was shown to have relatively high potency in the blockage of the beta adrenergic metabolic effect in contrast to their relatively low potency in the blockade of cardiac effect [18]. α-Methyl DCI has much lower beta-blocking activity in cardiac effect as compared with that of DCI; however, they are equipotent in the blockade of vasodilatory effect [19]. Thus the substitution of alpha carbon atom dissociates the beta adrenergic blocking activity in the heart, but may increase other beta-blocking activities.

Hydroxy-substitution at the beta carbon atom seems to be a necessary feature of the beta adrenergic blocking drugs. Its presence results in the formation of an asymmetric center. It has been shown by Howe [20] and Pratesi et al. [21] that pharmacological activity is much greater in the l-isomers for both beta adrenergic agonists and antagonists.

Local anesthetic activity has been found in some beta adrenergic blocking drugs. This activity appears to be equipotent in both d- and l-isomers [22]. However, no correlation between the beta-blocking

effect and the local anesthetic activity has been found. Thus propranolol and pronethalol were shown to be equally effective as compared to procaine in the guinea pig wheal test, but propranolol is ten
times more active in the prevention of tachycardia than is pronethalol
[23]. INPEA and pronethalol have equipotency in the cardiac effect.
Yet the former does not exhibit any activity in local anesthesia [24].

Expanding the aliphatic side chain by addition of —OCH$_2$ group results in producing a series of potent beta adrenergic blocking drugs,
including propranolol which is frequently employed as a reference
compound for the comparison of activities among the beta-blockers.
The pharmacological activity of this series will be described along
with their chemical features of ring substitution.

The phenolic hydroxy-groups of catecholamines have been shown
to be essential for their pharmacological activity. Corrodi et al.[17]
demonstrated that the meta-OH group is more important than the
para-OH group for the activity on the beta receptors. Elimination
of both —OH groups resulted in marked decrease of the intrinsic
activity of the beta adrenergic drugs. However, the affinity of these
compounds for the beta adrenergic receptors remained. Thus phenyl-
ethanolamine and its N-methyl and N-isopropyl derivatives have a
beta adrenergic blocking activity with respect to the tachycardia induced by beta adrenergic drugs [25]. 3-Methoxyisoproterenol, a
metabolite of isoproterenol, was found to have antagonistic properties
to the beta adrenergic agonists [26, 27]. Replacement of the phenolic-
OH groups with chlorine atoms or with methyl groups results in an
increase of beta adrenergic blocking activity [8, 17, 26]. Substitution
of the para-hydroxy group by a methylsulfonamide, acetamide, or nitro
group also forms potent beta adrenergic blocking drugs such as
MJ1999 [28], practolol [29, 30], and INPEA [31], respectively. Among
them, practolol has been shown to be a specific cardiac blocker with
very little effect on vasodilation or bronchial dilation. Attachment
of another benzene moiety to the 3,4-positions of the original ring
system has produced another series of potent beta adrenergic blocking drugs, such as pronethalol [32], butidrine [33], and propranolol[34].
All of these agents decrease the resting heartbeat, cardiac output,
contractility, and blood pressure. It is interesting that substitution
of a saturated ring at the same positions decreases the beta-blocking
activity [9], yet introducing a ketone group at the saturated ring,
as in bunolol [35], restores the beta-blocking activity. Substitutions
at the 2- or 2,5-positions of the ring retain the beta-blocking activity.
However, variable activities were found among these beta-blockers.
In addition to the 2-substitution, alprenolol and oxprenolol [36] also

contain the —OCH_2 group which favors beta-blocking activity. On the other hand, the 2,5-dimethoxy series (N-isopropylmethoxamine, methoxamine, and butoxamine) bears the α-methyl group which decreases the beta-blocking activity. Thus the potency contributed by the 2- or 2,5-substitutions is obscured.

DRUG METABOLISM

Although information on the biotransformation of beta-blockers is still far from complete, activity in this area has increased in recent years. It is interesting to compare the metabolic pathways of beta adrenergic blockers and the catecholamines.

Dichloroisoproterenol

The metabolism of DCI was studied by Mayer [37] in dogs and mice. After a single dose by intravenous administration, DCI disappeared from dog plasma in three phases. The first one was very rapid, with a half-life of only 1.4 min. The second and third phases had considerably longer half-lives, 32 and 110 min, respectively. Thus the investigator suggested rapid binding and distribution of DCI to the tissues during the first phase of the drug disappearance from the plasma, with subsequent release of the drug and/or its metabolites back to the plasma during the second and third phases. Preferential binding of the drug to various tissues was evidenced by its relatively high concentration in lung, liver, and kidney. It is interesting that DCI penetrated through the blood-brain barrier with rapid accumulation in the brain. A peak value, ten times higher than the plasma level, was observed 10 min after the intravenous administration.

The pharmacological significance of the binding of DCI in tissue was examined in the heart and brain. The appreciable concentration of DCI in the dog ventricle correlated directly with its cardiac adrenergic blocking effect for the first 6 hr. The rapid uptake of DCI in the central nervous system was reflected by the central blocking action in the dog [38] and by the clonic seizures in mice [39].

In addition to the unchanged drug, which is extractable by toluene under alkaline conditions, two metabolites were observed in the plasma. One was extractable by toluene under acidic conditions and the other remained in the aqueous residue as nonextractable. Despite the fact that the metabolites of DCI rapidly accounted for most of the radioactivity in plasma, the drug was unchanged in most of the tissues examined, except kidney. Thus it was suggested that the metabolites did not display the same affinity for tissues as demonstrated by the parent drug. Since the metabolites were excreted primarily in the urine, this might account for the relatively high concentration of metabolites in the kidney, particularly if the metabolites were found there. Biliary excretion was observed in the cannulated dog but was considered to be a minor route of excretion.

The acid-extractable metabolite was identified by paper chromatography as 3,4-dichloromandelic acid. An attempt to crystallize the isolated substance for further identification by comparing the melting point with an authentic sample of the compound was not successful. The formation of 3,4-dichloromandelic acid was presumed to follow the same pathway of oxidative deamination as established for catecholamines. After hydrolysis with β-glucuronidase and aryl sulfatase, 50% of the nonextractable metabolite was recovered as DCI. Thus it was concluded that DCI was excreted as conjugate. However, the nature of the conjugate has not been established.

Pronethalol

Extensive studies on the metabolism of pronethalol were carried out by Bond and Howe [40]. After oral administration, ^{14}C-pronethalol appeared to be well absorbed with 70% of the total dose accounted for in the excreta. Most of the radioactivity was found in urine collected in the first 24 hr after drug administration. Complete recovery of the radioactivity in urine was reported in three female patients, each of whom had received a single oral dose of the ^{14}C-drug.

Pronethalol was distributed in most of the organs of dogs with the highest concentrations in liver or kidney. The drug was also found in the brain with fairly constant amounts throughout the observation period (96 hr).

The urinary metabolites obtained from eight species of animals and man were separated by paper electrophoresis into three groups; acidic, basic, and amphoteric compounds, according to their electrophoretic mobility. Upon further separation by countercurrent chromatography, the acidic fraction was found to contain two major metabolites, 2-naphthylglycollic and 2-naphthoic acids. In addition, 2-naphthylglyoxylic acid was also obtained as a minor metabolite in rat, rabbit, and human urine. The basic metabolite was identified as 7-hydroxy-pronethalol. Treatment with β-glucuronidase resulted in liberation of the 7-hydroxy-pronethalol. Thus two metabolic path-

ways have been established; one involves oxidative deamination of
the side chain, and the other ring hydroxylation. The latter reaction
appeared to be the major pathway in most species of animals except
guinea pigs, which excreted more than 70% of the total dose in urine
as acidic metabolites. The metabolic pathways of pronethalol are illustrated in Fig. 2. The scheme of oxidative deamination was elucidated
by the in vitro study with the post-mitrochondrial fraction (9000 × g
supernatant) of guinea pig liver. The system required NADPH and
oxygen and was inhibited by mebanazine, a monoamine oxidase inhibitor.

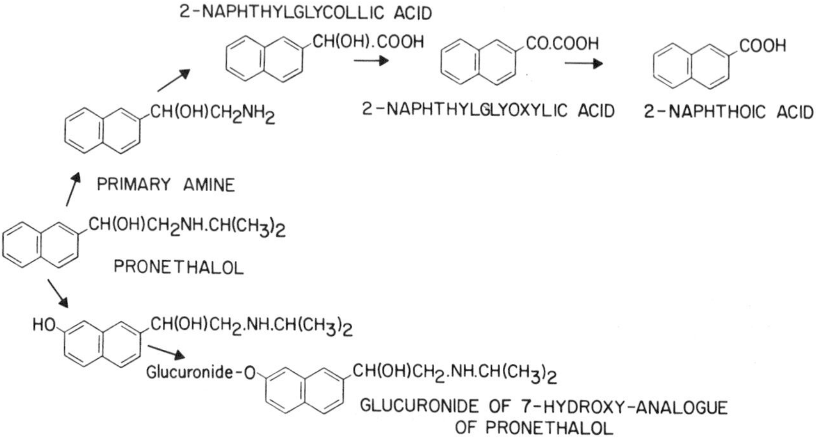

Fig. 2. Metabolic pathways of pronethalol.

Practolol

Preliminary studies in rats [41] with a single dose (20 mg/kg,
intraperitoneally) of (1-^{14}C) acetyl-labeled practolol showed that
99.5% of the dosed radioactivity was recovered within 7 days, with
3.5% as $^{14}CO_2$ expired in air and the remainder excreted in urine.
Electrophoresis revealed that 85% of the radioactivity was accounted
for as unchanged drug. Similar findings were obtained in rats chronically dosed with nonradioactive drug at high dosages (100 and 500
mg/kg) for up to 6 weeks prior to the administration of radioactive
drug. Thus it was suggested that the metabolic pattern is independent
of dose, duration of dosing, or route of administration.

Subsequent investigation with ^{14}C-ring labeled drug showed that
the drug was preferentially accumulated in some tissues, particularly

in liver, lung, and heart. The lowest tissue level was consistently found in the brain during the first 24 hr after oral administration, suggesting that the drug also readily traverses the blood-brain barrier. The finding of a high concentration of practolol in heart correlates with its cardio-selectivity.

Two metabolites of practolol in urine were separated on a silica gel column. They were identified by thin-layer chromatography as 2-hydroxy-4-(2-hydroxy-3-isopropylaminopropoxy) acetanilide and glucuronide of 1-(4-amino-3-hydroxyphenoxy)-3-isopropylamino-propan-2-ol. The structure of the glucuronide conjugate was further shown to be a phenolic conjugation. Thus the metabolic scheme of practolol can be illustrated as in Fig. 3.

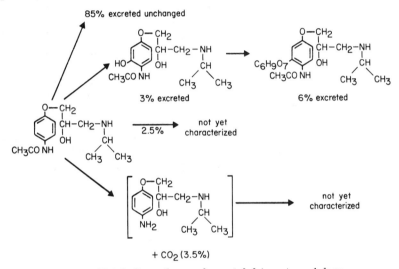

Fig. 3. Metabolic pathway of practolol in rats and dogs.

Propranolol

The absorption of propranolol was found to be essentially complete after oral administration of the ^{14}C-drug to rat, dog, and monkey [42]. Marked species differences in the mode of excretion were observed. The rat and dog excreted approximately 20 to 25% of the radioactive dose in the feces, whereas the monkey and man [38, 43] excreted only a small amount by that route. Despite the low excretion in the feces, a considerable amount of radioactivity was found in the bile of the monkey. Thus enterohepatic circulation was suggested; this might also account for the longer plasma half-life observed in the monkey than in dogs and rats.

In the dog, after intravenous or oral administration of ^{14}C-propranolol, considerable amounts of radioactivity were found in lung, liver, and kidney. Drug was also present in brain and heart. Further studies showed that most of the radioactivity present in the liver and kidney was naphthoxylactic acid, whereas unchanged drug remained in the lung and brain. This accounts for the pharmacological activity of propranolol in the heart, since release of the drug from the lung may serve as a continuous source of propranolol to the heart.

The metabolism of ^{14}C-propranolol was postulated early by Bond [44] (Fig. 4). Two metabolites were extracted in urine of the rabbit, rat, and man as 4-hydroxy-propranolol and naphthoxylactic acid. Recent investigations [42] from the same laboratory showed that naphthoxylactic acid was found in the urine of all animal species examined, but 4-hydroxy-propranolol was essentially absent. Further studies indicated that the 4-hydroxy derivative appeared only in the blood of an orally dosed dog, leading to the speculation that 4-hydroxy-propranolol was formed only when a large amount of the drug was present in the liver. An alternative explanation was that, under normal conditions, 4-hydroxy-propranolol was further metabolized; thus, after oral administration, the metabolic pathway was overwhelmed and free 4-hydroxy-propranolol, therefore, appeared in the blood.

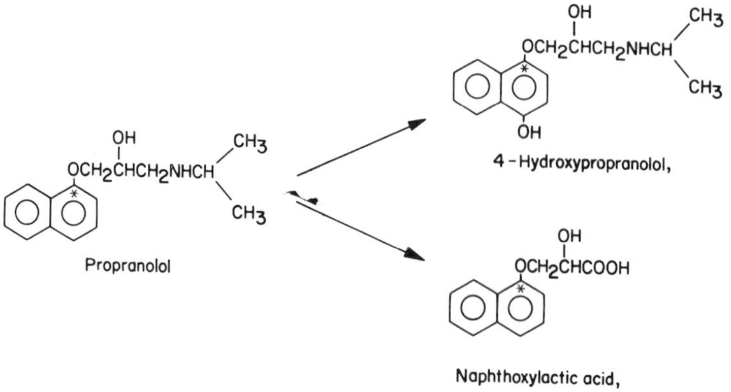

Fig. 4. Metabolic pathways of propranolol.

Bunolol

[14]C-Bunolol was absorbed extensively in dogs [45]. The peak value of radioactivity in the blood was reached within 1 hr, with a half-life of disappearance approximately 2-3 hr. The major portion of the administered radioactivity (53.8-75.4%) was excreted in urine and 14.8-17.2% was excreted in feces. While most of the radioactivity in urine was recovered in the first 24 hr, gradual elimination of radioactivity was observed via feces. In addition, a considerable amount of radioactivity was found in the gastrointestinal tract and liver, suggesting that enterohepatic circulation was taking place. Residual amounts of radioactivity were found in heart, brain, kidney, spleen, and fat, 72 hr after oral administration of the drug.

The metabolites of bunolol [46] in urine were extracted by ether. Both acidic and basic metabolites in free and conjugated forms were obtained. So far, two acidic metabolites were identified as 3-[(5,6,7,8-tetrahydro-5-oxo-1-naphthyl)-oxy]-lactic acid and the corresponding acetic acid. Thus the metabolic pathways for bunolol have been constructed in Fig. 5.

Isopropylmethoxamine and Methoxamine

IMA was administered to rats and dogs [47]. The drug was extensively metabolized with only small amounts (2%) remaining in the urine as unchanged form. Most of the metabolites excreted in urine were found to be conjugated. After hydrolysis with sulfuric acid, the metabolites were identified by paper chromatography as 5-hydroxy or 2-hydroxy derivatives of IMA. Further studies showed that methoxamine and its 2-hydroxy, but not the 5-hydroxy, derivatives were also present in urine. The metabolism of IMA is summarized in Fig. 6. Unlike other beta-blockers, the metabolism of IMA involves only dealkylation and conjugation. Oxidative deamination has not been demonstrated.

Oxprenolol

Oxprenolol was readily absorbed in dogs and men after oral administration of the drug [52]. Whole-body autoradiography in the mouse, one minute after an intravenous dose of 25 mg/kg of ^{14}C-labelled drug, showed that oxprenolol was quickly and widely distributed throughout the animal. It was also demonstrated that the level of oxprenolol increased linearly in the organs of rats in response to increasing doses ranging from 34.2 to 1140.0 μg/kg with preferential accumulation of the drug being found in the lung, kidney,

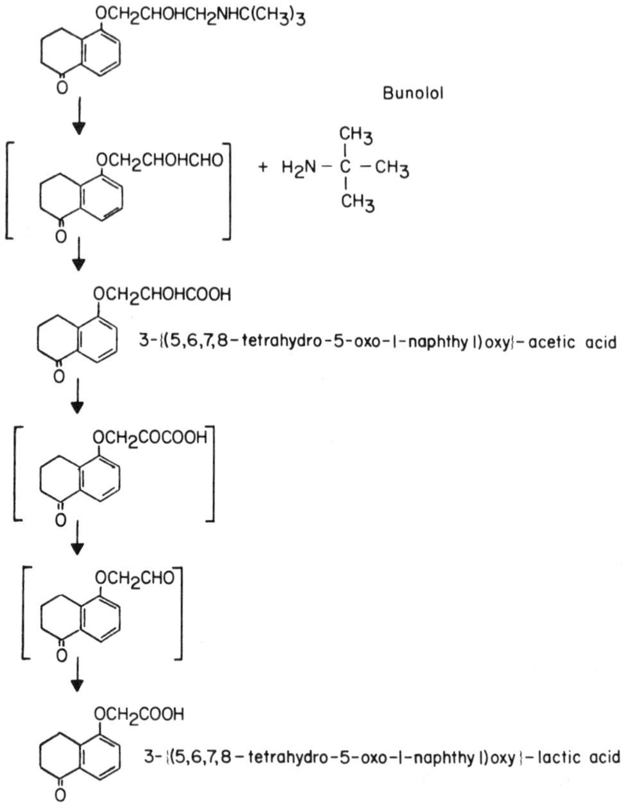

Fig. 5. Metabolism of bunolol.

and liver. The concentrations of drug in the brain were the lowest among the organs examined and were equivalent to the blood levels of the drug throughout the range of dosages. In man, over 70% of the drug was excreted in urine with the major portion formed as glucuronide conjugate. No metabolite of oxprenolol was detected in human urine.

Garteiz [53] administered oxprenolol to rats at 20 mg/kg/day for three days. Both conjugated and free drug were found in urine. Metabolites were also found. Both the conjugated drug and its conjugated metabolites were hydrolyzed by glucuronidase, then treated with trifluoroacetic anhydride to form the corresponding trifluoro-acetylated derivatives. These were then separated and identified by combination of gas chromatography and mass spectrometry. The metabolic pathways of oxprenolol in rats were postulated (Fig. 7),

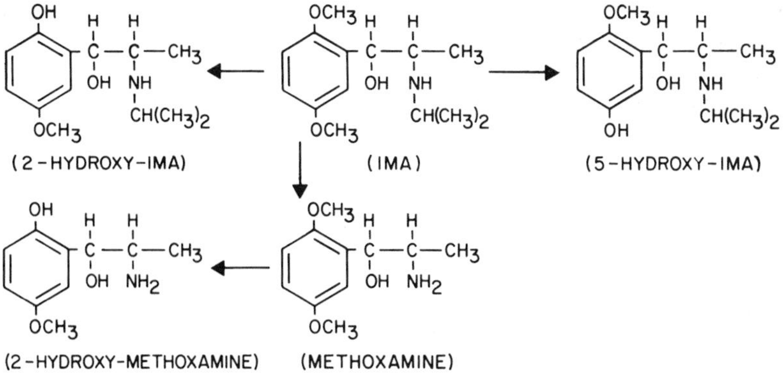

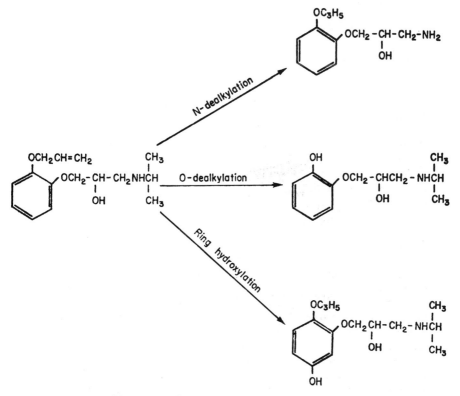

Fig. 6. Metabolic pathways of isopropylmethoxamine.

Fig. 7. Metabolic pathways of oxprenolol in rats.

based on the structure of the derivatives. It appeared that trifluoro-
acetylated derivatives of the beta-hydroxy-N-isopropylamino side
chain, typical pharmacophoric group of beta blockers, can serve as
a valuable tool for the metabolic study on this class of compounds.

CONCLUSIONS

Three interesting aspects have emerged from the metabolism of
beta adrenergic blockers.

1) Structurally, beta-blockers are related to the catecholamines.
Most of the blocking agents rapidly entered into the central nervous
system, while little epinephrine [48] or norepinephrine [49] penetrated the blood-brain barrier. This was attributed to the high lipoid
solubility of many beta-blockers, such as DCI and propranolol. However, water-soluble compounds, such as practolol, are also absorbed
in the brain. Furthermore, no appreciable amount of drugs was found
in the adipose tissue as evidenced by the study of DCI. Thus selective
absorption, rather than solubility, could be the underlying mechanism.
2) The binding of epinephrine and norephinephrine to tissues was
reported by Axelrod [48] and Whitby [49] as a cause of inactivation
for the catecholamines. The pharmacological activity of beta adrenergic blockers appears to be associated with the tissue binding of
the drugs. The nonspecific activity of DCI and propranolol was associated with their broad distribution among many tissues. On the
other hand, the selectivity of practolol is thought to be due to its high
affinity for heart tissue and low affinity for brain.
3) The major metabolic pathway for circulating catecholamines
is the O-methylation, as opposed to oxidative deamination at nerve
endings [50]. Oxidative deamination is considered to be only a secondary route of drug alteration for epinephrine and norepinephrine
in the circulation. Isoproterenol [51] is converted to 3-O-methyl
derivative, but no acidic metabolite has been found. This suggests
that N-deisopropylation could be more difficult than N-demethylation among the catecholamines. However, N-deisopropylation is
commonly observed in the metabolism of beta-blockers. Oxidative
deamination is predominant in the biotransformation of these drugs,
except for the methoxamine series. It can be argued that the lack of
a phenolic group in the beta blocking agent prevents the O-methyl
transfer. However, hydroxylation of the aromatic ring system has
been shown in some beta-blockers. Furthermore, O-demethylation,
rather than O-methylation, has been shown in the metabolism of IMA
and methoxamine. Both the methoxy- and hydroxy-derivatives have

the same pharmacological activity. Thus the metabolic studies of beta-blocking agents has further illustrated the different characteristics between the agonists and the antagonists of beta adrenergic drugs.

References

[1]   J. N. Langley, *J. Physiol.*, **33**, 374 (1905).

[2]   H. H. Dale, *J. Physiol.*, **34**, 163 (1906).

[3]   R. P. Ahlquist, *Amer. J. Physiol.*, **153**, 586 (1948).

[4]   N. C. Moran and M. E. Perkins, *J. Pharmacol. Exp. Ther.*, **124**, 223 (1958).

[5]   M. Nickerson and L. S. Goodman, *J. Pharmacol. Exp. Ther.*, **89**, 167 (1947).

[6]   M. DeV. Cotten, N. C. Moran, and P. E. Stopp, *J. Pharmacol. Exp. Ther.*, **121**, 183 (1957).

[7]   M. Nickerson, J. W. Henry, and G. M. Nomaguchi, *J. Pharmacol. Exp. Ther.*, **107**, 300 (1953).

[8]   C. E. Powell and I. H. Slater, *J. Pharmacol. Exp. Ther.*, **122**, 480 (1958).

[9]   E. J. Ariens, *Ann. N.Y. Acad. Sci.*, **139**, 606 (1967).

[10] R. P. Ahlquist, *Ann. Rev. Pharmacol.*, **8**, 259 (1968).

[11] C. T. Dollery, J. W. Paterson, and M. E. Conolly, *Clin. Pharmacol. Ther.*, **10**, 765 (1969).

[12] J. E. Biel, E. G. Schwarz, E. P. Sprengeler, H. A. Leiser, and H. L. Friedman, *J. Amer. Chem. Soc.*, **76**, 3149 (1954).

[13] H. D. Moed, J. Van Dijk, and H. Hiewind, *Rec. Trav. Chim. Pays-Bas*, **74**, 919 (1955).

[14] H. Langecher, and H. Friebel, *Arch. Exp. Path. Pharmak.*, **226**, 493 (1955).

[15] A. M. Lands and M. I. Tainter, *Arch. Exp. Path. Pharmak.*, **219**, 76 (1953).

[16] K. Wiemers, *Arch. Exp. Path. Pharmak.*, **213**, 283 (1951).

[17] H. Corrodi, H. Persson, A. Carlsson, and J. Roberts, *J. Med. Chem.*, **6**, 751 (1963).

[18] B. Levy, *J. Pharmacol. Exp. Ther.*, **146**, 129 (1964).

[19] D. R. Van Deripe and N. C. Moran, *Fed. Proc.*, **24**, 712 (1965).

[20] R. Howe, *Biochem. Pharmacol. Suppl.*, **12**, 85 (1963).

[21] P. Pratesi, A. LaManna, A. Campiglio, and V. Ghislandi, *J. Chem. Soc.*, **426**, 2069 (1950).

[22] A. M. Barrett and V. A. Cullum, *Brit. J. Pharmacol.*, **34**, 43 (1968).

[23] A. Morales-Aguilera and E. M. Vaughan Williams, *Brit. J. Pharmacol.*, **24**, 332 (1965).

[24] P. Somani and B. K. B. Lum, *J. Pharmacol. Exp. Ther.*, **147**, 194 (1965).

[25] P. Pratesi and E. Grana, *Advan. Drug. Res.*, **11**, 127 (1965).

[26] J. W. Paterson, M. E. Conolly, D. S. Davies, and C. T. Dollery, *Lancet*, **2**, 426 (1968).

[27] E. Philippot, Z. M. Bacq, and F. G. Sulman, *Arach. Int. Pharmacodyn.*, **156**, 234 (1965).

[28] D. C. Kvam, D. A. Riggilo, and P. M. Lish, *J. Pharmacol. Exp. Ther.*, **149**, 183 (1965).

[29] D. Dunlop and R. G. Shanks, *Brit. J. Pharmacol.*, **32**, 201 (1968).

[30] J. D. Fitzgerald and B. Scales, *Int. J. Clin. Pharmacol.*, **5**, 465 (1968).

[31] U. M. Teotino, L. P. Friz, G. Steis, and D. D. Bella, *J. Pharm. Pharmacol.*, **15**, 26 (1963).

[32] J. W. Black and J. S. Stephenson, *Lancet*, **ii**, 314 (1962).

[33] R. Ferrini, *Arzneimittelforschung*, **18**, 48 (1968).

[34] J. W. Black, W. A. M. Duncan, and R. G. Shanks, *Brit. J. Pharmacol.*, **25**, 577 (1965).

[35] R. D. Robson and H. R. Kaplan, *J. Pharmacol. Exp. Ther.*, **175**, 157 (1970).

[36] B. Ablad, M. Brogard, and L. Ek, *Acta Pharmacol. Toxicol.* (Suppl. 25), **2**, 9 (1967).

[37] S. E. Mayer, *J. Pharmacol. Exp. Ther.*, **135**, 204 (1962).

[38] L. Goldstein and C. Munoz, *J. Pharmacol. Exp. Ther.*, **132**, 345 (1961).

[39] S. E. Mayer, R. P. Maickel, and B. B. Brodie, *J. Pharmacol. Exp. Ther.*, **127**, 205 (1959).

[40] P. A. Bond and R. Howe, *Biochem. Pharmacol.*, **16**, 1261 (1967).

[41] B. Scales and M. B. Cosgrove, *J. Pharmacol. Exp. Ther.*, **175**, 338 (1970).

[42] A. Hayes and R. G. Cooper, *J. Pharmacol. Exp. Ther.*, **176**, 302 (1971).

[43] J. W. Paterson, M. E. Conolly, C. T. Dollery, A. Hayes, and R. G. Cooper, *Pharmacol. Clin.*, **2**, 127 (1970).

[44] P. A. Bond, *Nature*, **213**, 721 (1967).

[45] F-J. Leinweber, L. J. Haynes, M. C. Crew, and F. J. DiCarlo, *J. Pharm. Sci.*, **60**, 1512 (1971).

[46] F-J. Leinweber, R. C. Greenough, C. F. Schwender, L. J. Haynes, and F. J. DiCarlo, *J. Pharm. Sci.*, **60**, 1516 (1971).

[47] A. Klutch and M. Bordun, *J. Med. Chem.*, **10**, 860 (1967).

[48] J. Axelrod, H. Weil-Malherbe, and R. Tomchick, *J. Pharmacol. Exp. Ther.*, **127**, 251 (1959).

[49] L. G. Whitby, J. Axelrod, and H. Weil-Malherbe, *J. Pharmacol. Exp. Ther.*, **132**, 193 (1961).

[50] J. Axelrod, *Physiol. Rev.*, **39**, 751 (1959).

[51] G. Herting, *Biochem. Pharmacol.*, **13**, 1119 (1964).

[52] W. Reiss, T. G. Rajagopalan, P. Imhof, K. Schmid, and H. Keberle, *Post-grad. Med. J.*, **46**, 32 (1970).

[53] D. A. Garteiz, *J. Pharmacol. Exptl. Therap.*, **179**, 354 (1971).

Metabolism of Carbamate Insecticides

T. R. FUKUTO
Department of Entomology and Department of Chemistry
University of California at Riverside
Riverside, California 92502

The past decade has seen remarkable progress made in the understanding of the metabolism of carbamate insecticides in biological
systems. During this period the metabolic fate of a number of com-
mercially important insecticidal carbamate esters has been elucidated in plants and animals. As in the case of other insecticides,
these studies have been necessary for the proper assessment of
potential hazards arising from the use of insecticidal carbamates
and for the understanding of their mode of action. Studies on carbamate metabolism also have been instrumental in stimulating research on the role and importance of the mixed-function oxidases in
general insecticide metabolism and on basic aspects of these enzymes.
The available evidence indicates that carbamate esters are metabolized by at least two different processes. The principal route of
metabolism is oxidative in nature and is generally associated with
the mixed-function oxidases [1-3]. Depending on the functional groups
in the molecule, a variety of reactions catalyzed by these enzymes
may occur. These include hydroxylation of aromatic rings, O-dealkylation, N-methyl hydroxylation and N-dealkylation, hydroxylation
and subsequent oxidation of aliphatic groups, and thioether oxidation
to sulfoxides and sulfones. Further, metabolites containing hydroxyl
groups usually are conjugated to give water-soluble products, i.e.,
glucuronides, sulfates, and glucosides, depending on the biological
system. The variety of reactions which may be ascribed to the mixed-

117

function oxidases will be discussed further in relation to the metabolism of specific carbamates.

Cleavage of the carbamate moiety by enzymatic action evidently is another important metabolic pathway owing to the inevitable liberation of the phenolic or equivalent moiety, either directly or in a conjugated form. Direct esterase catalyzed hydrolysis has been

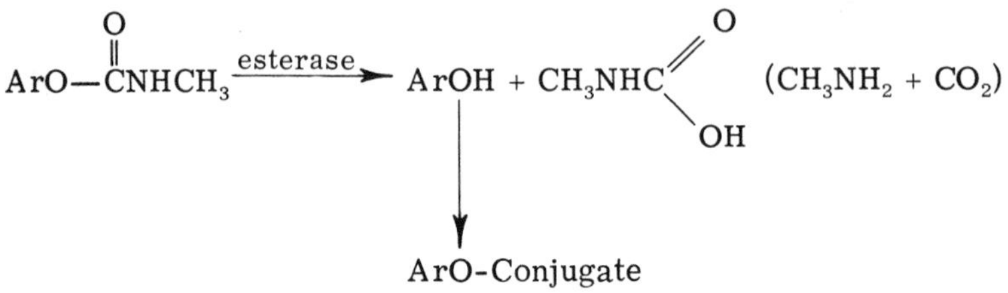

$$\underset{\displaystyle ArO-\overset{\displaystyle \overset{O}{\parallel}}{C}NHCH_3}{} \xrightarrow{\text{esterase}} ArOH + CH_3NHC\overset{\displaystyle \overset{O}{\diagup\!\!\!\diagdown}}{\underset{OH}{}} \quad (CH_3NH_2 + CO_2)$$

$$\downarrow$$

ArO-Conjugate

shown to occur with carbaryl (1-naphthyl methylcarbamate) and p-nitrophenyl methylcarbamate by a plasma albumin fraction that can be separated from the aliphatic and aromatic esterases, and cholinesterase from several mammalian and avian sources [4]. In addition, the ethyl-, propyl-, and i-propylcarbamates of p-nitrophenol also were shown to be hydrolyzed by the same plasma albumin fraction, but not by arylesterase, cholinesterase, chymotrypsin, lipase, papain, pepsin, or egg albumin [5]. An esterase present in rabbit plasma and another present in rabbit liver have been found to catalyze the hydrolysis of dimethylcarbamyl fluoride [6]. Later evidence showed that neither dimethylcarbamyl fluoride nor dimethylamine produced formaldehyde by the action of rat liver microsomes, indicating that hydrolysis occurred directly and not through an oxidized intermediate [7].

There is evidence indicating that the carbamate moiety may be cleaved after oxidation and eventual dealkylation of the N-methyl or N-alkyl moiety as depicted here. Support for this type of mechanism

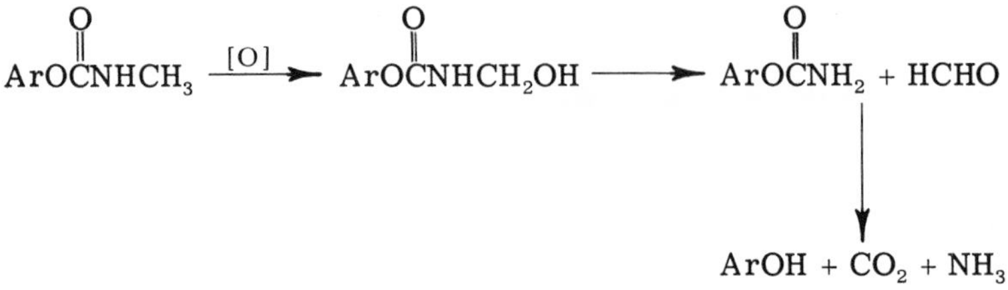

$$\underset{ArO\overset{O}{\overset{\parallel}{C}}NHCH_3}{} \xrightarrow{[O]} \underset{ArO\overset{O}{\overset{\parallel}{C}}NHCH_2OH}{} \longrightarrow \underset{ArO\overset{O}{\overset{\parallel}{C}}NH_2}{} + HCHO$$

$$\downarrow$$

$$ArOH + CO_2 + NH_3$$

was first demonstrated for carbamate esters by Hodgson and Casida [7, 8] who showed that dimethylcarbamates of various structures were

oxidized by a rat liver microsomal preparation to the N-hydroxymethyl intermediate which liberated formaldehyde upon treatment
with strong mineral acids. The reaction required molecular oxygen
and $NADPH_2$. The formation of the N-hydroxymethyl intermediate
also was demonstrated in rats treated orally with p-nitrophenyl dimethylcarbamate and in houseflies and the American cockroach.
N-Methylcarbamates treated with the microsomal system also produced formaldehyde. The dealkylated carbamates are substantially
less stable to hydrolysis than the monoalkyl- or dialkylcarbamates
[9, 10] and rapid hydrolysis of the carbamoyl moiety by enzymatic
or purely chemical action may be expected.

    Additional evidence supporting an oxidative mechanism for the
degradation of the carbamoyl moiety is found in $^{14}CO_2$ expiration
studies [11, 12]. Rats treated with various N-$^{14}CH_3$ labeled carbamates have been shown to expire from 25-77% of the applied dose
during a 48-hr period, providing direct evidence from N-demethylation. Similar results also were obtained with houseflies. N-Dealkylation reactions involving other types of molecules have been well
demonstrated in biological systems [13, 14].

CARBARYL

    The metabolism of carbaryl (1) or 1-naphthyl methylcarbamate,
the first monomethylcarbamate insecticide of commercial significance, has been examined extensively in animals and to a much lesser
extent in plants. The first study on carbaryl metabolism was carried
out by Eldefrawi and Hoskins [15] who showed that carbaryl is rapidly
metabolized in the common housefly (Musca domestica) and the German cockroach (Blatella germanica). By means of ring-labeled ^{14}C-
material and paper chromatography the metabolism of carbaryl into
at least three major products in the housefly and six major products
in the cockroach was demonstrated. The chromatographic behavior
of these metabolites indicated that they were all more polar than the
parent material. Although none of the metabolites were identified,
parallel experiments using ^{14}C-labeled 1-naphthol also gave the same
series of polar products, suggesting that the first step in carbaryl
metabolism in these insects is the hydrolysis of the carbamate to
the naphthol. Further, the pyrethrin synergist sesamex, when used
in conjunction with carbaryl, decreased the rate of carbaryl metabolism, providing evidence that inhibition of metabolic deteoxication
was, at least in part, responsible for the synergistic action of sesamex.

    Later studies by Casida et al. [16, 17] have demonstrated the im-
portance of oxidative processes in the metabolism of carbaryl. In an

initial study, incubation of carbaryl with rat liver microsomes fortified with NADPH$_2$ resulted in at least eight different metabolic products, three of which were tentatively identified (and later verified)
as 1-naphthyl hydroxymethylcarbamate (2), 4-hydroxy-1-naphthyl
methylcarbamate (3) and 5-hydroxy-1-naphthyl methylcarbamate (4).
Similar results were obtained from the housefly and American cockroach (Periplaneta americana) after topical treatment. Two other
metabolites with the ester linkage intact were detected, but not
identified, making a total of five metabolites in which the carbamate
moiety was not cleaved. Further studies [17] showed that the urine
from rabbits treated subcutaneously with carbaryl contained 2, 3, 4,
and also 5,6-dihydroxy-1-naphthyl methylcarbamate (5), 1-hydroxy-
5,6-dihydro-5,6-dihydroxynaphthalene (6), and 1-naphthol (7). Several
other unidentified minor metabolites also were detected. The same
pattern of metabolism also was found when carbaryl was incubated
with enzyme preparations obtained from the liver of rats, mice, and
rabbits.

Evidently, the metabolism of carbaryl in the various biological
systems cited above is quite complex and the principal reactions that
occur may be depicted as shown here. The transitory epoxide intermediate given in brackets, although not isolated or detected, was
postulated because of the presence of 4 and 5 which may be formed
by epoxide opening and proton migration to give 4 and epoxide opening by water to give 5. Support for an intermediate such as this is
found in a recent communication describing the first isolation and
identification of 1,2-naphthalene oxide from the incubation of naphthalene with rat liver microsomes [18]. In addition to the organosoluble unconjugated metabolites represented by 2-7, the urine from
carbaryl treated rabbits contained at least four or five other water-
soluble metabolites which probably were conjugates of hydroxylated
products of carbaryl, i.e., glucuronides or sulfates. The structure
of another metabolite with the carbamate linkage cleaved and three
ether-soluble metabolites were not determined. To emphasize further the complexity of the problem, in some cases the urine from
carbaryl treated rabbits contained at least 15 metabolites and in
vitro experiments with rabbit, mouse, and rat liver microsomal
preparations showed the presence of at least 20 metabolites. Examination of the major metabolites, particularly those with the carbamate moiety intact, showed that they were all of little toxicological
significance.

The metabolism of carbaryl also has been examined in a variety
of other mammals including the rat [19, 20], man, guinea pig [19, 21],
monkey, pig, sheep [21], dog [22], and chickens [23]. Carbaryl is

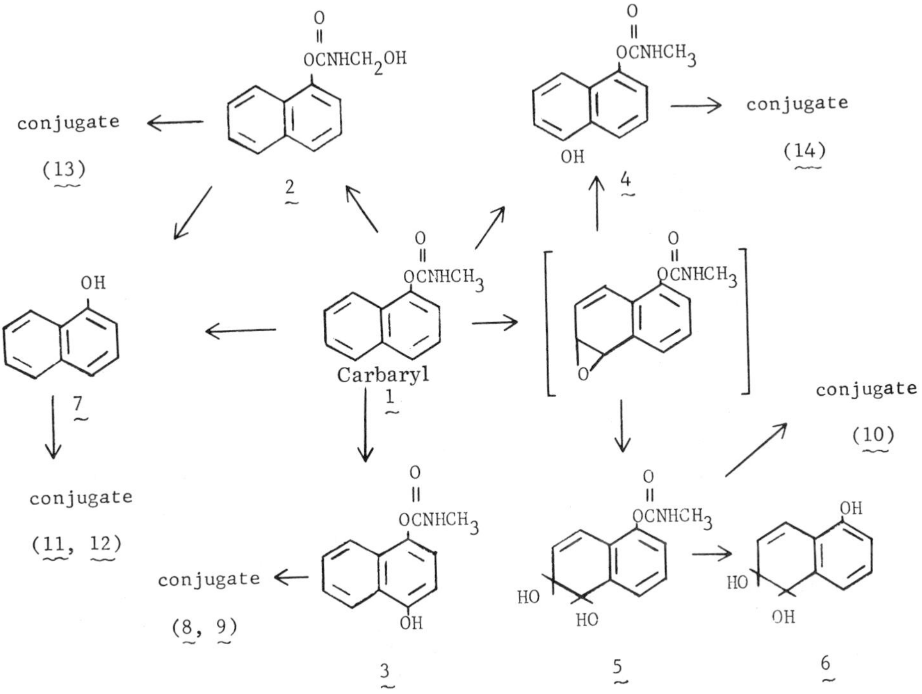

$$\text{OCNHCH}_2\text{OH}$$

conjugate ← (13)

$$\text{OCNHCH}_3 \quad \rightarrow \quad \text{conjugate}$$

OH (14)

OH

←

2

$$\text{OCNHCH}_3$$

7

Carbaryl
1

$$\text{OCNHCH}_3$$

conjugate

conjugate

(11, 12)

→

(10)

$$\text{OCNHCH}_3$$

conjugate ←

(8, 9)

$$\text{OCNHCH}_3$$
HO
HO

$$\text{OH}$$
HO
OH

3   5   6

4

rapidly metabolized, conjugated, and eliminated from these animals, principally in the urine as glucuronides or sulfates. For example, the excretion of ring- and carbonyl-labeled carbaryl was essentially completed 3 days following oral administration to rats [19]. Similarly, excretion was rapid in the pig and sheep. Depending on the animal approximately eight water-soluble metabolites were found in the urine. The major metabolites recovered from urine were 4-(methylcarbamoyloxy)-1-naphthyl glucuronide (8), 4-(methylcar-bamoyloxy)-1-naphthyl sulfate (9), and a metabolite tentatively identified as 1-naphthyl methylimidocarbamate O-glucuronide (10) [19, 21]. More recent evidence indicates, however, that 10 is actually 5,6-dihydro-5,6-dihydroxycarbaryl glucuronide, i.e., the glucuronide of 5 [24]. Other water-soluble metabolites identified in varying amounts depending on the animal were 1-naphthyl glucuronide (11) and 1-naphthyl sulfate (12). At least two other metabolites with the carbamate moiety intact were detected but not identified. In a separate study [20] evidence has been obtained, although by no means conclusive, that carbaryl is metabolized by rats after intraperitoneal

administration and eliminated in the urine principally as the glucuronide of N-hydroxymethyl-carbaryl (13), i.e., as the conjugate
of 2. In a more recent study [23] chickens treated orally with carbaryl produced as the major urinary metabolites 11 (6-16%), 12
(41-46%), and 9 (7-12%). A total of about 15 different metabolites
were detected, including 1-naphthol (7) and 5-(methylcarbamoyloxy)-
1-naphthyl sulfate (14). Evidence also was obtained indicating that
one of the metabolites was a conjugate of 5,6-dihydroxy-carbaryl, a
metabolite hitherto unreported by other investigators. In the whole
animal carbaryl evidently is metabolized in a manner similar to
that occurring in in vitro systems but the products are generally
found as conjugates.

Compared to animals, relatively little is reported on the metabolism of carbaryl in plants [25-27]. In the cotton plant [25], after
entering through the root system, about half of the absorbed carbaryl
is metabolized in 3 days. Approximately 47% was degraded by hydrolysis of the carbamate moiety, the remaining 53% presumably
by hydroxylation of the naphthalene ring. Injection of carbaryl into
the bean plant [26, 27] produced water-soluble metabolites attributable to hydroxylation of the ring or N-methyl group followed by conjugation, mainly as glycosides. Hydrolysis of the glycosides by β-
glucosidase gave the N-hydroxymethyl (2), 4-hydroxy (3), 5-hydroxy
(4), and 5,6-dihydro-5,6-dihydroxy [5] derivatives of carbaryl, i.e.,
the same carbaryl metabolites produced in mammals and insects.

ZECTRAN

The metabolism of Zectran, 4-dimethylamino-3,5-xylyl N-methylcarbamate, has been examined in plants [28-30], insects [31, 32], and
mammals [33, 34]. Zectran applied to the stem of broccoli flowers
gave, after 10 days, a number of metabolic products [28]. Elucidation of the metabolic pathway was accomplished by paper chromatography and a tedious fractionation procedure which evidently accounted for all of the radioactivity. Of the total radioactivity, 17.9%
was incorporated in the lignin and the remaining 82.1% was accounted
for as shown in Table 1. The nature of the metabolites suggests that
the initial step in Zectran metabolism in broccoli is hydrolysis of
the carbamate moiety and the metabolic scheme shown was proposed.

In contrast to results with broccoli, Zectran injected into the bean
plant produced a number of metabolites in quantities ranging from
1.5-10.9% of the recovered radioactivity in which the carbamate
moiety remained intact [29]. These metabolites were tentatively
identified by co-chromatographic procedures as 4-methylform-

Table 1

Distribution of Radioactivity (Ring-Label-^{14}C)
in Broccoli Treated with Zectran

	Metabolites	Total radioactivity (%)
1	Unchanged Zectran	5.1
2	4-Dimethylamino-3,5-xylenol	1.4
3	4-Dimethylamino-3,5-dimethyl-o-benzoquinone	11.2
4	2,6-Dimethyl-p-benzoquinone	13.6
5	Conjugated 4-dimethylamino-3,5-xylenol	23.4
6	Conjugated 2,6-dimethylhydroquinone	27.4

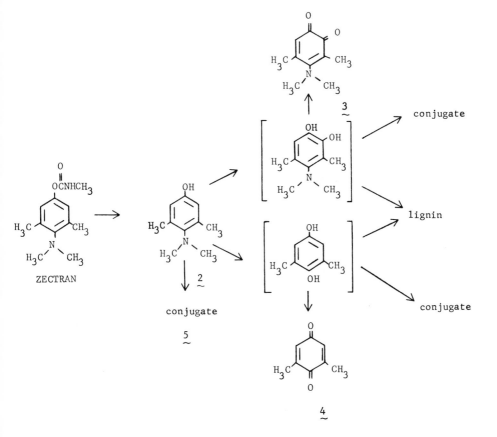

amido-3,5-xylyl (7), 4-methylamino-3,5-xylyl (8), 4-formamido-3,5-xylyl (9), and 4-amino-3,5-xylyl (10) methylcarbamate. Several other metabolites also were detected but unidentified. However, the major portion of the radioactivity remained as unextractables from the plant material, e.g., 62% after 3 days, indicating incorporation of Zectran degradation products into plant tissue as was demonstrated with broccoli. The same metabolites, but in substantially larger amounts were obtained when Zectran was exposed to sunlight on the surface of bean leaves [30]. Thus one of the metabolic pathways of Zectran in or on the bean plant may be depicted as shown. Of considerable interest is the finding that 8 and 9 are significantly more toxic to mice than is Zectran.

The principal metabolite, consisting of 89.1% of the total radioactivity in the urine of a dog treated orally with radioactive Zectran, was found to be conjugated 4-dimethylamino-3,5-xylenol (2) either as the sulfate or glucuronide (5) [33]. Of the total radioactivity excreted, 75% was in the urine and the rest was in the feces. The other metabolites in the urine were conjugated 2,6-dimethylhydroquinone (6), unconjugated 4-dimethylamino-3,5-xylenol (2), an unidentified neutral material, and an unconjugated acidic substance [32].

In in vitro studies [34], Zectran incubated with rat liver microsome and NADPH$_2$ was converted into at least nine different ether-soluble products. Two of the major metabolites were identified as

8 and 4-dimethylamino-3,5-xylyl N-hydroxymethylcarbamate (11),
and two minor metabolites as 7 and 10. The same metabolic products and also 9 and 11 were produced when Zectran was incubated
with the microsomal fraction from housefly abdomen [31].

Zectran applied topically to the spruce budworm (Choristoneura
occidentalis), tobacco budworm (Heliothis virescens), and housefly
larvae produced a total of 9 metabolites in the budworm species and
10 in the housefly [32]. The major metabolites were identified as
8, 10, 7, and 9, in order of decreasing quantities, and another metabolite was tentatively identified as the N-hydroxymethylcarbamate 11.
Of particular interest was the observation that the carbamate moiety
in Zectran is not hydrolyzed in these insects since no $^{14}CO_2$ was expired when carbonyl-labeled Zectran was applied, and the oxidative
pathway appears to be the primary route of metabolism.

In a study related to the metabolism of Zectran, the fate of N-
acetyl-Zectran in the mouse and spruce budworm was investigated
[35]. N-Acetylation of Zectran did not greatly alter its toxic effect
on spruce budworm, but virtually eliminated toxicity to mice, and the
N-acetyl derivative was examined to obtain a rationale for its
selective toxicity. In mice, N-acetyl-Zectran is rapidly detoxified
by hydrolysis of the carbamate ester moiety to produce 4-dimethyl-
amino-3,5-xylenol, CO_2, and an unknown water-soluble compound.
In spruce budworm the major products isolated and identified were
Zectran, unchanged N-acetyl-Zectran, and 4-methylamino-3,5-xylyl
methylcarbamate (8). The evidence, therefore, indicates that N-
acetyl-Zectran is nontoxic to mice because the animal is able to
degrade it to nontoxic products, but it is toxic to the spruce budworm
because deacetylation occurred before hydrolysis, producing in turn
toxic Zectran and 8.

AMINOCARB

Aminocarb or 4-dimethylamino-m-tolyl methylcarbamate is
closely related in structure to Zectran and its metabolic fate in
biological systems is expectedly similar to that of Zectran. In the
bean plant, after injection into the stem, aminocarb was converted
into at least two identifiable metabolites, 4-formamido-m-tolyl and
4-methylamino-m-tolyl methylcarbamate [29]. The major portion of
the radioactivity (carbonyl ^{14}C-labeled), however, was unextractable
from leaf tissue. Exposure to sunlight on the surface of the bean leaf
converted aminocarb in significant amounts into the four expected
products; 4-methylformamido- (1), 4-methylamino- (2), 4-formamido-
(3), and 4-amino-m-tolyl (4) methylcarbamate [29, 30]. Incubation of

aminocarb with the microsomal fraction from housefly abdomen resulted in 2, 3, and 4 and also hydroxymethylaminocarb (5) as separable
metabolites [31]. Similarly, rat liver microsomes effected the conversion of aminocarb to 2 and 5 as the major products and 1 and 4
as minor products [34]. Over-all the oxidative metabolic pathway
for aminocarb in plants and animals may be depicted as shown.

FORMETANATE

Formetanate or m-[(dimethylamino)methylene]aminophenyl methylcarbamate hydrochloride, a carbamate ester with excellent broad
spectrum acaricidal activity, has been studied in the rat [36] and
orange seedling [37]. When formetanate was administered orally
to the rat, 86% of the dose was eliminated via the urine and 8% in
the feces after 72 hr. Approximately 20% (72 hr) to 32% (6 hr) of
the total metabolites partitioned into ethyl acetate from the urine.
The principal organosoluble metabolite in the urine was m-form-
amidophenyl methylcarbamate (1) which constituted 15% of the total
in the 6-hr urine and 8.5% in the 72-hr urine. Other metabolites
present in small but significant amounts were the methylformamidine
or N-demethyl derivative (2), m-formamidophenol (3), m-amino-
phenol (4), and m-acetamidophenol (5). Small quantities of unchanged

formetanate also were recovered but the amounts gradually diminished with time. Hydrolysis of the water-soluble metabolites in the presence of β-glucuronidase, or a combination of β-glucuronidase and aryl sulfatase, or hydrochloric acid produced the same metabolites present in the organosoluble fraction. The major product obtained from hydrolysis by the various treatments was 5 (18 to 49% of total). The metabolism of formetanate in the rat, therefore, may be depicted as shown. Formetanate and metabolites 1 through 5 exist also in the form of conjugates in rat urine. Metabolites 3, 4, and 5 probably are conjugated as the O-glucuronides but the nature of the conjugates of formetanate, 1, and 2 remains unknown. The presence of large amounts of 5 is not unexpected since other studies [38] have shown that aminophenols are readily N-acetylated in mammals.

The rate of metabolism of formetanate was much slower in orange seedlings than in the rat [37]. For example, over 57% of a stem-injected dose of formetanate remained unaltered 20 days after treatment. Formetanate injected into the stem showed considerable systemic movement and 65% of the injected material had moved into the leaf after 20 days. Metabolites recovered as organosoluble materials from the stem and leaf were 1, 2, 3, 4, and m-aminophenyl methylcarbamate (6). Approximately 25% of the total metabolites in stems and leaves was in the form of water-soluble materials which when hydrolyzed in the presence of β-glucosidase gave 1, 3, 4, and formetanate. The major aglycone was $\underline{3}$ (35-39%), followed by $\underline{1}$ (10-12%). Treatment of orange seedlings by foliar application also resulted in the same metabolites in the leaves. In addition, small amounts of the phenol of formetanate ($\underline{7}$) were recovered. This metabolite was not detected in the plant following stem injection.

It appears that hydrolytic processes are as important as oxidative processes in the metabolism of formetanate in both the rat and orange seedling. It is difficult to establish at this time whether degradation of the dimethylformamidine side-chain is oxidative or hydrolytic. Based on the chemical properties of amidines, a plausible mechanism for the formation of $\underline{1}$ from either formetanate or $\underline{2}$ is the direct attack of a water molecule on the formyl carbon atom with simultaneous displacement of the amino moiety. This would suggest that $\underline{1}$ is formed by a hydrolytic process.

ALDICARB

Aldicarb or 2-methyl-2-(methylthio)propionaldehyde O-methylcarbamoyl oxime is an outstanding systemic insecticide [39]. In contrast to most carbamate insecticides, aldicarb is unusual in that it does not contain an aromatic moiety and, also, it is a carbamate ester of an oxime. Owing to its high toxicity to warm blooded animals, aldicarb has been extensively examined for metabolism and the toxicological properties of its metabolites evaluated.

In general, the metabolism of aldicarb in plants, insects, and mammals is the same. Because of its usefulness in control of cotton pests, practically all of the work in plants has been done with cotton [40-42]. The metabolic reactions of aldicarb are similar to the oxidative and hydrolytic pathways found in the thioether containing organophosphorus esters such as demeton [43]. In the cotton plant the thioether moiety is rapidly oxidized to the sulfoxide and the sulfoxide much more slowly to the sulfone [40-42]. Aldicarb sulfoxide ($\underline{1}$) is relatively stable in the plant and is the major intact metabolite present in mature cotton plants, even as long as 2 months after treatment. In terms of relative amounts of the total metabolites present in the cotton plant, as much as 80% has been found as $\underline{1}$ [40]. Because of the persistence of $\underline{1}$ in plants and its higher anticholinesterase activity compared to aldicarb itself, systemic activity after treatment of plants with aldicarb has been attributed to $\underline{1}$. Aldicarb sulfone ($\underline{2}$), on the other hand, is generated from $\underline{1}$ at a much slower rate. For example, the maximum amount of $\underline{2}$ found in the leaf 21 days after injection into the petiole was 10% of the total metabolites

present [41]. The relative amounts of aldicarb and the intact metabolite 1 and 2 recovered from cotton leaves at different time intervals
after petiole injection are shown graphically in Fig. 1. This figure
serves to point out the relationship between the toxic forms of aldicarb present in the plant after different time intervals and illustrates the importance of metabolism studies in the evaluation of
hazards arising from residues of systemic insecticides.

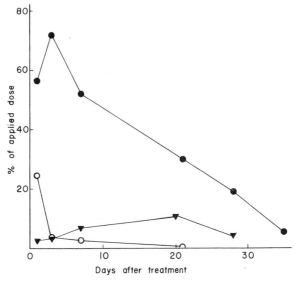

Fig. 1. Relative amounts of aldicarb (O), aldicarb sulfoxide (●), and aldicarb
sulfone (▼) in the cotton plant at different intervals after treatment.

Apparently, 1 and 2 are the only metabolites formed in which the
carbamate moiety remains intact. No evidence has been found indicating the formation of the N-hydroxymethyl or N-demethyl derivatives
of aldicarb, aldicarb sulfoxide, and aldicarb sulfone. A large number
of metabolites representing products from the hydrolysis of the carbamate moiety of the oxidative metabolites of aldicarb have been isolated and identified. Among the organosoluble hydrolytic metabolites,
the oxime sulfoxide (3) generally was recovered in largest amounts
although results are conflicting between different laboratories, e.g.,
Metcalf et al. [40] found 3 as the major hydrolytic metabolite while
Coppedge et al. [41] recovered the nitrile sulfoxide (4) in greater
quantities than 3. Nevertheless, both 3 and 4 are two of the principal

metabolic products arising from cleavage of the carbamate moiety of
1. Evidence also has been obtained indicating the presence of oxime
sulfone in the cotton plant [40] but this was not confirmed by a later
study [41].

In the early studies by Metcalf et al. [40] and Coppedge et al. [41]
on aldicarb metabolism in cotton, several unknown metabolites were
isolated by chromatographic methods but remained unidentified. In
a recent investigation by Bartley et al. [42] the identity of six water-
soluble metabolites was elucidated by chromatographic and mass
spectral analysis, and it is probable that some of these are the same
as the unknown metabolites of the earlier investigations. The major
organoinsoluble metabolite, apparently formed by a reductive pathway was a conjugate (presumably glycoside) of 2-methyl-2-(methylsulfinyl)propanol (5) which was recovered as 70-80% of the total
organoinsoluble metabolites. Small quantities of conjugated 2-methyl-
2-(methylsulfonyl)propionaldehyde oxime (oxime sulfone) (6), 2-
methyl-2-(methylsulfonyl)propanol (7) and oxime sulfoxide also were
found. Other metabolites which were identified were 2-methyl-2-
(methylsulfinyl)propionamide (8), 2-methyl-2(methylsulfinyl)pro-
pionic acid (9), and 2-methyl-2-(methylsulfonyl)propionic acid (10).
Toxicological studies with these metabolites showed that they were
all virtually nontoxic to rats.

Over-all, the metabolism of aldicarb in the cotton plant may be
depicted as shown. The two aldehydes in brackets were not detected
and were suggested as logical intermediates to subsequent metabolites. At least three metabolites of unknown structure also were detected. The scheme shows that the initial metabolic reactions are
oxidative and hydrolytic, producing organosoluble metabolites (1, 2,
3, and 4) which are eventually converted to water-soluble materials.
Unexpectedly, the chief metabolic reaction to the formation of water-
soluble metabolites was reductive, leading to 5 as the principal metabolite in the form of its glycoside.

Initial studies by Knaak et al. [44] showed that rats given oral sub-
lethal doses rapidly metabolized aldicarb and excreted the metabolic
products in the urine principally as 1 and 3 in approximately 40 and
30% of the applied dose, respectively. The remaining 30% consisted
of a large number (approximately nine) of more polar metabolites
which were not identified but believed to be acidic materials based
on their elution pattern from an ion exchange column. These metabolites undoubtedly are identical to some of the water-soluble metabolites formed in plants. Evidence, although not conclusive, was
obtained for the presence of trace quantities of unchanged aldicarb,

aldicarb oxime, and 6. A subsequent investigation by Andrawes et al.
[45] confirmed earlier results that 1 and 3 were the major metabolites
produced by rats but also showed the presence in rat urine of large
amounts of nitrile sulfoxide (4) and small but significant quantities of
2, 6, nitrile sulfone, unchanged aldicarb, and aldicarb oxime. Approximately 37% of the total metabolites consisted of organoinsoluble
polar metabolites. Thus in gross aspects the metabolism of aldicarb
in the cotton plant and the rat is similar.

The metabolism of aldicarb in a lactating cow also has been examined with particular attention paid to metabolites in milk [46, 47].
Aldicarb is rapidly metabolized in the cow and eliminated in the
urine, e.g., 83% of a single oral dose after 24 hr, but significant
quantities of metabolites (3% of applied dose) also are found in milk.
The metabolites in the milk were the same as those detected in the
urine. Among the 12 metabolites recovered from milk 1, 2, 3, 4, 6,
nitrile sulfone, and aldicarb oxime were identified. 3 and 4 were
present in largest amounts 3-6 hr after treatment, but each of these
decreased with time along with an increase in the nitrile sulfone
which became the major metabolite after 12 hr. 1 and 2, the toxic
intact metabolites, although found in significant amounts up to 12 hr
after treatment, were not present after 24 hr. However, the milk of
cows given aldicarb on a daily basis for 14 days at a dose equivalent
to 0.12, 0.6, and 1.2 ppm in the feed contained on a daily average 4.4
and 7.3 ppb, 25.6 and 35.9 ppb, and 43.6 and 66.5 ppb 1 and 2, respectively [47]. The over-all spectrum of metabolites on a long-
term feeding basis was the same as in the case of a single oral
treatment.

The same pattern of oxidative and hydrolytic reactions occurs
when insects are treated with aldicarb [40, 48]. In houseflies [40]
as much as 70% of the recovered metabolites after topical application was 1 with much less 2. A small amount of unchanged aldicarb
also was recovered as well as at least two unknown metabolites.
Unchanged aldicarb, 1, and 2 also have been recovered after topical
treatment of adult boll weevils (Anthonomous grandis Boheman),
and injection in the tobacco budworm (Heliothis virescens) [48]. Depending on the time interval after treatment, aldicarb or 1 were the
major metabolites. Other metabolites recovered but in minor quantities were 3, 4, 6, several unidentified materials and, in some cases,
the nitrile sulfone. Thus the metabolic pathways of aldicarb in insects are similar to those occurring in plants and mammals.

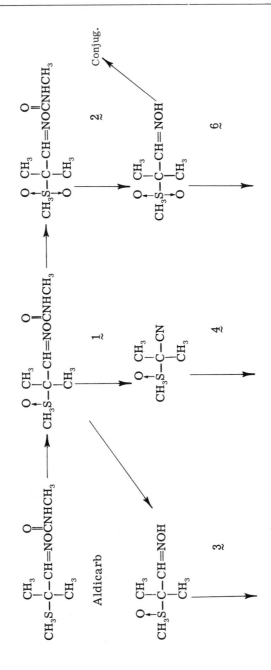

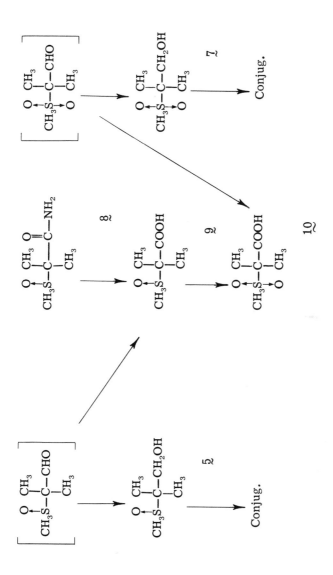

MOBAM

The metabolism of Mobam or 4-benzothienyl methylcarbamate appears to have been studied only in mammals [49, 50]. The primary route of metabolism of Mobam in rats is hydrolytic in nature [49]. Rats given oral dosages of 2.0 and 13.0 mg/kg ^{14}C-ring-labeled Mobam eliminated 87 and 76%, respectively, of the radioactivity in the urine within 24 hr as water-soluble metabolites. Most of the remaining radioactivity was found in the feces and a minor amount (<1%) was contained in various tissues of the rat. Analysis of the urine revealed at least six metabolites. Two metabolites, 4-benzothienyl sulfate (1) and 4-benzothienyl glucuronide (2), accounted for 83 and 87% of the total metabolites at the low and high dosages, respectively. The sulfate (1) was by far the major metabolite, constituting 63 and 79% of the metabolites at the two respective dosages. Both of these conjugates were isolated in the pure state and excellent agreement of infrared spectra was obtained between authentic samples of 1 and 2 and the purified metabolites. No attempt was made to identify the remaining minor metabolites. Evidently, Mobam is rapidly hydrolyzed in the rat to 4-hydroxybenzothiophene, which in turn is even more rapidly conjugated to the sulfate and glucuronide. The fast degradation of Mobam to hydrolytic products is consistent with its moderately low mammalian toxicity (rat oral LD_{50} 234 mg/kg).

Degradation of Mobam to water-soluble products was noticeably faster in the goat than in the rat, e.g., 96% was excreted in the urine after 24 hr [50]. Significant amounts of labeled materials also were detected in the milk of a goat and cow treated orally with Mobam. Analysis of the urine and milk revealed that the same five metabolites were present in each phase. The principal metabolite in milk, 96-98% of the total, was identified as the sulfate ester of 4-hydroxybenzothiophene-1-oxide (3) based on its chemical properties, infrared, and mass spectral data. However, all attempts to synthesize 4-hydroxybenzothiophene-1-oxide by another method for structural confirmation of 3 were unsuccessful. Metabolite 3 also was found in

3

abundance in goat and cow urine (26-60%). The remaining metabolites were present in minor amounts and were not identified. Significantly, however, one of the major metabolites recovered from rats, 2, was not found.

METHIOCARB

Methiocarb or 4-(methylthio)-3,5-xylyl methylcarbamate is a compound closely related in structure to Zectran, but it contains a methylthio moiety in place of dimethylamino. In the bean plant the methylthio group is oxidized to the sulfoxide (1) which in turn is more slowly converted to the sulfone (2) [29]. Oxidation of the methylthio group in methiocarb to the sulfoxide is somewhat slower than the analogous oxidation of aldicarb and as much as 20% unchanged methiocarb was present in the plant 24 hr after injection. At this time 1 and 2 constituted 32% of the total metabolites, the rest being unidentified breakdown products. Degradation of methiocarb or 1 and 2 was quite rapid and over 85% of the plant-injected methiocarb was in the form of hydrolyzed products after 2 days.

CARBOFURAN

Carbofuran or 2,2-dimethyl-2,3-dihydrobenzofuranyl-7 methylcarbamate is a relatively new systemic insecticide with broad spectrum activity. Studies in plants, insects, and mammals have shown that the most vulnerable position for metabolic attack is the 3-position in the dihydrobenzofuranyl ring, giving rise to 3-hydroxy-carbofuran (1) as the initial metabolic product [51-53]. This substance

evidently is the first intermediate formed en route to a number of
other metabolites in the biological systems examined. The vulner-
ability of the 3-position to hydroxylation is of considerable interest,
particularly since this position was preferred over hydroxylation of
the aromatic ring.

The various metabolic transformations which carbofuran undergoes in the cotton plant are presented in the scheme [51]. As indicated, the formation of 1 is the first step in plant oxidative metabolism and this compound was always present in substantial amounts
in the early stages after absorption of carbofuran. For example, in
an isolated leaf experiment 4 days after treatment as much as 93%
of the total materials recovered from a column was 1 and this declined to 39% after 8 days. The principal pathway for the disappearance of 1 was by oxidation to 3-keto-carbofuran (2). However,
2 was hydrolytically unstable and did not accumulate to large quantities in the plant, e.g., 10% of the total metabolites was 3 after 10
days. The three intact carbamate esters, carbofuran, 1, and 2, were
hydrolyzed to their respective phenols 3, 4, and 5 and these were in
turn rapidly conjugated to the corresponding glucosides (6, 7, and 8).
However, small but significant amounts of the phenols were detectable by thin-layer chromatography. The glucosides, 6, 7, and 8, increased with time of exposure of carbofuran in the cotton leaf and
after 8 days these became the major metabolites in the leaf. The
glucoside of 1, i.e., 9, also was present as a conjugate. Toxicological studies showed that 1 and 2 were approximately 5 and 50 times
less effective in inhibiting fly-head cholinesterase than carbofuran
and both were nontoxic to the housefly.

The metabolism of carbofuran in the intact cotton plant after its
introduction into the lower stem through a capillary funnel also was
studied. Over-all, metabolism was the same as in isolated leaf experiments except for evidence suggesting the formation of 6-hydroxy-
3-keto-carbofuran (10). Also experiments similar to those described
for isolated cotton leaves were conducted with 10-day-old corn seedlings cut off above the roots and placed in carbofuran solution. Although the rate of metabolism in corn was slower than that observed
in cotton leaves under similar conditions, the over-all metabolic pattern was the same.

Carbofuran metabolism also has been examined in the white mouse
[51], rat [52], and lactating cow [53] and found to be virtually identical
to metabolism in plants except for the formation of N-hydroxymethyl
derivatives. Mice given 2 mg/kg carbofuran eliminated on the average about 50% of the administered oral dose after 24 hr. The urine
contained 1 as the major metabolite along with small amounts of 3,

5, and their conjugates, and 2 [51]. Carbofuran appears to be metabolized much more rapidly and extensively in the rat to produce a larger number of metabolites including N-hydroxymethyl derivatives. For example, 92% of an oral dose of 0.4 mg/kg was excreted in the urine within 32 hr, of which over 90% could not be extracted with organic

solvents. Organosoluble metabolites present in rat urine were unmetabolized carbofuran, 1, 2, 3, 5, 3-hydroxy-N-hydroxymethyl-
carbofuran (11), N-hydroxymethyl-carbofuran (12), and two unidentified metabolites. Acidic hydrolysis of the organoinsoluble conjugates
produced 1, 3, 4, 5, and 11. Of these, 5, the 3-keto-phenol, was present in quantity greater than 50% of the total metabolites, suggesting
that the principal metabolic pathway for carbofuran in the rat is
identical to that occurring in cotton. Parallel experiments using
rat liver oxidase gave qualitatively identical results.

11   12

Carbofuran administered orally to a cow was metabolized and excreted mainly in the urine (about 94%) but as much as 2% of the dose
in the form of metabolites was found in the milk [53]. Analysis of
the milk indicated the presence of unchanged carbofuran, 1, 2, 4, and
11 and conjugates of 1, 3, 5, and 11. There was a gradual decrease
in the amount of organosoluble metabolites in milk with time with
concommitant increase in water-soluble metabolites. For example,
75% was organosoluble 2 hr after treatment compared to 20% after
12 hr. Of the organosolubles, 1 was consistently the major metabolite while 4 (in the form of its conjugate) was by far the predominant
water-soluble metabolite.

Houseflies treated with carbofuran produced 1, 2, 11, and an unidentified substance as the organosoluble metabolites and conjugates
of 1, 11, and 12 as water-soluble metabolites [52]. A substantial
quantity of unchanged carbofuran (42% of total dose of 0.05 μg per
fly) also was recovered. 3-Hydroxy-carbofuran (1) was the major
metabolite present in houseflies 1 hr after topical application. Evidently carbofuran is metabolized at a slower rate in houseflies compared to mammals. Carbofuran ingested by the saltmarsh caterpillar
(Estigmene acrea), was rapidly metabolized and excreted via the
feces as 8% 2, 2% 3, and approximately 88% as water-soluble conjugates [51]. The major conjugate (79%) was the glucoside of 5,
i.e., 8. Again, the isolation of 8 as the principal metabolite strongly
indicates that the major pathway for carbofuran is the same in plants,
insects, and mammals.

MEOBAL

The metabolism of Meobal or 3,5-dimethylphenyl methylcarbamate
has been investigated in rats and found to be very complex [54]. Within
a period of 48 hr after oral administration of ^{14}C-ring-labeled Meobal,
greater than 90% of the radioactivity was metabolized and eliminated
via the urine. Examination of the urine showed the presence of at least
28 different metabolic products. Only about 0.5% of the total products
was unchanged Meobal. Of the 28 metabolites, 11 were identified
with a reasonable amount of certainty. The metabolic scheme given
is based on identified products and accounts for 65% of the total
products from Meobal metabolism in rats.

The major metabolite found in urine was 3-methyl-4-carboxy-
phenyl methylcarbamate (8) which accounted for 31% of the total
radioactivity. Metabolites 9 (4.9%), 10 (10.1%), and 11 (trace),
combined with 8 accounted for approximately 46% of the total metabolites, indicating that oxidation of the 4-methyl to 4-carboxy was one
of the principal metabolic pathways. In spite of evidence indicating
this to be one of the major metabolic pathways, definitive proof for
the presence of the 4-hydroxymethyl-3-methylphenyl methylcarbamate (in brackets) could not be obtained. However, support for the
presence of the conjugate (7a or 7b) of 4-hydroxymethyl-3-methyl-
phenol was obtained. Apparently oxidation of the 4-hydroxymethyl
moiety to 4-carboxy is faster than the oxidation of 4-methyl to 4-
hydroxymethyl. In direct contrast, oxidation of the 3-hydroxymethyl
group to 3-carboxy apparently is comparatively slow since significant amounts of 4 (2.2%), the 3-hydroxymethyl-4-methylphenyl
methylcarbamate, was recovered from urine. Also, about 8% of the
3-hydroxymethyl derivative was in the form of its glucuronide (5).
No evidence was obtained for the presence of 3-carboxy-3-methyl-
phenyl methylcarbamate, the 3-analog of 8, even though 8 was the
major metabolite isolated from rat urine.
The metabolites, 3,4-dimethylphenol and its conjugates (1, 2, and
3), were minor metabolic products, representing only 5% of the total
radioactivity in the urine. This suggests that Meobal is somewhat
resistant to hydrolysis in vivo in rats and that metabolism proceeds
mainly by oxidative processes. However, it should be emphasized
again that 35% of the radioactivity present in the urine represents
unidentified materials and the possibility remains that part of these
are products resulting from initial hydrolysis of Meobal.
Concurrent studies with rat liver homogenate, microsomes, and
supernatant showed Meobal is readily converted to 3-methyl-4-hy-
droxymethylphenyl and 4-methyl-3-hydroxymethylphenyl methyl-
carbamates as the predominant products. Relatively little was oxidized further to the carboxy derivative.

LANDRIN

Landrin consists of a mixture of approximately 75% of 3,4,5-tri-
methylphenyl methylcarbamate and 18% of the 2,3,5-isomer. The
metabolism of each isomer has been examined in plants, insects,
and mammals [55]. Expectedly, the metabolism of Meobal and the
Landrin isomers is quite similar.
3,4,5-Trimethylphenyl Methylcarbamate. The various metabolic
reactions which 3,4,5-trimethylphenyl methylcarbamate undergoes

in different biological systems are presented in the scheme. The identity of the metabolites in the scheme was accomplished by co-chromatographic methods.

Incubation of 3,4,5-isomer with mouse-liver microsomes resulted in over 20 different organosoluble metabolites, over half of which remained as unidentified materials. The major metabolite (32% of total recovered) was the 4-hydroxymethyl derivative (3), followed by the 3-carboxy derivative (8) in 13% recovery. The remaining identified metabolites including 1, 2, 5, 6, 7, and 9 were found in minor amounts (3.5% or less). The large amount of 3 and the absence of the corresponding 4-carboxy derivative suggest that steric effects from the adjacent 3- and 5-methyl groups prevents further oxidation of 4-hydroxymethyl to carboxyl. Only about 1% of the parent 3,4,5-isomer was recovered unchanged, indicating that this molecule was highly susceptible to attack by mouse-liver microsomal oxidase. In comparison, only 25% of the parent compound was metabolized after incubation with housefly-abdomen microsomes, the major products being 3 (8%) and 5 (5.5%). Only 1% of the 3-carboxy derivative (8) was recovered from housefly microsomes compared to 13% from mouse-liver microsomes. Thus housefly enzyme was generally less efficient in metabolizing the 3,4,5-isomer.

Metabolism in vivo in the mouse and housefly was in general similar to microsomal metabolism except for conjugation taking place in the whole animal. The principal metabolites found in mouse urine after hydrolysis of the conjugates by glusulase were 6 (4.6%) and 8 (9.6%); 3, 4, 5, and 9 were minor metabolites present in less than 1.5%. In light of the small amounts of initial oxidation products, 3 and 5, the 3,4,5-isomer evidently is rapidly and extensively metabolized in the live mouse. The housefly, on the other hand, was less capable of extensive metabolism and about 70% of the recovered material from excreta of houseflies treated by injection was in the form of conjugates of 3 (59%) and 5 (11%). Over-all, the metabolic products in vitro were consistent, quantitatively and qualitatively, with in vivo results in the mouse and housefly.

The principal metabolite formed in bean plants after stem injection was 3, present mainly in the form of the glucoside. For example, 6 days after treatment 57% of the applied radioactivity was recovered as 3. The other identified metabolite, besides unchanged parent compound, was the conjugate of the N-hydroxymethylcarbamate (1), which was present in 6-18% 6 days after treatment. Two unidentified metabolites also were isolated. Metabolism of 3,4,5-isomer, therefore, appears to be much less complex in plants than in animals.

2,3,5-Trimethylphenyl Methylcarbamate. The metabolic reactions experienced by the 2,3,5-isomer generally were similar to those of the 3,4,5-isomer. However, only the ^{14}C-carbonyl labeled material was available for this study and, therefore, metabolic products arising from cleavage of the carbamate moiety were not detected. The various metabolites produced from carbonyl-labeled 2,3,5-trimethylphenyl methylcarbamate in plants and animals are shown in the scheme.

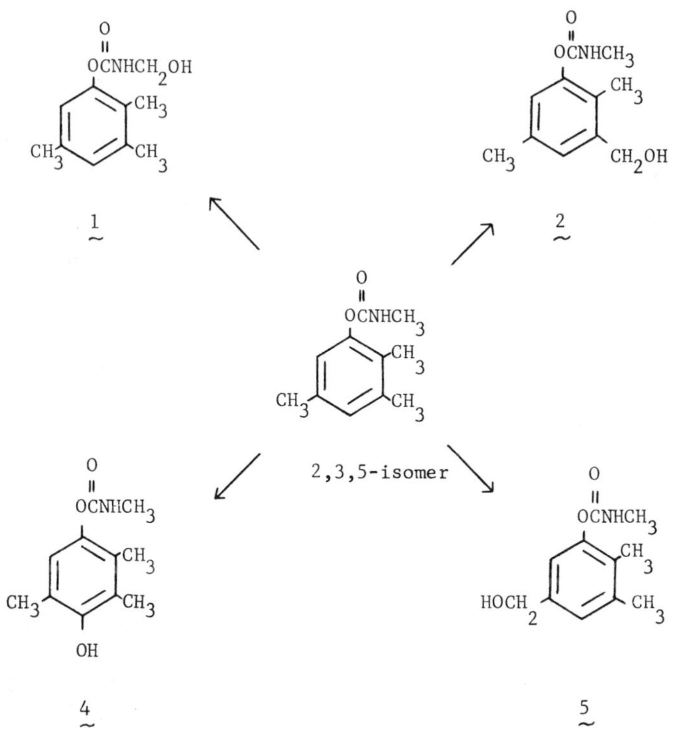

O
‖
OCNHCH$_2$OH
CH$_3$
CH$_3$ CH$_3$

1

O
‖
OCNHCH$_3$
CH$_3$
CH$_3$ CH$_2$OH

2

O
‖
OCNHCH$_3$
CH$_3$
CH$_3$ CH$_3$

2,3,5-isomer

O
‖
OCNHCH$_3$
CH$_3$
CH$_3$ CH$_3$
OH

4

O
‖
OCNHCH$_3$
CH$_3$
HOCH$_2$ CH$_3$

5

In spite of the limitations imposed by the carbonyl label, approximately 15 different metabolites were detected when the 2,3,5-isomer was incubated with mouse liver microsomes. The principal metabolites isolated were the 3-hydroxymethyl (2) and 5-hydroxymethyl (5) derivatives in 26 and 8% of the total recovered radioactivity, respectively. Also detected in trace amounts were unchanged 2,3,5-isomer, 1, and 4. Approximately 11 metabolites remained as unknowns. Housefly microsomes produced 2 and 5 in virtually equal amounts, each in approximately 10% of the recovered metabolites. However, about 75% of the parent compound was recovered unchanged, a situation similar to the 3,4,5-isomer.

The 2,3,5-isomer was extensively degraded when administered orally to the mouse and only 36% of the administered dose could be recovered. The only intact carbamate derivative which was recovered from urine, after treatment with glusulase, was 2 in only 2.5% of the administered amount. Approximately 9 metabolites representing the remaining radioactivity were not identified. As in the case of the 3,4,5-isomer, metabolism of the 2,3,5-isomer was less extensive in houseflies. Approximately 65% of the total radioactivity present in excreta of houseflies after treatment by injection were 2 and 5 in the form of conjugates.

In the bean plant the 2,3,5-isomer was converted principally to the glucosides of 2 (53%) and 5 (25%). However, about 7% was detected as 1 and 1% was recovered as unchanged parent material.

In gross aspects, the evidence indicates that both isomers of Landrin are metabolized primarily by oxidative processes in all the biological systems studied except in the mouse where hydrolytic degradation is important. In bean plants, houseflies, and in the housefly microsomal system, methyl oxidation generally stops at the hydroxymethyl stages because of conjugation or the dehydrogenases involved in the enzyme systems are of low activity. In the mouse, however, the intermediate hydroxymethyl derivatives are metabolized further to the carboxylic acid.

CARBANOLATE

Carbanolate or 2-chloro-4,5-dimethylphenyl methylcarbamate is closely related structurally to Meobal and the Landrin isomers but contains a chlorine atom adjacent to the carbamoyl moiety. The metabolic transformations which carbanolate undergoes in biological systems, however, are less defined. Carbanolate is readily absorbed through the root system of a bean plant from an aqueous solution and metabolized [56]. After 7 days, 97-98% of the carbanolate was converted into at least three metabolic products. The major metabolite, representing 44-74% of the radioactivity in the plant, was a water-soluble substance which when hydrolyzed in the presence of β-glucosidase produced an organosoluble material containing the intact carbamate moiety. Therefore, the major pathway for carbanolate metabolism in the plant is oxidative. Mass spectral analysis showed that an oxygen atom was introduced into the molecule on the ring system, leading to the four suggestions shown for the structure of the aglycone. Mass spectroscopic evidence favored either 1 or 2 over 3 or 4, but at this point it is not possible to assign the structure of the metabolite on a firm basis. Structures 3 and 4, however, are closely related to the principal metabolites produced from the Landrin isomers in the bean plant. Further, the chlorine atom on the ring is expected to have a deactivating effect on ring hydroxylation and, therefore, assignment of 3 or 4 as the metabolite still remains a strong possibility.

$$
\underset{\underset{\sim}{1}}{\text{Cl}\text{-}\underset{\text{CH}_3}{\overset{\overset{\text{O}}{\overset{\|}{\text{OCNHCH}_3}}}{\underset{\text{CH}_3}{\bigcirc}}}\text{-OH}}
\qquad
\underset{\underset{\sim}{2}}{\text{Cl, HO}\text{-}\underset{\text{CH}_3}{\overset{\overset{\text{O}}{\overset{\|}{\text{OCNHCH}_3}}}{\bigcirc}}\text{-CH}_3}
\qquad
\underset{\underset{\sim}{3}}{\text{Cl}\text{-}\underset{\text{CH}_3}{\overset{\overset{\text{O}}{\overset{\|}{\text{OCNHCH}_3}}}{\bigcirc}}\text{-CH}_2\text{OH}}
\qquad
\underset{\underset{\sim}{4}}{\text{Cl}\text{-}\underset{\text{CH}_2\text{OH}}{\overset{\overset{\text{O}}{\overset{\|}{\text{OCNHCH}_3}}}{\bigcirc}}\text{-CH}_3}
$$

Carbanolate is rapidly metabolized in the rat to give water-soluble products [57]. Use of carbonyl-labeled ^{14}C-carbanolate showed that greater than 50% of the administered radioactivity was expired as $^{14}CO_2$, indicating that hydrolysis was an important degradation mechanism in the rat. Parallel studies with ring-methyl-labeled ^{14}C-carbanolate showed that the bulk of the metabolites was eliminated through the urine as water-soluble conjugates. At least seven different metabolites were detected but none was identified with any degree of certainty. One of the major urinary metabolites was believed to be the N-glucuronic acid derivatives of carbanolate but evidence for this was indirect.

PROPOXUR

The metabolism of propoxur (also known as aprocarb) or 2-isopropoxyphenyl methylcarbamate has been studied extensively in insects [58-60]. In the housefly propoxur is metabolized into approximately 10 organosoluble products and at least 6 water-soluble products [58]. Organosoluble metabolites identified by comparison of their chromatographic properties with authentic synthetic samples were 5-hydroxy-propoxur (1), 2-hydroxyphenyl methylcarbamate (2), N-hydroxymethyl-propoxur (3), and 2-isopropoxyphenyl carbamate or N-demethyl-propoxur (4). The known metabolic pathways for propoxur metabolism in the housefly are shown. Metabolites 1, 2, and 3 also were present as water-soluble conjugates. The most abundant metabolite present was 1 (20-28% of total after 4 hr) followed by 2 and 3 in substantially lower amounts. Degradation of propoxur by hydrolysis of the carbamate moiety was of minor metabolic importance since little $^{14}CO_2$ was liberated when carbonyl-labeled ^{14}C-propoxur was used.

In housefly strains resistant to intoxication by propoxur the rate of metabolism was three times greater than in susceptible strains, indicating that tolerance to the toxic effect of propoxur is dependent on metabolism rates. Qualitatively, the spectrum of metabolites in resistant flies was identical to that found in susceptible flies although there were significant quantitative differences. Pretreatment of flies with piperonyl butoxide and other synergists markedly reduced the rate of metabolism of propoxur in both susceptible and resistant strains of houseflies. For example, the amount of unchanged propoxur found in the two strains of flies was twofold or more greater after pretreatment with piperonyl butoxide. In general, there was a direct correlation between toxicity to propoxur and reduction in metabolism rates attributable to the action of the synergist.

The in vitro metabolism of propoxur by the enzyme present in housefly abdomen was similar to that occurring in the live insect with the exception that relatively small amounts of the products were in the form of conjugates. Addition of bovine serum albumin increased the activity of the enzyme, and activity was inhibited by synergist. Further, examination of enzyme preparations from a variety of different housefly strains showed good correlation between the resistance level of the strain and the metabolizing activity of their enzyme preparations. Genetic analysis in relation to resistance to propoxur and metabolism of propoxur in living flies and enzyme preparations have shown that resistance and metabolism is largely associated with the 5th chromosomal gene(s) [59].

The metabolism of propoxur in mosquito larvae (Culex pipiens fatigans) is similar to that taking place in houseflies [60]. Propoxur is absorbed by mosquito larvae from a water medium and metabolized into at least 10 different products. The major metabolites were identified by chromatographic methods as 1, 2, 3, and 4. Incubation of propoxur with mosquito larvae homogenate also produced the same metabolites. Comparison of resistant and susceptible strains of larvae showed that propoxur was metabolized at a faster rate by the resistant strain, both in vivo and in vitro.

Incubation of propoxur with rat liver microsomes produced 11 metabolites separable by thin-layer chromatography [34]. Metabolites identified by cochromatography and their relative amounts were 1 (5-6%), 2 (9-12%), 3 (15-19%), and 2-isopropoxyphenol (3.3%). Related studies [60] using a mouse-liver microsome-plus-soluble enzyme preparation also showed that propoxur was metabolized to 1, 2, and 3. Again, the N-hydroxymethyl derivative (3) was obtained in consistently larger amounts than 1 or 2. It appears that hydroxylation of the N-methyl moiety is the major metabolic reaction with mammalian enzyme compared to ring hydroxylation in the 5-position with insect enzyme.

Less information is available concerning propoxur metabolism in plants [26, 29]. Analysis of products in the bean plant 6 days after injection showed that over 30% of the applied propoxur was recovered as water-soluble metabolites in the form of conjugates. Over 80% of these metabolites contained the intact carbamate moiety, indicating that the major pathways for metabolism were nonhydrolytic. Hydrolysis of the conjugates using β-glucosidase resulted in approximately 10 different products. Chromatographic evidence indicates that two of these were 2 and 3. Over 90% of the total metabolites recovered was 2, and it appears that O-dealkylation is the principal pathway for propoxur degradation in plants.

In limited experiments, the analysis of urine from humans given small dosages of propoxur showed that the major portion of the administered dose was eliminated as a conjugate of 2-isopropoxyphenol, presumably as the glucuronide [61].

DIMETILAN

Dimetilan or 1-(dimethylcarbamoyl)-5-methyl-3-pyrazolyl dimethylcarbamate differs from previously discussed carbamates in that it is an ester of dimethylcarbamic acid. Although of high insecticidal activity, dimetilan is rapidly metabolized in houseflies and cockroaches with a half-life of less than 30 min [62]. Hydrolysis of the dimethylcarbamate moiety in the 5-position is responsible for part of the metabolic products formed, but the majority of the various metabolites recovered from these insects is attributable to reactions not involving cleavage of the ester linkage. Nine metabolites were detected by thin-layer chromatography from extracts of dimetilan-treated German roaches, six from the American cockroach, and four from houseflies. Of the five metabolites isolated from the American cockroach, none showed any changes in the 3-methylpyrazole ring since 3-methyl-5-pyrazole was recovered when the metabolites were subjected to hydrolysis. Analysis of other fragmentation products after extensive hydrolysis of each of the metabolites showed that dimetilan metabolism occurs principally through oxidative conversion of the methyl groups on the 2- and 5-dimethylcarbamoyl moiety. Although none of the metabolites was identified with satisfaction, the evidence pointed to the scheme shown for dimetilan metabolism in the cockroach. Of the various metabolites, the metabolite tentatively identified as 4 and another unidentified metabolite were highly toxic to houseflies and the American cockroach, and they undoubtedly contribute to the intoxication of these insects after treatment with dimetilan.

SUMMARY

From this brief review it is evident that carbamate insecticides act as typical foreign molecules in biological systems, and are metabolically transformed by a variety of chemical reactions into molecules with increased polar properties. The initial step in carbamate ester metabolism is usually oxidative in nature and probably involves the mixed function oxidases in animals and related enzymes in plants. In most cases the oxidative reaction introduces a functional group, usually a hydroxyl moiety, which serves as a center for secondary conjugation reactions. Because of the labile nature of the carbamate ester group, hydrolysis of the carbamate linkage also is an important metabolic reaction, usually leading to phenolic compounds which also are conjugated to water-soluble products.

The exact point of attack in the carbamate molecule varies with the nature of the functional groups in the molecule but is usually the same in plants and animals. Groups which are most susceptible to oxidation, e.g., thioethers as in the cases of aldicarb and methiocarb, normally are attacked first. The benzylic 3-carbon atom in carbofuran is another example of a functional group highly vulnerable to enzymatic oxidation. Hydroxylation and ketonization of this carbon readily occurs with the usual chemical oxidizing agents in good yields [46].

Although metabolism of carbamate ester generally leads to nontoxic products, there are a number of examples where toxic metabolites are produced, e.g., aldicarb sulfoxide, N-demethyl dimetilan, and N-demethyl and N-formyl Zectran. However, on an over-all basis metabolism constitutes a defense mechanism against the toxic action of carbamate esters.

References

[1] E. Hodgson (ed.), *The Enzymatic Oxidation of Toxicants*, North Carolina State Univ., Raleigh, 1968.
[2] R. J. Kuhr, *J. Agr. Food Chem.*, 18, 1023 (1970).
[3] H. W. Dorough, *J. Agr. Food Chem.*, 18, 1015 (1970).
[4] J. E. Casida and K. B. Augustinsson, *Biochem. Biophys. Acta*, 36, 411 (1959).
[5] J. E. Casida and K. B. Augustinsson, *J. Econ. Entomol.*, 53, 205 (1960).

[6]   K. B. Augustinsson and J. E. Casida, *Biochem. Pharmacol.*, **3**, 60 (1959).

[7]   E. Hodgson and J. E. Casida, *Biochem. Pharmacol.*, **8**, 179 (1961).

[8]   E. Hodgson and J. E. Casida, *Biochem. Biophys. Acta*, **42**, 184 (1960).

[9]   L. W. Dittert and T. Higuchi, *J. Pharm. Sci.*, **52**, 852 (1963).

[10] T. R. Fukuto, M. A. H. Fahmy, and R. L. Metcalf, *J. Agr. Food Chem.*, **15**, 273 (1967).

[11] J. G. Krishna and J. E. Casida, *J. Agr. Food Chem.*, **14**, 98 (1966).

[12] R. L. Metcalf, M. F. Osman, and T. R. Fukuto, *J. Econ. Entomol.*, **60**, 445 (1967).

[13] D. V. Parke, *The Biochemistry of Foreign Compounds*, Pergamon, Oxford, 1968.

[14] L. Shuster, *Ann. Rev. Biochem.*, **33**, 571 (1964).

[15] M. E. Eldefrawi and W. M. Hoskins, *J. Econ. Entomol.*, **54**, 401 (1961).

[16] H. W. Dorough and J. E. Casida, *J. Agr. Food Chem.*, **12**, 294 (1964).

[17] N. C. Leeling and J. E. Casida, *J. Agr. Food Chem.*, **14**, 281 (1966).

[18] D. M. Jerina, J. W. Daly, B. Witkop, P. Zaltzman-Nirenberg, and S. Udenfriend, *J. Amer. Chem. Soc.*, **90**, 6525 (1968).

[19] J. B. Knaak, M. J. Tallant, W. J. Bartley, and L. J. Sullivan, *J. Agr. Food Chem.*, **13**, 537 (1965).

[20] A. Hassan, S. M. A. D. Zayed, and F. M. Abdel-Hamid, *Biochem. Pharmacol.*, **15**, 2045 (1966).

[21] J. B. Knaak, M. J. Tallant, S. J. Kozbelt, and L. J. Sullivan, *J. Agr. Food Chem.*, **16**, 465 (1968).

[22] J. B. Knaak and M. J. Sullivan, *J. Agr. Food Chem.*, **15**, 1125 (1967).

[23] G. D. Paulson, R. G. Zaylskie, M. V. Zehr, C. E. Portnoy, and V. J. Feil, *J. Agr. Food Chem.*, **18**, 110 (1971).

[24] L. J. Sullivan, J. M. Eldridge, J. B. Knaak, and M. J. Tallant, Abstract No. 6, PEST, 159th National Meeting of the American Chemical Society, Toronto, May 25, 1970.

[25] I. Y. Mostafa, A. Hassan, and S. M. A. D. Zayad, *Z. Naturforsch. B*, **21**, 1060 (1966).

[26] R. J. Kuhr and J. E. Casida, *J. Agr. Food Chem.*, **15**, 814 (1967).

[27] H. W. Dorough and O. G. Wiggins, *J. Econ. Entomol.*, **62**, 49 (1969).

[28] E. A. Williams, R. W. Meikle, and C. T. Redemann, *J. Agr. Food Chem.*, **12**, 453 (1964).

[29] A. M. Abdel-Wahab, R. J. Kuhr, and J. E. Casida, *J. Agr. Food Chem.*, **14**, 290 (1966).

[30] A. M. Abdel-Wahab and J. E. Casida, *J. Agr. Food Chem.*, **15**, 479 (1967).

[31] M. Tsukamoto and J. E. Casida, *Nature*, **213**, 49 (1967).

[32] R. B. Roberts, R. P. Miskus, C. K. Duckler, and T. T. Sakai, *J. Agr. Food Chem.*, **17**, 107 (1969).

[33] E. A. Williams, R. W. Meikle, and C. T. Redemann, *J. Agr. Food Chem.*, **12**, 457 (1964).

[34] E. S. Oonnithan and J. E. Casida, *J. Agr. Food Chem.*, **16**, 28 (1968).

[35] R. P. Miskus, T. L. Andrews, and M. Look, *J. Agr. Food Chem.*, **17**, 842 (1969).

[36] A. K. Sen-Gupta and C. O. Knowles, *J. Econ. Entomol.*, **63**, 10 (1970).

[37] C. O. Knowles and A. K. Sen-Gupta, *J. Econ. Entomol.*, **63**, 615 (1970).

[38] H. G. Bray, R. C. Clowes, and W. V. Thorpe, *Biochem. J.*, **51**, 70 (1952).

[39] L. K. Payne, Jr., H. A. Stansbury, Jr., and M. H. J. Weiden, *J. Agr. Food Chem.*, **14**, 573 (1966).

[40] R. L. Metcalf, T. R. Fukuto, C. Collins, K. Borck, J. Burk, H. T. Reynolds, and M. F. Osman, *J. Agr. Food Chem.*, **14**, 579 (1966).

[41] J. R. Coppedge, D. A. Lindquist, D. L. Bull, and H. W. Dorough, *J. Agr. Food Chem.*, **15**, 902 (1967).

[42] W. J. Bartley, N. R. Andrawes, E. L. Chancey, W. P. Bagley, and H. W. Spurr, *J. Agr. Food Chem.*, **18**, 446 (1970).

[43] T. R. Fukuto, J. P. Wolf, III, R. L. Metcalf, and R. B. March, *J. Econ. Entomol.*, **49**, 147 (1956).

[44] J. B. Knaak, M. J. Tallant, and L. J. Sullivan, *J. Agr. Food Chem.*, **14**, 573 (1966).

[45] N. R. Andrawes, H. W. Dorough, and D. A. Lindquist, *J. Econ. Entomol.*, **60**, 979 (1967).

[46] H. W. Dorough and G. W. Ivie, *J. Agr. Food Chem.*, **16**, 460 (1968).

[47] H. W. Dorough, R. B. Davis, and G. W. Ivie, *J. Agr. Food Chem.*, **18**, 135 (1970).

[48] D. L. Bull, D. A. Lindquist, and J. R. Coppedge, *J. Agr. Food Chem.*, **15**, 610 (1967).

[49] J. D. Robbins, J. E. Bakke, and V. J. Feil, *J. Agr. Food Chem.*, **17**, 236 (1969).

[50] J. D. Robbins, J. E. Bakke, and V. J. Feil, *J. Agr. Food Chem.*, **18**, 130 (1970).

[51] R. L. Metcalf, T. R. Fukuto, C. Collins, K. Borck, S. Abd. El-Aziz, R. Munoz, and C. C. Cassil, *J. Agr. Food Chem.*, **16**, 300 (1968).

[52] H. W. Dorough, *J. Agr. Food Chem.*, **16**, 319 (1968).

[53] G. W. Ivie and H. W. Dorough, *J. Agr. Food Chem.*, **16**, 849 (1968).

[54] J. Miyamoto, K. Yamamoto, and T. Matsumoto, *Agr. Biol. Chem.*, **33**, 1060 (1969).

[55] M. Slade and J. E. Casida, *J. Agr. Food Chem.*, **18**, 467 (1970).

[56] A. R. Friedman and A. J. Lemin, *J. Agr. Food Chem.*, **15**, 830 (1967).

[57] R. L. Baron and J. D. Doherty, *J. Agr. Food Chem.*, **15**, 830 (1967).

[58] S. P. Shrivastava, M. Tsukamoto, and J. E. Casida, *J. Econ. Entomol.*, **62**, 483 (1969).

[59] M. Tsukamoto, S. P. Shrivastava, and J. E. Casida, *J. Econ. Entomol.*, **61**, 50 (1968).

[60] S. P. Shrivastava, G. P. Georghiou, R. L. Metcalf, and T. R. Fukuto, *Bull. World Health Org.*, **42**, 931 (1970).

[61] J. A. Dawson, D. F. Heath, J. R. Rose, E. M. Thain, and J. B. Ward, *Bull. World Health Org.*, **30**, 127 (1964).

[62] M. Y. Zubaire and J. E. Casida, *J. Econ. Entomol.*, **58**, 403 (1965).

Microsomal* Drug Metabolizing Enzymes in Insects

C. F. WILKINSON and L. B. BRATTSTEN
Department of Entomology
Cornell University
Ithaca, New York 14850

*Use of the term "microsomal" to describe the drug metabolizing enzymes in insects is not always strictly correct as many studies have employed only homogenates or mitochondrial supernatants. Furthermore, few insect microsomal fractions have been characterized by electron microscopy and microsomal marker enzymes have not been used to define the fractions biochemically or to establish their homogeneity. Although the authors fully recognize the limitations of their use of the term "microsomal" (see Section III.D.3), they have used it throughout the manuscript for the sake of simplicity.

I. INTRODUCTION

Until quite recently, interest in the biotransformation of foreign compounds (xenobiotics) has been focused almost exclusively on mammalian species with direct reference to their ability to metabolize drugs and related materials. As a result, we have accumulated a great deal of information on the types of metabolic reactions that take place in mammals and have gained considerable insight into the biochemical properties of the enzyme systems catalyzing these conversions. Combined with a knowledge of the influence on these enzymes of physiological factors, such as sex, age, hormonal status, and genetic makeup, and an understanding of the effects of a variety of exogenous environmental factors, it is often possible to assess with some accuracy the biological longevity of a given material and to predict its ultimate metabolic fate. It is now clear that the degree and duration of the effects of biologically active materials can be modified considerably and often determined entirely by their metabolic interactions, and the ability of an animal to survive exposure to a potentially toxic substance often stands or falls on its capacity first to detoxify and subsequently to remove the material from its body.

Recent years have seen a growing concern regarding the general deterioration of the environment and the potential hazards to living organisms posed by the increasing environmental levels of a plethora of synthetic chemicals released by man. In response to this concern and in recognition of the critical role that biotransformation reactions play in determining the continued wellbeing of living organisms, more emphasis is being placed on the comparative aspects of drug metabolism. Such comparative studies, involving mammals, birds, fish, and a variety of other vertebrate and invertebrate species, establish how animals differ from one another in their ability to metabolize foreign compounds and indicate those forms of life that are least equipped to withstand exposure to certain chemicals and that are consequently in need of greater environmental protection. Not all forms of life, however, are deemed to warrant protection and, indeed, in many cases man expends a great deal of time and effort in

contriving methods of controlling a variety of organisms classified
as pests. This is particularly true with insects.

Thus, although the class Insecta contains many fascinating species
worthy of protection, the major driving force behind drug metabolism
studies in insects is the desire to control those species which are
pests of agricultural or public health importance. The critical role
of metabolism in relation to selective toxicity and insect resistance
to insecticides is now well established and consequently interest in
the detoxication mechanisms of insects is directed toward obtaining
information that might indicate flaws in the systems that may be
exploited in the more efficient use of existing insecticide chemicals
or in the design of new materials. Most of our existing insecticides
are lipophilic organic compounds that, because of their broad spectrum of toxicity, often pose a real threat to nontarget species.
Clearly, it will be advantageous to design and develop new insecticides that can selectively control an undesirable species with a minimal effect on other more beneficial forms of life with which it coexists.

Quite apart from the practical expediency arising from a desire
to control pest species, insects constitute an extremely interesting
group of organisms for comparative studies. Not only is the phylum
Arthropoda the largest one in the animal kingdom, comprising
approximately 75% of all known animal species, but its members constitute models for all conceivable modes of life from such diverse
aspects as nutrition to locomotion. The class Hexapoda or Insecta,
which includes about 26 major orders, constitutes approximately
90% of the known species of Arthropods and is estimated to contain
from 2 1/2 to 10 million species. At the present time in-depth studies
on the biochemistry of foreign compound metabolism have been effected on only about 20 insect species, most of which are limited to
those readily reared under laboratory conditions.

The comparative aspects of drug metabolism have received considerable attention in a number of books [1-3] and review articles
[4-14] and several interesting papers are to be found on the proceed-
ings of a symposium devoted to the subject [15-21]. Most of these reviews are primarily concerned with comparative patterns of drug
metabolism in terrestrial and aquatic vertebrates, and relatively few
[8-14] give any consideration to foreign compound metabolism in insects and other invertebrate species. Furthermore, the majority of
the discussions are based mainly on the qualitative patterns of metabolites produced in vivo by different species and do not include a great
deal of information on in vitro studies concerning the nature and properties of the enzymes concerned. Major exceptions to this are the reviews of Terriere [10,11] and a recent contribution by Hodgson and
Plapp [14].

This review represents an attempt to provide a comprehensive summary of the current state of knowledge of foreign compound metabolism in insects. Emphasis will be placed on in vitro studies of the enzymes responsible for the primary oxidation of xenobiotics and on some of the problems encountered in working with insect species.

II. HISTORICAL BACKGROUND

The introduction of synthetic organic chemicals for insect control during World War II was an important technological milestone responsible for opening up several vast new areas of research. The ability of insects to metabolize such materials in vivo was first fully recognized during the late 1940's, when it was discovered that one of the major factors associated with the rapid development of insect resistance to DDT was the capacity of the insect to dehydrochlorinate it to the relatively nontoxic DDE. Investigations on the metabolism of other insecticides, including the cyclodienes and other chlorinated hydrocarbons, the organophosphates, and later the carbamates, were initiated during the early to mid 1950's and as this period was one that saw intense activity in the commercial development of insecticide chemicals, industry provided a constant supply of new compounds with which to work. Metabolic investigations were further aided by improved methodology, particularly the use of radiotracer techniques, and by the increased availability of more sophisticated instrumentation for the resolution, detection, and identification of very small amounts of metabolites. It soon became clear that insects and other organisms were indeed capable of metabolizing almost all organic insecticides to some extent and where comparative investigations were carried out it was evident that the nature of the metabolites produced by both insects and mammals were essentially similar. Almost all of these investigations were effected in vivo and, consequently, only the end products of metabolism were normally observed. Because these were often secondary conjugates, the investigations yielded little information on the nature of the primary or intermediary metabolites or on the enzymes responsible for their production. Dehydrohalogenation was of course well established with DDT and the importance of hydrolysis and desulfuration was recognized in the metabolic interactions of the organophosphates. Although several types of metabolites, such as epoxides, sulfoxides, and sulfones, appeared to result from oxidative reactions, the general importance of enzymic oxidation in insects was not fully recognized during the 1950's.

Meanwhile, there was intense activity in the field of pharmacology, where by the mid 1950's it was already clear that in
mammals, the primary metabolism of a large number of drugs and
other foreign compounds was effected by relatively few pathways
catalyzed by mixed-function oxidases (MFO's) associated with the
hepatic microsomes [5]. For some time, the relevance of these important findings escaped many investigators involved in studies of
insecticide metabolism and it was not until the early 1960's that in
vitro systems from mammalian liver were employed to any great
extent in such studies. Following the success achieved with these
systems, the next logical step was the development of similar in
vitro preparations from insects. Although as will emerge from this
review, the use of in vitro systems from insects is still in its in-
fancy and our basic knowledge of the insect microsomal enzyme
system is still meager, it has now become common practice to employ such preparations in metabolic studies where they are often
extremely useful in reproducing reactions occurring in the living
organism.

It is not the purpose of this review to attempt any survey of
the vast literature concerning insecticide metabolism in vivo.
Readers interested in this area are referred to some of the many
recent excellent books and reviews on the subject [22-26].

III. PREPARATION OF INSECT MICROSOMES

In mammals, in vitro studies of the microsomal drug metabolizing enzymes are facilitated by the fact that enzyme activity
is associated primarily with the liver, which provides a readily available, relatively homogeneous source of tissue for biochemical investigations. In contrast, the preparation of microsomal enzymes from
various insect species has presented many problems and continues
to be a major stumbling block in in vitro studies. Two major problems exist, which are closely interrelated. The first of these constitutes the choice of a suitable tissue source from which to prepare
the enzyme and the second involves a thorough evaluation of the optimum preparatory procedure by which the enzyme can be obtained.

A. Tissue Sources

In evaluating a suitable tissue source for enzymic studies,
one problem that is immediately obvious and that is in itself
often sufficient to damp the spirits of even the most enthusiastic
investigator is the relatively small size of most insect species and

the small amount of tissue consequently available. This problem was initially obviated by the use of homogenates and various subcellular fractions derived from whole insects. Indeed, this procedure is still being employed in several laboratories.

In one of the first in vitro studies with insects, Agosin et al. [27], employing NADPH-fortified microsomal preparations from homogenates of whole German cockroaches (Blattella germanica), American cockroaches (Periplaneta americana), and several strains of insecticide-resistant and -susceptible houseflies (Musca domestica), demonstrated the oxidative metabolism of DDT. Whole housefly preparations have subsequently been used in in vitro studies of the hydroxylation of naphthalene [28-34], the epoxidation of aldrin [32, 35-40], heptachlor [39-41], and isodrin [39,40] and the oxidative metabolism of a variety of other cyclodiene insecticides [36, 42-45]. Microsomes obtained from whole blowflies (Phormia regina) have been shown to be active in hydroxylation [29, 46], dealkylation, and epoxidation [46] and similar preparations from whole larvae of Triatoma infestans catalyze the oxidative metabolism of DDT [47].

Such whole-insect preparations do in some cases provide a qualitative indicator of microsomal enzyme activity and their use has established that the pathways of microsomal metabolism in insects are basically similar to those occurring in mammalian liver. Unfortunately, however, the successes achieved with these preparations prove to be the exceptions rather than the general rule. More usually, enzyme activity in homogenates of whole insects is either nonexistent or extremely low and bears little or no relationship to that which is expected from the in vivo metabolic capability of an equivalent amount of living insects. Thus, Brodie and Maickel [6], in the first major comparative study of drug metabolism, were unable to demonstrate any microsomal enzyme activity in preparations from the house cricket (Acheta domesticus) in spite of the fact that the insect was found capable of metabolizing a variety of drugs in vivo; in another study, whole homogenates of nine other insect species, each of which was metabolically active in vivo, were found to possess no oxidizing activity [48, 49]. Although active microsomal preparations can sometimes be obtained from whole lepidopterous larvae [50-52], it is more commonly found that such preparations are devoid of measurable oxidative activity [53-57].

Even at best, it is highly questionable whether the activity measured in these whole preparations provides a realistic indicator of the enzymic capability of the insect under investigation and large day-to-day variations make it very difficult to obtain satisfactory data. Furthermore, enzyme activity is usually extremely labile and because the preparations must be used without delay all biochemical investigations inevitably assume some of the characteristics of

an athletic contest. It is indeed somewhat surprising that whole-
insect preparations exhibit any activity at all and it would be interesting to see how much activity could be demonstrated in analogous preparations from whole mammals!

The microsomal fraction derived from homogenates of whole
insects is clearly a heterogeneous mixture of material from all
parts of the insect and as it has now been firmly established that
there are marked differences in the microsomal activity of various
insect tissues (Section III.C) there will be a substantial dilution factor associated with the presence in the final pellet of enzymically
inert material derived from inactive tissues. This factor alone can
probably account for the low in vitro activity often observed in
homogenates of whole insects. Even more important, however, is
that the homogenization of whole insects results in the release of a
large number of endogenous materials that have potentially inhibitory effects on one or more components of the microsomal enzyme
complex. Under the conditions of physiological and biochemical com-
partmentation existing in vivo, such materials will not, of course,
come into contact with the endoplasmic reticulum. Following the dis-
ruption of cellular organization, however, the endoplasmic reticulum
is exposed to a multitude of enzymes, lipids, steroids, and other cell
components, any of which may interfere with microsomal enzyme
activity. The chances of encountering such materials are of course
greatest when whole insects are employed and, for this reason,
either specific body regions of the insect, for example, housefly
abdomina [14, 58], or individual organs (Section III.C) have in recent
years been found to provide more satisfactory tissue sources from
which to prepare microsomes; even with these, however, endogenous
inhibitors can sometimes be important artifacts.

B. Endogenous Inhibitors

The presence of endogenous inhibitors of microsomal oxidation in preparation from rat liver has been recognized for some
time [59, 60] and recent studies have established that inhibition results at least in part from the interaction with NADPH-cytochrome c reductase of products formed during the action of NADPH-
pyrophosphatase on NADPH [61].

The possibility that insect homogenates might contain materials that inhibit MFO activity was first suggested by Nakatsugawa and Dahm [62] working on the parathion activation enzymes in
cockroach (Periplaneta americana) fat body and was subsequently
amply verified by numerous researchers working with a variety of
insect species. Unfortunately, the data from different laboratories
are often incomplete and their marked lack of agreement has until

quite recently made it difficult to reach any firm or unifying conclusions regarding the nature of these materials. It is quite clear, however, that one or more of several different types of inhibitors or
inactivators may be involved in any one species and that these can
often seriously impede progress in in vitro investigations of the
microsomal enzymes in insects.

The presence of inhibitory materials in preparations from the
housefly (Musca domestica) was first demonstrated by Matthews
and Hodgson [63], who found that the 15,000 $\times$ g supernatant
from homogenates of whole insects was unable to oxidize p-nitrophenyl N,N-dimethylcarbamate without first being dialyzed against
either distilled water or phosphate buffer. The freeze-dried dialyzate
inhibited enzyme activity in mouse liver microsomes and the inhibitory factor was found to be water soluble and heat stable. Subsequent
studies confirmed the inhibitory activity of whole housefly homogenates and established that different inhibitory factors were associated
with different body regions of the insect [49, 64-68]. Thus, although
some inhibition was found to be associated with a heat-labile factor
localized in the abdomen [49, 67], the major factor contributing to
the inhibitory activity of whole housefly homogenates appeared to be
heat stable and to be concentrated in the head and thorax of the insect
[49, 64, 65, 67]. The first major breakthrough with regard to identification was the observation by Jordan and Smith [68] that the heat-
stable oxidase inhibitor was absent in a strain of houseflies possessing a mutant yellow eye color. The relationship between inhibition and
eye pigmentation was further confirmed by the fact that inhibitory
activity in head preparations from nine strains of houseflies occurred
only in those possessing the wild-type eye color and was not related
to differences in sex, microsomal enzyme levels, or degree of insecticide resistance of the insects employed [69]. The absence of any
marked inhibitory activity in the heads of strains with white or ocra
eyes strongly suggested that inhibition might be associated with an
ommochrome pigment, such as xanthommatin [69], because it has
been known for some time that the lack of eye color in various mutant
strains results from genetic blocks on the biosynthesis of these pigments from tryptophan [70]. That xanthommatin is indeed the major
inhibitory component in housefly heads has now been firmly established in independent investigations in three different laboratories
[71-74] and studies with eye-color mutants of Drosophila melano-
gaster and honey bee (Apis mellifera) drones have confirmed its general importance in other insect species [73]. Xanthommatin either
isolated from housefly heads or produced synthetically by the oxidation of 3-hydroxykynurenine is an extremely potent inhibitor of MFO
activity in both insects and mammals and causes substantial inhibi-

tion of housefly microsomal epoxidase activity at concentrations as
low as 5×10^{-7} M [71, 72].

The inhibition of MFO activity is accompanied by a marked
increase in NADPH oxidation [71-74] indicating that xanthommatin acts as an electron sink and consequently impedes the flow of
electrons from NADPH to cytochrome P-450. When a variety of arti-
ficial electron acceptors was employed, it was established that xanthommatin accepts electrons from the flavoprotein NADPH-cytochrome
c reductase [71, 72] and this has subsequently been substantiated using
a purified NADPH-cytochrome c reductase from housefly microsomes
[74]. The increase in NADPH oxidation caused by xanthommatin also
occurs in the presence of CO and the absence of any direct interaction
with P-450 is further confirmed by the fact that the inhibitor does not
interfere with substrate binding to this cytochrome [74]. It is quite
clear, therefore, that xanthommatin is acting in a similar manner to
Methylene Blue and is diverting the flow of electrons required to reduce P-450 (Fig. 1). The ability of dihydroxanthommatin to undergo
autooxidation or to reduce cytochome c and dichlorophenol indophenol
nonenzymically indicates the probable involvement of a reversible

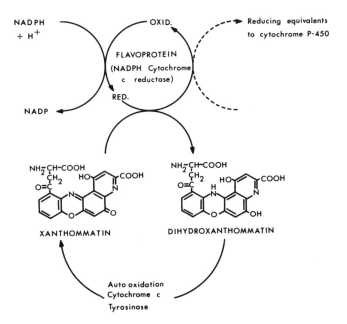

FIG. 1. Mechanism of inhibition of microsomal oxidation by xanthommatin.

reaction that results in the cyclic regeneration of xanthommatin and
a consequent enhancement of its overall inhibitory potential [71, 72].
It is probable that the reported enhancement of housefly microsomal
activity by cyanide [35, 68] results at least in part from the ability of
cyanide to prevent reoxidation of dihydroxanthommatin by either cytochrome c oxidase or tyrosinase, although it may also occur to some
extent through blockage of the reaction between DOPA, tyrosinase,
and 3-hydroxykynurenine, which can produce xanthommatin in situ in
housefly homogenates [71, 72]. The marked stimulation of NADPH
oxidation reported to occur in housefly head preparations in the presence of menadione (2-methyl-1,4-naphthoquinone) and catechol (which
can be readily oxidized to o-benzoquinone by tyrosinase) [66] may
result from the ability of these materials to reoxidize dihydroxanthommatin, although the quinones themselves may conceivably accept
electrons directly from the microsomal electron transport chain.

Considerable confusion has resulted from various reports that
the major inhibitor in housefly preparations is soluble and dialyzable [63], in the 10,000 × g supernatant [66, 68] and in the 800 × g
sediment [64, 65]. Some of this confusion clearly results from the
fact that xanthommatin is only sparingly soluble in aqueous solution
and will consequently have a fairly broad distribution in both soluble
and particulate fractions, depending on the method of preparation employed [71, 72].

Although the eye pigments are clearly of primary importance
in determining microsomal enzyme activity in preparations from
whole houseflies and other species, it should not be construed
that these are the only or even the most important inhibitory factors
in all insect preparations. Thus, the absence of microsomal enzyme
activity in whole homogenates of the southern armyworm (Prodenia
eridania) has been shown to result from the presence of a potent
endogenous inhibitor in the gut contents of the larvae [53, 54, 75]. The
material has been purified approximately 70-fold and characterized
as a soluble proteinase with a molecular weight of about 26,000 [75].
In the crude form it is remarkably heat stable but becomes progressively more labile on purification. The proteolytic (caseinolytic)
activity of the inhibitor can be blocked with well-known serine hydrolase reagents, such as diisopropyl phosphorofluoridate and phenyl-
methane sulfonyl fluoride, and although these materials will afford
some degree of protection for the microsomal enzymes in the presence of the inhibitor, the reagents themselves cause some inhibition
at the rather high concentrations (1 mM) required to obtain this effect.
Bovine serum albumin (BSA) has a marked protective effect on the
microsomes in the presence of this inhibitor and when employed at a
concentration of 80 μg per incubation it resulted in a sevenfold enhancement of epoxidase activity in armyworm gut preparations [75].

It was concluded that the inhibitor effects a direct proteolytic attack on the microsomal protein and that the BSA reduces this by providing the inhibitor with an alternative protein substrate. A subsequent study [76] has established that the inhibitor markedly decreases the reduction of cytochrome P-450 by NADPH in rat liver microsomes through solubilization of NADPH-cytochrome c reductase. It had little or no effect on cytochromes b_5 or P-450 and caused no apparent decrease in the ability of the latter to bind hexobarbital [76]. These effects are similar to those previously reported for trypsin [77] and it is entirely possible that the gut contents inhibitor is a naturally occurring larval digestive proteinase. If this is the case, similar proteolytic enzymes will be expected to have broad significance in homogenates of whole insects and, indeed, inhibitory activity has been found to be associated with the gut contents of several other species of lepidopterous larvae [53, 56, 57], the house cricket (Acheta domesticus) [78], and a caddis-fly larva [79].

The marked enhancement of microsomal enzyme activity that results from adding BSA to homogenates of whole houseflies [35, 64, 65] may be caused in part by the presence of a proteinase of this type, as substantial caseinolytic activity has been demonstrated in 10% (w/v) homogenates of whole houseflies and other insects [75]. This possibility is further supported by the fact that the BSA-sensitive inhibitory factor in houseflies is heat labile and is concentrated largely in the abdominal region of the insect [65, 67, 68]. The fact that BSA can also reduce the inhibition caused by xanthommatin [74] may explain the BSA enhancement of MFO activity in housefly heads and thoraces [65], although other investigators [71, 72] have been unable to show any effect of BSA on xanthommatin inhibition. The possibility that BSA may act as a microsomal stabilizing agent was initially investigated as a result of its reported ability to bind and thereby reverse fatty acid inhibitors of oxidative phosphorylation in mitochondria [64]. Although a search for such inhibitors proved negative, it did establish the existence of an ether extractable inhibitory factor(s), possibly a neutral organic material, in homogenates of whole houseflies [64]. The identity of this factor remains unknown.

Investigations on the microsomal enzymes of orthopteran insects have revealed the presence of several endogenous inhibitors in homogenates of whole insects and isolated organs. A material occurring in the 800 × g sediment of cockroach (Periplaneta americana) fat body homogenates interferes with the activation of parathion (desulfuration) by microsomes from this tissue [62] and what are probably similar materials have subsequently been reported in the 10,000 × g sediment from homogenates of locust (Schistocerca gregaria) and cockroach (unspecified) fat bodies [49, 66]. The inhibitor associated with the 10,000 × g sediment from locust fat body is heat stable (15 min at 100°C) and causes an irreversible inhibition of p-nitrotoluene oxidation by a rabbit liver preparation [49, 66]. The inhibitory factor is reported to have two distinct modes of action. One of these, which occurs on exposure of a rabbit liver preparation to the inhibitor at 0°C, results in the immediate removal of a portion of the microsomal activity; the amount of enzyme activity lost has been found to increase only slightly following further periods of incubation at 0°C and the inhibitor can subsequently be removed by centrifugation at 10,000 × g to leave an active microsomal enzyme preparation. If instead the inhibitor is allowed to remain in suspension during the microsomal assay at 37°C, what is described as a second type of inhibitory action results in a complete block of enzyme activity [49, 66]. There seems to be little reason why these "two types of inhibitory activity" cannot be fully explained in terms of the temperature difference.

In addition to these particulate materials, the nature of which remains unknown, inhibitors have also been reported in the soluble fractions from American cockroach (Periplaneta americana) fat body and midgut homogenates and from whole German cockroach (Blattella germanica L.) homogenates [80]. The inhibitor in the soluble fraction of American roach midgut homogenates is not dialyzable, is heat labile, and is associated with a protein fraction precipitated with $(NH_4)_2SO_4$ at 70-80% saturation. Based on its chromatographic behavior on Sephadex gel, it is estimated to have a molecular weight of between 6000 and 15,000 and is tentatively characterized as an enzyme [80]. If this characterization is correct, it is possibly another proteolytic enzyme similar to those previously discussed but unfortunately no mention is made about its localization in the gut contents or the gut tissues themselves; this is also true of the potent inhibitor reported in the whole midgut homogenates of the locust (Schistocerca gregaria) [49, 66]. The presence of an inhibitor in the gut contents of the house cricket (Acheta domesticus L.) has recently been reported [78, 81] and work in this laboratory is currently in progress to characterize this material [82].

A quite different type of endogenous inhibitor has recently been encountered in the midgut tissues of the honey bee (Apis mellifera) [83]. Unlike the materials previously discussed this inhibitor is intracellular and furthermore is found only in larvae or adult worker (female) bees; it appears to be entirely absent from the gut tissues of drones (males). Preliminary investigations indicate that it is a soluble nucleic acid or nucleoprotein (mol wt ~ 18,000) and although it is a potent inhibitor of insect microsomal enzymes it appears to have little or no effect on those from mammalian liver [83].

Endogenous inhibitors, such as eye pigments or digestive proteinases, are likely to be encountered to some extent throughout the entire life cycle of the insect. Others, however, may attain significance only at certain stages of development and may be associated with specific age-dependent changes in the insect's biochemistry. One example of the latter is the microsomal enzyme inhibition caused by soluble products of the darkening reaction or melanization process in preparations of whole late-instar lepidopterous larvae [50, 52]. This type of inhibition becomes important as a result of enhanced polyphenoloxidase activity in the larvae at this stage of development and its effects can be obviated by the addition of 1-phenyl-2-thiourea to the preparations [50, 52].

C. Tissue Distribution of Oxidase Activity

Although preparations from whole insects have proved useful in gross metabolic studies, it is obvious that they constitute a highly unsatisfactory source from which to initiate meaningful biochemical investigations on the nature and properties of the microsomal enzymes. In recent years, therefore, increasing attention has been given to establishing more homogeneous tissue sources for such studies.

Early investigations established the ability of several intact insect organs and tissues to catalyze metabolic reactions now considered typical of mammalian microsomal enzymes. In the American cockroach (Periplaneta americana) desulfuration activity was reported to occur in the Malpighian tubules [84]*, the gastric caeca [86], the gut [87], or the fat body [87-89], depending apparently on the substrate employed. The gut and fat body were also reported to be most active in desulfuration in the cattle grub (Hypoderma bovis) [90] and the desert locust (Schistocerca gregaria) [91], and a more detailed investigation on p-nitrotoluene oxidation by intact tissues of the latter species showed activity to be in the order fat body > gastric caeca > foregut = midgut > Malpighian tubules > hindgut [48, 49].

Early attempts to prepare cell-free preparations from insect tissues were in most cases unsuccessful when it was found that homogenization resulted in a marked decrease or complete loss of enzymic activity [48, 49, 87, 88, 91-93]. Fenwick [89, 94], however, was able to retain schradan activation activity in homogenates and subcellular fractions of locust (Schistocerca gregaria) fat bodies and the 10,000 × g supernatant (but not whole homogenate) from this tissue was shown to catalyze the oxidation of p-nitrotoluene [48]. Nakatsugawa and Dahm [85] had more success and were able to make a direct comparison between Guthion activation activity in NADPH-fortified homogenates of American cockroach tissues and that in the corre-

---

*Originally reported as foregut but subsequently corrected [85].

sponding intact tissues. The most active whole tissues, in descending order and measured in terms of activity per microgram protein nitrogen were Malpighian tubules > fat body > heart > nerve cord > caeca, whereas with homogenates the order was midgut and caeca > Malpighian tubules > fat body > foregut and hindgut. In homogenates, the variation in activity between different tissues was not as great as that observed with whole tissues and it was concluded that the enzymes were fairly broadly distributed throughout the insect. It was, however, pointed out that because of its relatively large mass, the fat body might have the greatest enzyme activity per insect and this has been confirmed in a more recent investigation [78]. Studies with other orthopteran species support the view that several different tissues are capable of microsomal oxidation. In crude tissue homogenates (2,000 × g supernatant) of the house cricket (Acheta domesticus) maximum epoxidase and hydroxylase activities are associated with the Malpighian tubules when measured either per milligram protein or per insect [78, 81], whereas in the Tampa cockroach (Nauphoeta cinerea) and the Madagascar cockroach (Gromphadorhina portentosa), the midgut and caeca appear to possess the most activity [78, 95]. In the latter species, the fat body, in spite of its low specific activity, contributes substantially to the total enzymic capability of the insect as a result of its large mass. The relative ease with which orthopteran fat body tissue can be obtained has made it a favorite source for studies on insect microsomes and insecticide metabolism [62, 80, 95-99]. Although the fat body has also been shown to be the most active organ for the hydroxylation of carbaryl(1-naphthyl N-methylcarbamate) in larvae of the blowfly (Calliphora erythrocephala) [100] it should not be assumed that this organ is of equal importance in all insect species.

Studies on the enzyme distribution patterns in approximately 40 species of lepidopterous larvae have clearly established that maximum drug metabolizing activity is associated with the tissues of the alimentary tract and is particularly high in the midgut [53, 54, 55, 75, 101-104]. The lone exception to this general pattern appears to be the cabbage looper (Trichoplusia ni), where preparations from the fat body are more active than those from the gut [56, 57]. Active oxidase preparations have been obtained from the gut tissues of adult houseflies [65] and larvae of the sawfly (Macremphytus varianus) [105], the honey bee (Apis mellifera) [83], and the Colorado potato beetle (Leptinotarsa decemlineata) [106]. The gut and fat body of a caddisfly larva (Limnephilus sp.) are also active with respect to epoxidation [79].

It is clear, therefore, that unlike mammals, insects do not have any one specific organ in which the drug metabolizing enzymes are predominantly localized and that the patterns of tissue

distribution vary considerably not only between different orders of
insects but also between different species within a single order. Consequently, in working with any new insect species it becomes necessary to undertake a thorough evaluation of the tissue most suitable
as an enzyme source.

D. Preparatory Procedures for Obtaining Insect Microsomes

Initial attempts to prepare insect microsomes were based
on the tacit assumption that the subcellular fractionation of homogenates of whole insects or insect tissues could be satisfactorily accomplished by procedures identical to those used for mammalian liver.
Thus, using a tissue grinder or mechanical blender, the insect tissue
under consideration was homogenized in some isotonic or hypertonic
medium and the resulting brei was subjected to differential centrifugation under conditions similar to those described in the classic work
of Palade and Siekevitz [107]. It was taken for granted that the various
subcellular fractions obtained in this way were morphologically and
biochemically similar to those from liver [107-109]. Through a combination of such factors as practical convenience and personal prefer-
ence, modifications have been effected in this general procedure with
the result that the methods presently being employed in different laboratories often vary considerably. Once a procedure has been adopted
there is usually a marked reluctance on the part of the investigator to
accept any further change.

In view of the considerable variations in the nature of the
insect tissues employed, it is of course to be expected that differences
in the optimum preparatory procedures for obtaining microsomes will
occur. This is particularly true in preparations from such heterogeneous tissue sources as whole insects or insect body regions where
the procedures employed can markedly affect the interference from
endogenous inhibitors or other artifacts present in the tissues. Consequently, most of the detailed studies on preparatory procedures
have been carried out on these rather crude tissue sources and have
considered such factors as the method of homogenization, the homogenization medium, and the optimum centrifugal conditions for subcellular fractionation.

1. Homogenization Procedure

The method of homogenization can clearly play an important
role in determining the yield and final activity of the microsomes
and although several methods have been employed there is a general
consensus of opinion that the procedure should be relatively gentle
and be accomplished as quickly as possible. With mammalian liver

it has been reported that, because of the better yields of microsomal protein obtained, the Waring Blendor provides a more effective method of homogenization than the Potter Elvehjem tissue grinder [110]. In contrast, Schonbrod and Terriere [31] found approximately twice the yield of microsomal protein and at least 50% greater naphthalene hydroxylation activity in microsomes prepared from whole houseflies homogenized in a tissue grinder compared with those from insects initially processed in a Waring Blendor; similar results were obtained with regard to the activities of microsomes from housefly abdomina homogenized with a teflon pestle and an Omni-mixer [58]. The yield of microsomal protein is not, however, the only criterion to be considered in determining the suitability of a homogenization procedure with insects. A recent report has indicated that although a mechanical blender provides an almost 3-fold higher yield of microsomal protein from whole houseflies, the naphthalene hydroxylating activity of the microsomes obtained by this procedure is 25-fold lower than that of microsomes from houseflies homogenized by a gentle pounding action in a mortar [34]. It was concluded that the latter procedure is superior because it retained the integrity of the sarcosomes and therefore prevented the release of a mitochondrial cytochrome that not only interfered with their measurement of cytochrome P-450 but also inhibited the microsomal enzyme activity. Philpot and Hodgson [111] have recently suggested that in view of the close similarity between the CO-difference spectrum of the microsomes from whole blended houseflies [34] and that previously described for preparations from adrenal mitochondria [112], the interfering material is probably cytochrome oxidase. It seems unlikely that this material would seriously interfere with microsomal enzyme activity and it is more probable that the inhibition associated with the so-called "sarcosomal microsomes" [34] is caused instead by xanthommatin derived from the insect's head; this view is supported by the finding that the sarcosomal microsomes cause a marked increase in NADPH oxidation [34]. Other workers have successfully employed a mortar and pestle for homogenizing whole insects [27, 46, 113, 114].

When a tissue grinder is employed, the degree of homogenization of whole houseflies or housefly abdomina is important and although several different motor drive speeds have been used it appears that only very few (2-10) passes of the plunger are required [31, 58, 67, 68]. If grinding is prolonged, or if the pestle used is too tight, the activity of the resulting brei becomes progressively lower [68]. Although this may be caused in part by enzyme denaturation through excessive abrasive action of chitinous portions of the insect, it probably results mainly from the more efficient release of endogenous inhibitors. Jordan et al. [67] found that the decreased enzyme

activity in hard homogenates of housefly abdomina could be enhanced
by the addition of 1-2% w/v BSA and it was also demonstrated that
such homogenates inhibited oxidase activity in more gently prepared
homogenates [67, 68]. Protein yields are reported to increase as a
linear function of the number of insects homogenized in the tissue
grinder [31] although, according to Jordan et al. [67], the activity per
insect in homogenates of housefly abdomina decreases progressively
with increasing concentration of tissue employed, probably as a result of the increased concentration of inhibitory materials.

2. Homogenization Medium

The medium employed in the initial homogenization of insect
tissues can also be important. Schonbrod and Terriere [31] reported that homogenization of whole houseflies in 0.1 M phosphate
buffer (pH 7.4) rather than 0.15 M KCl almost doubled the activity of
the microsomes obtained, and in a more recent study using housefly
abdomina it was shown that 0.25 M phosphate buffer (pH 7.8) was
better than 0.25 M sucrose, 0.15 M KCl, 0.71 M KCl, or 0.25 M
sucrose plus 0.15 M phosphate buffer as an initial homogenization
medium [58]. Further investigation revealed that the ionic strength
of the medium was more important than either its molarity or pH,
and although 0.2 M phosphate buffer (ionic strength 0.57) proved optimum for this buffer, KCl buffered with Tris to the same pH and ionic
strength was equally satisfactory [58]. Again, it is possible that by
minimizing the release of endogenous inhibitors, the homogenization
medium plays a more critical role in determining the activity of
preparations from heterogenous tissues, such as whole insects, than
of those from individual insect organs, although the possibility of a
more direct effect on the membranes cannot be overlooked.
    In order to counteract the effects of endogenous inhibitors,
BSA (1-2% w/v) is often incorporated in the homogenization
medium [58,64,65,115].

3. Subcellular Fractionation

The methods employed for the subcellular fractionation of
of homogenates of whole insects or insect tissues vary somewhat
between different laboratories but all rely basically on the technique
of differential centrifugation described by Siekevitz [108,109]. Thus,
microsomes are typically prepared by centrifuging at 100-200,000 ×
g for approximately 60 min a postmitochondrial supernatant resulting from a previous spin of 10-12,000 × g for about 30 min. In order
to remove the often substantial amounts of chitinous debris and lipids
released during the homogenization of insect tissues, the initial brei

is usually filtered through cheese cloth, cotton, or glass wool and/or subjected to a low speed centrifugation step (300-2000 × g for about 10 min). This general procedure, which is based on the assumption that the sedimentation characteristics of the subcellular particles of insect tissues are similar to those from mammalian liver, has proved satisfactory in many investigations although it has been established that buffering systems and centrifugation speeds must be varied from one insect to another and even between different tissues of the same insect [116]. Several investigators, however, have encountered more serious difficulties in achieving subcellular fractionation by this procedure.

Nakatsugawa and Dahm [62], employing a variety of centrifugal forces and times, found it impossible to obtain a clear separation between the microsomal parathion activating enzymes and cytochrome oxidase (employed as a biochemical marker for mitochondria) in fat body preparations from the American cockroach (Periplaneta americana). Centrifugation at 40-50,000 × g for 30 min was considered sufficient to sediment all the parathion activation activity and indeed a considerable amount could be brought down during short spins at forces as low as 1500 × g. A subsequent, more comprehensive investigation, which also included an electron microscopic examination of the fractions obtained [99,117], established that about 77% of the parathion activation activity in an American cockroach fat body homogenate could be recovered in a microsomal pellet sedimenting at 55,680 × g (45 min) from a mitochondrion free supernatant obtained by centrifuging at 650 × g (120 min). Attempts to change these sedimentation characteristics by incorporating a variety of buffers and other additives into the suspension medium failed and, indeed, it was found that if buffer was omitted entirely, the parathion activation enzymes were sedimented under force-time conditions as low as 340 × g for 10 min [99,117]. Similar, although not quite as dramatic, results were obtained by Price and Kuhr [100] working on the oxidative metabolism of carbaryl in homogenates and subcellular fractions of blowfly larva (Calliphora erythrocephala) fat body. These workers reported that the highest enzyme activity occurred in an intermediate pellet sedimenting at 30,000 × g (15 min) whether isolation took place in 0.15 M KCl or in 0.25 M sucrose (both unbuffered). The modifying effect of the suspension medium was clearly demonstrated by the fact that with KCl the next highest activity was in the mitochondrial fraction (10,000 × g, 16 min) and with sucrose in the microsomes (105,000 × g, 60 min). The particulate nature of the 30,000 × g pellet was not investigated but it was surmised to consist of "light" mitochondria and "heavy" microsomes.

Work in this laboratory has shown that when homogenates of cricket (Acheta domesticus) Malpighian tubules or Madagascar

cockroach (Gromphadorhina portentosa) gut-caeca tissues in 0.15 M
KCl or 0.25 M sucrose are subjected to differential centrifugation
almost all the microsomal epoxidation activity is sedimented during
a 15 min spin at 12,000 × g [78,81,95]. If, instead, the crude homogenates are layered on 1.6 M sucrose and centrifuged for 45 min at
150,000 × g in a swinging bucket rotor, two major protein fractions
are obtained, a dense pellet that sediments to the bottom of the tube
and a light protein band that remains at the sucrose-KCl interface.
Most of the epoxidation activity is associated with this latter fraction
and an electron microscopic investigation shows it to consist largely
of membranous vesicles probably derived from the endoplasmic reticulum [78,81,95].

The reasons for the apparently anomalous sedimentation characteristics of these fractions are not immediately obvious. It would
appear that under certain conditions the microsomal particles
can either clump together to form aggregates that subsequently be-
have as larger particles or that the vesicles become adsorbed or
otherwise attached to the surfaces of larger particles, such as mitochondria. It is also possible that some insect tissues contain adhesive
materials that tend to bind the particles together. Clearly, the suspension medium has an important effect on this behavior possibly by
modifying the physicochemical forces involved. A similar problem
has been encountered in microsomal enzyme studies with fetal rat
livers where the 9,000 × g pellet was found to contain both microsomal membranes and mitochondria and the 105,000 × g pellet was
comprised mainly of free ribosomes [118].

Whatever the cause of this phenomenon, it clearly emphasizes
the danger in assuming that similar centrifugal fractions from
different tissues of different organisms consist of the same subcellular particles. At the same time, it indicates that the preparatory procedures developed for the fractionation of microsomes from mammalian liver are not necessarily satisfactory for other mammalian
tissues or for the tissues of other organisms. This latter is of some
interest from a semantic viewpoint because the initial definition of
"microsome" as "the high speed pellet (from 100,000 to 200,000 × g
for 60-120 min) resulting when the supernatant fluid from the mitochondrial fraction is sedimented" [109] is based solely on the preparative technique of differential centrifugation. If, as seems the case,
this procedure is inappropriate with some insect tissues, the question is raised as to whether it is strictly correct to refer to insect
microsomes, or whether another definition should be employed that
is based more on the morphological character of the particles.

Not all types of studies on the drug-metabolizing enzymes in
insects require that microsomal suspensions be employed. Indeed,
in some cases, particularly in comparative studies where a measure

of the total enzyme activity is sought and where the speed of preparation and assay may be important, the use of less homogeneous fractions, such as the postmitochondrial supernatant, can provide valuable information and may be advantageous. The use of such fractions is also likely to be less dependent on the addition of cofactors than is the use of the microsomal fraction, and although these are now fairly well characterized, there are cases where unknown factors in the soluble fraction are required for microsomal activity [49,117]. The 10,000 × g supernatant of whole houseflies or housefly abdomina has been used with some success [49,66,68], as has a similar fraction from locust fat body homogenate [48,49]. Brattsten [46], working with pupal and adult fleshflies (Sarcophaga sp.) and blowflies (Phormia regina), employed a 60,000 × g supernatant for in vitro assays of epoxidation, N- and O-demethylation, and ring hydroxylation. Cruder fractions consisting of the 800-1000 × g (10 min) supernatant have been found a satisfactory enzyme source with various tissues of lepidopterous larvae [53,54,56,57] and several species of Orthoptera including the house cricket (Acheta domesticus) and the Madagascar cockroach (Gromphadorhina portentosa) [78,81,95].

As a consequence of the many problems referred to, the question arises as to what constitutes an acceptable unit on which to base measurements of microsomal enzyme activity in insects. This is of particular importance in all comparative investigations [11]. In mammalian studies, it is common practice to describe enzyme activity in terms of either specific activity (per milligram microsomal protein) or on the basis of the wet weight of tissue employed. Use of the latter is precluded in many insect preparations and although the specific activity can be measured, it has often little or no meaning in heterogeneous preparations, such as those from whole insects or whole body regions. Even when single organs are employed, the specific activity varies in a manner that reflects the method of preparation. Furthermore, because of the relatively broad tissue distribution patterns often found in insects, the specific MFO activity of a single tissue may have little relevance to the in vivo enzymic capability of the whole insect. Nor does specific activity take into account the relative masses of the different tissues on which their total enzyme activity ultimately depends. At the present time, it is probable that "enzyme units per insect" constitutes the most satisfactory unit on which to base measurements of MFO activity.

E. Storage Stability of Insect Microsomes

In contrast to liver microsomes, which can be stored under certain conditions for considerable periods of time without significant loss in drug metabolizing activity [110,119], the marked lability of most insect preparations is a serious practical problem that complicates in vitro biochemical investigations. Consequently, insect microsomes or other subcellular fractions must usually be used without delay following their preparation. Agosin et al. [27] reported that microsomal suspensions from whole German cockroaches lost all DDT metabolizing activity within 48-72 h of preparation when stored at 2°C in 0.15 M KCl and similar preparations from whole houseflies could not be stored for more than 47 h without serious loss of activity [31]. Although prior to homogenization whole houseflies can be satisfactorily stored at −15°C for periods of up to 3 months, and although detached abdomina retain activity when kept at room temperature for up to 2 h, a rapid fall in enzyme activity occurs immediately following homogenization [49, 67, 68]. The rate of decay is a function of the method of homogenization employed and increases in a manner proportional to the concentration of tissue in the homogenate [49, 68]; no significant difference was observed in the rate of loss at 0°C or 20°C. Decay of the enzyme could, however, be prevented by the addition of substrate and cofactors [49, 68], and the addition of BSA (1% w/v) or KCN (10^{-3} M) prior to incubation could reactivate the decayed enzyme. Hansen and Hodgson [58] reported that when microsomes from housefly abdomina were resuspended at a concentration of 30 flies/ml in Tris-HCl buffer (0.1 M, pH 7.9) containing 2% BSA they lost considerable activity when stored for 2 days at 0-4°C. Most of this loss occurred during the first 2 h of storage and was dependent on the molarity of the homogenization medium, being most marked when high ionic strength buffers were employed. In the presence of 1.5% BSA microsomes from housefly abdomina retained full activity when held for 5 h at below 5°C or at 20°C and with BSA no significant loss occurred after 1 month of frozen storage [64]. Activity was, however, rapidly lost in the absence of BSA.

Schonbrod and Terriere [31] established that although microsomes from whole houseflies lost enzymic activity when stored at 0°C in concentrated suspensions or frozen well-drained pellets, preparations stored at 0-4°C for periods of up to 1 month as dilute suspensions (3.5 mg protein/ml) in Tris-HCl buffer (pH 8.2) retained about 80% of their initial naphthalene hydroxylase activity and even exhibited an increase in activity during the first 7 days. In contrast, microsomes from the larval gut tissues of the silkworm (Antheraea pernyi) and the southern armyworm (Prodenia eridania) were more stable when stored at 0°C as a concentrated suspension (6 mg protein/ml) in 0.066 M phosphate buffer (pH 7.8) than in a more dilute form (1.5 mg protein/ml) and the preparations retained full activity for at least 4 weeks when held as frozen well-drained pellets at −15°C [53,101]. It is of interest that in spite of the changes that occurred in epoxidase, hydroxylase, and N-demethylase activities under these different storage conditions cytochrome P-450 levels were found to remain relatively constant.

In other studies Nakatsugawa and Dahm [62] were able to store cockroach (Periplaneta americana) fat body microsomes at −15°C for 1 week without any significant decrease in desulfuration activity (conditions unspecified) and at the same temperature microsomal suspensions of cricket (A. domesticus) Malpighian tubules in buffered (0.05 M Tris-HCl, pH 7.4) or unbuffered 0.25 M sucrose lost only 7-17% of their initial epoxidation activity for periods of up to 3 weeks [78,81].

It is likely that much of the lability that has been observed with insect microsomes is caused by artifacts, such as endogenous inhibitors in the preparations, and does not reflect any basic difference in the nature of the tissue. The establishment of suitable storage conditions will greatly facilitate biochemical investigations by allowing the accumulation of material when it is most readily available or when the insects are in a physiological condition of particular interest.

IV. PROPERTIES OF INSECT MICROSOMES

A. Morphological Characteristics

Subcellular fractions from homogenates of insect tissues have been defined almost solely in terms of their biochemical and enzymic properties and by direct analogy from studies with mammalian liver it is usually assumed that the fraction containing maximum MFO activity is the microsomal fraction. Thus, in spite of the often anomalous sedimentation behavior of insect microsomes surprisingly little attention has been given to investigating their ultrastructural characteristics and to determining whether indeed they have similar morphological properties to those described from mammalian liver [108,109].

Cassidy et al. [116] examined microsomal preparations from Musca domestica abdomina and Prodenia eridania gut and fat body by electron microscopy and found their structural components similar to those of smooth microsomes from mammalian liver [120]. These were membranous vesicles, broken membranes, and free ribosomes, although clusters of glycogen granules were observed in Prodenia gut preparations and both gut and fat body microsomes from this species contained microbial contaminants. Centrifugation at 10,000 × g for 15 min was sufficient to remove all mitochondria from the housefly preparation but to satisfactorily accomplish this with Prodenia gut tissues it was necessary to increase the preliminary

spin to 30,000 × g. In the housefly abdomen and Prodenia gut preparations, the fine structure of the membranes was retained but Prodenia
fat body microsomes prepared under similar conditions contained
disrupted vesicles and showed a general loss of structural integrity.
This became even more marked when potassium phosphate buffer
was substituted for Millonig's sodium phosphate-sucrose buffer and
it was concluded that both buffering systems and centrifugation speeds
must be varied among different insects and even among different tissues of the same insect. Unfortunately, this investigation tended to
overemphasize the importance of ultrastructural homogeneity of the
fractions and relied solely on NADPH oxidase as a biochemical
marker for microsomal enzyme activity. It was subsequently shown
[53] that microsomal fractions prepared from the 10,000 × g (15 min)
supernatant of homogenates of Prodenia gut tissues were composed
largely of smooth membrane fragments and vesicles and, in contrast
to the observations of Cassidy et al. [116], contained only minimal
numbers of mitochondria, microbes, or glycogen granules. It was,
however, observed that the homogenization medium had a profound
effect on the ultrastructure of the gut microsomes. Fractions prepared in 0.15 M KCl were generally heterogeneous and contained
irregularly shaped membrane fragments in a matrix of free ribosomal particles, whereas those prepared in 0.25 M sucrose-1 mM
EDTA appeared as smooth oval membrane vesicles and were almost
entirely free of ribosomal material. In spite of these obvious ultrastructural differences, the epoxidase, hydroxylase, and N-demethylase activities of these fractions were essentially identical. Subsequent studies using sucrose density gradient centrifugation confirmed
that MFO activity in Prodenia gut tissues was associated with a fraction composed mostly of smooth membrane vesicles [53].

Studies on the parathion activation enzymes in cockroach (Periplaneta americana) fat body established that 77% of the activity
could be sedimented by centrifugation at 55,680 × g for 45 min [117].
An electron microscopic examination of this fraction revealed that
although the lower part of the pellet contained significant numbers
of bacteria and mitochondria it was composed primarily of rough-
surfaced membrane fragments, probably derived from the rough-
surfaced endoplasmic reticulum of the fat body cells [117]. Glycogen
granules were evenly distributed throughout the pellet. In contrast
to the observations with M. domestica and P. eridania microsomes,
there was a notable absence of smooth membrane fragments, and in
view of the established association between MFO activity and the
smooth endoplasmic reticulum of mammalian liver [120-122], this
observation appears somewhat anomalous. It was, however, supported
by the fact that only rough-surfaced endoplasmic reticulum could be
identified with certainty in sections of intact fat body tissue [117].

An electron microscopic examination of fractions obtained by sucrose density centrifugation from cricket (A. domesticus) Malpighian tubules and cockroach (G. portentosa) gut-caeca tissues showed that in each case the fraction exhibiting most epoxidation activity contained membrane fragments and vesicles derived from both rough- and smooth-surfaced endoplasmic reticulum [78,81,95,123]. The fractions were essentially free from mitochondrial contamination.

Electron micrographs of sections of intact guts of P. eridania and G. portentosa show that the epithelial cells are richly endowed with microvilli that project into the lumen of the gut. These clearly provide an extensive surface area for absorption of materials from the alimentary tract and as there is evidence that the endoplasmic reticulum extends into these microvilli it is possible that they constitute important sites of MFO activity [78,95,123]. Sections of intact cricket (A. domesticus) malpighian tubules also show numerous microvilli extending into the lumen of the tubule, and again both rough- and smooth-surfaced endoplasmic reticulum are clearly visible in the cells [78].

From these few investigations it can be concluded that the MFO activity in subcellular fractions of insect tissues is associated with membrane particles derived from the endoplasmic reticulum of the cell and that these fragments and vesicles are quite similar in appearance to the microsomes from mammalian liver. No attempts have yet been made to separate the rough and smooth membrane particles from insect cells and because both types are usually present in active fractions it is not possible to conclude with any certainty whether MFO activity is associated more with one than the other.

B. Biochemical Characteristics

1. Reactions Catalyzed

During the last decade, it has been demonstrated that a large number of foreign compounds, including insecticides, drugs, and a variety of model substrates, are oxidatively metabolized by isolated microsomes or other subcellular fractions derived from insects. The nature and diversity of the reactions catalyzed clearly indicate that insect microsomes possess a similar degree of metabolic versatility and substrate nonspecificity as those from mammalian liver [1,2,5,124,125]. As shown in Table 1, the types of reactions effected by insect microsomes include the hydroxylation of aromatic and alicyclic rings, the hydroxylation of aliphatic side chains, the dealkylation of aromatic and cyclic ethers, the dealkylation of substituted amines, the epoxidation of double bonds, the oxi-

dation of thioethers, and the oxidation (desulfuration) of phosphoro-
thionates (P = S) to phosphates (P = O). With insecticidal compounds,
most of these constitute detoxication reactions but in some cases,
especially in the desulfuration of phosphorothionates, the reaction is
responsible for activating an intrinsically inactive material to one
that is highly toxic. In addition to these oxidative reactions, insect
microsomes also catalyze the reduction of aromatic nitro and azo
compounds and effect the hydration of epoxide rings.

Most of the studies in which these reactions have been demonstrated have been primarily concerned with establishing metabolic pathways and have employed insect microsomes mainly as biochemical tools for generating primary oxidative metabolites. The
success of these investigations is usually measured in terms of the
ability of the system to convert x to y and, consequently, in most
cases only minimal attention has been given to establishing optimum
incubation conditions or the essentiality of added cofactors. Few
in-depth studies have yet been directed toward more clearly defining
the biochemical characteristics of insect microsomes and the in vitro
conditions under which they can best be studied.

2. Incubation Conditions

The type, strength, and pH of the buffer employed in in vitro
assays with insect microsomes are important parameters that
should be evaluated. In most studies, either Tris or phosphate buffer
has been used and there is a general lack of agreement about which
is most satisfactory. Several investigators, using a variety of tissues,
have found that phosphate is better than Tris [56,115,129], whereas
others have either shown the opposite [31,79] or have found no
marked difference between the two [37,53,54]. It has recently been
established that if the ionic strength and pH are carefully controlled,
either Tris or phosphate provides an equally suitable medium for
incubations of housefly abdomina microsomes [14,58] and it is therefore probable that most of the reported variations reflect differences
in ionic strength rather than basic differences in the suitability of the
buffers per se.

The pH optima for a variety of reactions catalyzed by insect
microsomes appear to be characteristically higher than those observed with mammalian liver microsomes, although the curves are
often fairly broad. The hydroxylation of naphthalene [28,31] and
demethylation of Hempa [115] in housefly microsomes are optimal at
pH 7.8-8.0 and 8.0, respectively, and hydroxylation and N- and O-
dealkylation in microsomes from housefly abdomina all occur optimally between pH 7.7 and 8.1 [58]. Epoxidation in housefly abdomina
is highest at pH 7.8 [129] and maximum carbaryl hydroxylation activ-

TABLE 1

Reactions Catalyzed by Insect Microsomes[a]

Reaction Type and Substrate	Species	Tissue	Fraction	Reference
Hydroxylation (aromatic)				
naphthalene	housefly (A) (Musca domestica)	I	M	28-34, 40, 126
	housefly (A) (Musca domestica)	Abd	M	14, 127
	blowfly (A) (Phormia regina)	I	M	29
aniline	southern armyworm (L) (Prodenia eridania)	G	M	128
	M. domestica (A)	Abd	M	58, 129
carbaryl	cabbage looper (L) (Trichoplusia ni)	G, FB, MT, SG	800 S	56, 57
	P. regina (L)	FB	M	100
	M. domestica (A)	I	M	130
	M. domestica (A)	Abd	M	64, 65
biphenyl	M. domestica (A)	I, Abd	H, 10,000 S	49, 67, 68
	blowfly (A) (Lucilia sericata)	I, Abd	H, 10,000 S	68
Baygon	M. domestica (A)	Abd	H, M	64, 65, 130-133
Hydroxylation (alicyclic)				
dihydroaldrin	M. domestica (A)	I	M	36, 37
dihydroisodrin	P. eridania (L) + other lepidopterous larvae	G, FB, MT, Hd		53, 101, 102, 134

	house cricket (N, A) (Acheta domesticus)	MT, G, FB	2,000 S, M	78, 81
	Madagascar cockroach (N, A) (Gromphadorhina portentosa)	MT, G, FB, GC	2,000 S, M	78, 95
	sawfly (L) (Macremphytus varianus)	G	M	105
	honey bee (A, L) (Apis mellifera)	G, Hd, T	M	83
dihydrochlordene and related cyclodienes	M. domestica (A)	I	M	44
photoisodrin and photodieldrin	M. domestica (A)	Abd	M	128
rotenone	M. domestica (A)	Abd	M	65, 135, 136
	American cockroach (A) (Periplaneta americana)	FB	H	80, 136
Hydroxylation (aliphatic) hexobarbital	M. domestica (A)	Abd	M	129
p-nitrotoluene and other alkylbenzenes	M. domestica (A)	Abd	10,000 S	137
	locust (Schistocerca gregaria)	FB	H, 10,000 S	48, 49, 66, 137
DDT	M. domestica (A)	I	M	27, 138
	M. domestica (A)	Abd	H, M	65, 132, 139
	Triatoma infestans (L)	I	M	47
	German cockroach (A) (Blattella germanica)	I	M	27
	P. americana (A)	I	M	27
Landrin	M. domestica (A)	Abd	M	140

(continued)

TABLE 1 (continued)

Reaction Type and Substrate	Species	Tissue	Fraction	Reference
pyrethroids	M. domestica (A?)	Abd	H, M	141, 142
Epoxidation				
aldrin	M. domestica (A)	I	M	32, 35-41, 69, 71, 72, 143-145
	M. domestica (A)	Abd	H, M	14, 65, 129, 132, 69
	M. domestica (L and P)	I	M	39
	P. regina (A)	I	M	143
	P. regina (A)	I	60,000 S	46
	fleshflies (A) (Sarcophaga bullata and S. crassipalpis)	I	60,000 S	46
	caddisfly (L) (Limnephilus sp.)	G, FB	H	79
	corn earworm (L) (Heliothis zea) and 4 other species of lepidopterous larvae	I	M	50
	P. eridania (L)	I	M	52
	P. eridania (L) and approximately 40 other species of lepidopterous larvae	G, FB, MT	2000 S, M	53, 54, 75, 101, 102, 104, 128
	H. Zea (L) and polyphemus moth (L) (Antheraea polyphemus)	G, FB, MT	M	55
	A. domesticus (N, A)	G, FB, MT	2000 S, M	78, 81, 146
	G. portentosa (N, A)	G, FB, MT, GC	2000 S, M	78, 95
	P. americana (A)	G, FB, MT, GC	2000 S	78

Compound	Species	Tissue	Amount	Reference
2000	Tampa roach (A) (Nauphoeta cinerea)	G, FB, MT, GC	2000 S	78
	Colorado potato beetle (L, A) (Leptinotarsa decemlineata)	G, FB	M	106
	A. mellifera (L, A)	G, Hd, T	M	83
	M. varianus (L)	G	M	105
heptachlor	M. domestica (A)	I	H, M	39-43, 126, 145, 147
	M. domestica (A)	Abd	H	41
	P. americana (A)	FB	H	41
isodrin	M. domestica (A)	I	M	39,40
O-Dealkylation p-nitroanisole	M. domestica (A)	Abd	M	14, 58, 74, 127, 129, 148
	P. regina (A)	I	60,000 S	46
	S. bullata and S. crassipalpis (A, P)	I	60,000 S	46
	wax moth (L) (Galleria mellonella)	G	H	103
	P. eridania (L)	G	H	82
	A. mellifera (L, A)	G	M	83
methoxychlor	M. domestica (A)	Abd	M	129
Baygon	M. domestica (A)	Abd	H, M	64, 65, 131-133
N-Dealkylation p-nitrophenyl-N,N-dimethylcarbamate	M. domestica (A)	I	15,000 S, M	63

(continued)

TABLE 1 (continued)

Reaction Type and Substrate	Species	Tissue	Fraction	Reference
p-chloro-N-methylaniline	M. domestica (A)	Abd	M	14, 58, 127, 148
	P. eridania (L) and several other species of lepidopterous larvae	G, FB, MT	2000 S, M	53, 75, 82, 101, 102
	M. varianus (L)	G	M	105
	A. mellifera (L, A)	G	M	83
4-dimethylaminopyrene	P. regina (P, A)	I	60,000 S	46
	S. bullata and S. crassipalpis (P, A)	I	60,000 S	46
hempa	M. domestica (A)	Abd	9,000 S, M	115, 149
several insecticidal N-methyl carbamates	M. domestica (A)	Abd	H, M	64, 65, 131-133
N-Methyl hydroxylation several insecticidal N-methyl carbamates	M. domestica (A)	Abd	H, M	64, 65, 133
banol	cockroach (A) (Blaberus giganteus)	FB	M	97
Sulfoxidation Mesurol	M. domestica (A)	Abd	H, M	64, 65
Desulfuration schradan	S. gregaria (N)	FB	H, M	89, 94
Guthion	P. americana (A)	G, FB, MT, other tissues	H	85

Reaction/Substrate	Species			References
parathion	P. americana (A)	FB	M	62, 98, 99, 117, 150, 151
	rice stem borer (L) (Chilo suppressalis)	I	M	51
several phosphorothionates	M. domestica (A)	Abd	M	65, 132, 133, 152-154
Cyclic ether cleavage				
piperonyl butoxide and several other 1,3-benzodioxoles	M. domestica (A)	Abd	M	155-158
3,4,5,6-tetrachloro-1,3-benzodioxole	P. eridania (L)	G	H, M	128, 157
Organophosphate degradation (oxidative ester cleavage)				
parathion, diazinon and other phosphorothionates	M. domestica (A)	Abd	M	98, 148, 150, 154
	P. americana (A)	FB	M	150, 151
EPN	G. mellonella (L)	G	M	103
propylparaoxon	M. domestica (A)	Abd	M	98
paraoxon and diazoxon	M. Domestica (A)	Abd	M	148, 152-154, 159
Reduction				
nitrobenzene	M. domestica (A)	I	M	160
	P. eridania (L)	G	M	160
	G. portentosa (A)	G, FB, MT, GC	H, M	160
p-nitrobenzoic acid	G. portentosa (A)	G	M	160
neoprontosil	G. portentosa (A)	G	M	160

TABLE 1 (continued)

Reaction Type and Substrate	Species	Tissue	Fraction	Reference
CPA (1,2-dimethyl-4- (p-carboxyphenylazo)- 5-hydroxybenzene)	G. portentosa (A)	G	H	161
Epoxide hydration several cyclodiene epoxides	M. domestica (A)	I	M	162

[a]Abbreviations employed: A, adult; abd, abdomen; FB, fat body; G, gut; GC, gastric caeca; H, homogenate; Hd, head; I, whole insect; L, larva; M, microsomes; MT, Malpighian tubules; N, nymph; P, pupa; S, supernatant (g force indicated); SG, silk gland; T, testis.

ity in fat body microsomes of the blowfly larva (C. erythrocephala) occurs at pH 8.0 [100]. In some cases, the optima appear quite high. Thus, for DDT hydroxylation in microsomes from the German cockroach (B. germanica), the housefly, and T. infestans, the pH optima are 8.5-8.8, 8.5, and 9.0, respectively [27,47,138] and the pH curves for epoxidation and hydroxylation in housefly microsomes indicate that although maximum activity is observed at pH 8.0-8.2, only a slight decrease in activity occurs up to pH values as high as 10.0 [35, 37]. Similar pH profiles have recently been reported for epoxidation in tissues of a caddisfly larva (Limnephilus sp.) [79]. In other insect species, pH optima are somewhat lower, being 7.0-7.5 for desulfuration in cockroach (P. americana) fat body [62,151] and 7.4 and 7.6-7.8 for both epoxidation and hydroxylation in preparations from cricket (A. domesticus) Malpighian tubules and Madagascar cockroach (G. portentosa) gut-caeca, respectively [78,81]. Epoxidation, hydroxylation, and N-demethylation in gut microsomes from P. eridania and epoxidase activity in the gut tissues of 12 other species of lepidopterous larvae occurred optimally at pH 7.8 [53,54,102]. In gut preparations from the cabbage looper (T. ni), however, epoxidation [53] and carbaryl hydroxylation [56,57] activities are optimal at pH 6.9, although maximum hydroxylation activity in fat body homogenates is obtained at pH 7.8-8.2 [56,57]. This clearly demonstrates that optimal in vitro assay conditions can vary even between different tissues of the same insect species.

Most of these studies indicate that with any particular enzyme source the pH optima for different microsomal reactions are quite similar. This is not always true, however, as in microsomes from whole blowflies (P. regina) and fleshflies (Sarcophaga sp.) O-demethylation and epoxidation activities are highest at pH 7.7-8.1 whereas N-demethylation and ring hydroxylation are maximal at pH 7.0-7.5 [46].

The temperature at which assays are conducted can also have a marked effect on enzyme lability and, consequently, on in vitro activity, and in view of the fact that insects are poikilothermic organisms, there is little reason to assume that their enzymes, like those of mammals, function optimally at 37°C [11]. Based on this assumption, most of the early studies with insect microsomes were conducted at 37°C [27,48,89,94]. Subsequent investigations have established that although this temperature may be satisfactory in a few cases, the enzymes in most insect tissues exhibit maximum in vitro activity at somewhat lower temperatures. Housefly microsomes are reported to function optimally at 34°C for naphthalene hydroxylation [28] and at 37°C for DDT hydroxylation [138], although microsomes from housefly abdomina exhibit maximum hydroxylation and N- and O-dealkylation activity between 30° and 33°C [14, 58]; this is in agreement with an earlier report that preparations from housefly abdomina are more stable on incubation at 30°C than at 37°C [65]. Epoxidation, hydroxylation, and N-demethylation in microsomes from whole blowflies (P. regina) and fleshflies (Sarcophaga sp.) are found to be greatest at 30°C [46] as is DDT hydroxylation in T. infestans microsomes [47]. The enzymes in cockroach (B. giganteus) fat body are most active at 35°C [97] and epoxidation and hydroxylation in preparations from cricket (A. domesticus) Malpighian tubules occur optimally at 30°-35°C [78, 81]. The latter temperature range is also optimal for oxidase activity in gut microsomes from larvae of P. eridania [53] although fat body preparations from another lepidopterous larva, the cabbage looper (T. ni), metabolize carbaryl best over the considerably lower range of 20°-25°C [56, 57]. A recent report indicates that aldrin epoxidase in gut and fat body preparations from a caddisfly larva (Limnephilus sp.) also exhibits a low temperature optimum (20°-25°C) and has marked lability above 30°C [79]. With this species, considerable activity is retained at temperatures as low as 10°C, and in view of the fact that the larva is aquatic, it is interesting to speculate on a possible relationship between the low enzyme temperature optimum and the low ambient temperature of the insect's natural habitat. This relationship has been established in fish [3, 19, 163] and other aquatic vertebrates [164].

Because of the presence of endogenous inhibitors in many insect preparations (Section III.B), the incorporation of BSA (1-2% w/v) in the incubation medium often increases the activity observed [35,50, 53, 58, 64, 65, 67, 68, 115, 129, 132, 133, 148]. As previously discussed (Section III.B), BSA probably serves as an alternative protein substrate for proteolytic enzymes, although it may also bind unsaturated fatty acids [165], which are potential inhibitors of MFO activity [166, 167]. The use of BSA, however, must be approached with some caution because its effects are not clearly understood. If it is employed in excess, it can result in a decrease in enzyme activity [58], possibly by binding lipophilic substrates and consequently limiting their availability at the active site. In some cases, BSA stimulates MFO activity in the absence of endogenous inhibitors [53] and as this is particularly marked at low concentrations of enzyme protein it may result from an enhanced solubilization of the substrate [168]. Each of these effects is likely to change both the K_m and V_{max} of the reaction [127] and consequently may markedly modify the results obtained. Furthermore, the presence of a variety of added proteins in the incubation medium can cause an apparent change in enzyme activity by reducing the efficiency of product extraction [68].

3. Effects of Cofactors, Metal Ions, and Other Materials

In attempts to improve the in vitro activity of insect preparations and to further characterize the enzymes involved, several studies have been made on cofactor and other requirements. Although these are not always strictly comparable because of differences in the tissue source and subcellular fraction employed and variations in the methods of preparation and incubation, some fairly typical data are shown in Table 2.

TABLE 2

Effect of Cofactors and Other Materials
on in Vitro Microsomal Enzyme Activity in Insect Preparations

Incubation medium	Percent Activity[a]				
	A	B	C	D	E
Complete[b]	100	100	100	100	100
Minus NADPH[c]	1	18	6.4	41	70.7
Minus NADPH[c] plus NADH[c]	4	51	—	47	65.3
Plus FAD (10^{-3} M)	107	89	—	58	73.7
Plus FMN (10^{-3} M)	88	77	—	56	59.3
Plus EDTA (10^{-3} M)	112	106	93.6	99	96.6
Plus nicotinamide (10^{-3} M)	100	93	86.2	89	55.7
Plus glutathione (10^{-3} M)	100	99	—	—	99.5
Plus KCN (10^{-3} M)	—	—	124	—	92.3
Minus O_2	4	26	9.9	—	20.5

[a]A, epoxidation in P. eridania gut microsomes [53, 54]; B, epoxidation in A. domesticus Malpighian tubule microsomes [78, 81]; C, carbaryl metabolism in whole M. domestica microsomes [130]; D, epoxidation in G. portentosa caeca microsomes [78, 95]; E, carbaryl metabolism in T. ni fat body homogenates [56].

[b]Complete incubation media contained either Tris-HCl or phosphate buffer (5.0 × 10^{-2} M); G6-P (2.4 × 10^{-3} M); G6-PDH (1-2 units); NADP (0.5-1.0 × 10^{-4} M) or NADPH (10^{-4} M) and the appropriate enzyme preparation.

[c]Cofactor added directly or produced by appropriate generating system.

There is general agreement that MFO activity is dependent on NADPH. It appears to make little difference whether this is added directly to the incubations or produced in situ by a suitable generating system [58], although experience in this laboratory suggests that the time linearity of the reaction is extended when a generating system is employed. Because crude homogenates of insect tissues apparently often contain quite high endogenous levels of glucose 6-phosphate dehydrogenase (G6-PDH), its addition may not always be required for the G6-P/G6-PDH/NADP generating system. The extent to which

NADH can satisfy the enzymic requirements appears to vary with the
tissue source employed and the reaction under consideration. Column
A of Table 2 indicates that for epoxidation in P. eridania gut microsomes the requirement for NADPH is quite rigid and cannot be satis-
fied by NADH [53, 54]. This is also true for DDT hydroxylation in B.
germanica microsomes [27], epoxidation of aldrin in whole lepidopterous larvae [50], schradan activation in locust fat body [89], and
banol metabolism in microsomes from B. giganteus fat body [97]. In
the latter, however, NADH is observed to stimulate activity in the
presence of subminimal concentrations of NADPH, a phenomenon
similar to that sometimes observed in mammalian liver microsomes
[169]. In contrast, NADH (1.7 μM) was found to inhibit naphthalene
hydroxylation in microsomes from whole blowflies [29]. Most studies
indicate that NADH can partially (40-60%) support enzyme activity
(Table 2, columns B-E) [56, 57, 62, 65, 78, 81, 85, 95] although the
hydroxylation of DDT in microsomes from T. infestans nymphs is
reported to occur equally well in the presence of either NADPH or
NADH [47]. The mechanism by which NADH can transfer reducing
equivalents to cytochrome P-450 is not yet understood, and the presence of transhydrogenases and NADP in crude insect preparations
cannot be discounted.

In addition to the requirement of NADPH, oxygen is also found to
be necessary for optimum in vitro enzyme activity [27, 28, 53, 54,
56, 57, 62, 78, 81, 83, 95, 97, 130]. The extent by which activity is
reduced under anaerobic conditions appears to vary considerably
(Table 2) but it is probable that much of this variation results from
incomplete removal of oxygen from the incubation medium or from
the presence of traces of oxygen in the nitrogen usually employed in
such studies. The need for both NADPH and O_2 strongly suggests that
the microsomal enzymes in insects are indeed mixed function oxidases according to the definition proposed by Mason [170] but this
has not yet been unequivocally established by the use of $^{18}O_2$.

The addition to insect microsomes of FMN or FAD is found to have
either no effect or to inhibit oxidase activity (Table 2) [53,54,56,57,
78, 81, 95, 130] and the inhibition of MFO activity in housefly microsomes resulting from illumination of the incubations has been attributed to the presence of free flavins in the preparations [170,171]. Removal of these by repeated washing reduced the light sensitivity as
did the addition of potassium iodide, a fluorescence quencher. In addition, it was shown that the illumination of housefly and mammalian
liver microsomes containing free riboflavin decreased the level of
P-450 and reduced the rate of insecticide metabolism [170,171].

Nicotinamide, which is often added to mammalian liver microsomes to prevent NADPH degradation by pyridine nucleotidases [172],
has no stimulatory effect on insect preparations [29,48,53,54,66,

89] and often results in some inhibition [56, 57, 78, 81, 95, 130]. The one exception to this appears to be DDT hydroxylation in microsomes from T. infestans nymphs, which is reported to have an absolute requirement for nicotinamide [47].

In mammalian liver microsomes, an active NADPH-requiring lipid peroxidation system sometimes competes with drug and insecticide oxidation and can be effectively blocked with EDTA, antioxidants, Mn^{2+}, and Co^{2+} [38]. Lipid peroxidation cannot be detected in housefly microsomes [38] and the failure of EDTA to cause any marked stimulation of MFO activity in preparations from other species [53, 54, 56, 57, 78, 81, 83, 130] suggests that this reaction is of only minor consequence in insects.

The effects of several metal ions have been evaluated on the oxidative activity of insect microsomes but no consistent requirements have been observed. In some cases, the addition of Mg^{2+} to mammalian liver microsomes has been reported to increase drug metabolizing activity [172, 173, 174], possibly through its interaction with a heat-stable activating factor in the preparations. Therefore, magnesium is often added to insect preparations and, although it sometimes enhances MFO activity [27, 29, 47, 58, 89, 100], it is more usually found to have no marked effect [53, 54, 56, 57, 78, 81, 83, 97] and may cause inhibition at high concentrations [58, 100]. Some metal ions, including Cu^{2+}, Cu^+, and Zn^{2+}, are potent inhibitors of insect microsomal enzymes [53, 54, 56, 57, 78, 81], whereas most are found to have little or no effect on in vitro activity.

4. Inhibitors

The inhibition of microsomal enzyme activity is probably the only aspect of drug metabolism that has received more attention in insects than in mammals to date. This stems from the fact that materials that inhibit MFO activity have the potential to act as insecticide synergists in vivo and thereby enhance the insecticidal potency of a variety of materials with which they are combined. The practical advantages to be gained from the use of such materials in insect control programs are obvious, and considerable commercial interest in the development of new insecticide synergists has stimulated a great deal of research in this area. A comprehensive discussion of the vast amount of data on synergism and MFO inhibition would be out of context here, and because these subjects have been discussed at some length in several recent reviews [158, 171, 175, 176], they will be given only brief consideration.

Structures of some of the major groups of materials that have been investigated are shown in Fig. 2. These include the 1,3-benzodioxoles (Fig. 2a), the aryloxyalkylamines, such as SKF 525-A (Fig. 2b), and

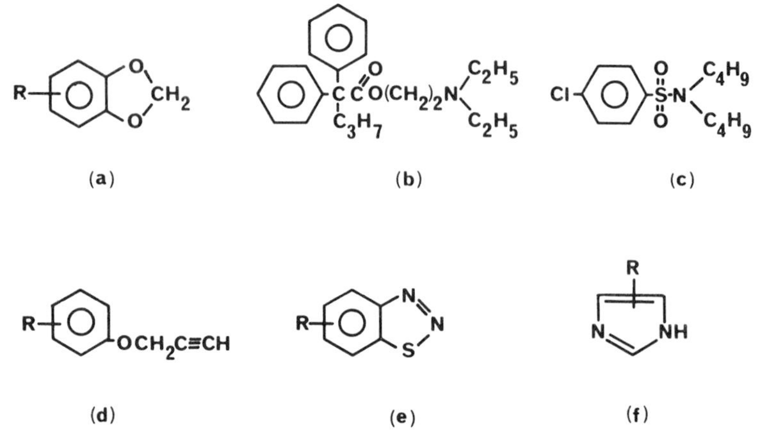

(a)   (b)   (c)

(d)   (e)   (f)

FIG. 2. Inhibitors of microsomal oxidation. (a) 1,3-benzodioxole; (b) SKF 525-A; (c) WARF antiresistant; (d) aryl-2-propynyl ether; (e) 1,2,3-benzothiadiazole; (f) 1- or 4(5)-arylimidazole.

other N-alkyl compounds, such as WARF antiresistant (Fig. 2c), the aryl-2-propynyl ethers (Fig. 2d), the 1,2,3-benzothiadiazoles (Fig. 2e), and the 1- and 4(5)-arylimidazoles (Fig. 2f). Compounds representing each of these groups can effectively synergize the toxicity of a variety of insecticides to insects and it is now well established that this results from their ability to inhibit the microsomal enzymes responsible for insecticide detoxication [12, 158, 171, 175, 176].

The 1,3-benzodioxoles are the most extensively investigated materials and a large number of these have been evaluated as in vitro inhibitors of a variety of reactions catalyzed by insect microsomes. Compounds studied range from natural products, such as safrole and isosafrole [30, 56, 57], to the more complex synthetic materials piperonyl butoxide [30, 56, 57, 62, 80, 97, 115, 127, 131, 133, 137], sesamex [30, 35-38, 44, 45, 62, 79, 97, 115, 127, 129, 177, 178], sulfoxide [30, 62, 80, 127, 137], propyl isome [30, 62, 137], and Tropital [115]. Indeed, almost any material possessing the 1,3-benzodioxole nucleus is an effective MFO inhibitor in vitro and in recent years many more simply substituted compounds have been employed in inhibition studies [30, 38, 53, 54, 78, 81, 100, 128]. The 1,3-benzodioxoles are general microsomal enzyme inhibitors, although the degree of inhibition observed often varies considerably with the reaction being studied [127] and the insect preparation employed (Table 3). It is somewhat surprising that this group of materials has not been more widely employed in inhibition studies with mammalian liver microsomes. In general, the latter are found to be 10-100 times

TABLE 3

Inhibitory Activity of Selected Materials on Microsomal Oxidation in Insects

Inhibitor	I_{50} Molar Concentration[a]			
	A	B	C	D
Piperonyl butoxide	3×10^{-5}		1.8×10^{-5}	
Sesamex	5.5×10^{-5}	8×10^{-4}		3.2×10^{-5}
5,6-Dichloro-1,3-benzodioxole		4.8×10^{-6}	6.6×10^{-6}	3.3×10^{-4}
SKF 525-A	3.5×10^{-3}	6×10^{-4}	1.3×10^{-5}	1.4×10^{-5}
2,4,5-Trichlorophenyl 2-propynyl ether			1.6×10^{-6}	
5,6-Dichloro-1,2,3-benzothiadiazole			5.7×10^{-6}	1.6×10^{-5}
Metyrapone		1.1×10^{-6}		
1-Phenylimidazole			3.4×10^{-6}	

[a] A, Naphthalene hydroxylation in whole housefly microsomes [30]; B, expoxidation in whole housefly microsomes [37, 38]; C, epoxidation in P. eridania gut microsomes [54, 191, 192]; D, epoxidation in A. domesticus microsomes [78, 81].

less susceptible to inhibition by the 1,3-benzodioxoles [37, 38, 158, 171] but it is not yet clear whether this indicates a basic difference at the enzyme level or whether it is artifactual.

Despite the accumulation of a considerable amount of information on the inhibitory properties of the 1,3-benzodioxoles, the exact mechanism by which these materials interact with the microsomal enzyme system remains a matter for some speculation [158, 171, 175, 176].

It is now well established that the 1,3-benzodioxoles are themselves metabolized to the corresponding catechols by the microsomal enzymes [128, 155-158] and as a consequence of this it has been suggested that they act competitively as oxidizable alternative substrates. This mechanism is supported by some kinetic analyses that indicate competitive inhibition [30, 127, 176, 179] but the type of inhibition appears to vary with the substrate and the inhibitor and, in some cases, even with the inhibitor concentration [127, 179, 180]. The fact that curved Lineweaver-Burk plots are sometimes obtained [35, 38] makes the interpretation of kinetic data extremely difficult. Alternative substrate inhibition is characterized by the fact that the Michaelis constant (K_m) of the compound when employed as a substrate is the same as its inhibition constant (K_i) when serving as an inhibitor [181, 182]. Measurements of this type have not yet been made with the 1,3-benzodioxoles, and although it is likely that some inhibition results from the alternative substrate mechanism, it seems equally probable that other factors are involved. Hennessy [183, 184] has suggested that inhibition could result from hydride-ion transfer from the methylene group of the ring and proposed that the electrophilic benzodioxolium ion thus formed could interact by ligand displacement or addition at the hemochrome of cytochrome P-450. More recently, Hansch [185] has suggested the possible involvement of homolytic free radicals in the inhibitory mechanism and this has received some support from the finding that the 1,3-benzodioxoles can interact with certain nonenzymic free-radical generating systems [62, 175, 186, 187]. The ability of piperonyl butoxide to bind to reduced cytochrome P-450 to produce a difference spectrum similar to that obtained with ethyl isocyanide [188] (see Section IV.C.1) may also be associated with the mode of action of the 1,3-benzodioxoles and it is possible that the inhibitory activity of these materials results from a combination of two or more different mechanisms.

SKF 525-A, which is widely used as an inhibitor of the drug metabolizing enzymes in hepatic microsomes [189], also inhibits the microsomal enzymes from insects [30, 37, 38, 54, 78-81, 115, 127], although in some cases rather high concentrations are required [30, 127]. Kinetic analyses indicate that the inhibition of naphthalene hydroxylation and p-nitroanisole demethylation in housefly abdomina microsomes is almost competitive but plots of $1/v$ versus $[I]$ are nonlinear

[127]. Curved Lineweaver-Burk plots were obtained in a study of SKF 525-A inhibition of aldrin epoxidation in microsomes from whole lepidopterous larvae [50]. SKF 525-A appears to act mainly as an alternative substrate in hepatic microsomes [182, 189] but the situation is complicated by the fact that it is metabolized to at least one product which is a more potent inhibitor [190] and that it appears to bind irreversibly to the type I site but not the type II site [189]. Preincubation of SKF 525-A with housefly abdomina microsomes enhanced the inhibition of O-demethylation [127] and may indicate metabolism to a more potent inhibitor. Two other N-alkyl compounds, MGK 264 and WARF antiresistant, have also been shown to be effective inhibitors of insect microsomes [62, 80] and the latter material is competitive with respect to the parathion activation enzymes from P. americana fat body [62].

Most of the other groups of compounds shown in Fig. 2 have not yet been extensively studied in vitro, although the data available suggest that they are general inhibitors of MFO activity. The aryl-2-propynyl ethers have been shown to inhibit oxidase activity in microsomes from A. domesticus Malpighian tubules [78, 81] and P. eridania gut [191] (Table 3) and a recent study has established that a large series of 1,2,3-benzothiadiazoles are inhibitors of epoxidation and hydroxylation in both insect and hepatic microsomes [192]. Both of these groups of materials are effective synergists for several insecticides [193, 194]. More recently, several series of 1- and 4(5)-phenylimidazoles have been found to be extremely potent inhibitors of MFO activity in P. eridania gut and rat liver microsomes with I_{50} values as low as 10^{-8} M [191, 195]. Inhibitors of steroid hydroxylation in mammals, including Metyrapone and some related substituted pyridines, are also effective inhibitors of epoxidation and hydroxylation in housefly microsomes [37, 171]. Other materials reported to inhibit insect microsomes include p-chloromercuribenzoate [89] and p-chloromercuriphenyl sulfonate [127], α,α'-dipyridyl [85, 89], 2,4-dinitrophenol [89, 100], and a variety of electron acceptors, such as neotetrazolium and Methylene Blue [71, 72].

Competitive inhibition is observed in insect microsomes when the effect of one substrate on the metabolism of another is studied. Thus, the epoxidation of aldrin by housefly microsomes is competitively inhibited by dihydroaldrin [36, 37] and γ-hexachlorocyclohexane [37] and the hydroxylation of dihydroaldrin is similarly inhibited by dieldrin and γ-hexachlorocyclohexane [37]. It is of interest that neither of the two latter materials are metabolized by the microsomal enzymes and consequently cannot be classified as substrates. Because of their lipophilic character, however, they are clearly bound either at or close to the active site of the microsomes in a manner that precludes the binding of and subsequent metabolism of oxidizable substrates. Competitive inhibition of aldrin epoxidation by p-nitroanisole, hexobarbital, and naphthalene is also observed in housefly microsomes and the sum total of the epoxides produced from combinations of two or three epoxidizable substrates is approximately equal to that formed when only one is employed [40, 129].

5. NADPH Oxidation and Oxygen Consumption

Although both NADPH and oxygen are required for optimal activity in insect microsomes (Section IV.B.3), few studies have been conducted to determine the rate at which these materials are consumed and to investigate whether any stoichiometric relationship exists between NADPH oxidation, oxygen consumption, and the amount of substrate metabolized. Stoichiometric relationships of this type have in some cases been demonstrated in hepatic microsomes [196, 197] but are often difficult to obtain because of the presence of enzymes, lipids, and other endogenous materials that consume NADPH and oxygen in the absence of any exogenous substrate [198]. This problem is also encountered in the few insect preparations that have been investigated. In microsomes from housefly abdomina, NADPH and NADH are both rapidly oxidized in the absence of any substrate, and the fact that NADPH oxidation is markedly reduced by CO indicates that much of this activity is mediated through cytochrome P-450 [199]. The K_m values for NADPH and NADH are 1.8×10^{-5} M and 1.6×10^{-4} M, respectively [199]. NADPH oxidation was inhibited by each of nine sulfhydryl inhibitors, p-chloromercuriphenyl sulfonate being the most effective [199]. In contrast to hepatic microsomes, where type I substrates are reported to enhance and type II substrates to reduce the rate of NADPH oxidation [200], the addition of phenobarbital, pyridine, SKF 525-A, sulfoxide, and MGK 264 to the housefly preparations all decreased NADPH oxidation and aniline caused a slight stimulation [199]. These results are difficult to interpret, although one possibility is that endogenous NADPH oxidation is substantially inhibited in the presence of an exogenous substrate and that in the in vitro situation the substrate-dependent NADPH oxidation is actually less than the level of endogenous activity.

The rate of oxygen consumption by microsomal preparations from housefly abdomina is dependent on the concentrations of NADPH and enzyme, and the effects of various substrates and inhibitors are similar to those observed for NADPH oxidation [201]. Both oxygen uptake and NADPH oxidation are inhibited by treating the housefly microsomes with sodium cholate, sodium deoxycholate, proteinases, snake venoms, and phospholipases A and C [202].

C. Microsomal Electron Transport

Of central importance in the microsomal oxidation of foreign compounds in mammalian liver is an electron transport pathway that
transfers electrons or reducing equivalents through a series of redox
components from NADPH to cytochrome P-450 [169, 203-206]. The
latter constitutes the terminal oxidase of the microsomal electron
transport chain and it is at the heme moiety of this cytochrome that
molecular oxygen is bound, activated, and ultimately incorporated
into the drug or insecticide substrate. Although full details of the
electron transport chain remain to be elucidated, a somewhat simpli-
fied and generally accepted scheme is shown in Fig. 3. This indicates

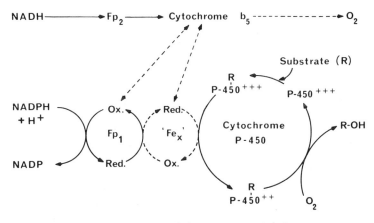

FIG. 3. Microsomal electron transport chain.

that the foreign compound first forms a complex with the oxidized
form of P-450, which is then reduced by the flow of electrons from
NADPH. The reduced P-450 substrate complex subsequently combines with molecular oxygen and the resulting complex rapidly breaks
up to give the oxidized substrate and water and, at the same time,
regenerates oxidized P-450 for further substrate binding. A flavoprotein (Fp_1), NADPH-cytochrome c reductase, is the major intermediate between NADPH and P-450 [204, 207] and, although there is
some evidence suggesting another component Fe_x between the flavoprotein and P-450 [208, 209], it now seems likely that the flavoprotein
can reduce P-450 directly [210]. Considerable controversy exists
regarding the physiological significance in drug metabolism of another
redox pathway that transfers electrons from NADH to cytochrome b_5

via a flavoprotein, NADH-cytochrome b_5 reductase (Fp_2) [211, 212].
It is possible that through a process of electron crossover (Fig. 3)
this pathway may provide some reducing equivalents for P-450 [169]
although it has been suggested that it may play a more direct role in
the oxidative desaturation of fatty acids [213] or in the reduction of
ascorbate [214].

1. Cytochrome P-450

The presence of a CO-binding pigment in mammalian liver microsomes was first recognized in 1958 [215, 216]. The pigment was subsequently characterized as a b-type cytochrome and because in its
reduced form it combines with CO to form a complex with an absorption maximum at 450 nm it was designated cytochrome P-450 [217,
218]. It is now well established that this cytochrome constitutes the
site of oxygen activation [203, 206, 219, 220] and of substrate interaction in the oxidative metabolism of foreign compounds by liver
microsomes. Treatment of microsomes with a variety of reagents
causes a change in the spectral properties of the CO complex and the
absorption maximum shifts from 450 to 420 nm. Although the peak at
420 nm is more typical of b-type cytochromes, the so-called cytochrome P-420 is catalytically inactive and its formation probably
results from a change of conformation on the microsomal membrane.

The first reports of a similar CO-binding pigment in insect microsomes were those of Ray [35, 221], who worked with preparations
from whole houseflies, M. vicina, and cockroaches, B. germanica
and P. americana. The difference spectrum obtained by passing CO
through a suspension of NADPH or dithionite-reduced housefly microsomes showed a sharp peak at 450 nm [35] that was rapidly converted
to cytochrome P-420 on standing or following treatment with deoxycholate. Subsequent investigations have confirmed the presence of
cytochrome P-450 in microsomes from whole houseflies [34, 130]
and housefly abdomina [14, 111, 113, 114, 148, 222] and have established its existence in preparations from blowfly larva (C. erythrocephala) fat body [100], cockroach (P. americana) gut and fat body
[80], cockroach (G. portentosa) tissues [78], cricket (A. domesticus)
Malpighian tubules [78], and several species of whole lepidopterous
larvae [50] and larval tissues [53, 56, 57, 101, 102]. Insect microsomes typically exhibit a greater contamination with cytochrome
P-420 than do those from mammalian liver, and it is likely that this
and the generally greater instability of insect cytochrome P-450 is
associated with the method of preparation employed and/or the presence of endogenous inhibitors [111]. Some investigators have encountered problems in measuring cytochrome P-450 in microsomes from
whole houseflies and have reported CO-difference spectra with a

trough at 440-445 nm and a peak at about 420-430 nm [34, 113]. It is probable that these anomalous spectra result from the presence of cytochrome oxidase in the preparations [111] and can be obviated by the use of milder homogenization techniques [34] that minimize mitochondrial rupture.

Quantitative measurements of cytochrome P-450 have been made in several insect preparations and the concentrations reported vary considerably, ranging from 0.004-0.034 nmoles/mg protein in various microsomes from tissues of the cockroach (G. portentosa) [78] to 1.48 nmoles/mg protein in those from P. eridaniá gut [53,101]. More typically, values lie within the range 0.2-0.5 nmoles/mg protein [34, 35], or approximately one fifth those reported for mammalian liver microsomes [210]. Such measurements have little meaning, however, as all are calculated on the basis of the single extinction coefficient of 91 cm^{-1} mM^{-1} reported for the cytochrome P-450 from rabbit liver microsomes [218]. Because there is now considerable evidence for the existence of more than one type of P-450 in mammalian liver microsomes [223, 224], the validity of using this extinction coefficient even in mammals is open to serious question and its application to insects must be considered as nothing more than an academic exercise. The quantitative assessment of cytochrome P-450 in insect microsomes will have to await its solubilization and detailed physicochemical characterization; at the present time, measurements of ΔOD/mg protein are more appropriate. Unfortunately, the treatment of housefly microsomes with many enzymes and reagents known to solubilize particulate enzymes often leads to a rapid conversion of cytochrome P-450 to P-420 [202]. This is true when sodium cholate, trypsin, Russell's viper venom (containing phospholipase A), and phospholipase A are used, although sodium deoxycholate, subtilisin (purified Bacillus subtilis protease), Crotalus venom, and phospholipase C were found to have no effect [202].

The direct involvement of cytochrome P-450 in microsomal oxidation in insects is indicated by the marked inhibition of enzyme activity by CO [35, 53, 56, 57, 78, 79, 81, 105, 115, 130]. In housefly microsomes, the CO inhibition of aldrin epoxidation [35] and carbaryl hydroxylation [130] was reversed by light by only 12 and 7%, respectively, but these apparently low levels of reversal may be caused partially by the inhibition of MFO activity observed following illumination of the microsomes with light in the 400-500 nm waveband (Section IV.B.3). The fact that insects are not dependent on hemoglobin for oxygen transport and will therefore survive in an atmosphere of oxygen and CO enabled Lewis [225] to demonstrate the in vivo inhibition of epoxidation by CO in houseflies. Similarly, houseflies kept in an atmosphere of 40% CO, 20% O_2, and 40% N_2 showed a 15-fold greater susceptibility to carbaryl than those maintained in

air, indicating the reduced ability of the flies to hydroxylate this
material in the presence of CO.

An association between cytochrome P-450 and MFO activity is
also evident from the results of studies on the patterns of enzyme
distribution in insect tissues [53, 78, 102] as well as those concerned
with variations in MFO activity with age and stage of development
[53, 78, 102, 113]. It is clear, however, that no quantitative relationship exists between the level of cytochrome P-450 and the rate of
microsomal metabolism. This has been demonstrated in comparisons
between strains of insecticide-resistant and -susceptible houseflies
[113, 148, 222] among which the strain differences in enzyme activity
are usually considerably greater than the differences in P-450 levels.
That factors other than the level of cytochrome P-450 are rate limiting on enzyme activity is also suggested by the results of microsomal
storage experiments [53,78,101] in which, under certain conditions,
MFO activity is observed to decrease and cytochrome P-450 levels
remain relatively constant. Such results clearly indicate that the level
of P-450 does not constitute a good quantitative index of MFO activity.

The spectral binding characteristics of several ligands other than
CO have also been studied in microsomes from housefly abdomina
[111, 222]. The n-octylamine-P-450 difference spectrum in microsomes from susceptible houseflies is similar to that reported with
normal rabbit microsomes [224], having an absorption peak at 432
nm and troughs at 410 and 394 nm [111]. In resistant flies, however,
the peaks are shifted slightly (maximum at 429 nm, minimum at 390
nm) and approach the spectrum obtained with microsomes from rabbits treated with 3-methylcholanthrene [224]. As in mammalian liver
microsomes [226], ethyl isocyanide combines with cytochrome P-450
in housefly abdomina microsomes to produce a difference spectrum
exhibiting double soret peaks at 455 and 430 nm [111, 222]. These are
in pH-dependent equilibrium and the equilibrium point is below pH
7.5 in preparations from susceptible houseflies [111]. In microsomes
from some insecticide-resistant strains of flies, however, the equilibrium point appears to be at a higher pH, as despite some probable
interference from the ethyl isocyanide-P-420 complex (absorption
maximum 433 nm) the 430 nm peak is considerably greater than that
occurring at 455 nm [111, 222]. These findings, combined with the
small differences that have been observed in the absorption maxima
of the CO-difference spectra [111, 114], have led to the interesting
suggestion that cytochrome P-450 may be qualitatively different in
insecticide-resistant and -susceptible houseflies [111] (Section V.A.3).

Piperonyl butoxide, a microsomal enzyme inhibitor and insecticide
synergist (Section IV.B.4), complexes with reduced cytochrome P-450
in both mouse liver [188] and housefly abdomina [111] microsomes to
produce a difference spectrum that resembles that obtained with ethyl

isocyanide. This has been designated as a type III spectrum [188].
Absorption maxima are at 455 and 427 nm in preparations from both
species and are in pH-dependent equilibrium [188]. Piperonyl butoxide
produces a typical type I substrate difference spectrum with the oxidized form of P-450 [188]. The 1,2,3-benzothiadiazoles, another group
of MFO inhibitors and insecticide synergists (Section IV.B.4), also
exhibit different binding spectra with oxidized and reduced cytochrome
P-450 [192, 227]. With oxidized P-450, a typical type II difference
spectrum is obtained (absorption maximum 432 nm, minimum 390 nm)
in both rat liver and insect microsomes [192], whereas with reduced
P-450 the absorption maximum occurs at 444-446 nm [192, 227]; the
latter peak is displaced to 450 nm following treatment with CO [192,
227].

Little information is available on substrate binding to cytochrome
P-450 in insect microsomes, which probably results mainly from the
practical problem of obtaining the relatively high concentrations of
microsomal protein required to produce measurable substrate difference spectra. The data that are available indicate that substrate binding spectra in insect preparations are similar to those reported for
hepatic microsomes [228-232]. Microsomes from housefly abdomina
show a characteristic type I difference spectrum with piperonyl butoxide (peak at 390 nm, trough at 420 nm) [14] and (+)benzphetamine
[111], and a type II spectrum (peak at 426 nm, trough at 390 nm) was
obtained with pyridine [14, 111]. An identical type II spectrum was
obtained from aniline in microsomes from G. portentosa gut and the
K_s (spectral dissociation constant) was found to be 0.014 M [233]. It
is somewhat surprising that most of the substrates that are commonly
used in insect microsomal enzyme studies have not yet been characterized as type I or type II.

2. NADPH-Cytochrome c Reductase

NADPH-cytochrome c reductase is known to be an important component of the electron transport pathway in hepatic microsomes [204,
207] and has been purified and characterized from pig [209] and rat
[234] liver. The enzyme has been solubilized recently from housefly
abdomina microsomes, purified, and its properties compared with
the enzymes from pig and rat liver [14, 235-237]. All are flavopro-
teins and have molecular weights of 57,000 to 68,000. The prosthetic
group in the mammalian enzyme is FAD, but as FAD and FMN were
both capable of restoring activity to the housefly apoenzyme [235, 236]
and as the quantity of enzyme available was too small for analysis,
the nature of the prosthetic group in the housefly could not be determined. The electron donor and acceptor properties are similar,
although higher K_m values for NADPH, cytochrome c, and dichloro-

phenolindophenol indicate that the insect enzyme has a lower affinity
for these materials than do those from mammalian liver [14, 235,
237]. It is noteworthy that the housefly NADPH-cytochrome c
reductase also appears to be more susceptible to inhibition by sulfhydryl reagents [237].

NADPH-cytochrome c reductase activity has also been demonstrated in microsomes from cricket (A. domesticus) Malpighian
tubules [78] and in the mitochondrial supernatant from mosquito
larvae and adults [238, 239]. Reductase activity in cricket Malpighian
tubules was observed to increase 4- to 5-fold during the first 9 days
of adult life and exhibited an activity pattern that paralleled that of
MFO activity [78].

3. Cytochrome b_5

In 1950, Sanborn and Williams [240] reported the discovery of a
pigment, cytochrome x, in larval tissues of the silkworm (Hyalophora
cecropia) and subsequent studies [241, 242] revealed that this pigment was in fact identical to the cytochrome b_5 discovered independently in mammalian liver microsomes [243]. The cytochrome b_5
from liver microsomes was purified and characterized [211, 212] and
simultaneous discovery of the flavoprotein, NADH-cytochrome b_5
reductase, clearly established the existence of a microsomal electron transport pathway from NADH to cytochrome b_5 (Fig. 3). Although
the electron transport pathway from NADPH to cytochrome P-450 is
clearly of primary importance in drug metabolism, the possible
involvement of the pathway from NADH cannot be discounted entirely
[169].

Cytochrome b_5 has been demonstrated in microsomes from whole
houseflies [35], housefly larvae [244], and housefly abdomina [222],
as well as in preparations from lepidopterous larvae [50] and cricket
(A. domesticus) Malpighian tubules [78]. Cytochrome b-555 [245] has
been purified from housefly larvae [244] and is considered to be a
solubilized form of cytochrome b_5. The purified cytochrome has a
molecular weight of 13,700, contains protoheme as the prosthetic
group, and does not combine with either CO or cyanide [244]. Its
other properties closely resemble those described for cytochrome b_5
purified from rabbit liver microsomes [211, 212]. Purified cytochrome
b-555 was reduced by NADH in the presence of NADH-cytochrome b_5
reductase purified from rat liver microsomes, and the fact that reduction by NADH also occurred with the housefly larval microsomal fraction strongly suggests the presence of the flavoprotein in this preparation. The presence of NADH-cytochrome b_5 reductase has not yet
been demonstrated unequivocally in insect microsomes.

The association, if any, between cytochrome b_5 and MFO activity in insect microsomes is unknown but its concentration does not appear to be rate limiting. Thus, the cytochrome b_5 content in microsomes from the abdomina of several strains of insecticide-susceptible and -resistant houseflies remained the same despite large variations in microsomal enzyme activity [222], and the levels of cytochrome b_5 in cricket Malpighian tubule microsomes showed a poor correlation with epoxidation activity in insects of different age and sex [78].

V. FACTORS AFFECTING MICROSOMAL ACTIVITY

A. Physiological Factors

1. Effect of Age and Stage of Development

It is well established that microsomal enzyme activity in mammalian liver is lacking in fetal and newborn animals. The enzymes usually start to appear within a few days after birth and subsequently increase to attain maximum adult levels of activity during the next few weeks or months depending on the animal concerned [246-248]. Because of the presence of the relatively inflexible sclerotized exoskeleton, growth and development in insects is a discontinuous process characterized by the occurrence of several molts, during which the growing animal replaces its cuticle with a new and larger one. Insects also undergo a metamorphosis during their development, the immature stages of many species being quite different from the adult with respect to morphology, physiology, and feeding habits and often having distinct modes of living and behavior. Metamorphosis may be either holometabolous (complete) or hemimetabolous (gradual or incomplete). The latter term describes those species in which the young on hatching generally resemble the adult except for their smaller size and sexual immaturity. During development, these insects, which include the orders Orthoptera and Homoptera, pass through several nymphal instars, each of which more closely resembles the adult. Holometabolous insects, including the Diptera, Lepidoptera, and Coleoptera, are characterized by having larval and pupal stages during their development. In view of the fact that these complex patterns of development are often closely associated with changes in the biochemistry of the insect, it is perhaps not surprising that large changes in enzyme activity, including drug metabolizing activity, may occur with age and stage of development. The importance of this factor has often been overlooked in studies of MFO activity in insects and it is likely that the frustrating lack of data reproducibility that is often experienced is in some cases a direct reflection of age variations in the insects employed. The problem is

exacerbated by the fact that the entire life cycle of many insect species is completed within a period of only a few weeks and, consequently, large changes in enzyme activity may occur within days or
even hours. Unfortunately, the data on the nature of these changes are
not always in agreement and until fairly recently few general patterns
have become evident.

Most of the MFO studies on houseflies and other dipteran species
have concentrated on adult insects and have paid little attention to
changes in enzyme activity during development and metamorphosis.
Khan's results [39] indicate that in the housefly (M. domestica)
epoxidase activity first appears in newly hatched larvae (only traces
were found in eggs) and after attaining a maximum after 1 day,
steadily declines during the remainder of the larval period. Fresh
pupae were found to have slightly higher activity than late larvae, but
here again activity decreased with age and only trace levels were
found just prior to the adult emergence [39]. These data differ sharply
from those obtained in a more recent study [249], which indicate that
heptachlor epoxidase activity appears only in late third-instar larvae
(3.23 days old) about 15 h prior to pupation. At this stage the enzyme
shows a dramatic 24 h burst of activity that, after reaching a maximum about 11 h before pupation, rapidly declines to only trace levels
in pupae and phorate adults (Fig. 4). This age-activity pattern correlates quite well with changes in the level of cytochrome P-450 that
have been observed during larval development [113] (Fig. 4). Carbaryl
metabolizing activity in blowfly larvae (C. erythrocephala) fat body
was observed to decrease markedly from the fourth to the eighth day
in larvae reared at 25°C but passed through a maximum at 9-11 days
(about halfway through the larval period) when the insects were reared
at 10°C [100]. Presumably, the lower temperature merely serves to
slow down maturation, which suggests that a similar bell-shaped
curve might have been obtained in the study at 25°C if 1 to 4-day-old
larvae had been included. Studies with another blowfly (P. regina), as
well as several species of fleshfly (Sarcophaga sp.), indicate that
hydroxylation and N-demethylation activities decrease during pupal
development [46].

Most workers are in agreement that MFO activity in adult flies
undergoes a general increase following emergence, although in view
of the fact that the rate of maturation and longevity of flies depend
on factors such as rearing conditions and nutrition, it is not unexpected that some variations occur between different laboratories.
Naphthalene hydroxylation and epoxidation activities in microsomes
from whole houseflies increased markedly during the first week of
adult life [28, 29, 39, 249] (Fig. 4) and in preparations from housefly
abdomina a similar postemergence increase was observed for O- and
N-dealkylation [58] and cytochrome P-450 [113] (Fig. 4). In female

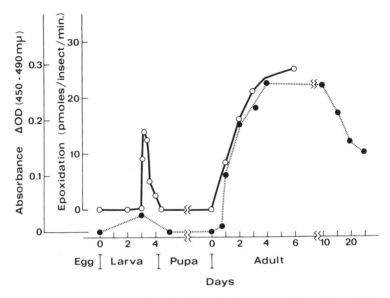

FIG. 4. Changes in microsomal epoxidation activity (O—O) and cytochrome P-450 content (● · · · ●) in houseflies of different age and stage of development. (Data from Yu and Terriere [249] and Perry and Buckner [113].)

flies, maximum activity was attained about 1 week after emergence [39, 58], but in males peak activity occurred at about 4 days, possibly because of earlier maturation [58]. After this initial increase, enzyme activity either remains relatively constant [29] or exhibits a steady decline [39, 58] with increasing senescence. In contrast to these data, it has been reported that the ability of fly abdomen microsomes to metabolize a number of carbamates did not change during the period from 1 to 15 days after emergence [65] and the increasing susceptibility of older flies to carbamates [250] provides indirect evidence suggesting that in some strains MFO activity may even decrease with age. With microsomes from adult blowflies (P. regina), ring hydroxylation in both sexes increased substantially from 1 to 8 days of age, whereas N-demethylation remained relatively constant [46]. The increase in hydroxylation activity corresponded favorably with an increase in the in vivo tolerance of the insects to carbaryl and an increase in the synergistic ratio with piperonyl butoxide-carbaryl combinations. Similar, although more variable, patterns of MFO activity were observed in adult fleshflies (Sarcophaga bullata and S. crassipalpis) and in the former species a peak of activity was consistently observed at 1 day, followed by a decline at 2 days and a steady increase during the next 6 days. The validity of this somewhat

unusual age-activity profile was supported by the observed changes
in in vivo susceptibility of the flies to carbaryl during this period of
time [46].

Dramatic changes in MFO activity occur during development and
metamorphosis in Lepidoptera. Thus, although no activity could be
detected in eggs or young larvae, the larval gut tissues of the southern armyworm (P. eridania) exhibited a 30-fold increase in epoxidase
activity during development from the fourth to the sixth instar and
subsequently showed an equally remarkable decline as the sixth instar
larvae began burrowing into the soil in preparation to pupate [53, 54]
(Fig. 5a). A qualitatively similar pattern that is not unlike that

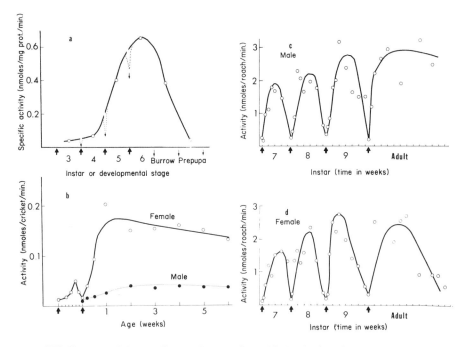

FIG. 5. Age-activity profiles of microsomal epoxidation in three insect species:
(a) Southern armyworm (P. eridania); (b) house cricket (A. domesticus); (c and d)
Madagascar cockroach (G. portentosa). (Data from Krieger and Wilkinson [54], Benke
and Wilkinson [81], and Benke et al. [95].)

described for housefly larvae [249] was observed with each of 16
other species of lepidopterous larvae included in this study [53, 102].
In another investigation, it was shown that carbaryl metabolizing
activity in the larval gut and fat body tissues of several strains of the
cabbage looper (T. ni) also increased throughout larval development

and attained a maximum level in final instar larvae and prepupae [56, 57]. In all species examined, MFO activity is greatest in actively feeding final instar larvae and as enzyme levels are measured in terms of specific activity the increases do not merely reflect the larger size of the tissues in older larvae. The increase in activity through larval development does not, however, occur in a smooth, continuous manner but, as indicated in Fig. 5a (dotted lines), undergoes marked changes within the course of each instar. As the larva prepares to molt into a new stadium, it usually enters a period of quiescence and reduces feeding. Epoxidase activity in the gut tissues of the larvae of several species decreases at this stage and remains at a low level for a period that extends through the molt and into the early part of the next instar before increasing again [53]. Consequently, particularly in early instar larvae, where the entire stadium occupies a period of only about 2 days, MFO activity is probably in a constant state of change. Perhaps the most dramatic changes in enzyme activity occur during the larval-pupal metamorphosis. The onset of this stage is marked by the cessation of larval feeding and this is shortly followed by a voiding of the gut contents and a general shrinking (dehydration) of the tissues. Depending on the species involved, the larva then either burrows into the soil or begins to spin a cocoon. Whatever the case, the cessation of feeding appears to signal a rapid decline in MFO activity, which usually approaches only trace levels by the time pupation occurs [53, 54, 56, 57, 102]. In P. eridania, the decrease in activity from feeding sixth instar larvae to prepupae was accompanied by a 25-fold decrease in cytochrome P-450 and a similar but less marked fall in the level of cytochrome b_5 [53]. No MFO activity was detected in the tissues of any of the adult moths and butterflies examined.

Studies with several species of orthopteran insects, which undergo gradual metamorphosis through a series of nymphal instars, emphasize the remarkable changes that may occur during insect development. Fenwick [89] observed that the erratic schradan activation activity in desert locust (S. gregaria) fat body resulted from age variation and a study of this revealed that, in fifth instar hoppers, activity declined sharply 2 days prior to the final molt and rose again slightly during the first 3 weeks of adult life. These results were subsequently confirmed for the oxidation of p-nitrotoluene [49] and it was concluded that "if an oxidation enzyme is required from an insect, it is best to avoid the period near molts." Parathion activation in homogenates of cockroach (P. americana) fat body was also found to be age-dependent and increased in adults up to about 3 months of age [62]. Detailed studies on the age variation in epoxidation and hydroxylation activities in the Malpighian tubules of male and female crickets (A. domesticus) established that activity was low during the molts from the eighth to the ninth instar and from the ninth instar to the adult [78, 81]. Enzyme activity passed through a peak about midway through the ninth instar and, in the female, epoxidation increased 10- to 12-fold during the first week of adult life (Fig. 5b). The increase was not as marked for hydroxylase activity and both types of activity remained at a much lower level in the male insect. As the adult insects matured, enzyme activity steadily declined over a period of 5 to 6 weeks. The in vivo importance of the Malpighian tubules in insecticide detoxication is indicated by the fact that these patterns of enzyme activity correlate well with observed changes in the toxicity of carbaryl and its synergism by piperonyl butoxide to crickets of different age and sex [146].

Facilitated by the larger size of the insect, age-activity profiles with gut-caeca preparations from the Madagascar cockroach (G. portentosa) were studied over several instars and with both sexes distinct patterns of epoxidation and hydroxylation activity were observed [78, 95]. Figure 5, c and d, clearly shows that activity follows a characteristic rhythmic cycle, being low during the molt and passing through a maximum about midway through each instar. In the adult male, activity is maintained at a uniformly high level (Fig. 5c), whereas in the female it exhibits a decrease from the fifth to the eleventh week (Fig. 5d). This period coincides with the development of the young inside the female (they are produced viviparously at about the twelfth week) and consequently the decline in activity at this stage provides an interesting parallel with the observed decreases in microsomal activity associated with pregnancy in mammals [251]. There is also evidence with the Madagascar cockroach, in which MFO activity is distributed in several different tissues, that epoxidase activity in the fat body does not undergo the same degree of change with age as that in the gut and caeca and retains some activity even during the molt [78, 95].

These investigations strongly suggest that MFO activity in insects is under strict metabolic control and that the control mechanism is closely linked with the process of metamorphosis. This association immediately suggests a possible interrelationship between enzyme activity and the levels of insect hormones, particularly juvenile hormone [252, 253] and the ecdysones [253-255], during insect development. Changes in the titer of ecdysone (the molting hormone) during larval development in the silkworm (Samia cynthia ricini) exhibit an almost inverse pattern to that observed for MFO activity, being highest immediately before and during the molt, and lowest during the midinstar period [256, 257]. Juvenile hormone levels, as well as protein and RNA synthesis, are highest during the immediate postmolt period and show a steady decline as the instar progresses [257]. The onset of pupation is marked by a rapid increase in ecdysone titer and a corresponding decrease in the level of juvenile hormone [257]. Yu and Terriere [249] have suggested that the sudden burst of MFO activity that takes place in last instar housefly larvae just before pupation may be associated with the increasing ecdysone titer occurring at this time. Ecdysterone (β-ecdysone) has in fact been found to stimulate MFO activity in adult houseflies, but no conclusive evidence has been obtained concerning any similar activity in housefly larvae [249]. If, indeed, MFO activity is stimulated by ecdysone, one would not expect to observe a decrease in activity at the onset of pupation as the elevated ecdysone titer is maintained during this period.

An alternative viewpoint is that the microsomal enzymes may play an important role in regulating the levels of juvenile hormone and/or ecdysone but, unfortunately, the involvement of the MFO's in hormone biosynthesis or degradation has not yet been established in insects. The presence of the epoxide ring in juvenile hormone and the several hydroxy functions in ecdysone suggest that these or similar, perhaps more specific, enzymes may have biosynthetic importance. Furthermore, the juvenile hormone activity of several 1,3-benzodioxoles that are known inhibitors of MFO activity (Section IV.B.4) [252, 258] may result from either a blockage of the pathway of ecdysone synthesis or an inhibition of juvenile hormone degradation, although the latter does not appear to be mediated by MFO enzymes [259, 260]. The fact that in lepidopterous larvae ecdysone levels are low when MFO activity is high, and vice versa [53, 257], suggests the possibility that ecdysone may be degraded by the drug metabolizing enzymes. The highly hydroxylated ecdysone, however, appears an unlikely substrate for the MFO's and, in addition, it has been established that ecdysone is degraded largely by a soluble enzyme present in the fat body of the blowfly larva (C. erythrocephala) [261]. Clearly, the relationship, if any, between MFO activity and hormone levels must await more information on the biosynthetic and degradative pathways of hormone metabolism. It is, of course, entirely possible that there is no direct association between the two and that the decline of MFO activity during molting or ecdysis is just one consequence of the general biochemical and physiological reorganization of the tissues that occurs at this time.

2. Sex

Very few studies have been made on sex-linked variations in microsomal activity in insects and the results must be interpreted with some caution because they may be age-dependent and reflect different rates of maturation and senescence (Section V.A.1). It is fairly clear that in several insect species MFO activity does vary between the sexes although the differences observed are often small and depend to some extent on the methods of preparation and the manner in which the results are expressed. Where sex differences are observed, the female insect invariably has the higher titer of activity.

The greater tolerance of female houseflies to many insecticides [131, 250], has long been recognized and as a consequence of this it has become common practice to employ only female flies in insecticide screening programs. That this greater tolerance to insecticides is in some cases caused by an increased detoxication capability has been established by in vitro studies. Microsomes from whole female houseflies have greater epoxidation activity than those from males [39] and preparations from housefly abdomina show a similar trend with regard to O- and N-dealkylation [58, 115]. However, female flies are considerably larger than males and as they yield more microsomal protein the sex differences appear much greater when enzyme activity is measured on a per fly basis than when it is expressed per milligram protein. In some cases the relative activities can be completely reversed. Thus, although the cytochrome P-450 levels are greater in female flies than in males [113, 222] the cytochrome content per milligram protein is actually highest in the male insects [222]. No consistent sex differences have been demonstrated for naphthalene hydroxylation in housefly microsomes [29] or for several microsomal reactions in preparations from whole blowflies (P. regina) and fleshflies (Sarcophaga sp.) [46].

In vitro epoxidation and hydroxylation activity in microsomes from cricket (A. domesticus) Malpighian tubules is higher in females than in males [78, 81] but no sex differences are observed in preparations from cockroach (G. portentosa) gut-caeca [78, 95], locust (S. gregaria) fat body [89], or gut and fat body of three species of lepidopterous larvae [53].

3. Strain Differences

The ability of insects to gain resistance to almost all types of synthetic organic insecticides is an extremely important practical problem that seriously threatens our continued ability to control insect pests by means of chemicals [262, 263]. It is now recognized that resistance is a preadaptive phenomenon and that the insecticide acts as a powerful agent to select those members of the population that for one reason or another have the ability to survive exposure. When the selection pressure is maintained over several generations, substantial levels of resistance are often rapidly attained. The problem is further complicated by the fact that the development of resistance is not confined to the insecticide used as the selective agent but may extend through a phenomenon termed "cross-resistance" to include other groups of materials to which the population has never been exposed. Although resistance may occur through one or more of

several mechanisms, it is established that one of the major causes
of DDT resistance is an enhanced ability to detoxify this insecticide
by dehydrochlorination

Early in vitro studies on the microsomal enzymes in insects,
mostly the housefly, showed that the levels of activity often varied
considerably between different laboratory strains exhibiting various
degrees of resistance to insecticides. As a consequence of this observation, it was suggested that in some cases there might be a relationship between MFO activity and insecticide resistance [29] and subsequent investigations indeed confirmed that many strains of resistant
insects had high in vitro levels of microsomal activity [10-12, 14, 29,
32, 33, 39, 40, 55, 57, 64, 65, 113, 129, 131-133, 139, 142, 144, 148,
149, 153, 154, 158, 177, 265]. In most of these cases, the development
of resistance appears to be associated with a general increase in all
types of microsomal activity. Thus, houseflies selected for resistance
with either a carbamate or DDT may simultaneously attain high epoxidation, hydroxylation, and O- and N-demethylation activities that, in
addition to enhancing the metabolism of the insecticide used in the
selection process, also facilitate the metabolism of a large number
of other unrelated insecticides by pathways involving microsomal
oxidation. This, of course, provides a ready explanation of cross-
resistance and at the same time suggests the interesting possibility
of controlling resistant insects with insecticides that require activation (intoxication) by microsomal oxidation [12]. It should not, however, be construed that insect resistance to insecticides is caused
solely by enhanced MFO activity or that there is any simple relationship between the two [113, 148]. On the contrary, it is important to
recognize that in most of these strains the enhanced microsomal
activity is probably only one of several contributing factors and that
its relative importance is likely to vary among different strains. The
role played by the MFO's in determining the in vivo susceptibility of
resistant insects to several insecticides can often be clearly demonstrated by the degree to which toxicity is enhanced when the insecticide is applied in combination with a synergist known to inhibit the
microsomal enzymes [131, 139, 153, 158, 266, 267]. Usually, synergism occurs in both resistant and susceptible strains, although in
resistant insects the degree of synergism is much greater.

Improvements in the in vitro techniques for working with insect
microsomes combined with genetic crossing experiments employing
a variety of visible mutants as chromosomal markers have in recent
years led to a considerable increase in our understanding of the biochemical genetics of insect resistance in the housefly [14, 265]. Semi-
dominant genes on chromosomes II and V are now considered to be
largely responsible for controlling microsomal enzyme activity and,
depending on the strain involved, either one or both of these may play

a primary role in determining resistance [14, 133, 265, 268]. The gene(s) on chromosome II has been shown to cause as much as a 10-fold increase in microsomal hydroxylation and epoxidation activity, [33, 39, 40, 129] and its presence is of primary importance in strains of houseflies selected for resistance to naphthalene [33] and to carbamates [14,32,39,40,129,132,265]. In other strains, however, carbamate resistance has been shown to be associated primarily with an increase in oxidase activity controlled by the gene(s) on chromosome V [132, 133], which has also been implicated in DDT resistance [14, 132, 139]. It is probable that in some resistant strains the genes on chromosomes II and V both contribute to the final level of resistance attained [14, 33, 133, 265] and their effects may be still further modified by the presence of other genes not directly associated with metabolism. A factor associated with chromosome III is known to have an effect on cuticular penetration of insecticides in the housefly [33, 269].

In agreement with the observed increases in MFO activity cytochrome P-450 levels in microsomes from the abdomina of several resistant strains of houseflies are up to 2-fold higher than those in preparations from susceptible insects [111, 113, 148, 222]. There is also evidence that suggests that the P-450 in resistant houseflies may be qualitatively different from that in susceptible strains. Thus, in microsomes from some strains of resistant flies the peak of the CO-difference spectrum consistently occurs at 448 or 449 nm compared with 451 nm for the susceptible flies [111, 114], and both quantitative and qualitative differences are also observed in the spectral parameters of a variety of other substrates and ligands, including pyridine (type II), (+)benzphetamine (type I), octylamine, ethyl isocyanide, and piperonyl butoxide (type III) [111, 222]. Such spectral differences may well indicate that the cytochrome P-450 in resistant flies is qualitatively different from that in susceptible insects and, as pointed out by Philpot and Hodgson [111], it is interesting to speculate whether the genes on chromosomes II and V are responsible for the synthesis of two different types of cytochrome P-450. The differences in MFO activity between resistant and susceptible strains of insects are quantitative rather than qualitative but it is quite possible that even a relatively small change in the conformation of cytochrome P-450 may markedly increase either the affinity or the metabolic turnover of different insecticide substrates and lead to some of the resistance spectra that are observed.

4. Effect of Nutrition and Diet

Little attention has been given to the possible effects on MFO activity of the nutritional status of the insect and it is likely that in laboratory-reared insects some variation in data between laboratories may result from this factor. It is well known that the susceptibility of insects to insecticides is influenced by diet [113, 270] but few attempts have been made to relate this to changes in metabolism. Adult houseflies maintained on a diet of sugar and water were found to be consistently more susceptible to m-isopropylphenyl N-methylcarbamate than those fed on milk [250] and that this may result from changes in MFO activity is suggested by the higher in vitro carbamate [65] and hempa [115] metabolizing activity in milk-fed flies. It has also been established that the levels of P-450 in microsomes from one insecticide-susceptible and six -resistant strains of flies maintained on a sugar diet are only about 50% of those observed in preparations from the same strains provided with milk [113]. These studies clearly indicate that the activity of the drug metabolizing enzymes of insects, like those in mammals [271], is depressed as a result of protein deficiency.

In several species of polyphagous lepidopterous larvae, the host plant on which the insect is maintained appears to have little or no influence on MFO activity in the gut tissues. This was established with silkworm (Telea polyphemus) larvae reared on sweet cherry, sour cherry, dogwood, and oak [53, 102] and for larvae of the southern armyworm (P. eridania) feeding on leaves of tomato, potato, lima bean, and red kidney bean [53].

B. Environmental Factors

1. Enzyme Induction

The marked increase in the drug metabolizing activity of liver microsomes that occurs following in vivo treatment of mammals with a large variety of lipophilic drugs, insecticides, and other foreign compounds is now a well-established phenomenon and is termed "enzyme induction" [272-275]. Induction appears to represent a temporary biochemical adaptation that enables the animal to survive exposure to potentially hazardous foreign chemicals and that in both acute and chronic situations can often substantially modify the duration and intensity of action of biologically active materials. The increased MFO activity is usually associated with an increase in liver weight [276] and a marked proliferation of the smooth endoplasmic reticulum of the liver cell [277, 278]. That MFO induction represents an increase in protein synthesis is shown by the increased incorporation of labeled amino acids into protein [279] and of labeled bases into RNA [280] and by the increase in template activity of liver chromatin. Furthermore, inhibitors of protein synthesis, such as ethionine, puromycin, and actinomycin D, are known to block enzyme induction. Other changes associated with induction in mammals include an increase in microsomal phospholipid content [278] and variations in the relative concentrations of the several components of the microsomal electron transport chain [275].

The first attempt to demonstrate microsomal enzyme induction in insects was that of Morrello [281] and was instigated largely by the possibility that induction might be associated with the tolerance or resistance of insects to certain insecticides, particularly the chlorinated hydrocarbons, such as DDT and the cyclodienes. Morrello [281] showed that the treatment of Triatoma infestans with 3-methylcholanthrene led to an 11% increase in the in vivo production of polar metabolites from DDT and at the same time caused a 12% decrease in mortality from DDT poisoning. Subsequent investigations established that pretreatment of the same species with phenobarbital caused an increase in DDT metabolism in isolated microsomes [47, 282].

Several workers have clearly demonstrated induction in houseflies, although the magnitude of the observed increases in MFO activity varies considerably depending on the nature of inducing agent and the strain of flies employed. Walker and Terriere [126] have shown substantial increases in both naphthalene hydroxylase and heptachlor epoxidase activities following treatment of flies of the Orlando-DDT resistant strain with dieldrin. The increased MFO activity was associated with an accelerated incorporation of isoleucine into microsomal protein and a reduction in the susceptibility of the flies to carbaryl [126]. Feeding the same strain of flies on a diet containing 100 ppm of dieldrin resulted in an increase in microsomal epoxidase activity as well as an increase in the microsomal metabolism of several insecticides [14, 283] although similar treatment of the R-Baygon strain appeared to lead to a decrease in epoxidase activity. Dieldrin treatment also resulted in increased levels of cytochromes P-450 and b_5 in this strain and caused changes in the spectral parameters of the ethyl isocyanide difference spectrum [222]. Perry et al. [114] established that although increases in MFO activity and levels of cytochrome P-448* were observed following treatment of several strains of flies with phenobarbital there appeared to be no linear relationship between the two.

DDT and its analogs appear to be generally less potent inducers in houseflies than dieldrin [126, 145, 283, 284] and significant MFO induction by DDT is usually observed only in strains of flies showing some degree of resistance to this insecticide [138, 282, 285]. This is not always true, however, because Oppenoorth and Houx [139] were unable to demonstrate any DDT-induced activity in flies of the F_c

*This refers to the reported shift in the P-450 spectrum that is observed in some insecticide-resistant strains of houseflies (see Section V.A.3).

strain, which are known to be resistant to DDT by a mechanism
involving microsomal oxidation. A similar relationship with resistance has been observed in the inducibility of heptachlor epoxidase
by dieldrin in housefly strains with either high or low initial levels
of oxidase activity [147]. The strains with initially high oxidase capacity had a greater tendency to be induced than did the low oxidase
strains, and the F_1 hybrids resulting from crosses between the two
showed an intermediate level of induction. It was suggested that the
high oxidase strain might have a greater capacity for increasing its
microsomal enzymes through possession of more genes or gene
sequences for enzyme regulation. Although there is little doubt that
resistance per se is "a case of pure Darwinian selection" [26] and
should not therefore be confused with the noninheritable phenomenon
of enzyme induction, it is possible that an enhanced ability to be tem-
porarily induced may assist the survival of those members of the
population preadapted to resistance.

Other biochemical changes associated with induction have also
been demonstrated but, as with MFO activity, these only occur to any
significant extent in resistant strains of insects. DDT treatment
increases the incorporation of ^{14}C-labeled amino acids into total protein [286], polysomal protein [287], and microsomal protein [285, 288]
in resistant houseflies and into total protein of Triatoma infestans
nymphs [289]. Similar increases in the incorporation of labeled bases
into RNA have also been observed in these species [138, 282, 285,
287, 288, 290] and when the time course of these events has been followed it appears to precede the increase in protein synthesis [282,
287, 290, 291]. The isolated mRNA from DDT-treated houseflies
possesses up to 7-fold higher template activity in a cell-free protein
synthesis system than does that from control insects [287, 290]. Further studies on the mechanism of DDT induction in houseflies have
revealed that DDT binds to components in the nucleus and, as in
mammals [292], appears to have a direct effect on the DNA-dependent
RNA polymerase that shows in vivo a rapid increase in activity following treatment with the inducer [282]. This occurs prior to the
increases in mRNA and protein synthesis. As a result of these investigations, it was suggested that DDT might act at the chromatin level
or have a more direct effect on the polymerase itself. A direct effect
on transcription is indicated by the fact that actinomycin D blocks
both dieldrin-induced MFO activity [145] and DDT-induced ^{14}C-uracil
incorporation into RNA in houseflies [290], although Ishaaya and
Chefurka [288] have observed that this material has no effect on the
incorporation of ^{14}C-leucine into membranes following treatment of
flies with DDT. Puromycin, which inhibits protein synthesis at the
translation level by releasing peptides from RNA ribosome complexes,
had no effect on dieldrin induction when injected into houseflies at

levels as high as 10 μg/fly [145], although in vitro it caused peptide
release from housefly ribosomes [287]. It is possible that the failure
of puromycin to cause any effect in vivo resulted from inadequate
translocation within the insect. Cycloheximide, another inhibitor of
protein synthesis, blocked dieldrin-induced MFO activity and protein
synthesis in houseflies [126].

In addition to these changes, which are directly associated with
the detoxication enzymes, DDT treatment is reported to induce the
enzyme NAD-kinase in T. infestans nymphs [286, 293] and it is suggested that this increases the amount of NADP available for reduction via the pentose phosphate pathway for glucose metabolism. This
pathway is itself found to be enhanced as a result of DDT treatment
[294], although if, as seems likely, it is involved in the generation of
NADPH for MFO activity, it will be expected to show greater activity
during periods of microsomal metabolism.

Not all attempts to demonstrate microsomal enzyme induction in
insects have been successful. Treatment of locusts (S. gregaria) with
phenobarbital or benzpyrene failed to cause any subsequent increase
in the oxidation of p-nitrotoluene in enzyme preparations from the fat
body [137] and attempts to induce P. eridania larvae with a variety of
materials produced no consistent data [53]. More recent studies indicate that lepidopterous larvae may be more refractory to induction
than adult insects and that exposure to much higher levels of the inducing agent is required to observe any effect [82]. Chlorcyclizine and
phenobarbital incorporated in the diet of wax moth larvae (Galleria
mellonella) at concentrations of 5000 and 10,000 ppm, respectively,
resulted in enhanced MFO activity in the larval gut tissues but even
at these high concentrations treatment for at least 2 days was required
to produce any significant effect [103]. The large and rapid changes in
MFO activity that are associated with normal larval development complicate induction studies in lepidoptera and can readily obscure any
inductive changes unless the control and treated insects are exactly
synchronized with respect to age.

2. Enzyme Inhibition

The ability of several groups of materials to inhibit MFO activity
in vitro in insect microsomes has already been discussed (Section
IV.B.4) and reference has also been made to the fact that many of
these same compounds are effective insecticide synergists in vivo
It is not entirely unexpected, therefore, that the in vitro activity of
microsomes prepared from insects pretreated with synergists is
found to be markedly depressed, although it is often difficult to assess
whether the inhibition observed truly reflects the state of the enzyme
in vivo or whether it occurs in vitro as a result of residual material

liberated during the preparation. Compared with controls, preparations from the abdomina of three strains of houseflies exposed to low concentrations of piperonyl butoxide for 24 h prior to assay showed a much reduced capacity to metabolize several insecticides, including aldrin, DDT, allethrin, and Baygon [132]. Similarly, microsomes from the abdomina of houseflies fed diets containing piperonyl butoxide and 2,3,6-trichlorophenyl-2-propynyl ether for 24 h prior to homogenization and assay had only traces of aldrin epoxidase activity [114] and reduced levels of cytochrome P-450 [114, 222]. The decrease in cytochrome P-450 content at various time intervals following topical application of piperonyl butoxide and sesamex showed a favorable correlation with the toxicity of Baygon to the treated insects [113]. The recent finding that piperonyl butoxide partially prevents CO binding to cytochrome P-450 in microsomes from both houseflies [111] and mammalian liver [188] provides a probable explanation of these data. This is strengthened by the fact that the in vivo treatment of mice with piperonyl butoxide leads to an initial decrease in the CO-difference spectrum in microsomes subsequently prepared from the animals [227, 295].

VI. EVOLUTIONARY CONSIDERATIONS

The evolutionary development of the microsomal detoxication system is a subject that attracts a great deal of speculative interest from both zoologists and biochemists and one that is of special significance for those involved in comparative investigations. Quite clearly, the MFO system existed long before the advent of modern drugs and pesticides and for this reason questions are continually raised regarding the natural substrates of these enzymes. Some hold the view that, in mammals, they perform a major physiological role in steroid hormone metabolism [273, 296, 297]. Teleologically, however, it seems unlikely that nature would rely on such remarkably nonspecific enzymes for this important purpose and although hepatic microsomes will indeed metabolize steroids in vitro there is some question regarding whether this is of physiological significance in regulating steroid hormone levels in vivo. Furthermore, it is by no means clear whether this hypothesis is applicable to all of the diverse forms of life now known to possess an MFO system. The ubiquitous occurrence of these enzyme systems throughout the animal and plant kingdoms suggests some common fundamental system. The ubiquitous entirely plausible that they have developed as a biochemical defense mechanism to protect organisms from the many naturally occurring lipophilic foreign compounds to which they are continually exposed [5, 6, 298].

Brodie and Maickel [6] suggested that the microsomal detoxication system only developed when, in the course of evolution, animals first emerged onto the land and hypothesized that aquatic species, because of their ability to dialyze foreign compounds into the surrounding medium, did not require such systems. Although it is now recognized that aquatic forms of life do possess MFO systems [19, 163, 299], it is true that in general the enzymes are not so well developed as in most terrestrial organisms. The enzymes comprising the MFO complex are admirably suited for their role in detoxication. They will accept as a substrate almost any lipophilic material with which they are presented and by one or more of the many reactions of which they are capable will convert it into a more polar, hydrophilic form that can be more readily removed from the body. The fact that in most cases this conversion simultaneously results in the detoxication of a toxic material is probably secondary to the purpose of increasing its polarity, because were it not for these enzymes, lipophilic materials of all types would steadily accumulate in the tissues of most living organisms.

If the MFO system is indeed an evolutionary adaptation to a terrestrial habitat, and if natural selection acts to reduce energetic and nutritional waste, it seems possible that phylogenetic relationships might exist between the levels of MFO activity in different species and the relative need for such enzymes based on the degree of natural exposure to foreign compounds. In most insect species, the major route by which foreign compounds enter the body is by ingestion and as the natural feeding habits of many taxonomically closely related groups are both diverse and yet fairly clearly defined, insects constitute an excellent group of model organisms with which to test the defense hypothesis. This is particularly true with the phytophagous lepidopterous larvae, which vary from being strictly monophagous to highly polyphagous with regard to their host plant specificity.

A recent study [104] has clearly established that MFO activity in the gut tissues of 35 species of lepidopterous larvae is significantly higher ($p > .01$) in polyphagous species (normally feeding on plants of more than ten families) than in oligophagous species (feeding on two to ten plant families) and that the activity in the latter group is significantly higher ($p > .01$) than in monophagous species that normally feed on plants within one family. These data strongly suggest that the MFO system in lepidopterous larvae has developed to enable them to metabolize secondary plant substances in the food and that the enzymic capability of the system has adjusted by natural selection to the quality and quantity of these materials likely to be encountered. This is in agreement with the suggestion made by Gordon [300] over a decade ago that "the extraordinarily high and generalized tolerance of the larval feeding stages of relatively polyphagous holometabolous insects to contact insecticides is probably the result of selection for endurance of prolonged and varied biochemical stresses associated with the diversity of their natural food plants." Conversely, the high susceptibility of honey bees to many modern insecticides reflects a poorly developed MFO system which may result from the fact that for much of their lives bees feed on a specialized diet [honey, pollen, etc.] and perhaps have not been subjected to high natural selection pressures from foreign compounds. The process of natural selection and evolutionary development is, of course, extremely slow but the rapid development of insect resistance to insecticides provides an excellent example of accelerated evolution and illustrates how strains of insects with enhanced MFO activity can result from selection by foreign compounds.

In most insect species, MFO activity is associated with the tissues of either the fat body or the alimentary tract (or both) (Section III.C.) and it is possible that the relative in vivo significance of these tissues in terms of detoxication depends on the route by which the foreign compound enters the insect. The possession of high enzyme activity in the gut tissues is clearly of advantage in metabolizing ingested compounds and for such insects as lepidopterous larvae that lead a fairly sedentary life in the relatively clean environment of the leaf surface, exposure to foreign compounds is almost exclusively in the ingested food. Consequently, MFO activity in these species is found almost entirely in the gut tissues. Such a distribution of enzyme activity, however, would be of little benefit in enabling the insect to survive exposure to materials that effect direct entry by cuticular penetration, and for such compounds it is likely that the fat body or Malpighian tubule enzymes play a more important role in detoxication. Experimental evidence supporting this hypothesis has recently been obtained with the Madagascar cockroach (G. portentosa) [95]. It is of interest that many of the insect species that have an active MFO system in the fat body are those, such as cockroaches, which as a result of their high mobility and the nature of their habitats are likely to be more exposed to foreign compounds by contact.

VII. SUMMARY

Despite the numerous problems encountered in working with insect microsomes, substantial progress has already been made in elucidating their biochemical and morphological characteristics and a fairly solid core of knowledge has now been established from which more sophisticated investigations can be initiated. It appears that the microsomal enzymes in insects are basically similar to those in mammalian liver but the possibility that subtle qualitative differences do exist cannot be discounted on the strength of the data presently available. If indeed differences exist, they will undoubtedly be revealed in future comparative studies with inhibitors or inducers, or following the solubilization, purification, and cross-reconstitution (insects versus mammals) of the major components of the microsomal enzyme complex. Unfortunately, the chances of finding major biochemical differences that can be exploited in the design of new selective chemicals for insect control appear to be rather more remote now than they did a few years ago and it would seem that selectivity based on differences in primary metabolism will have to rely more on quantitative than on qualitative variations in the enzymes concerned.

Nonetheless, it is probable that future biochemical studies on insect microsomes will complement those with mammalian liver and add considerably to our general knowledge of microsomal mixed-function oxidation and the mechanism by which organisms survive exposure to potentially harmful foreign compounds. In some types of studies, insects may even constitute a more suitable microsomal enzyme source than mammalian liver. This is likely to be particularly true with regard to studies of the biochemical genetics of the microsomal enzymes and the mechanism by which enzyme activity is regulated by physiological and environmental factors.

Acknowledgment

Work conducted in this laboratory was supported by grants from the U.S. Public Health Service (Nos. ES-00400 and ES-00098) and from the Rockefeller Foundation (RF 69073).

REFERENCES

[1] R. T. Williams, *Detoxication Mechanisms*, Wiley, New York, 1959.
[2] D. V. Parke, *The Biochemistry of Foreign Compounds*, Pergamon, Oxford, 1968.
[3] J. H. Dewaide, *Metabolism of Xenobiotics*, Drukkerij Leijn, Nijmegen, 1971.
[4] R. T. Williams and D. V. Parke, *Ann. Rev. Pharmacol.*, 4, 85 (1964).
[5] B. B. Brodie, J. R. Gillette, and B. N. LaDu, *Ann. Rev. Biochem.*, 27, 427 (1958).
[6] B. B. Brodie and R. P. Maickel, *Proc. Intern. Pharmacol.*, *1st Meeting*, Macmillan, New York, 1962, Vol. 6, p. 299.
[7] H. B. Hucker, *Ann. Rev. Pharmacol.*, 10, 99 (1970).
[8] J. N. Smith, in *Advan. Comp. Physiol. Biochem.* (O. Lowenstein, ed.), Academic, New York, 1968, Vol. 3, p. 173.
[9] J. N. Smith, in *Comparative Biochemistry*, (M. Florkin and H. S. Mason, eds.), Academic, New York, 1964, Vol. 6, p. 403.
[10] L. C. Terriere, *Ann. Rev. Entomol.*, 13, 75 (1968).
[11] L. C. Terriere, in *Enzymatic Oxidations of Toxicants* (E. Hodgson, ed.), North Carolina State Univ. Press, Raleigh, 1968, pp. 175-196.

[12] J. E. Casida, in *Microsomes and Drug Oxidations* (J. R. Gillette, A. H. Conney, G. J. Cosmides, R. W. Estabrook, J. R. Fouts, and G. J. Mannering, eds.), Academic, New York, 1969, pp. 517-531.

[13] R. M. Hollingworth, *Bull. World Health Org.*, 44, 155 (1971).

[14] E. Hodgson and F. W. Plapp, *J. Agr. Food Chem.*, 18, 1048 (1970).

[15] A. H. Conney, *Fed. Proc.*, 26, 1027 (1967).

[16] R. T. Williams, *Fed. Proc.*, 26, 1029 (1967).

[17] J. R. Gillette, *Fed. Proc.*, 26, 1040 (1967).

[18] C. C. Smith, *Fed. Proc.*, 26, 1044 (1967).

[19] R. H. Adamson, *Fed. Proc.*, 26, 1047 (1967).

[20] B. B. Brodie and W. D. Reid, *Fed. Proc.*, 26, 1062 (1967).

[21] G. T. Okita, *Fed. Proc.*, 26, 1125 (1967).

[22] C. M. Menzie, *Metabolism of Pesticides*, Special Scientific Report—Wildlife No. 127, U.S. Dept. Interior, July, 1969.

[23] T. R. Fukuto and J. J. Sims, in *Pesticides in the Environment* (R. White-Stevens, ed.), Dekker, New York, 1971, Vol. 1, Part 1, Chap. 2.

[24] T. R. Fukuto and R. L. Metcalf, *Ann. N.Y. Acad. Sci.*, 160, 97 (1969).

[25] L. Lykken and J. E. Casida, *Can. Med. Assoc. J.*, 100, 145 (1969).

[26] R. D. O'Brien, *Insecticides, Action and Metabolism*, Academic, New York, 1967.

[27] M. Agosin, D. Michaeli, R. Miskus, S. Nakasawa, and W. M. Hoskins, *J. Econ. Entomol.*, 54, 340 (1961).

[28] R. O. Arias and L. C. Terriere, *J. Econ. Entomol.*, 55, 925 (1962).

[29] R. D. Schonbrod, W. W. Philleo, and L. C. Terriere, *J. Econ. Entomol.*, 58, 74 (1965).

[30] W. W. Philleo, R. D. Schonbrod, and L. C. Terriere, *J. Agr. Food Chem.*, 13, 113 (1965).

[31] R. D. Schonbrod and L. C. Terriere, *J. Econ. Entomol.*, 59, 1411 (1966).

[32] R. D. Schonbrod, M. A. Q. Khan, L. C. Terriere, and F. W. Plapp, *Life Sci.*, 7, 681 (1968).

[33] J. A. Schafer and L. C. Terriere, *J. Econ. Entomol.*, 63, 787 (1970).

[34] A. Morello, W. Bleecker, and M. Agosin, *Biochem. J.*, 124, 199 (1971).

[35] J. W. Ray, *Biochem. Pharmacol.*, 16, 99 (1967).

[36] G. T. Brooks and A. Harrison, *Life Sci.*, 5, 2315 (1966).

[37] G. T. Brooks and A. Harrison, *Biochem. Pharmacol.*, 18, 557 (1969).

[38] S. E. Lewis, C. F. Wilkinson, and J. W. Ray, *Biochem. Pharmacol.*, 16, 1195 (1967).

[39] M. A. Q. Khan, *Biochem. Pharmacol.*, 19, 903 (1970).

[40] M. A. Q. Khan, *J. Econ. Entomol.*, 62, 388 (1969).

[41] T. Nakatsugawa, J. Ishida, and P. A. Dahm, *Biochem. Pharmacol.*, 14, 1853 (1965).

[42] G. T. Brooks, *World Rev. Pest Control*, 5, 62 (1966).

[43] G. T. Brooks, *Res. Rev.*, 27, 81 (1969).

[44] G. T. Brooks and A. Harrison, *Life Sci.*, 6, 681 (1967).

[45] G. T. Brooks and A. Harrison, *Life Sci.*, 6, 1439 (1967).

[46] L. B. Brattsten, Ph.D. Thesis, Univ. Illinois, Champaign-Urbana, 1971.

[47] M. Agosin, N. Scaramelli, L. Gil, and M. A. Letelier, *Comp. Biochem. Physiol.*, 29, 785 (1969).

[48] J. Chakraborty and J. N. Smith, *Biochem. J.*, 93, 389 (1964).

[49] G. E. R. Hook, T. W. Jordan, and J. N. Smith, in *Enzymatic Oxidations of Toxicants*, (E. Hodgson, ed.), North Carolina State Univ. Press, Raleigh, 1968, pp. 27-46.

[50] R. L. Williamson and M. S. Schechter, *Biochem. Pharmacol.*, 19, 1719 (1970).

[51] J. Fukami and T. Shishido, *Botyu Kagaku*, 28, 63 (1963).
[52] R. I. Krieger and C. F. Wilkinson, *Biochem. Pharmacol.*, 20, 2907 (1971).
[53] R. I. Krieger, Ph.D. Thesis, Cornell Univ., 1970.
[54] R. I. Krieger and C. F. Wilkinson, *Biochem. Pharmacol.*, 18, 1403 (1969).
[55] M. A. Q. Khan, *J. Econ. Entomol.*, 62, 723 (1969).
[56] R. J. Kuhr, *J. Agr. Food Chem.*, 18, 1023 (1970).
[57] R. J. Kuhr, *J. Econ. Entomol.*, 64, 1373 (1971).
[58] L. G. Hansen and E. Hodgson, *Biochem. Pharmacol.*, 20, 1569 (1971).
[59] J. Axelrod, *J. Pharm. Exp. Therap.*, 117, 322 (1956).
[60] J. Axelrod, *Biochem. J.*, 63, 634 (1956).
[61] H. A. Sasame and J. R. Gillette, *Arch. Biochem. Biophys.*, 140, 113 (1970).
[62] T. Nakatsugawa and P. A. Dahm, *J. Econ. Entomol.*, 58, 500 (1965).
[63] H. B. Matthews and E. Hodgson, *J. Econ. Entomol.*, 59, 1286 (1966).
[64] M. Tsukamoto and J. E. Casida, *J. Econ. Entomol.*, 60, 617 (1967).
[65] M. Tsukamoto and J. E. Casida, *Nature*, 213, 49 (1967).
[66] J. Chakraborty, C. H. Sissons, and J. N. Smith, *Biochem. J.*, 102, 492 (1967).
[67] T. W. Jordan, J. N. Smith, and N. Whitehead, *Australas. J. Pharmacy*, 49, (Suppl. 66), 584 (1968).
[68] T. W. Jordan and J. N. Smith, *Int. J. Biochem.*, 1, 139 (1970).
[69] R. D. Schonbrod and L. C. Terriere, *J. Econ. Entomol.*, 64, 44 (1971).
[70] S. Hiraga, *Japan J. Genet.*, 39, 240 (1964).
[71] R. D. Schonbrod, Ph.D. thesis, Oregon State Univ., Corvallis, 1971.
[72] R. D. Schonbrod and L. C. Terriere, *Pesticide Biochem. Physiol.*, in press, 1972.
[73] T. Nakatsugawa, personal communication, 1972.
[74] T. G. Wilson and E. Hodgson, *Pesticide Biochem. Physiol.*, 2, 64 (1972).
[75] R. I. Krieger and C. F. Wilkinson, *Biochem. J.*, 116, 781 (1970).
[76] S. Orrenius, M. Berggren, P. Moldeus, and R. I. Krieger, *Biochem. J.*, 124, 427 (1971).
[77] S. Orrenius, A. Berg, and L. Ernster, *Eu. J. Biochem.*, 11, 193 (1969).
[78] G. M. Benke, M.S. Thesis, Cornell Univ., 1971.
[79] R. I. Krieger and P. W. Lee, *J. Econ. Entomol.*, in press (1972).
[80] J. Fukami, T. Shishido, K. Fukunaga, and J. E. Casida, *J. Agr. Food Chem.*, 17, 1217 (1969).
[81] G. M. Benke and C. F. Wilkinson, *Pesticide Biochem. Physiol.*, 1, 19 (1971).
[82] L. B. Brattsten and C. F. Wilkinson, unpublished work, 1972.
[83] M. D. Gilbert and C. F. Wilkinson, unpublished work, 1972.
[84] R. L. Metcalf and R. B. March, *Ann. Entomol. Soc. Am.*, 46, 63 (1953).
[85] T. Nakatsugawa and P. A. Dahm, *J. Econ. Entomol.*, 55, 594 (1962).
[86] J. E. Casida, R. K. Chapman, M. A. Stahmann, and T. C. Allen, *J. Econ. Entomol.*, 47, 64 (1954).
[87] R. D. O'Brien, *J. Econ. Entomol.*, 50, 159 (1957).
[88] G. C. Kok and J. N. Walop, *Biochim. Biophys. Acta*, 13, 510 (1954).
[89] M. L. Fenwick, *Biochem. J.*, 70, 373 (1958).
[90] R. D. O'Brien and L. S. Wolfe, *J. Econ. Entomol.*, 52, 692 (1959).
[91] K. N. Mehrotra and S. Lal, *Indian J. Entomol.*, 29, 44 (1967).
[92] R. D. O'Brien and E. Y. Spencer, *J. Agr. Food Chem.*, 3, 56 (1955).
[93] M. L. Fenwick, J. R. Barron, and W. A. Watson, *Biochem. J.*, 65, 58 (1957).
[94] M. L. Fenwick, *Nature*, 182, 607 (1958).
[95] G. M. Benke, C. F. Wilkinson, and J. N. Telford, *J. Econ. Entomol.*, 65, 1221 (1972).

[96]   A. Vardanis and C. G. Crawford, *J. Econ. Entomol.*, **57**, 136 (1964).

[97]   E. G. Gemrich, *J. Agr. Food Chem.*, **15**, 617 (1967).

[98]   T. Nakatsugawa, N. M. Tolman, and P. A. Dahm, *Biochem. Pharmacol.*, **17**, 1517 (1968).

[99]   W. A. Brindley and P. A. Dahm, *J. Econ. Entomol.*, **63**, 31 (1970).

[100] G. M. Price and R. J. Kuhr, *Biochem. J.*, **112**, 133 (1971).

[101] R. I. Krieger and C. F. Wilkinson, *J. Econ. Entomol.*, **63**, 1343 (1970).

[102] R. I. Krieger, C. F. Wilkinson and E. F. Taschenberg, *J. Econ. Entomol.*, in press (1972).

[103] N. Ahmad and W. A. Brindley, *Toxicol. Appl. Pharmacol.*, **18**, 124 (1971).

[104] R. I. Krieger, P. P. Feeny, and C. F. Wilkinson, *Science*, **172**, 579 (1971).

[105] R. I. Krieger, M. D. Gilbert, and C. F. Wilkinson, *J. Econ. Entomol.*, **63**, 1322 (1970).

[106] S. Rehr and C. F. Wilkinson, unpublished work, 1970.

[107] G. E. Palade and P. Siekevitz, *J. Biophys. Biochem. Cytol.*, **2**, 171 (1956).

[108] P. Siekevitz, *Ann. Rev. Physiol.*, **25**, 15 (1963).

[109] P. Siekevitz, *Fed. Proc.*, **24**, 1153(1965).

[110] L. Leadbeater and D. R. Davies, *Biochem. Pharmacol.*, **13**, 1607 (1964).

[111] R. M. Philpot and E. Hodgson, *Chem.-Biol. Inter.*, **4**, 399 (1972).

[112] J. Kowal, E. R. Simpson, and R. W. Estabrook, *J. Biol. Chem.*, **245**, 2438 (1970).

[113] A. S. Perry and A. J. Buckner, *Life Sci.*, **9**, 335 (1970).

[114] A. S. Perry, W. E. Dale, and A. J. Buckner, *Pesticide Biochem. Physiol.*, **1**, 131 (1971).

[115] S. Akov, J. E. Oliver, and A. B. Borkovec, *Life Sci.*, **7**(II), 1207 (1968).

[116] J. D. Cassidy, E. Smith, and E. Hodgson, *J. Insect Physiol.*, **15**, 1573 (1969).

[117] W. A. Brindley, Ph.D. thesis, Iowa State Univ., 1966.

[118] I. B. Chaterjee, Z. H. Price, and R. W. McKee, *Nature*, **207**, 1168 (1965).

[119] T. Chan and L. C. Terriere, *Biochem. Pharmacol.*, **18**, 1061 (1969).

[120] T. E. Gram, L. A. Rogers, and J. R. Fouts, *J. Pharm. Exptl. Therap.*, **155**, 479 (1967).

[121] T. E. Gram and J. R. Fouts, in *Enzymatic Oxidations of Toxicants*, (E. Hodgson, ed.), North Carolina State Univ. Press, Raleigh, 1968, pp. 47-64.

[122] J. L. Holtzman, T. E. Gram, P. L. Gigon, and J. R. Gillette, *Biochem. J.*, **110**, 407 (1968).

[123] R. I. Krieger and J. N. Telford, unpublished work, 1971.

[124] The Chemical Society, Thanet Press, Margate, 1970, Specialist Periodical Reports, *Foreign Compound Metabolism in Mammals*, Vol. 1.

[125] L. Shuster, *Ann. Rev. Biochem.*, **33**, 581 (1964).

[126] C. R. Walker and L. C. Terriere, *Entomol. Exptl. Appl.*, **13**, 260 (1970).

[127] L. G. Hansen and E. Hodgson, *Pesticide Biochem. Physiol.*, **1**, 109 (1971).

[128] C. F. Wilkinson and L. J. Hicks, *J. Agr. Food Chem.*, **17**, 829 (1969).

[129] M. A. Q. Khan, J. L. Chang, D. J. Sutherland, J. D. Rosen, and A. Kamal, *J. Econ. Entomol.*, **63**, 1807 (1970).

[130] R. J. Kuhr, *J. Agr. Food Chem.*, **17**, 112 (1969).

[131] S. P. Shrivastava, M. Tsukamoto, and J. E. Casida, *J. Econ. Entomol.*, **62**, 483 (1969).

[132] F. W. Plapp and J. E. Casida, *J. Econ. Entomol.*, **62**, 1175 (1969).

[133] M. Tsukamoto, S. P. Shrivastava, and J. E. Casida, *J. Econ. Entomol.*, **61**, 50 (1968).

[134] R. I. Krieger and C. F. Wilkinson, *Pesticide Biochem. Physiol.*, **1**, 92, (1971).

[135] J. Fukami, I. Yamamoto, and J. E. Casida, *Science*, **155**, 713 (1967).

[136] J. Fukami, T. Mitsui, K. Fukunaga, and T. Shishido, in *Biochemical Toxicology of Insecticides* (R. D. O'Brien and I. Yamamoto, eds.), Academic, New York, 1970, p. 159.

[137] J. Chakraborty and J. N. Smith, *Biochem. J.*, **102**, 498 (1967).

[138] L. Gil, B. C. Fine, M. L. Dinamarca, I. Balazs, J. R. Busvine, and M. Agosin, *Entomol. Exp. Appl.*, **11**, 15 (1968).

[139] F. J. Oppenoorth and N. W. H. Houx, *Entomol. Exp. Appl.*, **11**, 81 (1968).

[140] M. Slade and J. E. Casida, *J. Agr. Food Chem.*, **18**, 467 (1970).

[141] I. Yamamoto and J. E. Casida, *J. Econ. Entomol.*, **59**, 1542 (1966).

[142] I. Yamamoto, E. Kimmel, and J. E. Casida, *J. Agr. Food Chem.*, **17**, 1227 (1969).

[143] T. M. Chan, J. W. Gillett, and L. C. Terriere, *Comp. Biochem. Physiol.*, **20**, 731 (1967).

[144] M. A. Q. Khan and L. C. Terriere, *J. Econ. Entomol.*, **61**, 732 (1968).

[145] S. J. Yu and L. C. Terriere, *Pesticide Biochem. Physiol.*, **1**, 173, (1971).

[146] G. M. Benke and C. F. Wilkinson, *J. Econ. Entomol.*, **64**, 1032 (1971).

[147] L. C. Terriere, S. J. Yu, and R. F. Hoyer, *Science*, **171**, 581 (1971).

[148] M. D. Folsom, L. G. Hansen, R. M. Philpot, and R. S. H. Yang, *Life Sci.*, **9**(II), 869 (1970).

[149] S. Akov and A. B. Borkovec, *Life Sci.*, **7**(II), 1215 (1968).

[150] P. A. Dahm, in *Biochemical Toxicology of Insecticides* (R. D. O'Brien and I. Yamamoto, eds.), Academic, New York, 1970, p. 51.

[151] T. Nakatsugawa and P. A. Dahm, *Biochem. Pharmacol.*, **16**, 25 (1967).

[152] S. ElBashir and F. J. Oppenoorth, *Nature*, **223**, 210 (1969).

[153] F. J. Oppenoorth, *Bull. World Health Organ.*, **44**, 195 (1971).

[154] R. S. H. Yang, E. Hodgson, and W. C. Dauterman, *J. Agr. Food Chem.*, **19**, 14 (1971).

[155] J. E. Casida, J. L. Engel, E. G. Esaac, F. X. Kamienski, and S. Kuwatsuka, *Science*, **153**, 1130 (1966).

[156] E. G. Esaac and J. E. Casida, *J. Agr. Food Chem.*, **17**, 539 (1969).

[157] C. F. Wilkinson, *J. Agr. Food Chem.*, **15**, 139 (1967).

[158] J. E. Casida, *J. Agr. Food Chem.*, **18**, 753 (1970).

[159] F. J. Oppenoorth, S. Voerman, W. Welling, N. W. Houx, and J. Wouters van den Oudenweijer, *Nature-New Biol.*, **233**, 187 (1971).

[160] H. A. Rose, unpublished work, 1972.

[161] R. G. Young, unpublished work, 1972.

[162] G. T. Brooks, A. Harrison, and S. E. Lewis, *Biochem. Pharmacol.*, **19**, 255 (1970).

[163] D. R. Buhler and M. E. Rasmusson, *Comp. Biochem. Physiol.*, **25**, 223 (1968).

[164] P. J. Creaven, W. H. Davies, and R. T. Williams, *Life Sci.*, **6**, 105 (1967).

[165] P. D. Boyer, F. G. Lum, G. A. Ballou, J. M. Luck, and R. G. Rice, *J. Biol. Chem.*, **162**, 181 (1946).

[166] R. P. DiAugustine and J. R. Fouts, *Biochem. J.*, **115**, 547 (1969).

[167] S. Orrenius and H. Thor, *Eu. J. Biochem.*, **9**, 415 (1969).

[168] A. P. Alvares, G. Schilling, A. Garbut, and R. Kuntzman, *Biochem. Pharmacol.*, **19**, 1449 (1970).

[169] R. W. Estabrook and B. S. S. Cohen, in *Microsomes and Drug Oxidations* (J. R. Gillette, A. H. Conney, G. J. Cosmides, R. W. Estabrook, J. R. Fouts, and G. J. Mannering, eds.), Academic, New York, 1969, pp. 95-105.

[170] S. E. Lewis, J. W. Ray, and R. J. Kuhr, in *Insect Toxicologists' Information Service* (F. J. Oppenoorth and N. W. H. Houx, eds.), Wageningen, Netherlands, 1968, Vol. 11, p. 170.

[171] G. T. Brooks, *Meded. Rijksfak. Landbouwwetensch. Gent.*, 33, 629 (1968).

[172] J. B. Schenkman, J. A. Ball, and R. W. Estabrook, *Biochem. Pharmacol.*, 16, 1071 (1967).

[173] L. C. Terriere and T. M. Chan, *Biochem. Pharmacol.*, 18, 1991 (1969).

[174] G. C. Mueller and J. A. Miller, *J. Biol. Chem.*, 176, 535 (1948).

[175] C. F. Wilkinson, in *Proc. 2nd Int. IUPAC Congr. Pesticide Chem.* (A. S. Tahori, ed.), Gordon and Breach, New York, 1971, Vol. 2, p. 117.

[176] C. F. Wilkinson in *Enzymatic Oxidations of Toxicants.* (E. Hodgson ed.), North Carolina State Univ. Press, Raleigh, 1968, p. 113.

[177] J. B. Lewis, *Nature*, 224, 917 (1969).

[178] J. B. Lewis and K. A. Lord, *Proc. 5th Brit., Insect. Fungic. Conf.*, 1, 465 (1969).

[179] M. W. Anders, *Biochem. Pharmacol.*, 17, 2367 (1968).

[180] S. Kuwatsuka, in *Biochemical Toxicology of Insecticides* (R. D. O'Brien and I. Yamamoto, eds.), Academic, New York, 1970, pp. 131-144.

[181] A. Rubin, T. R. Tephly, and G. J. Mannering, *Biochem. Pharmacol.*, 13, 1007 (1964).

[182] M. W. Anders and G. J. Mannering, *Mol. Pharmacol.*, 2, 319 (1966).

[183] D. J. Hennessy, *J. Agr. Food Chem.*, 13, 218 (1965).

[184] D. J. Hennessy, in *Biochemical Toxicology of Insecticides* (R. D. O'Brien and I. Yamamoto, eds.), Academic, New York, 1970, pp. 105-114.

[185] C. Hansch, *J. Med. Chem.*, 11, 920 (1968).

[186] R. S. Marshall and C. F. Wilkinson, *Biochem. Pharmacol.*, 19, 2265 (1970).

[187] R. S. Marshall, Ph.D. thesis, Cornell Univ., 1971.

[188] R. M. Philpot and E. Hodgson, *Life Sci.*, 10, 503 (1971).

[189] M. W. Anders, *Ann. Rev. Pharmacol.*, 11, 37 (1971).

[190] M. W. Anders, A. P. Alvares, and G. J. Mannering, *Mol. Pharmacol.*, 2, 328 (1966).

[191] J. C. Felton, D. W. Jenner, and P. Kirby, *J. Agr. Food Chem.*, 18, 671 (1970).

[192] C. F. Wilkinson, T. Yellin, and K. Hetnarski, submitted to *Biochem. Pharmacol.*, 21, 3187 (1972).

[193] R. M. Sacher, R. L. Metcalf, and T. R. Fukuto, *J. Agr. Food Chem.*, 16, 779 (1968).

[194] J. C. Felton, D. W. Jenner, and P. Kirby, *J. Agr. Food Chem.*, 18, 671 (1970).

[195] C. F. Wilkinson, T. Yellin, and K. Hetnarski, *Biochem. Pharmacol.*, 21, 3187 1972.

[196] D. M. Ziegler, C. H. Mitchell, and D. Jollow, in *Microsomes and Drug Oxidations* (J. R. Gillette, A. H. Conney, G. J. Cosmides, R. W. Estabrook, J. R. Fouts, and G. J. Mannering, eds.), Academic, New York, 1969, p. 173.

[197] S. Orrenius, *J. Cell. Biol.*, 26, 713 (1965).

[198] J. R. Gillette, B. B. Brodie, and B. N. LaDu, *J. Pharmacol. Exp. Therap.*, 119, 532 (1957).

[199] M. D. Folsom and E. Hodgson, *Comp. Biochem. Physiol.*, 37, 301 (1970).

[200] P. L. Gigon, A. M. Guarino, D. H. Schroeder, and J. R. Gillette, *Biochem. J.*, 113, 681 (1969).

[201] M. D. Folsom and E. Hodgson, *Comp. Biochem. Physiol.*, 39B, 599 (1971).

[202] M. D. Folsom, R. M. Philpot, and E. Hodgson, *Comp. Biochem. Physiol.*, 39B, 589 (1971).

[203] T. Omura, R. Sato, D. Y. Cooper, O. Rosenthal, and R. W. Estabrook, *Fed. Proc.*, 24, 1181 (1965).

[204] H. Kamin and B. S. S. Masters, in *Enzymatic Oxidations of Toxicants* (E. Hodgson, ed.), North Carolina State Univ. Press, Raleigh, 1968, pp. 5-25.

[205] H. Remmer, *Am. J. Med.*, 49, 617 (1970).

[206] J. R. Gillette, *Advan. Pharmacol.*, 4, 245 (1966).

[207] H. Kamin, B. S. S. Masters, Q. H. Gibson, and C. H. Williams, *Fed. Proc.*, 24, 1164 (1965).

[208] T. Yamano, Y. Hashimoto, and H. S. Mason, *Fed. Proc.*, 22, 586 (1963).

[209] C. H. Williams, and H. Kamin, *J. Biol. Chem.*, 237, 587 (1962).

[210] J. R. Gillette and T. E. Gram, in *Microsomes and Drug Oxidations* (J. R. Gillette, A. H. Conney, G. J. Cosmides, R. W. Estabrook, J. R. Fouts, and G. J. Mannering, eds.), Academic, New York, 1969, pp. 133-148.

[211] P. Strittmatter and S. F. Velick, *J. Biol. Chem.*, 221, 253 (1956).

[212] P. Strittmatter and S. F. Velick, *J. Biol. Chem.*, 221, 277 (1956).

[213] R. Sato, H. Nishibayashi, and A. Ito, in *Microsomes and Drug Oxidations* (J. R. Gillette, A. H. Conney, G. J. Cosmides, R. W. Estabrook, J. R. Fouts, and G. J. Mannering, eds.), Academic, New York, 1969, pp. 111-128.

[214] T. Hara and S. Minakami, *J. Biochem.*, 69, 325 (1971).

[215] M. Klingenberg, *Arch. Biochem. Biophys.*, 75, 376 (1958).

[216] D. Garfinkel, *Arch. Biochem. Biophys.*, 77, 493 (1958).

[217] T. Omura and R. Sato, *J. Biol. Chem.*, 239, 2370 (1964).

[218] T. Omura and R. Sato, *J. Biol. Chem.*, 239, 2379 (1964).

[219] R. W. Estabrook, D. Y. Cooper, and O. Rosenthal, *Biochem. Z.*, 338, 741 (1963).

[220] D. Y. Cooper, S. Levin, S. Narasimhulu, O. Rosenthal, and R. W. Estabrook, *Science*, 147, 400 (1965).

[221] J. W. Ray, in *Pest Infestation Research*, Her Majesty's Stationery Office, London, 1965, p. 59.

[222] H. B. Matthews and J. E. Casida, *Life Sci.*, 9(I), 989 (1970).

[223] N. E. Sladek and G. J. Mannering, *Biochem. Biophys. Res. Comm.*, 24, 668 (1966).

[224] C. R. E. Jefcoate, J. L. Gaylor, and R. L. Calabrese, *Biochemistry*, 8, 3455 (1969).

[225] S. E. Lewis, *Nature*, 215, 1408 (1967).

[226] Y. Imai and R. Sato, *Biochem. Biophys. Res. Comm.*, 23, 5 (1966).

[227] H. B. Matthews, M. Skrinjaric-Spoljar, and J. E. Casida, *Life Sci.*, 9(I), 1039 (1970).

[228] Y. Imai and R. Sato, *J. Biol. Chem.*, 62, 239 (1967).

[229] Y. Imai and R. Sato, *Biochem. Biophys. Res. Comm.*, 22, 620 (1966).

[230] H. Remmer, J. B. Schenkman, R. W. Estabrook, H. Sasame, J. R. Gillette, D. Y. Cooper, S. Narasimhulu, and O. Rosenthal, *Mol. Pharmacol.*, 2, 187 (1966).

[231] J. B. Schenkman, H. Remmer, and R. W. Estabrook, *Mol. Pharmacol.*, 3, 113 (1967).

[232] H. Remmer, J. B. Schenkman, and H. Greim, in *Microsomes and Drug Oxidations* (J. R. Gillette, A. H. Conney, G. J. Cosmides, R. W. Estabrook, J. R. Fouts, and G. J. Mannering, eds.), Academic, New York, 1969, pp. 371-386.

[233] L. Gil and H. Rose, unpublished work.

[234] A. H. Phillips and R. G. Langdon, *J. Biol. Chem.*, 237, 2652 (1962).

[235] T. G. Wilson, M. S. thesis, North Carolina State Univ., Raleigh, 1970.

[236] T. G. Wilson and E. Hodgson, *Insect Biochem.*, 1, 19 (1971).

[237] T. G. Wilson and E. Hodgson, *Insect Biochem.*, 1, 171 (1971).

[238] C. A. Lang, *Exp. Cell Res.*, 17, 516 (1959).

[239] C. A. Lang, *Fed. Proc.*, 20, 47 (1961).

[240] R. C. Sanborn and C. M. Williams, *J. Gen. Physiol.*, 33, 579 (1950).

[241] B. Chance and A. M. Pappenheimer, *J. Biol. Chem.*, 209, 931 (1954).

[242] A. M. Pappenheimer and C. M. Williams, *J. Biol. Chem.*, **209**, 915 (1957).

[243] C. F. Strittmatter and E. G. Ball, *Proc. Natl. Acad. Sci. U.S.*, **38**, 19 (1952).

[244] Y. Okada and K. Okunuki, *J. Biochem.*, **65**, 581 (1969).

[245] T. Yamanaka, S. Tokuyama, and K. Okunuki, *Biochim. Biophys. Acta*, **77**, 592 (1963).

[246] J. R. Fouts and R. H. Adamson, *Science*, **129**, 897 (1959).

[247] W. R. Jondorf, R. P. Maickel, and B. B. Brodie, *Biochem. Pharmacol.*, **1**, 352 (1959).

[248] S. J. Yaffe, J. Krasner, and C. S. Catz, *Ann. N.Y. Acad. Sci.*, **151**, 887 (1968).

[249] S. J. Yu and L. C. Terriere, *Life Sci.*, **10**(II), 1173 (1971).

[250] S. Abd El-Aziz, R. L. Metcalf, and T. R. Fukuto, *J. Econ. Entomol.*, **62**, 318 (1969).

[251] P. J. Creaven, D. V. Parke, and R. T. Williams, *Biochem. J.*, **91**, 12 p. (1964).

[252] W. S. Bowers, in *Naturally occurring Insecticides* (M. Jacobson and D. G. Crosby, eds.), Dekker, New York, 1971, Chap. 8.

[253] C. E. Berkoff, *Quart. Rev.*, The Chemical Society, London, **23**, 372 (1969).

[254] D. H. S. Horn, in *Naturally Occurring Insecticides* (M. Jacobson and D. G. Crosby, eds.), Dekker, New York, 1971, Chap. 9.

[255] W. F. Robbins, J. N. Kaplanis, M. J. Thompson, and J. A. Svoboda, in *Proc. 2nd Intern. IUPAC Congr. Pesticide Chem.* (A. S. Tahori, ed.), Gordon and Breach, New York, 1971, Vol. III, pp. 1-31.

[256] E. Shaaya and P. Karlson, *J. Insect Physiol.*, **11**, 65 (1965).

[257] N. Patel and K. Madhavan, *J. Insect Physiol.*, **15**, 2141 (1969).

[258] W. S. Bowers, *Science*, **164**, 323 (1969).

[259] M. Slade and C. H. Zibitt in *Proc. 2nd Intern. IUPAC Congr. Pesticide Chem.*, (A. S. Tahori, ed.), Gordon and Breach, New York, 1971, Vol. III, pp. 45-58.

[260] M. Slade and C. H. Zibitt, in *Insect Juvenile Hormones: Chemistry and Action* (J. J. Menn and M. Beroza, eds.), Academic, New York, 1972.

[261] P. Karlson and C. Bode, *J. Insect Physiol.*, **15**, 111 (1969).

[262] A. W. A. Brown, in *Pesticides in the Environment* (R. White-Stevens, ed.), Dekker, New York, 1971, Vol. I, Part II, Chap. 7.

[263] G. P. Georghiou, in *Agricultural Chemicals—Harmony or Discord for Food, People and the Environment* (E. Swift, ed.), Univ. of California, Division of Agricultural Sciences, 1971, p. 113.

[264] A. S. Perry and W. M. Hoskins, *J. Econ. Entomol.*, **44**, 850 (1951).

[265] F. W. Plapp, in *Biochemical Toxicology of Insecticides* (R. D. O'Brien and I. Yamamoto, eds.), Academic, New York, 1970, pp. 179-192.

[266] C. F. Wilkinson, *World Rev. Pest Control*, **7**, 155 (1968).

[267] C. F. Wilkinson, *Bull. World Health Organ.*, **44**, 171 (1971).

[268] G. P. Georghiou, *Exp. Parasitol.*, **26**, 224 (1969).

[269] F. W. Plapp and R. F. Hoyer, *J. Econ. Entomol.*, **61**, 1298 (1968).

[270] A. S. Perry, in *The Physiology of Insecta* (M. Rockstein, ed.), Academic, New York, 1964, Vol. 3, p. 285.

[271] J. V. Dingell, P. D. Joiner, and L. Hurwitz, *Biochem. Pharmacol.*, **15**, 971 (1966).

[272] A. H. Conney, *Pharmacol. Revs.*, **19**, 317 (1967).

[273] R. Kuntzman, *Ann. Rev. Pharmacol.*, **9**, 21 (1969).

[274] H. Remmer, R. W. Estabrook, J. Schenkman, and H. Greim, in *Enzymatic Oxidations of Toxicants* (E. Hodgson, ed.), North Carolina State Univ. Press, Raleigh, 1968, p. 65.

[275] H. Remmer, in *Proc. 2nd Intern. IUPAC Congr. Pesticide Chem.* (A. S. Tahori, ed.), Gordon and Breach, New York, 1971, Vol. II, p. 167.

[276] L. Golberg, *Proc. Eu. Soc. Study of Drug Toxicity*, 7, 171 (1966).

[277] J. R. Fouts and L. A. Rogers, *J. Pharmacol.*, 147, 112 (1965).

[278] H. Remmer and H. J. Merker, *Ann. N.Y. Acad. Sci.*, 123, 79 (1965).

[279] R. Kato, W. R. Jondorf, L. A. Loeb, T. Ben, and H. V. Gelboin, *Mol. Pharmacol.*, 2, 171 (1966).

[280] H. V. Gelboin, J. S. Wortham, and R. G. Wilson, *Nature*, 214, 281 (1967).

[281] A. Morello, *Nature*, 203, 785 (1964).

[282] M. Agosin in *Proc. 2nd Intern. IUPAC Congr. Pesticide Chem.* (A. S. Tahori, ed.), Gordon and Breach, New York 1971, Vol. II, p. 29.

[283] F. W. Plapp and J. E. Casida, *J. Econ. Entomol.*, 63, 1091 (1970).

[284] J. W. Gillett in *Proc. 2nd Intern. IUPAC Congr. Pesticide Chem.* (A. S. Tahori, ed.), Gordon and Breach, New York, 1971, Vol. II, p. 197.

[285] I. Ishaaya and W. Chefurka, *Riv. Parassit.*, 29, 289 (1968).

[286] M. Agosin, B. C. Fine, N. Scaramelli, J. Ilivicky, and L. Aravena, *Comp. Biochem. Physiol.*, 19, 339 (1966).

[287] S. Litvak and M. Agosin, *Biochemistry*, 7, 1560 (1968).

[288] I. Ishaaya and W. Chefurka, in *Proc. 2nd Intern. IUPAC Congr. Pesticide Chem.* (A. S. Tahori, ed.), Gordon and Breach, New York, 1971, Vol. II, p. 267.

[289] M. Agosin, L. Aravena, and A. Neghme, *Exp. Parasitol.*, 16, 318 (1965).

[290] I. Balazs and M. Agosin, *Biochim. Biophys. Acta*, 157, 1 (1968).

[291] S. Litvak, L. Tarrago-Litvak, P. Poblete, and M. Agosin, *Comp. Biochem. Physiol.*, 26, 45 (1968).

[292] H. V. Gelboin, L. R. Younger, D. W. Nebert, and J. M. Miller, *Proc. 4th Intern. Congr. Pharmacol.*, 1969, Vol. 4, p. 287.

[293] M. Agosin, J. Ilivicky, and S. Litvak, *Can. J. Biochem.*, 45, 619 (1967).

[294] M. Agosin, N. Scaramelli, M. L. Dinamarca, and L. Aravena, *Comp. Biochem. Physiol.*, 8, 311 (1963).

[295] R. M. Philpot and E. Hodgson, *Chem. Biol. Interact.*, 4, 185 (1971).

[296] D. Kupfer, *Residue Rev.*, 19, 11 (1967).

[297] A. H. Conney, R. M. Welch, R. Kuntzman, and J. J. Burns, *Clin. Pharmacol. Ther.*, 8, 2 (1967).

[298] C. P. Sherwin, *Physiol. Rev.*, 2, 238 (1922).

[299] D. R. Buhler, *Fed. Proc.*, 25, 343 (1966).

[300] H. T. Gordon, *Ann. Rev. Entomol.*, 6, 27 (1961).

GLOSSARY OF COMMON NAMES

Common, Trade, or Abbreviated Name	Chemical Name
Aldrin	1,2,3,4,10,10-hexachloro-1,4,4a,5,8,8a-hexahydro-1,4-endo,exo-5,8-dimethanonaphthalene
Allethrin	dl-2-allyl-4-hydroxy-3-hydroxy-3-methyl-2-cyclopenten-1-one esters of cis and trans dl chrysanthemum monocarboxylic acids
Banol	2-chloro-4,5-dimethylphenyl N-methylcarbamate
Baygon	2-iospropoxyphenyl N-methylcarbamate
Carbaryl	1-naphthyl N-methylcarbamate
DDT	1,1,1-trichloro-2,2,-bis(p-chlorophenyl)ethane
Diazinon	0,0-diethyl 0-(2-isopropyl-6-methyl-4-pyrimidinyl) phosphorothionate
Dieldrin	1,2,3,4,10,10-hexachloro-6,7-exo-epoxy-1,4,4a,5,6,7,8,8a-octahydro-1,4-endo,exo-5,8-dimethanonaphthalene
Dihydroaldrin	1,2,3,4,10,10-hexachloro-1,4,4a,5,6,7,8,8a-octahydro-1,4-endo,exo-5,8-dimethanonaphthalene
Dihydrochlordene	4,5,6,7,8,8a-hexachloro-3a,4,7,7a-tetrahydro-4,7-methanoindane
Dihydroisodrin	1,2,3,4,10,10-hexachloro-1,4,4a,5,6,7,8,8a-octahydro-1,4-endo,endo-5,8-dimethanonaphthalene
EPN	0-ethyl-0-p-nitrophenyl phenylphosphonothionate
Guthion	0,0-dimethyl S-4-oxo-1,2,3,-benzotriazin-3(4-H)-ylmethyl-phosphorodithioate
Hempa	hexamethylphosphorictriamide
Heptachlor	1-exo-4,5,6,7,8,8-heptachloro-3a,4,7,7a-tetrahydro-4,7-methanoindene
Isodrin	1,2,3,4,10,10-hexachloro-1,4,4a,5,8,8a-hexahydro-1,4-endo,endo-5,8-dimethanonaphthalene
Isosafrole	1,2-methylenedioxy-4-propenylbenzene
Landrin	mixture of 3,4,5- and 2,3,5-trimethylphenyl-N-methylcarbamate
Mesurol	4-methylthio-3,5-xylyl N-methylcarbamate
Methoxychlor	1,1,1-trichloro-2,2-bis (p-methoxyphenyl) ethane
Metyrapone	2-methyl-1,2-di(3-pyridyl)-1-propanone
MGK 264	N-(2-ethylhexyl)-5-norbornene-2,3-dicarboximide
Parathion	0,0-diethyl-0-p-nitrophenyl phosphorothionate
Piperonyl butoxide	α-[2-(2-butoxyethoxy)ethoxy]-4,5-methylenedioxy-2-propyltoluene
Propyl isome	di-n-propyl-3-methyl-6,7-methylenedioxy-1,2,3,4-tetrahydronaphthalene-1,2-dicarboxylate
Safrole	4-allyl-1,2-methylenedioxybenzene
Schradan	octamethylpyrophosphoramide
Sesamex	2-[3,4-(methylenedioxy)phenoxy]-3,6,9-trioxaundecane
SKF 525-A	2-(diethylamino)ethyl 2,2-diphenylpentanoate
Sulfoxide	1,2-methylenedioxy-4-[2-(octylsulfinyl)propyl] benzene
Tropital	piperonal bis[2-(2-butoxyethoxy)ethyl]acetal
WARF antiresistant	N,N-di-n-butyl-p-chlorobenzene sulfonamide

Effects of Environmental Organophosphorus Insecticides on Drug Metabolism

ROBERT E. STITZEL, JAMES T. STEVENS* AND
JOSEPH J. McPHILLIPS
Department of Pharmacology
West Virginia University Medical Center
Morgantown, West Virginia 26506

*Present address: Department of Pharmacology, Hershey Medical Center, Hershey, Pennsylvania 17033.

I. INTRODUCTION

The organophosphorus cholinesterase inhibitors are used extensively as agricultural insecticides. As a consequence, these compounds have now become a part of our environment, a fact that is of considerable toxicological significance. The principal action of the organophosphates is inhibition of cholinesterase and it is inhibition of this enzyme that is responsible for the signs of poisoning that are characteristic of that group of compounds; viz., excessive salivation, lacrimation, bronchoconstriction, sweating, nausea, abdominal cramps, vomiting, prostration, and death.

In addition to inhibiting cholinesterase the organophosphates will also act on other enzymes. One group of enzymes that is susceptible to inhibition is referred to as the "aliesterases" or "carboxyesterases." These enzymes are located primarily in the liver but are also found in plasma. Another important group of enzymes affected by organophosphates is the mixed-function oxidase system of the liver microsomes. The reaction of organophosphates with either carboxyesterases or mixed-function oxidases can produce alterations in the intensity and duration of action of a number of chemical substances to which organisms are exposed. The effects on enzymes other than cholinesterase, therefore, may prove to have important consequences for man.

This review is intended to focus on the interactions that occur between organophosphorus insecticides and the microsomal drug metabolizing enzymes. Particular emphasis has been placed upon insecticide-insecticide and insecticide-drug relationships because they may lead to profound changes in drug toxicity.

II. HYDROLASES

A. Hydrolytic Inactivation of Organophosphate Insecticides

All organophosphates are hydrolyzed by all organisms in which these compounds have been studied but the rate of hydrolysis varies depending upon the species studied. With few exceptions, the hydrolysis products of organic phosphates are nontoxic and do not inhibit cholinesterase [1]. Some of the enzymes that hydrolyze certain organophosphates are themselves subject to inhibition by organophosphates as well as by other compounds. Inhibition of hydrolysis is reported to be the basis for the lethal interaction that has been observed with certain combinations of organophosphates.

B. Lethal Interaction of Insecticides by Inhibition of
Mammalian Aliesterases

The ability of one organophosphate to potentiate the action of another was first observed by Frawley et al. [2] for the simultaneous administration of O-ethyl,O-p-nitrophenyl phenylphosphonothioate (EPN) and malathion. Malathion is an organic phosphate that is relatively nontoxic for mammals. The toxicity of this agent, however, is greatly enhanced when it is given with nontoxic doses of EPN. When malathion is given alone, the oral LD_{50} in male rats is 1400 mg/kg; the LD_{50} of EPN is 65 mg/kg. When given in combination, the LD_{50} of malathion is 165 mg/kg and the LD_{50} of EPN is 6.6 mg/kg, an increase in toxicity of approximately 10-fold [2]. In subsequent studies in which a number of pesticide combinations were examined, DuBois [3] reported malathion to be potentiated more frequently than any other compound. For a list of substances that will potentiate the toxicity of malathion the reader is referred to the articles by DuBois [3] and by Casida et al. [4].

Potentiation of malathion toxicity appears to be related to inhibition of carboxyesterases. Cook et al. [5-7] found that malathion is hydrolyzed by rat liver homogenates and that EPN prevents this hydrolysis. A subsequent study by Murphy and DuBois [8] revealed that liver from several species is capable of hydrolyzing malathion. Malathion, therefore, is very rapidly degraded by mammalian liver.

Malathion is a phosphorothionate and does not inhibit cholinesterase in vitro but is oxidized by liver microsomal enzymes to an oxygen analog, malaoxon, that does inhibit cholinesterase. Apparently, both malathion and malaoxon are subject to hydrolysis [8] and the enzyme responsible for hydrolyzing both of these substances has been identified by Main and Braid [9] as a carboxyesterase or aliesterase (Fig. 1). These liver esterases are the B-type esterases described and characterized by Aldrige [10]. They have a wide spectrum of activity and they hydrolyze both aromatic and aliphatic uncharged carboxylic esters. Main and Braid [9] studied the hydrolysis of malathion by rat and human liver and by rat plasma. Of all of the esterases examined only carboxyesterase (aliesterase) hydrolyzed malathion at significant rates.

C. Predicting Lethal Interaction

A method for predicting potentiation of malathion or any agent hydrolyzed by carboxyesterase was reported almost simultaneously in 1968 by DuBois et al. [11] and by Murphy and Cheever [12]. Be-

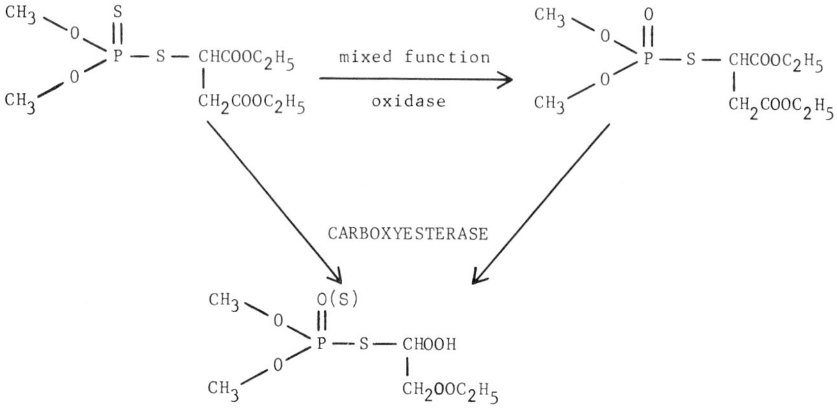

FIG. 1. Biotransformation of malathion and malaoxon.

cause malaoxon inhibits its own hydrolysis and the hydrolysis of malathion [13], triacetin and ethyl succinate are used as substrates for the carboxyesterase assay. Both groups of investigators found that aliesterases were much more susceptible to inhibition by organophosphates than was cholinesterase. For example, 4.5 ppm of EPN produced 50% inhibition of liver aliesterase, whereas 40 ppm were required to produce an equivalent degree of inhibition of brain cholinesterase [14]. A recent study by Cohen and Murphy [15], however, has shown that carboxyesterase inhibition in itself may not be sufficient to predict the relative capacities of various compounds to potentiate the toxicity of malathion. Parathion, for example, which produced significant inhibition of the hydrolysis of diethyl succinate, triacetin, and methyl butyrate, did not potentiate the toxicity of malathion. EPN, however, did potentiate the action of malathion and potentiation was closely associated with inhibition of hydrolysis of triacetin. Other factors, therefore, must be involved in potentiation of malathion toxicity.

D. Inhibition of Mammalian Acylamidase

Another enzyme that is subject to inhibition by organophosphates is an acylamidase which has been found in the liver of mammals [16]. This enzyme has been shown to be responsible for the hydrolysis of the herbicide 3,4-dichloroproprion anilide, the hydrolysis of which is inhibited by parathion [16]. In a later study, DuBois et al. [11] showed that both EPN and Delnav, at dietary levels of 5 and 25 ppm, caused significant inhibition of liver acylamidase.

It is clear, therefore, that organophosphates inhibit enzymes other than cholinesterase and that these enzymes are more susceptible to inhibition than is cholinesterase. Many of these enzymes are no doubt involved in the disposal of foreign compounds. It is important, therefore, to know which substances may inhibit these enzymes. It has been emphasized by DuBois [14] that if information on dietary levels that inhibit esterase activity were to be used in establishing tolerances for organophosphorus insecticides, adherence to such tolerances would insure that interaction through this mechanism would not occur.

III. EFFECTS ON MIXED FUNCTION OXIDASES

A. Microsomal Inactivation and Activation of Organophosphate Insecticides

In 1955, Brodie et al. [17] isolated the endoplasmic reticulum of the liver and proposed that it was the principal site involved in the biotransformation of foreign compounds. The endoplasmic reticulum of liver cells and other tissues is composed of a lipoprotein network of parallel stacks of tubules (cisternae) that randomly permeate to most parts of the cell cytoplasm. When the liver is homogenized, the cells are disrupted and the endoplasmic reticulum is fragmented to form small vesicles, known as "microsomes." Associated with the endoplasmic reticulum are enzymes, called "mixed-function oxidases," which require the reduced coenzyme $NADPH_2$ and oxygen, and it is these enzymes that are concerned in the metabolism of foreign compounds, steroids, and lipids.

The most common routes of microsomal metabolism involve oxidative, reductive, hydrolytic, or conjugative reactions. Often, a drug is subjected to several competing pathways simultaneously and the quantity of each metabolite formed will depend upon the relative rates of the various pathways. In addition, metabolic reactions can proceed sequentially. For instance, hydrolysis may take place only when preceeded by an oxidative step [18, 19]. Bidrin, a trialkylphosphate insecticide, undergoes N-demethylation, O-demethylation, and hydrolysis of the amide and alkylphosphate linkages [20].

Parathion is readily metabolized by mammals and insects into its oxygen analog, paraoxon. Paraoxon is further metabolized by hydrolysis to yield diethyl phosphate and p-nitrophenol and the latter is finally excreted in the urine as conjugates of p-aminophenol. It has been suggested that the hydrolytic cleavage occurs only subsequent to desulfuration [21].

Organophosphorus insecticides are usually degraded in animals by cleavage of phosphorus ester linkages. In the case of the phosphoro-thionates, the common route of metabolism is the one leading to the production of dialkylphosphorthioic acids [22-24]. It had long been assumed that the metabolites formed from the organophosphorus insecticides were the result of a hydrolytic action of blood and/or tissue phosphatases. Attempts to demonstrate these phosphatases, however, were not very successful except in the case of the housefly [25]. Recent studies, however, show that parathion is oxidatively cleaved by microsomal enzymes to yield diethyl phosphorothioic acid and 4-nitrophenol [26, 27]. Analogs of parathion containing a 4-nitrophenyl ester structure also undergo similar metabolic breakdown [28], as do diazinon and malathion [29]. It seems quite probable, therefore, that microsomal oxidative metabolism is not limited to 4-nitrophenyl analogs of parathion but probably occurs with many organophosphorus insecticides and may be a common metabolic pathway to many P-S compounds. The above studies emphasize the importance of microsomal metabolism in the biotransformation of organophosphorus esters.

As has been mentioned previously, certain organophosphorus insecticides are inefficient anticholinesterase agents in their original molecular form and must be oxidized (activated) in order to become potent anti-AChE agents. The hepatic system, which performs this biotransformation, is remarkably similar, if not identical, to the system responsible for drug metabolism. It requires the same cofactors, is sensitive to the same inhibitors, and is located in the microsomal fraction of the liver. The reaction product in the case of the phosphorothionates is the corresponding phosphate [30], whereas a phosphoramidate, such as OMPA, probably gives rise to its hydroxyl derivative [30, 31].

It should also be mentioned that such compounds as parathion, paraoxon, and EPN can serve as substrates for a nitroreductase system in liver microsomes of mammals, birds, and fishes [32]. Reduction of the nitro to the amino group probably proceeds via formation of the nitroso and/or hydroxylamino intermediates. The cofactor requirements of this system are again identical to that described by Fouts and Brodie [33] for the drug metabolizing system.

The phosphorodithioate insecticide, Dimethoate, has been shown to be metabolized by both a microsomal amidase and by cleavage of the S—C bond [34]. Hitchcock and Murphy [32] have suggested that in species in which hydrolytic degradation of the organophosphorus insecticides either does not occur or is slow, alternative metabolic pathways, such as reduction, may assume a much more important role in detoxication.

B. Biotransformational Activation of Parathion by Fishes

Contrary to reports that fishes lack significant microsomal enzyme activity, Ludke et al.[35] indicate that certain freshwater fishes have a pronounced ability to activate parathion in vivo. The reactions catalyzed by the fish enzymes are analogous to those demonstrated in mammals and insects. This observation supports the contention of Mayer et al. [36] that insecticides may influence the metabolism and/or toxicity of one another in the aquatic environment.

C. Inhibition of the Degradation of Organophosphates in Insects by Synergists

Piperonyl butoxide and other methylenedioxyphenyl (MDP) compounds are used as synergists for insecticide chemicals because they inhibit insect microsomal enzymes. They also have an effect on mammalian enzymes but are generally more effective and persist longer in insects than in mammals [37]. Housefly microsomes appear to metablize the insecticide synergists more slowly and thus are more easily inhibited by the in vitro addition of these substances [38]. The consequences of this microsomal inhibition usually are an increased toxicity and persistence of the insecticide in the organism. Treatment of houseflies [39] or mice [40] with insecticide synergists results in a reduced level of cytochrome P-450, a microsomal pigment thought to be important in the metabolism of steroids and drugs [41]. It is interesting that Jaffe et al. [42] have found that the MDP synergists may affect some microsomal pathways more than others. A factor that should not be ignored is that impurities in the insecticides themselves may contribute to insecticidal potentiation.

D. Insecticide-Drug Interactions

1. Hexobarbital Sleeping Time

Changes in the intensity and duration of action of clinically useful drugs has also been shown to be a consequence of exposure to insecticides. Rosenberg and Coon [43], for example, found that acute administration of the organophosphates ethyl p-nitrophenyl (thiobenzene phosphorate) (EPN), octamethyl pyrophosphoramide (OMPA), malathion, chlorothion, and Phostex increased hexobarbital sleeping time (HST) in mice. They suggested that the conversion of OMPA, parathion, and hexobarbital is an oxidative process that takes place both in the microsomal and in the supernatant fraction of liver homogenates.

Both OMPA and parathion are converted from relatively inactive substances to potent anticholinesterase compounds, whereas malathion,
chlorothion, and Phostex are partially inactivated by hepatic microsomes. Tetraethyl pyrophosphate (TEPP), which is neither activated
nor inactivated by liver microsomes, failed to increase HST. Serrone
and Fujimoto [44] observed an increase in HST following the acute
administration of N-methyl-3-piperidyl(N^1,N^1)diphenylcarbamate
hydrochloride (MPDC) to mice. Hart and Fouts [45] found that a single
dose of EPN to mice prolonged HST when hexobarbital was given as
long as 8 days after the initial injection of EPN. Parathion, paraoxon,
and malathion also significantly increased HST after a single injection, whereas OMPA had no effect. Proctor [46] found that a dose of
50 mg/kg of parathion caused the loss of righting reflex in mice treated
with a subanesthetic dose of hexobarbital, whereas OMPA failed to
enhance the sedative action of this barbiturate. Because the biotransformation of anticholinesterase insecticides by the liver may involve
the same enzyme system as that utilized in hexobarbital metabolism,
measurement of changes in HST after pesticide administration would
be a valid approach to the study of the effects of these agents on microsomal metabolism.

2. Liver Microsomes

Only a few studies have been concerned with the in vitro effects
of anticholinesterase pesticides on hepatic microsomal metabolism.
Conney et al. [47] have shown that both the acute and chronic administration of chlorothion inhibited the metabolism of steroids by the
hepatic microsomal system. These workers also found that parathion,
paraoxon, and malathion inhibited testosterone metabolism when added
in vitro. DuBois et al. [11] reported that organophosphate insecticides
were capable of inhibiting the detoxication of drugs and other chemicals containing ester linkages. MacDonald et al. [48] observed that
administration of parathion to female rats at 25% of its LD$_{50}$ inhibited
O-demethylase, O-dearylase, N-demethylase, azoreductase, and nitroreductase activity and that a single dose (1/4 LD$_{50}$) of carbaryl inhibited the enzymic activity of O-dearylase, N-demethylase, azoreductase, and nitroreductase but enhanced O-demethylase activity.

3. Acute Effects in Several Species

The toxic effects of the organophosphate insecticides have been
extensively studied in mammals. Furthermore, because studies by
other workers have implicated the cholinesterase inhibiting pesticides
with impaired microsomal metabolism and decreased drug detoxica-

tion, one might suspect that many drug-pesticide interactions would occur.

With such interactions in mind, our laboratory began an examination of the acute and subacute effects of selected anticholinesterase insecticides on hepatic microsomal drug metabolism.

Figure 2 shows that parathion, paraoxon, malathion, disulfoton, and carbaryl, when given 1 h prior to hexobarbital administration, significantly prolonged hexobarbital sleeping time [49, 50]. When

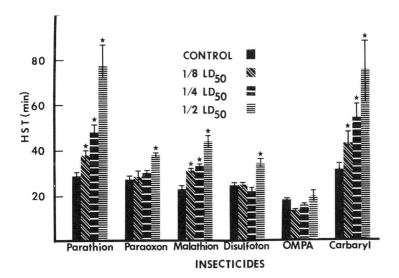

FIG. 2. Hexobarbital sleeping time (HST) in mice pretreated with various doses of insecticide. Animals were given either the insecticide or the appropriate vehicle orally 1 h prior to hexobarbital administration (100 mg/kg, i.p.). Values are the means ± S.E. obtained from 8 animals. Stars indicate significant differences (< 0.05).

this study was extended to the in vitro situation, it was found that parathion, malathion, disulfoton, and carbaryl were potent inhibitors of the metabolism not only of hexobarbital (Fig. 3), but also of aniline (Fig. 4) and ethylmorphine (Fig. 5). Paraoxon also inhibited the microsomal metabolism of ethylmorphine and hexobarbital in vitro and increased HST. However, paraoxon showed the ability to enhance rather than inhibit aniline metabolism [50]. OMPA, however, neither prolonged sleeping time in vivo nor impaired microsomal metabolism in vitro.

It is quite likely that a competition exists between the insecticides and the microsomal substrates used in our study. The existence of a competition is supported by our finding that increases in insecticide

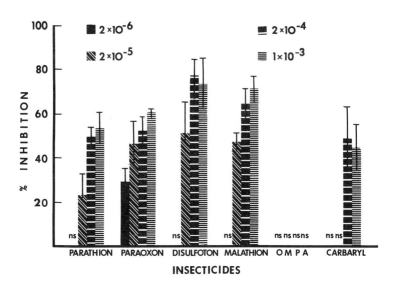

FIG. 3. Inhibition of the in vitro metabolism of hexobarbital produced by increasing molar concentrations of insecticide. Each value represents the mean ± S.E. of 3-5 experiments using mouse liver microsomes. (ns) No significant inhibition.

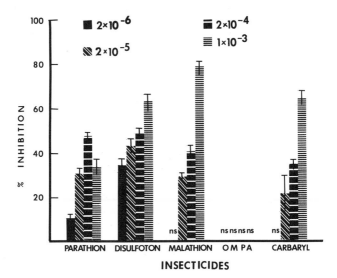

FIG. 4. Inhibition of the in vitro metabolism of aniline produced by increasing molar concentrations of insecticide. Each value represents the mean ± S.E. of 3-5 experiments using mouse liver microsomes. (ns) No significant inhibition.

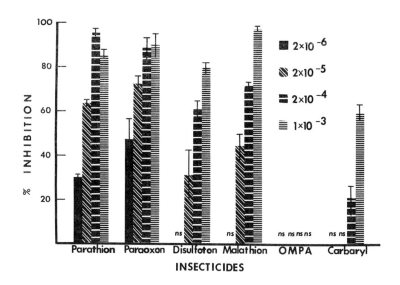

FIG. 5. Inhibition of the in vitro metabolism of ethylmorphine produced by increasing molar concentrations of insecticide. Each value represents the mean ± S.E. of 3-5 experiments using mouse liver microsomes. (ns) No significant inhibition.

concentration generally lead to increases in inhibition of substrate metabolism. The insecticides may be functioning as alternative substrates, as Lykken and Casida [51] have shown that many of them are metabolized by microsomal enzymes. A substrate competition for microsomal enzymes has already been established for some of the phosphorothionate insecticides and testosterone [52, 53].

The observation that OMPA has little inhibitory effect on the metabolism of hexobarbital, aniline, and ethylmorphine suggested that the ability of the insecticides to inhibit drug metabolism was not mediated through their action on cholinesterase. Although Proctor [46] has suggested that inhibition of brain cholinesterase may be a factor in prolonging the central action of hexobarbital, this does not appear to be the case in our study [50] because physostigmine, a drug that does inhibit brain cholinesterase [54], had no effect on the duration of hexobarbital anesthesia. Furthermore, the sensitivity of the central nervous system to hexobarbital did not appear to be significantly altered, because the brain concentration of barbiturate upon awakening was the same in control and insecticide-treated animals (Table 1). It appears from our studies that only those cholinesterase-inhibiting insecticides that are capable of competing for the microsomal enzyme system can alter the response of the animal to hexobarbital.

TABLE 1

Hexobarbital Sleeping Time (HST) and Brain Levels at Time of Awakening after
Acute Administration of Anticholinesterase Insecticides at ½ of Their LD_{50} to Mice

Treatment	Number of animals	HST ± S.E. (min)	Brain hexobarbital level (μg/g)
Control[a]	15	25.8 ± 2.6	44.0 ± 2.9
Parathion	15	60.8 ± 4.2[c]	51.6 ± 5.6
Malathion	15	86.5 ± 12.2[c]	48.6 ± 3.2
Disulfoton	15	33.6 ± 2.0[c]	43.0 ± 4.6
Carbaryl	15	33.6 ± 2.0[c]	39.2 ± 4.3
Control[b]	15	26.2 ± 1.7	45.4 ± 4.1
Paraoxon	15	34.5 ± 1.9[c]	50.0 ± 6.0
OMPA	15	31.8 ± 2.8	54.5 ± 9.3
Physostigmine	15	29.4 ± 1.9	56.7 ± 7.1

[a]Corn oil was used to solubilize all agents listed directly below in the column.
[b]Physiological saline used to solubilize all agents listed directly below in the column.
[c]Different from control at $p < 0.05$.

We have also studied the inhibition of microsomal drug metabolism
produced by the cholinesterase-inhibiting insecticides in the livers of
several species. This was done by comparing the rates of metabolism
of hexobarbital and aniline in a number of species, both in the presence
and in the absence of several of the insecticides [50]. Of the insecticides studied, only malathion and carbaryl were potent inhibitors of
hexobarbital metabolism in all species [Table 2]. Malathion inhibited
aniline metabolism in all species, whereas carbaryl was an inhibitor
of aniline hydroxylation only in the mouse and rat. Paraoxon, although
inhibiting hexobarbital oxidation in the mouse and rat, enhanced aniline metabolism in all species examined. OMPA, although not an inhibitor of drug metabolism, did appear to cause some degree of enhancement of hexobarbital oxidation in the rat and rabbit.

Because chemicals can affect hepatic drug and steroid metabolism
in man [55-57] as well as in experimental animals, we attempted to
determine whether insecticide-drug interactions can occur with therapeutic agents. We examined the effect that pretreatment with either
tolbutamide or bishydroxycoumarin had on the toxicity of carbaryl [50].
Both of these drugs, when administered 1 h prior to carbaryl, markedly
increased the toxicity of this compound. Potentiation of carbaryl toxicity may be explained on the basis of a competition of tolbutamide
and bishydroxycoumarin with carbaryl for microsomal enzymes, because all three compounds are inactivated by hepatic microsomes.
Such a competition would result in the enhancement of toxicity by preventing the biotransformation of carbaryl.

TABLE 2

Changes[a] in the in Vitro Liver Microsomal Metabolism of Hexobarbital and Aniline after the Addition of Insecticides

Pathway	Number of experimental animals	Species	Paraoxon	Malathion	Carbaryl	OMPA
Hexobarbital	3	Mouse	-60.6 ± 2.1^b	-71.6 ± 5.9^b	-44.6 ± 10.6^b	-10.0 ± 8.3
	3	Rat	-65.7 ± 10.0^b	-81.2 ± 3.3^b	-71.3 ± 2.3^b	$+30.5 \pm 5.2^b$
	3	Rabbit	$+19.0 \pm 3.9^b$	-26.2 ± 18.4	-74.0 ± 10.7^b	$+48.1 \pm 8.8^b$
	3	Dog	$+11.3 \pm 7.4$	-68.3 ± 3.4^b	-94.8 ± 5.2^b	$+11.2 \pm 5.2$
Aniline	3	Mouse	$+198.0 \pm 27.9^b$	-78.6 ± 3.2^b	-65.1 ± 3.1^b	$+1.4 \pm 11.4$
	3	Rat	$+287.0 \pm 37.0^b$	-78.8 ± 0.8^b	-27.1 ± 0.3^b	-2.3 ± 2.2
	3	Rabbit	$+248.0 \pm 31.0^b$	-54.7 ± 1.1^b	-13.2 ± 4.9	$+11.1 \pm 2.5$
	3	Dog	$+84.8 \pm 6.9^b$	-57.6 ± 4.1^b	-15.4 ± 7.6	$+7.4 \pm 7.0$
	1	Man (M)	—	-68.8	-25.0	-20.8
	1	Man (M)	$+13.9$	—	-15.8	$+2.5$

[a]Values expressed as percentage change in metabolism from the control; (−) indicates inhibition and (+) indicates stimulation.
[b]Different from their relative control at $p \leqslant 0.05$.

4. Chronic Exposure

Acute exposure was characterized by an inhibitory effect on drug metabolism. It was also of interest to determine the effect of more prolonged exposure to these insecticides on hepatic microsomal metabolism [58]. In contrast to the acute studies, the subacute administration (3-10 days) of parathion, malathion, disulfoton, carbaryl, and paraoxon shortened hexobarbital sleeping time in mice. This dose required to produce these effects, however, approached the toxic range because 1/2 the LD_{50} of each insecticide was necessary to shorten HST. At 1/8 the LD_{50}, only parathion and carbaryl shortened sleeping time, whereas OMPA had no effect at either 1/8 or 1/4 of its LD_{50}. At 1/2 its LD_{50}, all the mice treated with OMPA died.

The increased rate of drug metabolism that was suggested by the shortened barbiturate sleeping time was substantiated by our in vitro experiments [58]. The microsomal metabolism of hexobarbital and aniline was measured after 3 and 5 days of treating mice with 1/2 the LD_{50} of each insecticide. These time periods were chosen because mortality was considerably less at these intervals of drug administration. The metabolism of hexobarbital was more susceptible to stimulation than was the metabolism of aniline. Parathion, paraoxon, disulfoton, and carbaryl all produced substantial increases in the rate of hexobarbital oxidation after 5 days of insecticide treatment. Smaller increases in barbiturate metabolism were seen when animals were treated only 3 days (Table 3).

TABLE 3

Effect of Subacute Administration of Insecticides[a] on the in Vitro Metabolism[b] of Hexobarbital

| Treatment | Days of administration[c] | |
	3	5
None	94.5 ± 1.4 (3)	116.4 ± 5.2 (5)
Parathion	111.8 ± 6.8 (3)	155.2 ± 5.4[d] (5)
Paraoxon	150.1 ± 12.4[d] (3)	196.3 ± 14.1[d] (3)
Disulfoton	162.1 ± 20.7[d] (3)	160.0 ± 12.7[d] (5)
Carbaryl	144.1 ± 9.1[d] (3)	175.9 ± 19.0[d] (5)

[a]Insecticides were administered at ½ the LD50.

[b]Rate of metabolism is expressed as μmoles of hexobarbital metabolized per miligram of microsomal protein per hour.

[c]Numbers in parenthesis represent number of experiments. Each experiment was done with microsomes pooled from three mice.

[d]Significantly different from controls at the 0.05 level of probability.

Only carbaryl caused an induction of aniline metabolism after three daily doses of insecticide at 1/2 the LD_{50}. After 5 days, however, parathion, paraoxon, and disulfoton also increased the rate of aniline hydroxylation, although the increase was of a lesser magnitude than that observed for hexobarbital metabolism.

Because some of the anticholinesterase insecticides are able to both inhibit and stimulate drug metabolism, the action of the insecticides is not unlike the action of SKF 525A and other chemicals that affect drug metabolism in a biphasic manner [59]. It is obvious that this biphasic response of the drug metabolizing enzymes to anticholinesterase insecticides may be of some clinical importance, because humans may be subacutely or chronically exposed to these agents in their environment through serial spraying and ingestion of contaminated foodstuffs.

E. Enhancement of Drug Metabolism

In addition to induction of microsomal enzymes, a less clearly understood phenomenon of enhancement of drug metabolism may also occur. Anders [60] described enhancement as an increase in the in vitro metabolism of a compound produced by the addition of a second drug or chemical to the reaction mixture. Several workers have shown that certain chemically and pharmacologically unrelated compounds are able to enhance the metabolism of various substrates [61-64]. Studies in our laboratory [65, 66] have indicated that paraoxon is capable of enhancing the microsomal metabolism of aniline. The enhancing properties of paraoxon are not restricted to a single animal species. Although rat liver microsomes appear to be most responsive to the enhancing effects of paraoxon, aniline metabolism in the rabbit, mouse, and dog is also augmented (Table 4). It is interesting that Buhler and Rasmusson [67] have demonstrated enhancement of aniline metabolism in the rainbow trout. If human aniline hydroxylase activity is enhanced, the enhancement is not very marked because a paraoxon concentration of 1×10^{-3} M produced only slightly increased metabolic rates. One should bear in mind, however, that the period elapsed between the time of death and obtaining the human tissue sample (8-16 h) could have influenced the viability of the microsomes.

Although it was not possible to establish a mechanism for the enhancement of aniline metabolism by paraoxon, some observations may be made relative to its action compared with that of other known enhancers, such as acetone. When compared on a molar basis, paraoxon was much more potent than was acetone in enhancing aniline metabolism. A combination of the two chemicals did not produce additive

TABLE 4

Enhancement of Aniline Metabolism by Paraoxon in Liver
Microsomes from Different Species

Species	N	Mean control values ± S.E.[a]	Relative activity[b] ± S.E.		
			2×10^{-5} M	2×10^{-4} M	1×10^{-3} M
Mouse	4	71.6 ± 4.0	1.51 ± 0.10[c]	2.75 ± 0.31[c]	2.98 ± 0.39[c]
Rat	3	20.8 ± 5.2	1.14 ± 0.06	2.33 ± 0.16[c]	3.87 ± 0.37[c]
Rabbit	3	15.5 ± 0.7	1.46 ± 0.07[c]	2.56 ± 0.17[c]	3.48 ± 0.31[c]
Dog	3	25.8 ± 3.0	1.07 ± 0.02	1.44 ± 0.41[c]	2.10 ± 0.03[c]
Human	1	2.6	0.99	0.98	1.17
Human	1	0.8	1.09	1.10	1.14

[a]In nmoles/mg protein/h.
[b]With paraoxon/without paraoxon.
[c]Different from corresponding samples without paraoxon ($p < 0.05$).

effects but, in fact, actually reduced the degree of enhancement seen
with paraoxon alone. The enhancement produced by paraoxon appears
to resemble that brought about by 2,2'-bipyridine, because the latter
compound also produces some degree of blockade when incubated together with acetone [63].

The mechanism of activation produced by paraoxon is not dependent
upon the conversion of paraoxon to an active metabolite because the
addition of p-nitrophenol fails to cause enhancement of aniline hydroxylase activity in microsomal incubation mixtures [66]. It is of interest that the in vivo administration of paraoxon 1 h prior to sacrifice
resulted in an apparent in vitro enhancement of aniline hydroxylation.
It is probable that the latter stimulation was a true enhancement
rather than a microsomal induction, because it is unlikely that an increase in microsomal enzyme synthesis could have occurred in only
60 min; this view is based in part upon the observation that total
microsomal protein did not change during this time interval. Recent
studies by Kitagawa et al. [68] also point to an in vitro enhancement
of drug metabolism after in vivo drug administration.

Because the presence of paraoxon can change the kinetic properties
of aniline hydroxylation (Table 5), paraoxon-induced enhancement may
involve a direct interaction of paraoxon with the microsomal aromatic hydroxylases such that an alteration in the three-dimensional
structure of the enzyme(s) results. An examination of the allosteric
effects of all of the known enhancers may, in the future, offer a fruit-
ful approach to mechanistic studies.

TABLE 5

Effect of Acetone and Paraoxon on the Kinetics of
Aniline Hydroxylase of Mouse Liver

Enhancing agent	$K_m \times 10^{-4}$ M	V_{max}[a]
None	1.50 ± 0.13	69.2 ± 4.3
Paraoxon		
2×10^{-5} M	3.31 ± 0.27[b]	104.5 ± 9.0[b]
2×10^{-4} M	12.23 ± 0.95[b]	360.7 ± 29.2[b]

[a]V_{max} expressed as nmoles/mg protein/h $\pm$ S.E.
[b]Different from the control at $p < 0.05$.

IV. SUMMARY

The studies cited above indicate that many of the cholinesterase-
inhibiting insecticides can alter both the in vitro and in vivo rates of
drug metabolism. Although such insecticides as malathion and parathion become potent inhibitors of cholinesterase after metabolic conversion to their oxygenated analogs [69], such an oxidation does not
appear to be important for their effects on microsomal enzymes. The
observation that the subacute administration of both parathion and its
oxygenated metabolite, paraoxon, resulted in an induction of microsomal metabolism suggests that the ability of organophosphate insecticides to induce liver enzymes is independent of any oxidative biotransformation.

Although the relative potency of an individual insecticide varied
with the species being studied, inhibition of drug metabolism after
acute exposure was generally found among several species of animals,
including man. One exception to this was the observation that paraoxon enhanced aniline metabolism, whereas it inhibited ethylmorphine
and hexobarbital biotransformation. This enhancing property of paraoxon on aniline hydroxylase was observed consistently with hepatic
microsomal preparations from rats, mice, rabbits, dogs, and humans.
It is apparent that these findings cannot be dismissed as a species-
specific phenomenon and thus must represent another possible environmental hazard to man.

It is now clear that besides the inherent toxicity of these insecticides as cholinesterase-inhibiting agents, one must also consider
their potential to alter the toxicity and metabolism of drugs and other
substances to which man is exposed. The effects of anticholinesterase

insecticides on hepatic microsomal metabolism should be considered as another in an expanding list of interactions that can occur between environmental pollutants and clinically useful drugs.

Acknowledgments

The authors' work has been supported by Grants GM 16433, ES 00396, TO GM 0076, and FR 05433 from the U.S. Public Health Service. R. E. S. is a Research Career Development Awardee (1 KO4 GM 12522) of the U.S. Public Health Service.

REFERENCES

[1]   R. D. O'Brien, *Ann. N.Y. Acad. Sci.*, 123, 156 (1965).
[2]   J. P. Frawley, H. N. Fuyat, E. C. Hagan, J. R. Blake, and O. G. Fitzhugh, *J. Pharmacol. Exp. Ther.*, 121, 96 (1957).
[3]   K. P. DuBois, *Adv. Pest. Control. Res.*, 4, 117 (1961).
[4]   J. E. Casida, R. L. Baron, M. Eto, and J. L. Engle, *Biochem. Pharmacol.*, 12, 73 (1963).
[5]   J. W. Cook, J. R. Blake, and M. W. Williams, *J. Assoc. Off. Agr. Chem.*, 40, 664 (1957).
[6]   J. W. Cook, J. R. Blake, G. Yip, and M. Williams, *J. Assoc. Off. Agr. Chem.*, 41, 399 (1958).
[7]   J. W. Cook and G. Yip, *J. Assoc. Off. Agr. Chem.*, 41, 407 (1968).
[8]   S. D. Murphy and K. P. DuBois, *Proc. Soc. Exp. Biol. Med.*, 96, 813 (1957).
[9]   A. R. Main and P. E. Braid, *Biochem. J.*, 84, 255 (1962).
[10] W. N. Aldridge, *Biochem. J.*, 53, 110 (1953).
[11] K. P. DuBois, F. K. Kinoshita, and J. P. Frawley, *Toxicol. Appl. Pharmacol.*, 12, 273 (1968).
[12] S. D. Murphy and K. L. Cheever, *Arch. Environ. Health*, 17, 749 (1968).
[13] S. D. Murphy, *J. Pharmacol. Exp. Ther.*, 156, 352 (1967).
[14] K. P. DuBois, *Bull. World, Health Organ.*, 44, 233 (1971).
[15] S. D. Cohen and S. D. Murphy, *J. Pharmacol. Exp. Ther.*, 176, 733 (1971).
[16] C. L. Williams and K. H. Jacobson, *Toxicol. Appl. Pharmacol.*, 9, 495 (1966).
[17] B. B. Brodie, J. Axelrod, J. R. Cooper, L. E. Gandette, B. N. LaDu, C. Mitoma, and S. Udenfriend, *Science*, 121, 603 (1955).
[18] R. A. Neal and K. P. DuBois, *J. Pharmacol. Exp. Ther.*, 148, 185 (1965).
[19] R. E. Stitzel, L. A. Wagner, and R. J. Stawarz, *J. Pharmacol. Exp. Ther.* 182, 500 (1972).
[20] R. E. Menzer and J. E. Casida, *J. Agri. Food Chem.*, 13, 102 (1965).
[21] K. P. DuBois and F. K. Kinoshita, *Arch. Intern. Pharmacodyn. Ther.*, 156, 418 (1965).
[22] W. E. Robbins, T. L. Hopkins, and G. W. Eddy, *J. Agri. Food Chem.*, 5, 509 (1957).
[23] F. W. Phapp and J. E. Casida, *J. Agri. Food Chem.*, 6, 662 (1958).

[24]   H. R. Krueger, J. E. Casida, and R. P. Niedermeier, *J. Agri. Food Chem.*, 7, 182 (1959).

[25]   F. Matsumura and C. J. Hogendijk, *J. Agri. Food Chem.*, 12, 447 (1964).

[26]   T. Nakatsugawa and P. A. Dahm, *Biochem. Pharmacol.*, 16, 25 (1967).

[27]   R. A. Neal, *Biochem. J.*, 103, 108 (1967).

[28]   T. Nakatsugawa, N. M. Tolman, and P. A. Dahm, *Biochem. Pharmacol.*, 18, 1103 (1969).

[29]   T. Nakatsugawa, N. M. Tolman, and P. A. Dahm, *Biochem. Pharmacol.*, 18, 685 (1969).

[30]   R. D. O'Brien, *Toxic Phosphorus Esters*, Academic, New York, 1960.

[31]   R. D. O'Brien and E. Y. Spencer, *J. Agri. Food Chem.*, 3, 56 (1955).

[32]   M. Hitchcock and S. D. Murphy, *Biochem. Pharmacol.*, 16, 1801 (1967).

[33]   J. R. Fouts and B. B. Brodie, *J. Pharmacol. Exp. Ther.*, 119, 197 (1957).

[34]   A. Hassan, S. Zayed, and M. Bahig, *Biochem. Pharmacol.*, 18, 2429 (1969).

[35]   J. L. Ludke, J. R. Gibson, and C. I. Lusk, *Toxicol. Appl. Pharmacol.*, 21, 89 (1972).

[36]   F. L. Mayer, J. C. Street, and J. M. Newhold, *Bull. Environ. Contam. Toxicol.*, 5, 300 (1970).

[37]   M. Skrinjarie-Spoljar, H. B. Matthews, J. L. Engel, and J. E. Casida, *Biochem. Pharmacol.*, 20, 1607 (1971).

[38]   J. E. Casida, *J. Agri. Food Chem.*, 18, 753 (1970).

[39]   A. S. Perry and A. J. Buckner, *Life Sci.*, 9, 335 (1970).

[40]   H. B. Matthews, M. Skrinjaric-Spoljar, and J. E. Casida, *Life Sci.*, 9, 1039 (1970).

[41]   J. R. Gillette, in *Advances in Pharmacology* (S. Garattini and P. A. Shore, eds.), Academic, New York, 1964, Vol. 4, pp. 219-261.

[42]   H. Jaffe, K. Fujii, H. Guerin, M. Sengupta, and S. S. Epstein, *Biochem. Pharmacol.*, 18, 1045 (1969).

[43]   P. Rosenberg and J. M. Coon, *Proc. Soc. Exp. Biol. Med.*, 98, 650 (1958).

[44]   D. M. Serrone and J. M. Fujimoto, *J. Pharm. Exp. Ther.*, 133, 12 (1961).

[45]   L. G. Hart and J. R. Fouts, *Proc. Soc. Exp. Biol. Med.*, 114, 388 (1963).

[46]   C. D. Proctor, *Arch. Intern. Pharmacodyn. Ther.*, 150, 41 (1964).

[47]   A. H. Conney, R. M. Welch, R. Kuntzman, and J. J. Burns, *Clin. Pharmacol. Ther.*, 155, 167 (1967).

[48]   W. E. MacDonald, J. MacQueen, W. B. Deichman, T. Hamill, and K. Copsey, *Intern. Arch. Arbeitsmed.*, 26, 31 (1970).

[49]   J. T. Stevens, J. J. McPhillips, and R. E. Stitzel, *Pharmacologist*, 13, 289 (1971).

[50]   J. T. Stevens, R. E. Stitzel, and J. J. McPhillips, *J. Pharmacol. Exp. Ther.*, 181, 576 (1972).

[51]   L. Lykken and J. E. Casida, *Can. Med. Ass. J.*, 100, 145 (1969).

[52]   S. D. Murphy and K. P. DuBois, *Fed. Proc.*, 16, 324 (1967).

[53]   R. M. Welch, W. Levin, and A. H. Conney, *J. Pharmacol. Exp. Ther.*, 155, 167 (1967).

[54]   F. Bremer and J. Chatonnet, *Arch. Intern. Physiol. Biochem.*, 57, 106 (1949).

[55]   I. Bledsoe, D. P. Island, R. L. Ney, and G. W. Liddle, *J. Clin. Endocrinol. Metab.*, 24, 1303 (1964).

[56]   S. Burstein, and E. L. Klaiber, *J. Clin. Endocrinol. Metab.*, 25, 392 (1965).

[57]   S. A. Cucinell, A. H. Conney, M. Sansur, and J. J. Burns, *Clin. Pharmacol. Ther.*, 6, 420 (1965).

[58] J. T. Stevens, R. E. Stitzel, and J. J. McPhillips, *Life Sci.*, 11, 423 (1972).
[59] C. L. Rumke and J. Bout, *Arch. Pharmakol. Exp. Pathol. (Naunyn-Schmiedebergs)*, 240, 218 (1960).
[60] M. W. Anders, *Ann. Rev. Pharmacol.*, 11, 37 (1971).
[61] Y. Imai and R. Sato, *J. Biochem. (Tokyo)*, 63, 380 (1966).
[62] M. W. Anders, *Arch. Biochem. Biophys.*, 126, 269 (1969).
[63] M. W. Anders, *Biochem. Pharmacol.*, 18, 2561 (1969).
[64] K. E. Leibman, *Mol. Pharmacol.*, 5, 1 (1969).
[65] J. T. Stevens, R. E. Stitzel, and J. J. McPhillips, *Toxicol. Appl. Pharmacol.* 22, 288 (1972).
[66] J. T. Stevens, J. J. McPhillips, and R. E. Stitzel, *Toxicol. Appl. Pharmacol.* 23, 208 (1972).
[67] D. R. Buhler and M. E. Rasmusson, *Comp. Biochem. Physiol.*, 25, 223 (1968).
[68] H. Kitagawa, T. Kamataki, and Y. Tanabee, *Chem. Pharm. Bull. (Japan)*, 19, 221 (1971).
[69] J. C. Gage, *Biochem. Pharmacol.*, 54, 426 (1953).

Metabolic Fate of Hexobarbital (HB)

MILTON T. BUSH and WILLIAM L. WELLER
Department of Pharmacology
Vanderbilt University School of Medicine
Nashville, Tennessee 37203

I. INTRODUCTION

Hexobarbital is 1,5-dimethyl-5(1-cyclohexenyl)barbituric acid (HB). The structure is shown in Fig. 1.

In this review, those studies in which metabolites of HB have actually been identified will be emphasized; the much larger number of studies in which disappearance of HB has been measured will be discussed only briefly. Finally, we will discuss (and present some new data on) those physical and chemical properties of this drug and some of its metabolites which are important in its optimal and valid use as a pharmacological tool. Syntheses of labeled compounds will be outlined.

The metabolism of HB has been recounted briefly and partially in a number of previous articles; notably Williams [1], Mark [2], Williams and Parke [3], Bush and Sanders [4].

Knowledge of the metabolic fate of HB is of special interest because this drug has been used as a model substrate in hundreds of studies of the activity of the mixed-function oxidase system in the liver. The popularity of the drug for this purpose developed quite independently of any knowledge of its metabolic fate in the species most commonly used, the mouse and rat. The reasons for this appear to be several. The substance is sufficiently apolar to be rapidly absorbed and distributed in the body. Its hypnotic activity is such that suitable and convenient doses injected intraperitoneally produce a profound sleep of moderate duration, so that either shortening or lengthening of this (as may be brought about by an array of extrinsic

METABOLISM OF HEXOBARBITAL
(Known and Probable Routes)

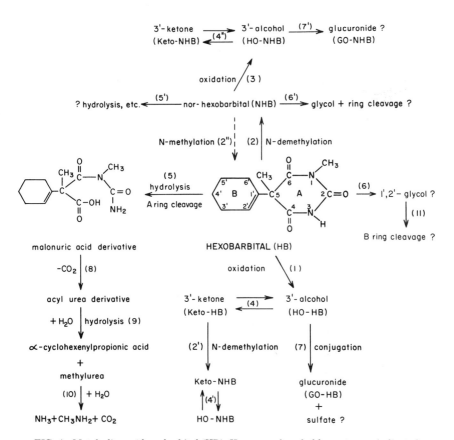

FIG. 1. Metabolism of hexobarbital (HB). Known and probable routes are indicated by the arrows. For discussion see the text.

and intrinsic factors) can be measured with acceptable accuracy. In addition, HB is in fact rather rapidly metabolized in animals, sufficiently so that there is not time for its extensive accumulation in the body fat. Thus, the duration of the hypnotic action is a reflection primarily of metabolism rather than of tissue redistribution (as is the case with thiopental). It is this unusual balance of properties (moderate apolarity, moderate hypnotic activity, and high susceptibility to chemical attack) that makes HB so well suited to the role of a model substrate.

II. STUDIES IN WHICH IDENTIFIED METABOLITES HAVE BEEN DETECTED OR QUANTIFIED

Metabolites of HB have been identified in relatively few species: dog, rabbit, mouse, rat, and man. There seem to be no published detailed studies in the rat and those reported in man are mostly the mention of spots on paper chromatograms. So few are the reports concerning all these species that we can conveniently consider them separately and in chronological order.

The liver is undoubtedly the major site of the metabolism of this drug, although this has been demonstrated only for the rabbit (only liver, kidney, brain, and skeletal muscle were tested). The known metabolites formed in vivo are excreted almost entirely in the urine.

In Fig. 1 we have sketched some probable as well as the known routes of metabolism of HB. It seems likely by analogy with our knowledge of the metabolism of other barbiturates that all these steps and others actually occur, but the major known metabolites are the alcohol (HO-HB via step 1), the ketone (keto-HB, via step 4 in the rabbit), the norketone (keto-NHB, mostly via step 2' in the dog and rabbit or possibly from HO-HB via HO-NHB), and the glucuronide (GO-HB via step 7). The minor known metabolites are nor-HB (NHB via step 2), the acylurea derivative (ureide) (via steps 5 and 8), and CO_2 (via step 10 or by a direct removal of the 2-carbonyl group from the malonyl urea ring of HB, not illustrated). The dashed arrow 2" indicates a purported but highly dubious reaction.

The fraction of the drug accounted for after its administration to animals has so far been rather modest: in the dog, about 7%; in the rabbit, about 35%; and in the mouse, 80% (with the aid of ^{14}C-labeled HB). The recoveries of identified compounds in some of the in vitro studies have been somewhat better. We will describe and discuss all of these in detail.

A. Fate of HB in the Dog

There still appears to be only one published study in this species, that of Bush, Butler, and Dickison [5]. This describes the first isolations of metabolites of HB. Most of the work was done just before the war of 1941-1945 and final characterization of the products was thus delayed. The methodology then available did not permit quantitation of the biologically inactive metabolites keto-HB and keto-NHB, which

were isolated from the urines of two dogs as pure crystalline substances in yields of about 1% and 6%, respectively. A valid quantitative estimate of the hypnotically active hypothetical urinary products
HB and NHB was possible. Based on calculated recoveries of over
90% of the amounts present in the urine, from countercurrent distribution (CCD) data and bioassays in mice, at most 0.2% of the dose of
HB was excreted unchanged and a similar amount was excreted as
apparent NHB. A minute amount of pure NHB was isolated from the
urine of one dog (in retrospect, the HB administered might have contained enough NHB as an impurity to account for this; see Section
IV.D). From the urine of one of the dogs a low-melting isomer of
keto-HB was isolated (0.5%). The two ketones were designated keto-
HB-I (mp 162°-164°C) and keto-HB-II (mp 141-142°C). They were found
to be practically identical in all ways except melting point: they had
the same partition coefficients in a number of solvent systems and
the same pK, elementary analyses, and ultraviolet absorption spectra
at various pH's. The nature of their isomerism remains undetermined
(see Section IV.E) (The amount of keto-HB-II now remaining for further characterization is 3 mg).

Because of their interest in N-demethylation of barbiturates [6],
Bush et al. [5] also studied the fate of NHB in similar experiments.
From the urines of two dogs two products were isolated as pure crystalline substances: unchanged NHB (13% of the dose) and keto-NHB
(20%).

This relatively large recovery of unchanged NHB, together with
the fact that only minute amounts of this substance were excreted
after the administration of HB, permitted the inference that relatively
little of the HB was N-demethylated. The source of the relatively
large amount of keto-NHB obtained from HB must then have been N-
demethylation of previously oxidized HB, presumably keto-HB (Fig. 1,
steps 1, 4 and 2', or possibly from HO-HB via HO-NHB). In their
studies in rabbits (Section II.B.2) Tsukamoto et al. [7] found good
evidence for the same pathway to keto-NHB.

No further studies of the fate of HB in the dog have been published,
apparently.

Recently in this laboratory we have begun to reinvestigate the fate
of HB in the dog with the aid of HB-2-^{14}C. This has permitted a great
improvement [8] of the methodology used in the earlier work [5]. So
far, only one dog has been worked up, incompletely. One gram (100 μc)
of the labeled drug was given to the animal (12 kg) by stomach tube.
Some 95% of the ^{14}C was collected in the urine during 48 h. Approximately half of this was readily extracted by ethyl acetate (the urine
was first made 2 M with NaH_2PO_4). Small aliquots of this material
have been put through a succession of CCD's [8]. Unchanged HB and

NHB have not been positively identified but the amounts present are
no more than 0.8% (of the dose) and 0.7%, respectively. HO-HB (20%)
and keto-HB (12%) have been clearly identified by their CCD behavior and keto-NHB has been tentatively identified (approximately 11%).
(The recoveries of these metabolites are considerably higher than
those reported by Bush et al. [5] because the earlier methodology
involved isolation of the pure crystalline products.) The labeled
material not extracted from the urine by ethyl acetate has been practically completely removed by a series of extractions with t-pentanol
but has not yet been investigated further. A considerable part of this
material could have been extracted by a more persistent use of ethyl
acetate. Some of the polar metabolite ($<10\%$) may be the result of
inadvertent overexposure of the original drug to excess NaOH during
dissolution prior to administration (the experiment was carried out
before we had all the data of Section IV.C).

Continuing work will include isolation of the identified labeled
metabolites in pure crystalline form as well as the identification of
the unknown highly polar metabolites.

B. Fate of HB in the Rabbit

The results in this species will be discussed in six main parts:
the classical work of Cooper and Brodie described in 1955 [9], which
was entirely in vitro; the extensive series of in vivo and in vitro
studies of Tsukamoto and his co-workers, beginning in 1956 [10];
reconciliation of these results; isolation of a glucuronide from rabbit
urine, and other studies.

1. In Vitro Studies of Cooper and Brodie

Cooper and Brodie were the first to examine the metabolism of HB
by isolated tissues. By means of the spectrophotometric method developed previously for pentobarbital [11] they measured the rate of
disappearance of HB from incubated slices of rabbit tissues: brain,
muscle, kidney, and liver. The drug was unchanged by all except
liver. They then proceeded to examine the activity of various fractions of liver and finally to ascertain the nature of the metabolites
produced by the action of the 9000 $\times$ g supernatant. They incubated
4 μmoles of HB (0.94 mg) with the fortified supernatant from 2.7 g
of rabbit liver for 75 min, when an analysis indicated that about 75%
of the HB had disappeared. For identification of the metabolite, the
bulk of the incubation mixture was extracted several times with chloroform, which removed "barbiturate" equivalent (by UV absorption) to
about 100% of the added HB. The concentrated extract was analyzed

by paper chromatography, using the solvent system butanol saturated with 1% ammonium hydroxide and visualizing the spots under a UV lamp. Only two spots were seen, one at Rf 0.80 (HB) and the other at Rf 0.30 (keto-HB-I and keto-HB-II). Although some 0.2 μmole of HB or ketone was required for detection, it was reasonable to conclude that "the major if not the only material formed from the HB was keto-HB." From a 100-fold scaleup of this experiment, they isolated pure crystalline keto-HB-I in unspecified yield. This experiment will be discussed in Section II.B.4.

2. In Vivo Studies of Tsukamoto et al.

Tsukamoto and his associates have published a series of excellent brief papers on the metabolism of HB. These span the period 1956-1965. They have added greatly to our knowledge of the fate of HB in the rabbit.

In their earlier reports [10, 12, 13] the Japanese workers described the isolation of several major metabolites from rabbit urine after oral administration of HB: keto-NHB and keto-HB-I (apparently identical with the corresponding products of Bush et al. [5] from the dog) together with larger quantities of two isomeric hydroxy derivatives, which they designated α-HO-HB and β-HO-HB, both optically active. These alcohols could be converted to keto-HB-I (optically inactive) by oxidation with chromium trioxide; this ketone could then be reduced back to a mixture of the diastereoisomeric α- and β-alcohols, both now optically inactive. Thus, the hydroxyl and keto groups were located in the same position (on the cyclohexenyl ring). This position was established as α to the double bond (that is, 3'-keto-HB and 3'-HO-HB) by a series of degradative reactions. In a similar manner, the structure of 3'-keto-NHB was established.

In a later more detailed paper, Tsukamoto et al. [14] described quantitative results obtained with a more refined methodology. The three main metabolites extracted from the urine by ethyl acetate were separated by paper chromatography and eluted and quantitated by UV spectrophotometry. Rabbits were fasted 24 h and given oral doses of 100, 200, and 300 mg/kg of HB dissolved in 1.1 equiv of NaOH (volume not specified). The three rabbits were given the three doses in turn at 7 day intervals. Analyses of aliquots of the 24 h urines revealed that the three metabolites were excreted in similar amounts by all the animals at all of the doses: keto-NHB 4-5% (average); keto-HB, 4-5%; and HO-HB, 16%. Thus, they accounted for some 25% of the dose. Control experiments showed 85-87% recovery of all three metabolites when these were added to blank urine. Very small amounts of two other substances were found in these experiments, a barbituate-like substance "HB-M" and the acylurea derivative. It seems highly likely that the latter is a chemical artifact rather than a bona fide metabolite (see Fig. 1, step 8). This will be discussed briefly in Section IV.C.

The metabolic fate of the major metabolites, keto-HB and HO-HB, was studied both in vivo and in vitro by Tsukamoto and his co-workers. The earlier work was done in vivo [14]. The three metabolites keto-HB-I, α-HO-HB, and β-HO-HB were given to each of three rabbits (strain not specified) in turn at 7 day intervals. The animals were fasted 24 h and dosed orally with 200 mg/kg; the drugs were dissolved in 10% excess aqueous NaOH. The 24 h urines were analyzed by the extraction-paper-chromatographic-spectrophotometric procedure. The α and β forms of HO-HB were not differentiated because they have the same Rf values and the same UV absorption spectra. Administration of these two compounds led to similar results: recovered HO-HB was 20-30%, keto-HB excreted was 8-11%, and about 1% of keto-NHB was found. After administration of keto-HB, 6-8% was excreted unchanged, 10-12% as HO-HB, and about 1% as keto-NHB. Thus, interconversion of alcohol and ketone was demonstrated but it remained uncertain which was formed first in the oxidation of HB.

3. In Vitro Studies of Tsukamoto et al.

Some time after their extensive studies in vivo, Tsukamoto et al. investigated the fate of HB as well as the known urinary metabolites in rabbit liver preparations in vitro [15]. They found that the microsomes and soluble fraction together produced both keto-HB and HO-HB from the parent compound. Incubation of HO-HB with soluble fraction alone produced appreciable amounts of keto-HB and addition of the microsomes decreased this amount.

In a subsequent more extensive study [16], it was demonstrated that the microsomal fraction of the liver can convert HB to HO-HB only and that the supernatant fraction contains most of the enzyme activity which is responsible for the further oxidation to the ketone. Later, a detailed study of this (crude) enzyme system was published [17], including a subcellular localization of activity, cofactor requirements, inhibitors, activators, and the effects of anaerobic conditions. The purification of this enzyme (3-hydroxy methylhexabital dehydrogenase) to 55-fold its activity in the crude soluble fraction was accomplished [18]. It was distinct from (ethyl) alcohol dehydrogenase and seemed to be specific for the cyclohexen-3-ol group; it had no action on many other hydroxy compounds, including hydroxysecobarbital.

4. Reconciliation of the Results of Cooper and Brodie with Those of Tsukamoto et al.

It is of special interest to note that the paper chromatographic solvent system used successfully by the Japanese workers to separate HO-HB (the two diastereoisomers had the same Rf values in all systems tested) from keto-HB-I was different from the one used by Cooper and Brodie. Tsukamoto et al. [19] state that they could not separate the alcohol from the ketone with butanol saturated with 1% ammonium hydroxide but that satisfactory separation with "compact spots" was achieved with butanol saturated with borate buffer of pH 11. Thus, even though Cooper and Brodie could not differentiate their major metabolite from the keto-HB-I or the keto-HB-II of Bush et al., it would seem quite possible, even likely that their rabbit liver preparations did in fact produce a certain amount of HO-HB. From a preparative run with 400 μmoles (94 mg) of HB and 300 ml of fortified rabbit liver 9000 $\times$ g supernate, Cooper and Brodie isolated crystalline keto-HB-I with correct melting point and mixed melting point, but they did not state the yield; and, although in their countercurrent distributions they pooled fractions containing material "with similar partition ratios," they did not specify any of the partition ratios. It is therefore not possible to calculate the composition of the (probable) mixture of keto-HB and HO-HB in their experiments, even with knowledge of the correct values of these partition coefficients. It would seem reasonable to assume that (except for possible strain differences) the metabolite pattern produced in the Cooper-Brodie experiments was similar to that found in the subsequent in vitro experiments by the Japanese workers. If the ketone were indeed the only metabolite, there would have been considerable interference with the determination tion of HB remaining after 75% was metabolized, by the method that Cooper and Brodie used [11]. They state that no interference was found by the method of comparative distribution ratios, but they did not state what proportion of HB had been metabolized in the tested samples. (See Sections IV.A and V.A for further considerations of this problem.)

5. Isolation of a Glucuronide from Rabbit Urine

The search for a conjugate of HO-HB in the urine was stimulated by the fact that only 25% of the dose of HB had been accounted for by the known metabolites. Toki and Takanouchi [20] gave several rabbits a total of 15.7 g of HB (total amount per animal, 400 mg/kg in divided doses) by gavage as a freshly prepared aqueous solution in 1.1 equiv of NaOH. The 24 h urine was worked up by a modification of the method of Kamil et al. [21] which involves repeated precipitation of the glucuronide as a lead salt and regeneration of the conjugate by precipitation of the lead with hydrogen sulfide. Final purification was achieved by column chromatography on silica gel, developing with wet ethyl acetate and eluting with methanol-ethyl acetate mixtures. The compound was obtained as a white powder and could not be recrystallized; but elementary analyses, the naphthoresorcinol test, and the UV absorption spectrum were in good agreement with the theoretical formula of a glucuronide of HO-HB (GO-HB in Fig. 1, step 7). The UV spectrum of the ionized form (pH 11) was virtually identical with those of HB and HO-HB; thus, the site of conjugation was on the 3'-hydroxyl group and not on the unsubstituted nitrogen in the malonyl-urea moiety. A paper chromatogram of the GO-HB showed only one spot and both acid hydrolysis and β-glucuronidase treatment gave modest yields of HO-HB.

The purified glucuronide was equivalent to approximately 6% of the dose of HB. No doubt much more than this is actually excreted.

6. Other Studies in the Rabbit

The production of CH_2O from HB by rabbit (and rat) liver 15,000 × g supernate was reported by McMahon [22] and is discussed in Section II.D.

The identification by thin-layer chromatography of metabolites of HB extracted from rabbit and mouse urine has been reported by No-ordhoek and Garritsen [23]. This will be discussed in Section II.C.3.

C. Fate of HB in the Mouse

1. The Question of the Interconversion of HB and NHB in Vivo

Several tentative reports of the N-methylation of several barbiturates in vivo were cited by Mark [2]. These involved only inconsistent findings of certain spots on paper chromatograms of urine and cannot therefore be taken seriously. There is one study, however, that seriously purports to have demonstrated such a metabolic reaction; that is, the conversion of NHB to HB in the mouse in vivo. In an extensive report of the effects of methyl donors on certain pharmacological actions of barbiturates in mice, Deininger [24] reported that appreciable amounts of HB were found in the blood of the animals after subcutaneous administration of NHB. If methionine were administered beforehand, this apparent N-methylation was considerably increased. He also reported that HB administered to the animals was N-demethylated to the extent of 50%, calculated from direct determinations of NHB in the blood. These conclusions were based on a paper chromatographic method in which the two barbiturates were separated and then quantitated by measuring the areas of the corresponding spots. The method would seem to be valid in principle but the sensitivity was very low. In addition, the blood levels of HB (measured at 30 and 60 min after dosage) were so low that in a typical experiment only 10 μg of "HB" were recovered from the pooled blood (5 ml) from ten mice 60 min after a dose of 200 mg/kg of NHB. Finally, there was no statistical evaluation of the results and simple recovery experiments in which HB and/or NHB were added to blank blood were not described. We can only conclude, with Maynert [25], that Deininger's results are unconvincing.

By use of an improved method of whole body analysis, Bush and Parrish [26] analyzed mice after the i.v. administration of 1 mg of HB or of NHB. They presented details of CCD fractionation which showed that 80-90% of either drug was recoverable unchanged (characterized by partition coefficients and UV spectra) 1 min after the injection. At either 30 or 60 min after administration of HB, NHB could not be detected; after administration of NHB, HB could not be detected. It was concluded that the interconversion, if any, was less than 5%. Recent studies [8] have confirmed that NHB is not present in significant amounts in mice after i.v. doses of 1 mg of HB-2-^{14}C (see Section II.C.4).

2. The Formation of $^{14}CO_2$ from HB-5-^{14}C and HB-2-^{14}C in Vivo

Metabolism studies of these two labeled forms of HB (and a number of other barbiturates) were described by Block and Ebigt [27]. They limited their measurements to the CO_2 formed in vivo by mice. They reported that approximately 1% of the dose of HB-2-^{14}C and about 0.2% of the dose of HB-5-^{14}C was found as $^{14}CO_2$ in the expired air. The syntheses of the labeled compounds were described.

3. Identification of HB Metabolites in Mouse (and Rabbit) Urine

Noordhoek and Gerritsen [23] have given a summary of qualitative studies of the urinary excretion of metabolites of HB by rabbits and mice. Large doses of the drug were administered orally and the 24 h urine extracted with ethyl acetate. By TLC, suitable spray reagents, and UV spectra, they identified keto-HB and HO-HB as well as NHB, HO-NHB, and keto-NHB. Additional amounts of the hydroxy derivatives were extractable from rabbit urine but not from mouse urine after glucuronidase treatment. The mice excreted much smaller

amounts of the demethylated metabolites than did the rabbits (no
quantitative data were given).

4. Quantitative Studies of the Disappearance of HB and of the
   Appearance of the Major Metabolites in Vivo and in Vitro
   with HB-2-^{14}C

Extensive studies of the metabolic fate of HB and NHB in mice
have been underway in the senior author's laboratory for a number
of years. The recent report on a major part of this work by Gerber
et al. [8] is apparently the first in which metabolites other than CO_2
have been quantitated in this species. A new methodology is described
for whole body analysis: homogenization with a large volume of acetone, removal of emulsifiers by treatment of this extract with charcoal, evaporation, and subjection of the residue to liquid-liquid extraction analysis (modified countercurrent distribution, according to
the procedure of Bush and Densen [28]) (see Section V.F). After the
i.v. administration of HB-2-^{14}C (1 mg and 1 μc per mouse, 20-25 g,
ICR males), the major metabolites were separated, identified, and
quantitated, along with the unchanged HB. The whole body half-life
(t/2) was 15 min and, at this time, 11% of the dose was present as
keto-HB, 40% as HO-HB. At 45 min, the amount of ketone had increased to 25%, of alcohol to 44%, and the remaining HB was 10%.
The approximately 20% loss (of ^{14}C) at 45 min is caused by adsorp-
tion of polar metabolites on the charcoal because the acetone extracts
always contained 100 $\pm$ 5% of the injected ^{14}C and HB itself was always recoverable in blank experiments in approximately 95% yield.
Thus, these recoveries of keto-HB and HO-HB do not necessarily
represent the maximum amounts produced by the animals (the excreta were included in the homogenizations) and the presence of small
amounts of other products in the acetone extracts is not ruled out.
After the treatment with charcoal, however, neither NHB not keto-
NHB could be detected (the treatment with charcoal is the only procedure so far found to remove the emulsifiers satisfactorily, making
possible the subsequent CCD's).

Gerber et al. determined the t/2 of HB in three strains of mice:
ICR (males), CFW, and A/HeJ; for the first two, t/2 was 15 min; for
the last it was 28 min. There was no difference between CFW or
A/HeJ males and females. Detailed studies of the disappearance of
HB and the formation of keto-HB and HO-HB in the 9000 $\times$ g supernatant fraction of liver revealed no differences between the three
strains in the pattern of metabolites produced. The ketone and alcohol accounted for practically all of the HB which disappeared. The
liver supernatant fraction from ICR mice pretreated with phenobarbital

metabolized HB twice as rapidly as the controls but the relative amounts of keto-HB and HO-HB formed did not change and no new metabolites were observed.

No experiments were done in which excreta were analyzed separately; all whole body analyses included whatever excreta were produced and no experiments were reported in which NHB-2-^{14}C was administered. Thus, there is still much to be learned about the fate of HB in the mouse.

D. Fate of HB in the Rat

There seem to be no published detailed studies in this species. Mention is made by Toki et al. [29] of the unpublished finding that in the 9000 × g supernatant fraction of rat liver HO-HB is the main metabolite and that keto-HB is a very minor metabolite.

Other in vitro work has been reported by McMahon [22]. In a comparative study of the N-demethylation of certain barbiturates and some related compounds, it was found that rat and rabbit liver microsomes produce formaldehyde from HB at a rather low rate, about one-half to one-third the rate from N-methylbarbital and about one-fifth the rate found for N,N'-dimethylbarbital. From 5 μmoles of HB incubated with the fortified 15,000 × g supernate equivalent to 200 mg of liver, CH_2O was produced at the rate of only 12 nmoles/h by the rat and 23 nmoles/h by the rabbit. Because these liver preparations also oxidize HB (much more rapidly than this) it is not known whether this CH_2O came directly from HB or from oxidized HB.

Extensive in vitro and in vivo studies of the fate of HB in the rat have been carried out in the senior author's laboratory during the last 3 years by Mr. Robert Holcomb. Two abstracts have been published [30, 31] and a complete manuscript will soon be submitted. After i.v. doses (13-33 μc/kg and 4-9 mg/kg) of HB-2-^{14}C in mature male animals (Sprague-Dawley) 95% of the label was put out in the 72 h urine, mostly in 12 h, with about 4% in the feces. By the CCD methodology it was shown that the major metabolites were keto-HB and HO-HB (together accounting for almost 80% of the dose), with quite small amounts of more polar material. Neither HB nor NHB were present in appreciable quantities (<1% of the dose). The feces contained only very polar material, probably conjugates. Tissue distribution measurements of HB and "metabolites," separately, showed an extremely rapid fall of both in all tissues, including blood and fat, after the early initial peak values (1-5 min). Studies in individual animals to which 40-60 mg/kg of HB-2-^{14}C (0.042 μc/mg) was given i.v. and from which blood samples were taken repeatedly by cardiac puncture [31] revealed that the level of unchanged HB declined to half its

1 min level in only 8 min. The rats had been protected reasonably
well from previous exposure to inducing agents and conditions. It was
inferred from these data together with the knowledge that HB concentrations were falling in all tissues, after 5 min, that metabolism rather than tissue redistribution played a dominant role in removing
HB from the blood (and tissues) even during the first 15 min or so.
This knowledge may require some reinterpretation of those estimates
of the rate of metabolism of HB which have been based on blood level
measurements during the time interval 60-120 min after administration [32], a time far greater than necessary to allow for practically
complete tissue equilibration of the drug, even when injected intraperitoneally, and a time during which the absolute rate of metabolism of
this drug is miniscule in comparison with the earlier rate.

E. Fate of HB in Man

There appear to be no quantitative studies in man and only one
identification of urinary metabolites beyond the observations of spots
on paper chromatograms. It is difficult to know when such data should
be taken seriously. Many common solvent systems fail to differentiate the barbiturates clearly and studies in man must therefore be especially carefully controlled; and even so, a spot developed by a single
solvent system is not conclusive.

The only reports before 1953 that we could find were those of
Fretwurst [33, 34] and Weese [35], both of whom reported "barbiturate" in the urine of human subjects after taking HB; neither author
described the methodology used. In more recent years, there seem
to be only two reports, both of paper chromatographic examinations
of human urine after dosage with HB. Tsukamoto et al. [36] extracted
the 8 h urine of men, given oral doses of 200 mg of HB, with ethyl
acetate. The residue from evaporation of the dried extracts was taken
up in methanol and chromatographed on paper impregnated with pH 11
borate buffer. The developing solvent was butanol saturated with this
buffer. Two major spots were revealed by spraying the chromatograms with 1% aqueous $NaIO_4$ and 1% aqueous $KMnO_4$. These corresponded with spots found with authentic keto-HB and HO-HB. The
authors also state that "the UV spectra of these products and authentic samples were identical." It was also stated that another spot on
the chromatograms corresponded to the ureide (see Section IV.C).

In his review, Mark [2] refers to a report by Frey et al. [37], in
which they found keto-HB in human urine by paper chromatography.

F. Studies of Other Barbiturates Containing the Cyclohexenyl Ring

Other than NHB, the only derivative that seems to have been extensively studied is cyclobarbital[5-ethyl-5(1-cyclohexenyl)barbituric acid] (EHB). Fretwurst et al. [38] found this drug to be excreted in the urine of men to the extent of about 7% along with much larger amounts (20%) of an oxidized product, a ketone. Tsukamoto and Kuroiwa [39] found this metabolite to be excreted by rabbits along with small amounts of the corresponding alcohol. They identified these products as 3'-keto-EHB and 3'-HO-EHB, by the same thorough techniques as for the HB studies. They also identified these metabolites of cyclobarbital in human urine [36], along with unchanged drug; the paper chromatographic results were confirmed by UV spectrophotometry. More recent quantitative studies in the rat with EHB-2-^{14}C have been reviewed by Maynert [25]. Tsukamoto and Kuroiwa [39] obtained similar results in studies with NHB.

NHB-2-^{14}C is presently under investigation in the senior author's laboratory, using the mouse, rat, and dog.

III. STUDIES INVOLVING QUANTITATION OF THE DISAPPEARANCE OF HB

A. General Considerations

Although we do not propose to review the huge number of publications in this area of HB metabolism, it seems important to cite a few representative studies and especially to comment on the rate of disappearance of the drug as a measure of its rate of metabolism.

HB has been widely used both in vivo and in vitro as a model substrate to monitor the activity of the mixed-function oxidase system in the liver. The disappearance of the drug is readily measured. The validity of this procedure in vitro depends only on the specificity of the method used for the measurement. In contrast, in vivo experiments are complicated by a number of factors in addition to the problem of method specificity. If we depend on the decline in blood level as a measure of the rate of metabolism, we must consider the effects of absorption, tissue redistribution, and renal excretion. If we are using whole body analyses (as is practical with mice and rats), these factors are ostensibly eliminated as far as the correctness of the analytical determination of the amount of HB remaining is concerned. One or the other of these factors may, nevertheless, have a profound influence on the value obtained for t/2.

B. Disappearance of HB in vivo

1. By Determination of Blood Levels

The great preponderance of in vivo studies has been based on blood analyses made at late times after administration when tissue redistribution is assumed complete. Renal excretion of unchanged HB has been ruled out (under normal conditions) in the rabbit [14,19], dog [5], and rat [30].

Perhaps the first discussion of this type of investigation was given by Brodie [40], who was then primarily concerned with thiopental in man. He did, however, present some data for HB. High doses (3 g) of this compound and of three thiobarbiturates were given to human subjects intravenously (by intermittent injection during 50 min) and the plasma levels followed for 24 h. The rate of decline of the HB levels was distinctly greater than for any of the other compounds, but all were remarkably slow. This was probably caused by the combination of large dose and accumulation in the fat, which was much less (in dogs) for HB than for the thio compounds. These data apparently did not permit a valid estimate of the rate of metabolism.

Blood levels of HB after oral administration to human subjects were reported by Bush et al. [41]. There was a considerable variation in the rates at which peak blood levels were reached and in the rates of decline. One subject (MTB) produced a sharp rise in blood level, which reached a peak in 30 min and then fell to half its peak value in the next 30 min. It is tempting and not unreasonable to interpret this as an indication of rapid metabolism, because absorption was clearly very rapid in this subject and tissue redistribution effects should be similar to those in the rat. Two other subjects achieved lower peak blood levels and apparently metabolized the drug less rapidly.

The first truly quantitative study of HB disappearance from blood appears to be that of Axelrod et al. [32], who investigated the inhibitory action of SKF 525-A (β-diethylaminoethyl diphenylpropylacetate) on the metabolism of a number of drugs in rats. Because it is typical of many later studies and illustrates the principles of the procedure, this work will be summarized here.

HB was injected i.p. (100 mg/kg) and 1 h was allowed for completion of absorption and development of steady-state conditions. Three blood samples were taken from each animal during the second hour and the plasma HB concentrations plotted on a logarithmic scale against time on a linear scale (the actual analytical results were not given). Extrapolation of a straight line drawn through these three points gave a hypothetical zero-time plasma level. The time at which this level was halved was called the "biological half-life" ("t/2").

actual values obtained for five control animals were within the range
28 ± 5 min. Pretreatment of other animals with SKF 525-A prolonged
the duration of the anesthesia and increased the "t/2", both by a factor
of approximately 2.5; the plasma levels of HB on awakening were essentially the same in both groups of animals. A separate study in the
same laboratory [42] had shown that SKF 525-A was a powerful inhibitor of HB metabolism by rat liver slices. This, along with the
correlations generated by the in vivo experiments, supported the
conclusion that SKF 525-A prolonged the anesthesia by inhibiting the
metabolism of HB.

Similar experiments and results in dogs were also reported.

These studies demonstrated the usefulness of this concept of biologic half-life, which has since been widely used with HB and other
drugs, and permits "t/2" to be estimated in man.

In the case of HB there are two more or less important sources of
(potential) error in the method as applied by Axelrod et al. [32] in the
rat. HB is metabolized so rapidly in this species that i.p. administration should not only withhold significant amounts of the drug for some
time from the metabolizing system in the liver but also, on absorption,
expose the molecules directly to this system. It would seem that i.v.
administration should give a less complicated picture of the in vivo
metabolism rate. Finally, blood samples taken as long as 2 h after
administration contain very low levels of the drug (about 6% of the
dose remains in the animal, calculated from "t/2" = 30 min), making
accurate analysis difficult. Relative values of "t/2" may, nevertheless,
be valid.

The ideal application of this method in the rat would seem to involve prompt i.v. administration, followed by sampling of the blood
at, say, 15, 30, and 45 min, and the data should, of course, be evaluated statistically.

For a consideration of the interference to be expected from metabolites in the blood, see Section V.

2. By Whole Body Analyses

Determination of the total amount of HB remaining in the body
should be the most accurate way of measuring the rate of its metabolism in vivo. It is required only that a reasonable number of animals
be analyzed by a specific method at suitable time intervals after administration of the drug. Because HB is metabolized quite rapidly
by both mouse and rat, i.v. administration is likely to give shorter
"t/2" values than other routes. There appears to be no comparative
study of this question.

Typical "t/2" values reported from various laboratories for mice are quite irregular: approximately 35 min [43], 19 ± 7 min [44], 81 min [45], 15 min for ICR mice and 28 min for A/HeJ mice [8]. It is clear from the last results that differences may be caused by the strain of the species used. Only the last study involved i.v. administration; the others involved i.p. It would also seem likely that the rate of i.v. injection, as well as the dose, might influence the results. Gerber et al. [8] injected 50 mg/kg in a volume of 0.25 ml within 2 sec. Much larger doses were given i.p. in the other reports. The data of Fouts and Brodie [43] permit estimation of "t/2" for the first half hour as about 35 min and for the second half hour as about 15 min; this difference is undoubtedly caused by the delayed exposure of a significant part of the dose to the metabolizing enzyme system.

The specificity of the method for HB determination becomes crucial in whole body analyses, because large amounts of metabolites are present. An analysis done 60 min after dosage involves only 12% of the administered HB (for "t/2" = 20 min). If a large proportion of the metabolite still present in the animal (or in the urine that was not excluded from the analysis) is keto-HB, as was the case in the experiment by Gerber et al. [8], this metabolite will appear in the UV analysis in significant quantities unless a buffer wash of the initial organic extract is introduced. Fouts and Brodie used such a procedure, namely, that of Axelrod et al. [32], but Quinn et al. [44] ostensibly used the method of Cooper and Brodie [9], which does not include a buffer wash. This ambiguity recurs many times in the literature and will be further discussed in Section V.

3. By Sleeping Time Measurements

The early reports, already discussed, which together established that the duration of the anesthesia produced by suitable large doses of HB was correlated with its chemical inactivation [32, 42] led to the frequent use of this measurement as an indicator of the rate of this chemical process. The method is advantageous because it requires no expensive equipment and large amounts of data are easily collected. A number of pitfalls are entailed, however, which we will not discuss here. Fouts [46] has presented a detailed and clear description of the principles and practical applications of the method.

That the basic correlations hold reasonably well in the mouse, rat, rabbit, and dog was confirmed by Quinn et al. [44]. Only in the mouse did they determine "t/2" by whole body analyses, but the duration of action was well correlated with "t/2" by blood analyses and relative enzyme activity (in vitro) in all these species. In spite of the apparent absence of whole body confirmatory data for the rat, it has seemed reasonable to accept the belief that metabolism is the only important mechanism responsible for the termination of the hypnotic action of HB in this species. Recent extensive time-concentration studies of the distribution of HB and its metabolites in some of the tissues of the rat by Holcomb et al. [30], together with detailed whole body analyses and excretion studies [47], have confirmed this belief.

In species that appear to metabolize HB less rapidly (dog and man) than the mouse and rat, it may be found that tissue redistribution is not a negligible factor in terminating the depressant action of the drug.

There are at least two other outstanding investigations of HB action in mice in which sleeping time and chemically determined HB remaining are shown to be in excellent correlation under many different experimental conditions. These are the detailed study of the effects of environmental and genetic factors by Vesell [48] and the elegant pharmacokinetic study by Noordhoek [49].

C. Disappearance of HB in Vitro

Typical investigations of the action of tissue preparations on HB involve slices, homogenates, or different fractions of the latter sedimented in the centrifuge. Since the demonstration by Cooper and Brodie [9] that slices of brain, kidney, and skeletal muscle of the rabbit had no action on HB and that slices of liver metabolized it rapidly, most if not all studies have been done with liver preparations. We have already referred to many of these. In recent years the isolated perfused rat liver has been used in a number of investigations [30, 50, 51].

Quantitation of the disappearance of HB under these various in vitro conditions has most often been carried out by the extraction-spectrophotometric method of Cooper and Brodie [9], more properly the method of Brodie et al. [11] to which the former authors refer. Occasionally, reference is made to the modification of this method first used by Axelrod et al. [32]. Remmer [45] used a still different modification of the 1953 method of Brodie et al. These, together with more recent, less familiar methodologies, will be discussed in detail in Section V.

D. The Optical Isomers of HB

The separation of the optical isomers of HB by Knabe and Krauter [52] and the finding by Wahlstrom [53] and by Rummel et al. [54] that these differ in anesthetic properties led to several studies of the metabolism of the isomers. These will be discussed briefly, even though only disappearance of the drug(s) has been measured.

Wahlstrom administered the compounds by controlled intravenous infusion in rats and monitored the onset of action by electroencephalographic (EEG) response (the "silent second"). For some duration measurements, small additional amounts were administered. His results showed marked differences between the antipodes: much less of the (+)HB (43 mg/kg) than of the (−) isomer (>114 mg/kg) was required to reach the EEG endpoint. At these doses, the sleeping time with the (−) isomer was much longer than with the (+) but the sleeping times with the same absolute doses were not measured. The two isomers were additive, not antagonistic, in their actions on the EEG.

Rummel et al. [54] found the (+) isomer to have lower serum and liver concentrations 10 min after i.p. administration to rats, but they did not estimate t/2. They found a higher brain/blood concentration for (+) than for (−). Degkwitz et al. [55] found distinct differences between the isomers' binding to the cytochrome(s) P-450 of rat liver and also that the (+) isomer was metabolized about 60% faster than was the (−) by liver microsomes. Furner et al. [56] administered 80 mg/kg of HB and the two isomers i.p. to rats and found rather small differences in rates of onset (loss of the righting reflex) and duration in male animals. In females, the onset rates were about the same as in the males (about 1.5 to 4 min) but the duration of sleep was vastly greater with the d (+) isomer (122 min) than with the l (−) isomer (33 min) or the dl compound (75 min). As would be expected, high blood levels persisted much longer in the females; in addition, the animals awoke at much higher blood levels of the l than of the d isomer. The authors did not offer an explanation of this phenomenon. Furner et al. found t/2 (by blood levels) in male rats to be 17 min for (+)HB, 48 min for (−)HB, and 41 min for HB (80 mg/kg, i.p.). Liver microsomes from males metabolized (+) twice as rapidly as (−) but those from females showed no differences between the isomers or the racemic drug, although they metabolized all much less rapidly than those from males.

A recent more detailed in vitro study of these isomers by McCarthy and Stitzel [57] has confirmed that (+)HB is more rapidly metabolized by rat liver microsomes than is (−)HB but no further experiments with sex differences were reported.

An impressive report [58] of investigations of the isomers of N-methyl cyclobarbital and N-methyl phenobarbital in vivo and in vitro serves to emphasize the complexity of this type of problem. Some of the results are comparable with those previously reported for HB and its isomers, but only female rats were used. No satisfactory theoretical basis for the differences between isomers was developed. It would seem that such a basis will probably require simultaneous involvement of tissue sensitivity, binding and distribution, and metabolism.

IV. PHYSICOCHEMICAL PROPERTIES OF HEXOBARBITAL
AND SOME OF ITS METABOLITES

A greater knowledge of the properties of HB than seems to be available would be useful, if not crucial, in guiding its use in the laboratory. Such factors as the degree of purity of the commercial commonly used HB-Na, or the closely related question of the actual rate of decomposition of HB in alkaline solutions, or the matter of optimizing the conditions for UV quantitation have apparently never been systematically investigated. In the authors' laboratory, these and other matters have long been of concern and many data have been accumulated. A summary of these in the present section may be useful as well as serve as a basis for further discussion of methodologies in Section V.

A. Melting points, Solubilities, Ionization Exponents, and Partition Coefficients

In Table 1 we have summarized the pertinent available data, some of which were taken from Bush et al. [5], Bush et al. [41], and Gerber et al. [8]. Other values were determined from time to time in this laboratory. Wherever discrepancies exist, recent data should be the more accurate. With few exceptions, these data for solubility and partition coefficients (C) are no more accurate than, say, ±10% and very large or very small values are likely to be in greater error. The pK_1 values are all certain to ±0.1, that of HB itself having been determined very carefully by Bush [59] by means of the hydrogen electrode and later checked a number of times in this laboratory by the spectrophotometric method of Butler et al. [60]. The latter method was used for all the other values, which have been repeatedly checked.

HB itself is the least unstable of all these compounds on melting. Only it and keto-HB give sharp reproducible melting points (capillary), and the latter substance becomes yellow in a very few minutes at the melting temperature.

A comparison of the C's reveals that more than one solvent system must be used to achieve efficient separation of these compounds. This problem will be discussed in Section V.

Most workers measuring the disappearance of HB have used the method of Brodie et al. [11], usually referred to as that of Cooper and Brodie [9] or as some modification of this. The initial step involves extraction (of blood, homogenate, etc.) with a large volume of heptane plus 1.5% isoamyl alcohol with salt saturation of the aqueous phase. Axelrod et al. [32] and Remmer [45] found that this solvent extracted some "metabolite," and that this could be removed by a buffer wash [32] or avoided by leaving out the i-amyl alcohol [45].

TABLE 1

Properties of Hexobarbital and Some of Its Metabolites

Substance	Melting point[a]	pK$_1$[b]	Solubility[c,d]			Partition coefficient[c,d]					
			Water	Methanol	B	B/0.1	B/2	E/0.1	E/2	A/w[e]	A/2[f]
HB	146	8.2	0.5	25	4	9	17	15		65	
NHB	208[h]	7.8	0.5	65		0.15	1.0	6		25	
Keto-HB-I	162	7.5	10.1[g]	50		0.09	0.7	0.49	4	6	20
Keto-HB-II	142	7.5		(10)[j]					4	6	
α-HO-HB	(195)[h,i,j]	8.0	2			0.01	0.07	0.25	2	2	
β-HO-HB	145	7.9									
Keto-NHB	216[h]	7.1	7	21[k]			0.004	(0.4)[j]	0.8		4

[a]Melting points are ±1°C and corrected except those marked with superscript i.

[b]Determined spectrophotometrically at 25° ± 2°C. A value for HB gotten by precise electrometric titration was given by Bush as 8.23 [59].

[c]At approximately 25°C unless otherwise noted; solubility values are mg/ml.

[d]B is 1-chlorobutane; E is diethyl ether; A is ethyl or isopropylacetate; lower phases are aqueous buffers of phosphate, pH 6.8; molarities as indicated. The partition coefficient (C) = concentration in upper phase/concentration in buffer. HB 10^{-3} to 10^{-6} M.

[e]The values from Bush et al. [5] were estimated gravimetrically and are for ethyl acetate/water.

[f]Isopropyl acetate/2M NaH$_2$PO$_4$, determined gravimetrically.

[g]At 32°-33°C.

[h]Decomposition; melting point varies greatly with rate of heating; ±4°C.

[i]This is 20°C below reported value (for α-HO-HB); product contains a very small amount of keto-HB-I.

[j]Parentheses indicate uncertain accuracy.

[k]At 5°-7°C.

So far as we have been able to find, no one has ever measured the C's under these various conditions, either with simple buffer-salt solutions or in the presence of blood or tissue. Using the ^{14}C-labeled compounds, we have made such measurements and the data are presented in Table 2. Here we have used isooctane instead of heptane because it has long been available as a pure compound. A number of barbiturates and thiobarbiturates have been checked with both these solvents and the C's have been practically identical.

It is seen that both the addition of i-amyl alcohol and of salt greatly enhance the C's for all the compounds and that the presence of whole blood or plasma significantly reduces them. It is clear that either the procedure of Axelrod et al. or that of Remmer should eliminate metabolite interference as long as the ratio of HB to NHB or HB to keto-HB is not too small. Whatever metabolite remains in the extract will be quantitatively carried along in the next steps of the Brodie et al. procedure and measured as HB. This will be further discussed in Section V.

For the solvent system 1-chlorobutane/0.1 M aqueous buffer (see Table 1), the relationships between C's and pH are shown in Fig. 2 for HB, NHB, keto-HB, and HO-HB.

B. Ultraviolet Absorption Spectra

All of these compounds, when dissolved in aqueous alkali, give spectra similar to those of other barbiturates. HB, keto-HB, and HO-HB have only one dissociable proton and therefore should give maximum absorption at pH = pK + 2 (99% ionized). At pH's above this, the absorption is the same [5], except for more or less rapid decomposition (see Section IV). NHB and keto-NHB have no N—CH$_3$ group and thus have two dissociable protons. The values of pK$_2$ have apparently not been determined. Like other barbiturates, HB and its derivatives exhibit very much weaker absorption in aqueous solutions at pH = pK$_1$ − 2 or lower, where ionization becomes negligible. This is the basis of the optical density difference (ODD) method of quantitating barbiturates, first described by Born [61], used by a few others, and modified and discussed in some detail by Bush [62]. The method involves the usual initial extraction (of blood, tissue, etc.) with organic solvent, buffer wash if necessary, and finally back-extracting the solvent-extract with a buffer of sufficiently high pH to remove most of the barbiturate. Brodie et al. [11] recommended pH 11 for HB and this is quite satisfactory (see Fig. 2). At this point, the usual procedure is to measure the optical density at the peak wave length, 245 nm, with a portion of the blank buffer solution in the reference cuvette. In the ODD method, aliquots of the pH 11 extract are suitably diluted or titrated with syrupy H$_3$PO$_4$ to give a reference solution of

TABLE 2

Effect of Blood and Plasma on Partition Coefficient[a]

Substance	Octane[b]/buffer, pH 6.8				Octane[b]/blood[c]		Octane[b]/plasma[d]		BuCl[e]/blood[f]
	0.1 M[g]	Sat'd NaCl[h]	1.5% AmOH[i]	NaCl[h] + AmOH[i]	Sat'd NaCl[h]	NaCl[h] + AmOH[i]	Sat'd NaCl[h]	NaCl[h] + AmOH[i]	
HB	0.16	0.9	0.38	8.2	0.24	2.2	0.20	2.7	5.6
NHB	0.00	0.01	0.05	0.3	0.002	0.08	0.002	0.11	0.08
Keto-HB-I	—	—	0.00	0.02	0.001	0.005	0.001	0.007	0.05
α-HO-HB	—	—	0.00	0.01	—	—	—	—	—

[a] Partition coefficient = concentration in organic phase/concentration in aqueous; molarity of drug in the aqueous phase is between 10^{-3} and 10^{-6} M. Temperature $25 \pm 2°C$.

[b] 2,2,4-Trimethylpentane.

[c] 1 ml of whole blood + 0.5 ml 0.1 M, pH 5.6 phosphate buffer.

[d] 1 ml of plasma + 0.5 ml 0.1 M, pH 5.6 phosphate buffer [10].

[e] 1-Chlorobutane; 2 vol. solvent to 1 vol. aqueous phase. All other volume ratios were 10.

[f] 1 ml of whole blood + 2 ml 0.1 M K_2HPO_4.

[g] 0.1 M phosphate.

[h] NaCl added to the aqueous phase.

[i] Isoamyl alcohol added to the octane.

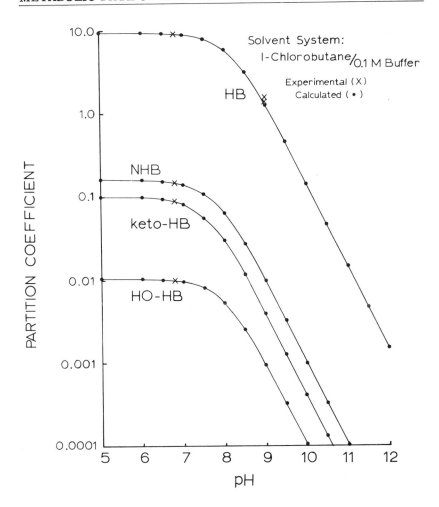

FIG. 2. Variation of partition coefficients with pH for HB and some of its metabolites. The calculated values (•) were obtained from experimental values (×) by the relationship

$$\log \left(\frac{C_a}{C_o} - 1 \right) = pH - pK_1$$

where C_a is the partition coefficient of the un-ionized acid and C_o is the partition coefficient of the total of ionized plus un-ionized acid. Solvent system: 1-chlorobutane/ 0.1 M buffer.

$pH = pK_1 - 2$ and a sample solution of $pH = pK_1 + 2$. The ODD between these two solutions is best scanned over the range 300–220 nm to check for interference, rather than simply measured at the peak wavelength. UV-absorbing substances present in the pH 11 extract but which do not change in absorbance over the pH range used are thus eliminated from the measurement.

In Fig. 3, the ODD's for HB at several concentrations are illustrated. The peaks of these curves occur at 245 ± 1 nm and when the absorbance is plotted against concentration on linear graph paper a straight line passing through zero is obtained. Such a graph serves as a reference for checking recoveries through the method.

We have determined similar values for the several available metabolites of HB (see Table 3). All follow Beer's law over the range of concentrations indicated. Similar calibration lines were reported by Tsukamoto et al. [14] for keto-NHB, keto-HB, and HO-HB, using the method of Brodie et al. [11].

The molar extinction difference coefficients between the singly ionized forms and the un-ionized forms of HB and its metabolites are listed in Table 3. Our values of ϵ and the peak wavelengths are in some cases slightly different from those of Tsukamoto et al. [14], because, in our ODD method, the absorbance of the un-ionized species is subtracted and because they used pH 11 (instead of pH = pK_1 + 2) where there is significant ionization of the second NH group in NHB and keto-NHB (which is accompanied by a shift of the peak to a longer wavelength as well as a diminution of ϵ; cf, [60]). Our values of ϵ for the ketones are quite a bit smaller than theirs and our λ_{max} values are higher because not only does the α,β-unsaturated ketone moiety absorb strongly but this absorbance does not change with pH.

C. Hydrolysis in Alkaline Solutions

HB and its metabolites are distinctly less stable in high pH aqueous solutions than are most of the commonly used barbiturates. We have investigated the nature of the products of hydrolysis of ^{14}C-HB by liquid-liquid extraction analysis and the rates of decomposition of HB, NHB, and keto-HB by UV analysis.

1. The Products of Hydrolysis

HB-2-^{14}C in a large excess of 1N NaOH (pH about 13.8) at room temperature decomposes rather rapidly (t/2 = 10 min) by A-ring cleavage (Fig. 1) at the peptide bond (3-4 or 1-6). Extraction analyses at a time when about 95% of the HB has disappeared indicate that the malonuric acid comprises about 80% of the mixture, the acyl urea derivative (ureide) about 5%, and methylurea about 10%. The acyl urea is readily extracted by 1-chlorobutane from aqueous buffer pH 9, whereas the carboxylic acid has a high partition coefficient into ethyl acetate from aqueous solution at pH 2. This malonuric acid is stable

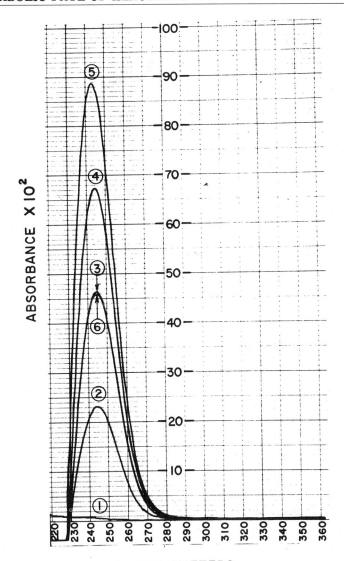

ABSORBANCE X 10^2

NANOMETERS

FIG. 3. Hexobarbital, UV absorbance difference (ODD). HB is at the same concentration in both cuvettes.

Curve	HB Concentration (nmole/ml)	Reference pH	Sample pH
1	0	6.2	10.2
2	30	6.2	10.2
3	60	6.2	10.2
4	90	6.2	10.2
5	120	6.2	10.2
6	120	6.2	8.2

TABLE 3

Molar Extinction Difference Coefficients

	pK_1	$\lambda max^{a,b}$	ϵ^b
HB	8.2	245	6,900
NHB	7.8	238	8,200
Keto-HB-I	7.5	247	10,100
α-HO-HB	8.0	245	7,900
β-HO-HB	7.9	246	7,100
Keto-NHB	7.1	242	11,900

[a] ±1 nm.

[b] Optical density differences were determined between buffered sample solutions of pH = pK_1 + 2 and buffered reference solutions of pH = pK_1 − 2. Concentrations of the buffers (borate-phosphate) were 0.1 M in the sample (high pH) solutions and approximately 0.2 M in the reference solutions (because of addition of H_3PO_4). The concentration of barbiturate was 10^{-4} M in both cuvettes.

enough to be isolated easily as the pure crystalline material (m.p. 135°-140°C, vigorous gas evolution). Heating an aliquot of the alkaline hydrolysis mixture at pH 2 and 95°C results in a relatively slow loss of CO_2 (formation of more of the ^{14}C-ureide, t/2 approximately 3 h) as well as the production of more ^{14}C-methyl urea. The latter has not been characterized beyond its partition coefficient (C = 0.01) between ethyl acetate and the pH 2 buffer.

If HB is heated in the presence of a large excess of aqueous 1N NaOH, the main products are the malonic acid and (presumably) methyl urea (see Section VI).

2. The Rates of Hydrolysis at Different pH's

It would seem highly desirable to know the rate of decomposition of HB in solutions prepared for administration. Concern about this is rarely expressed in the literature. Fouts [46] admonishes users that HB-Na solutions should be "used as quickly as possible" and a number of other workers have used "freshly prepared solutions." So far as we have been able to find, no one has made any quantitative study of the matter, although awareness of its importance clearly exists.

Because the products of hydrolytic breakdown of the barbituric acid ring do not have significant UV absorbance and give no interference by ODD, we have used this method to measure the rate of disappearance of substrate at various pH's.

The t/2 of HB at 0.03×10^{-3} M and $25° \pm 2°C$ is 10 min in 1N NaOH (pH approximately 13.8), 14 h at pH 12.0 (0.02 M KOH; HB, 9×10^{-5} M), and 372 h at pH 11.1 (commercial HB-Na in boiled distilled water; HB, 8.5×10^{-2} M) and at pH 10.3 the disappearance is $<5\%$ in 24 h (0.1 M borate buffer; HB, 9×10^{-5} M).

It is thus clear that solutions of commercial HB-Na prepared at the concentration recommended by Fouts [46] (20 mg/ml as HB) are stable enough to be useable during the whole day of preparation. On the other hand, HB dissolved in "1.1 equiv of NaOH" may not be so stable. If the acid is treated with a small volume of 1N NaOH (1.1 ml for 236 mg), for example, a considerable amount of hydrolysis is bound to occur during the several minutes required for complete dissolution. It is much better to treat the acid with less concentrated alkali even though the rate of dissolution may be slower. If it is desired to make 20 mg/ml (HB at 8.5×10^{-2} M), we suggest the following procedure: dissolve 267 mg of HB (1.13 mmoles) in 90 ml of BuCl and equilibrate this with 11.8 ml of 8.6×10^{-2} M NaOH (pH = 12.8) by shaking vigorously for 120 sec. The pH of the aqueous phase falls to 11.1 within 30 sec and to 11.0 in 120 sec, and analysis shows that the HB concentration is 8.5×10^{-2} M. The BuCl layer is aspirated off and the aqueous phase is freed of solvent by impingement with nitrogen. Hydrolysis should be less than 1 per cent.

The stability of HB at pH 11 or lower is good enough so that spectrophotometric measurements need not be hastened.

NHB is somewhat less unstable than is HB: t/2 = 41 h (0.02 N KOH, pH 12.0, and NHB 6×10^{-5} M). Keto-HB is much more unstable than the parent compound: t/2 = 18 h at pH 10.3 (0.1 M borate buffer; keto-HB, 4×10^{-5} M). Thus, if the ketone is to be quantitated, it must not be manipulated in high pH solutions.

We do not have data of this kind for HO-HB and keto-NHB.

If disappearance of HB is to be measured by UV analysis, the hydrolytic products will not interfere. If HB-2-^{14}C is to be quantitated by solvent extraction, however, the apolar hydrolytic product (the acyl urea derivative) described in Section IV.C.1 might very well interfere. We do not know the metabolic fate of this substance and have not detected it in any of the experiments with mice [8] or rats [47]. We were very careful, however, to avoid hydrolysis of the drug before administration.

D. Purity of Commercial HB

HB has long been available in bulk form from Winthrop Chemical Co. One recrystallization from alcohol gives material pure enough (m.p. 145°-6°C, corr.) for a reference standard. HB-Na has also been supplied by Winthrop, in 1 g batches in sealed ampules. This material is quite hygroscopic and even short exposure to moist air results in its becoming sticky and impossible to weigh accurately. Thus, Fouts [46] has suggested that the manufacturer's word be accepted as to the amount in the vial. This is indeed much more convenient than a direct determination but entails some risk. It is a simple matter, however, to compare the aqueous solution prepared from the HB-Na with a similar solution freshly prepared from pure HB as we have previously described, by spectrophotometry. Standard curves (Fig. 3) are quite reproducible.

Because so many workers have used HB-Na it has seemed to us desirable to check a few samples not only for the quantity in the vial but for purity as well. By direct weighing of unopened vials followed by opening and careful recovery of the washed glass sections, we have found three specimens to have a net weight within 1% of the labeled amount. These were all then checked by UV absorbance and found to contain 98 to 100% of HB-like material. Another specimen was analyzed by CCD. The solvent system was BuCl (300 ml) and 0.1 M borate buffer (pH 9.0, 100 ml). The whole 1 g specimen of HB-Na was put through a systematic fractionation using four batches of the organic solvent and two batches of the buffer. Calculation shows that the separation of HB from NHB should be better than 99% (see Figs. 2 and 4) and that the amount of NHB-like barbiturate present (some 90+% of which is in fraction "aqueous I") in the original gram of HB-Na was approximately 4.7 mg. This result does not, of course, guarantee this degree of purity for other batches of the drug.

E. Mass Spectra of HB and the Metabolites

Specimens of all the compounds listed in Table 1 have been examined in the LKB-9000 gas chromatograph-mass spectrometer by Dr. Keith H. Palmer at the Research Triangle Institute (present address: Brown University, Division of Biological and Medical Sciences, Providence, Rhode Island). He will report the results elsewhere.

It may be of interest here to anticipate his report concerning the relationship between keto-HB-I and keto-HB-II. The melting point of the latter compound is very close to that of β-HO-HB and it has been thought that these substances may be identical. The mass spectra of the two ketones are so closely alike, however, that Dr. Palmer feels certain that they are indeed isomeric. The measurements on β-HO-HB are incomplete but those on α-HO-HB show unmistakable differences between this substance and the two ketones.

V. METHODOLOGIES FOR THE QUANTITATION OF HB
(AND ITS METABOLITES)

A. General Considerations; Solvent Extraction

All present methods for quantitating HB involve extraction from aqueous biological material with an organic solvent. For the recovery of unchanged drug with a minimum of metabolite, Brodie et al. [63] suggested using the least polar solvent that would give reasonable quantitation. Petroleum ether and heptane were found too apolar on the latter count for pentobarbital [11] and HB [9]. The neat maneuver of adding a small amount of i-amyl alcohol (1.5%) solved this problem, in part, by greatly increasing the polarity of the solvent. When, in addition, they saturated the aqueous phase with sodium chloride, acceptable recoveries of the drug were achieved. Both of these additions increase not only the partition coefficients of HB but also those of the metabolites (Table 2, Section IV.A). This is not likely to lead to serious interference under conditions where the ratio HB/ metabolites is large (the early stages of a microsomal incubation or of disappearance from blood). However, under conditions where this ratio is small (blood, whole body, or microsomal analyses at late times, say, after 30 min) the interference, especially from keto-HB, may be quite significant. Axelrod et al. [32] washed the "petroleum ether extract" (presumably containing 1.5% i-amyl alcohol) twice with one-fifth volumes of pH 5.5 phosphate buffer in order to remove a metabolite of HB. It is not stated whether or not this buffer was saturated with salt. If not, the absolute recovery of HB would be drastically reduced to about 45% (see Table 2). These workers unquestionably corrected for this by carrying known amounts of HB through the method but low recoveries of the small amounts of HB remaining in such experiments would decrease even further the accuracy attainable by the method. Under some conditions no amount of buffer washing will remove the interference.

Cooper and Brodie [9] found their extraction procedure to be specific for HB (under their conditions) by measuring the partition coefficient of the extracted UV absorbing material "in a series of two phase systems consisting of heptane and various aqueous buffers" (the technique of comparative distribution ratios, a principle first suggested by Bush [64]) and comparing the values with those for authentic HB. No mention was made of the addition of i-amyl alcohol or salt to these systems and no data were presented. Our partition coefficients (Table 2) make it seem likely that they did, in fact, include one or the other or both of these adjuvants. In the subsequent literature involving HB quantitation, it would seem almost certain that all workers except

Remmer [45], and those few who refer to him, used both adjuvants although they may refer only to the Cooper-Brodie paper. Occasionally, it appears, some authors refer only to the latter paper yet have actually used the buffer-wash modification of Axelrod et al. [32].

Remmer [45] eliminated metabolite interference by leaving the i-amyl alcohol out of the Brodie solvent. This sufficed because NHB was probably present in his experiments (whole mice analyses) in negligible amounts.

The analysis of bile and urine, in which the ratio HB/metabolites is likely to be <0.01, requires more or less complete separation of the components before any of them can be identified or quantitated.

B. Spectrophotometry

In Section IV.B, we discussed the UV absorbance spectra of HB and its major metabolites and pointed out that the ODD method had certain advantages over the usual OD method. Both the specificity and sensitivity of the former procedure are somewhat greater because interference from impurities present in solvents and in biological material is reduced. The minimum amount of a pure oxybarbiturate that will give a significant UV peak is about 1 μg/ml in the cuvette. Extracts of blank microsomal preparations, liver perfusates, or blood generally give values of about this magnitude (with the ODD method and washed solvents, see below). The amount of blank interference from urine or whole body homogenate is very much larger, of course, and small amounts of barbiturate from such sources must be highly purified before even the ODD method can give significant values. (Methods in V.C, D, E and F may be more appropriate.) Some workers (Fouts and Brodie [43] and Remmer [45]) solved this problem by giving a sufficiently large dose (200 mg/kg) of HB to mice so that the absorbance of the blank material in the extract was small relative to that of the HB and could be diluted out. Bush and Parrish [26] gave doses of only 50 mg/kg and purified their whole mouse extracts by CCD. Tsukamoto et al. [14] extracted metabolites from rabbit urine with ethyl acetate, subjected aliquots of the concentrated extract to paper chromatography, eluted the spots with pH 11 buffer, and quantitated the purified HB metabolites by the OD method of Cooper and Brodie. The Japanese workers reported the absorbance maxima: keto-HB, 240 nm; HO-HB, 244 nm; and keto-NHB, 238 nm, at pH 11. They also gave a graph of extinction versus concentrations.

Solvents obtained from commercial sources have usually contained impurities that contribute considerable interference in the UV range used for oxybarbiturate determinations. Brodie et al. [11] washed their solvents with 1N NaOH, 1N HCl, and water until this interference was eliminated. The current availability of nanograde solvents (Mal-

linckrodt Chemical Works, St. Louis, Mo.) or distilled-in-glass solvents (Burdick and Jackson, Muskegon, Mich.) generally obviates the
need for further purification.

We have, on occasion, observed serious UV interference from commercial buffer solutions, probably due to phenolic antimicrobial
agents added by the manufacturer but not mentioned on the label!
This has also happened with 1N NaOH solutions. We now make up all
buffers involved in UV measurements from the reagent grade components.

When all these factors are taken into consideration, it may be concluded that the solvent extraction-spectrophotometric method aided
only by a buffer wash or two is most suitable for determination of HB
under circumstances where the unchanged drug is present in excess
over its metabolites and over the interfering materials extracted
from the biological sources. For other situations, one or another of
the procedures discussed in Sections V.C, D, E and F probably will
be the method of choice.

C. Paper and Thin-Layer Chromatography

Paper and thin-layer chromatography are not in themselves capable of quantitating HB or its metabolites. The use of paper chromatography in conjunction with UV spectrophotometry by Tsukamoto et
al. [14] has been discussed. Thin-layer chromatography (TLC) in
conjunction with ^{14}C counting has been applied satisfactorily by Holcomb [47] in his studies of HB metabolism in the rat. HB and the
metabolites were nicely separated on silica gel plates or "ChromAR"
sheets by the solvent chloroform/acetone (9/1) of Cochin and Daly
[65] and by a number of other solvents. Noordhoek and Gerritsen
[23] have separated some of the metabolites of HB in mouse urine by
TLC. They give no quantitative data but their discussion implies that
such data are forthcoming.

These methods of separation are, of course, also subject to interference from impurities that may be extracted with the drug and its
metabolites from some biological sources. Rf values may be more
or less seriously affected by the presence of large amounts of lipids
in solvent extracts of brain, liver, fat, or whole body homogenates.
The common precaution of suitable controls and rechromatographing
eluted materials should make the methods suitable for analysis of
such tissues especially if used in conjunction with ^{14}C labeling. Preliminary purification of crude extracts by liquid-liquid extraction
(see Section V.F) can be helpful.

Apparently these chromatographic methods have not been used in
quantitation procedures for HB and its metabolites other than in urine
and in liver supernatant studies.

D. Gas Chromatography

There appears to be only one description of this method as used
to quantitate HB. Anders [66] briefly reviews previous use of gas
chromatography (GC) for quantitation of barbiturates and describes
in detail a further variation of the method that is particularly suited
to rapid estimations of a number of barbiturates in small samples of
blood. HB was determined in 100 μl portions of rat blood by extraction
with equal volumes of chloroform, injecting aliquots of this extract
into the apparatus, and comparing the peak heights on the elution
graph with standards. After administration of 82 mg/kg i.p. to a rat,
samples of blood from the tip of the tail were analyzed at 30, 60, 90,
120, and 150 min. The half-life as estimated graphically was 36 min.
The sex and strain of the animals were not given. Whether metabolites
interfered or not was not mentioned but it would seem highly unlikely
that they did.

The sensitivity of the method makes it easy to detect HB (and other
barbiturates) in 0.1 ml portions of blood if these contain as much as
10 μg/ml. Mixtures of the barbiturates were not studied. A disadvantage of this particular method (not necessarily of other GC procedures)
seems to be the necessity of presaturation of the column by injecting
a relatively large quantity of the particular barbiturate being measured. This would be no disadvantage for studies of the disappearance
of a single drug, such as HB, however, and there would seem to be
no reason to doubt that a competent analyst should get perfectly valid
results.

HB seems not to have been included in the many other GC studies
of quantitation of barbiturates, probably because it is not of forensic
importance.

E. Liquid (Partition) Chromatography

Anders and Latorre [67] have included HB and keto-HB in a study
of the applicability of high-speed (high-pressure) liquid chromatography with an ion-exchange column to the resolution of mixtures
with a number of other barbiturates and hydantoins. It was shown
that mixtures of HB and keto-HB and of the other drugs and their
major metabolites can be separated satisfactorily by the procedure.
The effluents from the column were monitored by a nonspecific UV
detector. Application of the method to biological fluids is under study.

Simple mixtures of HB and keto-KB, phenobarbital and its p-hydroxy derivative, diphenylhydantoin and its p-hydroxy derivative, etc.,
can be separated readily by simple solvent extraction but this new
application of liquid chromatography promises to handle complex
mixtures of such drugs and their metabolites with a sensitivity com-

parable to that of TLC and GC and without the need to subject unstable substances to traumatic conditions or to derivatize polar compounds.

F. Countercurrent Distribution with ^{14}C-Labeled Materials

It was long recognized that labeling HB with ^{14}C would greatly
facilitate the working out of quantitative methods for elucidating its
metabolic fate. The label can be quantitated without extensive purification and the molecular species carrying the label can be identified
by comparing its distribution patterns with those of reference compounds in various separation processes.

After our successful synthesis of HB-2-^{14}C (see Section VI), we
applied our extensive experience with liquid-liquid extraction analysis to the problem. More conveniently called countercurrent distribution (CCD) but actually, as we use it, a simpler and more varied application of the same principles, the method involves the now classical
use of partition coefficients in suitable liquid-liquid, two-phase systems for separating and identifying components of mixtures [28, 68].

Our first application of the method to the labeled drug was to check
its purity. Several batches of drug have been prepared and checked
and the results of a typical analysis are shown in Fig. 4. These data
have been taken from the dissertation of Mr. Robert Holcomb [47].
The experimental procedure involved putting some 1.4 μc (5 mg) of
HB-2-^{14}C in the first tube of a four-tube machine [69] and equilibrating
it between 7 ml of 0.1 M pH 9.0 borate buffer and 14 ml of 1-chloro-
butane (BuCl). The other three tubes of the machine having been
charged, each with the same volume of buffer (preequilibrated with
the BuCl), the transfers, additions of fresh batches of BuCl (preequilibrated with the buffer), and equilibrations were then carried out in
the usual manner [28]. A total of four batches of BuCl were carried
through the machine, kept separate for analysis, and numbered 1, 2,
3, and 4. The four aqueous fractions remaining in the machine were
removed to holding tubes for analysis and numbered in reverse order
(fraction 8 from tube 1, fraction 7 from tube 2, etc.). All volumes
were checked. The results of the radiochemical analyses are plotted
in the usual way [28] in Fig. 4a and a theoretical distribution calculated from the amounts and ratios of the ^{14}C in the first three fractions.
The discrepancy between experimental and theoretical for fraction 4
is considered to be experimental error because the fractions on either
side show excellent agreement; the excess of ^{14}C over the theoretical
in fraction 8 is interpreted to represent a polar impurity, approximately 2% of the original material. The data plotted in Fig. 4b show
that the specific activity of the first four fractions is the same, the

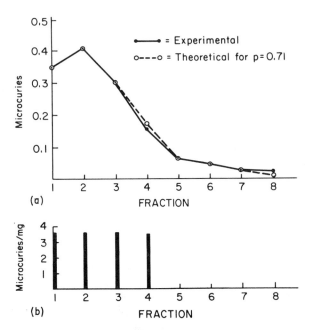

FIG. 4. Typical CCD pattern obtained with HB-2-^{14}C. The specimen examined here had been kept in crystalline form in a screw-capped vial at room temperature in the dark for 3 years. The solvent system was 1-chlorobutane (14 ml) and 0.1 M borate buffer pH 9.0 (7 ml). For other details, see the text. (●) Experimental; (○) theoretical for p = 0.71.

milligrams having been determined by UV analysis. The radiochemical purity was thus approximately 98%.

This analysis does not show the chemical purity of the labeled drug. That this was approximately 100 ± 2% was demonstrated by a UV absorbance per milligram comparison with pure HB of m.p. 146°C (Table 1); no qualitative or quantitative differences could be detected over the range pH 6-10. The m.p. of the white crystalline labeled material was 145°C.

The results of the application of this method of analysis to the separation, identification, and quantitation of HB, keto-HB, and HO-HB in the mouse (in vitro and by whole body analyses) have been summarized in Section II.C.4 of this review. The effectiveness of the method is attested to by the fact that 80% of the dose was accounted for as identified metabolites. The rationale of the choice of solvents, numbers of tubes required, etc. was not discussed. This may be of some interest.

Homogenization of mice in acetone has been demonstrated to recover 95-100% of 1 μc (1 mg) of intravenously administered HB-2-^{14}C, NHB-2-^{14}C, and keto-HB-2-^{14}C 1 min after injection (other barbiturates, bufotenine, and DDT are also recoverable in similar yields). The ^{14}C was similarly recoverable even 2 h after injection (excreta were included in the homogenization). After many trials of many procedures for removing emulsifiers from the acetone extract, we have so far had to accept the charcoal treatment as the only one that works [8], even though it appears to remove a portion of the metabolites (see discussion in Section II.C.4). Given the residue from the evaporation of the charcoal-treated acetone extract, the next steps were guided by the pertinent partition coefficients given in Table 1. As a solvent of low polarity we have long used BuCl (1-chlorobutane) instead of octane or heptane with i-amyl alcohol because we wished to have a pure, readily volatile solvent that would not leave a high boiling residue (i-amyl alcohol) on concentration of large volumes. The polarity of BuCl is about right to give easy separation of HB from its metabolites. This solvent is also transparent in the useful UV range. If the object of the procedure is only to determine unchanged HB, a buffer wash or two is necessary if either NHB or keto-HB is present.

If the object is to separate and determine the metabolites, more extensive fractionations must be done. Gerber et al. [8] reported that ten-tube CCD's (BuCl/2 M, pH6.8 buffer) showed that NHB was not present in significant amounts in the mouse at either 15 min or 45 min. (This is undoubtedly correct. A better solvent system would have been ether/0.1 M buffer, but this gave emulsions.) It was then feasible to analyze large numbers of animals with CCD's of only four tubes, to determine HB, keto-HB, and HO-HB simultaneously, with the solvent system BuCl/2 M, pH 6.8 buffer, the partition coefficients being respectively 17, 0.7 and 0.07; this was also used in several ten-tube CCD's for the unequivocal identification and quantitation of the metabolites in experiments with liver supernatant. Further characterizations of the partially purified biological keto-HB and HO-HB were made by four-tube CCD's with the solvent system ether/0.1M, pH 6.8 buffer, in which the partition coefficients are 0.49 and 0.25, respectively, a difference which is ample to permit differentiation and quantitation of the two substances but not sufficient to give complete separation from each other with small numbers of tubes.

The advantages of these small CCD's are several. Besides subjecting solutes to mild conditions, permitting quantitative recoveries of material, and being adaptable from the gram to the microgram scale (or lower), they permit a ready progression from one solvent system to another as these may give greater selectivity in successive separations of the components of a mixture. Separations can thus often be achieved which with any one solvent system, would require large numbers of tubes, expensive automation, and much laboratory space. The disadvantages are that complex mixtures of closely related components cannot be separated and that it is laborious to carry out even four-tube CCD's on a large number of samples.

A relatively inexpensive semiautomatic apparatus is now available [70] with which six four-tube CCD's (or four six-tube, or two ten-tube, or one thirty-tube) can be conveniently carried out simultaneously.

VI. BRIEF OUTLINE OF SYNTHESIS OF HEXOBARBITAL-2-^{14}C, NORHEXOBARBITAL-2-^{14}C, AND KETOHEXOBARBITAL-2-^{14}C

A. Hexobarbital-2-^{14}C

The malonic acid (m.p. 145°-150°C, gas evolution; neutral equivalent 102) was obtained from HB by alkaline hydrolysis and 2 mmoles were converted to the malonyl chloride with $SOCl_2$. Methylurea-2-^{14}C was prepared from urea-^{14}C by heating with excess methyl amine hydrochloride in a little water and then completing the reaction and drying by codistillation of the ammonia and water with dry pyridine. This solution, separated from crystals of salts by pipette, was added to 2 equiv of the malonyl chloride (freed of excess $SOCl_2$ by codistillation with dry toluene) in a little pyridine and the stirred mixture heated in a stoppered tube at 80°C for 60 h. The reaction solution was cooled, diluted with water, brought to pH 6 with HCl, and extracted three times with 2 vol portions of 1-chlorobutane (BuCl). These were washed with one portion of pH 6.8 buffer (0.1 M) and then equilibrated successively with a large volume (4 mmoles) of 0.02 N KOH. This aqueous extract was neutralized promptly and the product was extracted with BuCl. The dried extract was concentrated and gave crystals. Recrystallization from methanol gave a 20% yield of practically pure (white) material (m.p. 145°C corr.) The product of specific activity 1 mc/mmole is quite stable at room temperature, showing no change in its CCD pattern (Fig. 4) after 3 years.

B. Norhexobarbital-2-^{14}C

Norhexobarbital-2-^{14}C was prepared by the same procedure except for the use of ^{14}C-urea (added as a solution in warm pyridine). The product was extracted with ether and recrystallized from methanol. The yield of practically pure material was similar.

Although unlabeled NHB (Winthrop, recrystallized) seems to be reasonably stable at room temperature, the ^{14}C material has been rather unstable, perhaps because of trace impurities. Whereas a purity of about 98% was indicated by the original CCD-UV analysis, considerable decomposition was shown by a similar analysis after 1 year (Fig. 5). Repurification has thus been necessary before using the material.

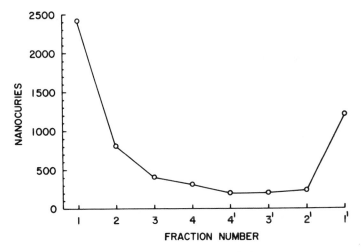

FIG. 5. CCD of NHB-2-^{14}C after 1 year storage in the dark at room temperature. Solvent system: octane-isoamyl alcohol (2/1) (22 ml) and 0.1 M phosphate pH 6.8 buffer (10 ml). The procedure was the same as that used for Fig. 4. The values for the aqueous fractions are plotted in the same order, although their numbering has been changed. The results are discussed in the text.

C. Ketohexobarbital-2-^{14}C

Ketohexobarbital-2-^{14}C was synthesized from labeled HB (5 mmoles) by oxidation with chromic anhydride in acetic anhydride solution, at room temperature, by a modification of the procedure outlined by Tsukamoto et al. [71]. The material was purified by CCD between ethyl acetate and pH 6 buffer and recrystallization from methanol. The pure product, specific activity 61 μc/mmole, was obtained in 21% yield. It has been quite stable at room temperature, the CCD analysis having remained unchanged in a year (Fig. 6).

Acknowledgments

Besides those co-workers who have already been acknowledged in the references, we are indebted to Betty Gray for help in the synthe-

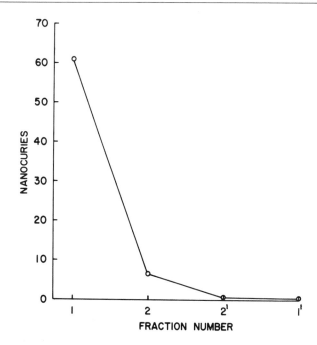

FIG. 6. CCD of keto-HB-2-^{14}C after 1 year storage in the dark at room temperature. Solvent system: ethyl acetate (20 ml) and 0.1 M phosphate pH 6.8 buffer (5 ml).
The experimental distribution (shown) and the theoretical distribution (not shown) are
practically identical.

sis of the first batch of HB-2-^{14}C, to Ellen Helman for some of the
physicochemical data, and to Herman Parrish and Bolton Smith for
many experiments in the development of the acetone-extraction method.
The senior author is especially indebted to his wife, Elaine Sanders-
Bush, for her skillful help and criticism, for collating references,
and doing a significant part of the typing.

The work has been supported in part by U.S. Public Health Service
Grant GM 15431 from the National Institute of General Medical Sciences and by Grant NS-03534 from the National Institute of Neurologi-
cal Disease and Stroke.

REFERENCES

[1]   R. T. Williams, *Detoxication Mechanisms*, 2nd ed., Wiley, New York, 1959,
      p. 610.
[2]   L. C. Mark, *Clin. Pharmacol. Ther.*, 4, 504 (1963).
[3]   R. T. Williams and D. V. Parke, *Ann. Rev. Pharmacol.*, 4, 85 (1964).
[4]   M. T. Bush and E. Sanders, *Ann. Rev. Pharmacol.*, 7, 57 (1967).

[5] M. T. Bush, T. C. Butler, and H. L. Dickison, *J. Pharmacol. Exp. Ther.*, **108**, 104 (1953).

[6] T. C. Butler and M. T. Bush, *J. Pharmacol. Exp. Ther.*, **65**, 205 (1939).

[7] H. Tsukamoto, S. Toki, and K. Kaneda, *Chem. Pharm. Bull. (Tokyo)*, **7**, 651 (1959).

[8] N. Gerber, R. Lynn, R. Holcomb, W. L. Weller, and M. T. Bush, *J. Pharmacol. Exp. Ther.*, **177**, 234 (1971).

[9] J. R. Cooper and B. B. Brodie, *J. Pharmacol. Exp. Ther.*, **114**, 409 (1955).

[10] H. Tsukamoto, H. Yoshimura, and S. Toki, *Pharm. Bull. (Tokyo)*, **4**, 368 (1956).

[11] B. B. Brodie, J. J. Burns, L. C. Mark, P. A. Lief, E. Bernstein, and E. M. Papper, *J. Pharmacol. Exp. Ther.*, **109**, 26 (1953).

[12] H. Yoshimura, *Pharm. Bull. (Tokyo)*, **5**, 561 (1957).

[13] H. Yoshimura, *Pharm. Bull. (Tokyo)*, **6**, 13 (1958).

[14] H. Tsukamoto, H. Yoshimura, and S. Toki, *Pharm. Bull. (Tokyo)*, **6**, 88 (1958).

[15] H. Tsukamoto, S. Toki, and K. Toki, *Chem. Pharm. Bull. (Tokyo)*, **8**, 561 (1960).

[16] S. Toki, K. Toki, and H. Tsukamoto, *Chem. Pharm. Bull. (Tokyo)*, **10**, 708 (1962).

[17] K. Toki, S. Toki, and H. Tsukamoto, *J. Biochem. (Tokyo)*, **53**, 43 (1963).

[18] K. Toki and H. Tsukamoto, *J. Biochem. (Tokyo)*, **55**, 142 (1964).

[19] H. Tsukamoto, H. Yoshimura, and S. Toki, *Pharm. Bull. (Tokyo)*, **6**, 15 (1958).

[20] S. Toki and T. Takenouchi, *Chem. Pharm. Bull. (Tokyo)*, **13**, 606 (1965).

[21] I. A. Kamil, J. N. Smith, and R. T. Williams, *Biochem. J.*, **50**, 235 (1951).

[22] R. E. McMahon, *Biochem. Pharmacol.*, **12**, 1225 (1963).

[23] J. Noordhoek and B. J. Gerritsen, *Acta Physiol. Pharmacol. Neerl.*, **15**, 414 (1969).

[24] R. Deininger, *Arch. exp. Path. Pharmakol.*, **227**, 316 (1956).

[25] E. W. Maynert, *Ann. Rev. Pharmacol.*, **1**, 45 (1961).

[26] M. T. Bush and H. Parrish, *Fed. Proc.*, **22**, 480 (1963).

[27] W. Block and I. Ebigt, *Arzneimittel-Forsch.*, **7**, 572 (1957).

[28] M. T. Bush and P. M. Densen, *Anal. Chem.*, **20**, 121 (1948).

[29] S. Toki, R. Yamasaki, and T. Wakiya, *Chem. Pharm. Bull. (Tokyo)*, **13**, 280 (1965).

[30] R. R. Holcomb, W. F. Woodside, and M. T. Bush, *Fed. Proc.*, **28**, 290 (1969).

[31] R. R. Holcomb, N. Gerber, and M. T. Bush, *Pharmacologist*, **11**, 261 (1969).

[32] J. Axelrod, J. Reichenthal, and B. B. Brodie, *J. Pharmacol. Exp. Ther.*, **112**, 49 (1954).

[33] F. Fretwurst, *Klin. Wchnschr.*, **12**, 1309 (1933).

[34] F. Fretwurst, *Med. Klin.*, **29**, 893 (1933).

[35] H. Weese, *Deutsche med. Wchnschr.*, **58**, 1205 (1932).

[36] H. Tsukamoto, S. Toki, and K. Kaneda, *Pharm. Bull. (Tokyo)*, **6**, 625 (1957).

[37] H. H. Frey, F. Sudeney, and D. Krause, *Arzneimittel-Forsch.*, **9**, 294 (1959).

[38] F. Fretwurst, J. Halberkann, and F. Reiche, *Munchen. med. Wchnschr.*, **79**, 1429 (1932).

[39] H. Tsukamoto and Y. Kuroiwa, *Chem. Pharm. Bull. (Tokyo)*, **7**, 731 (1959).

[40] B. B. Brodie, *Fed. Proc.*, **11**, 632 (1952).

[41] M. T. Bush, G. Berry, and A. Hume, *Clin. Pharmacol. Ther.*, **7**, 373 (1966).

[42] J. R. Cooper, J. Axelrod, and B. B. Brodie, *J. Pharmacol. Exp. Ther.*, **112**, 55 (1954).

[43] J. R. Fouts and B. B. Brodie, *J. Pharmacol. Exp. Ther.*, **115**, 68 (1955).

[44] G. P. Quinn, J. Axelrod, and B. B. Brodie, *Biochem. Pharmacol.*, 1, 152 (1958).
[45] H. Remmer, *Naunyn-Schmiedeberg's Arch. exp. Path. Pharmakol.*, 237, 296 (1959).
[46] J. R. Fouts, in *Methods in Pharmacology*, (Arnold Schwartz, ed.), Appleton, New York, 1971, Vol. 1, p. 287.
[47] R. R. Holcomb, Ph.D. dissertation, Vanderbilt Univ., Nashville, Tennessee, December, 1971.
[48] E. S. Vesell, *Pharmacology*, 1, 81 (1968).
[49] J. Noordhoek, *Eu. J. Pharmacol.*, 3, 242 (1968).
[50] R. E. Stitzel, M. W. Anders, and G. J. Mannering, *Mol. Pharmacol.*, 2, 49 (1966).
[51] R. E. Stitzel, T. R. Tephley, and G. J. Mannering, *Mol. Pharmacol.*, 4, 15 (1968).
[52] J. Knabe and R. Kraüter, *Arch. Pharm.*, 298, 1 (1965).
[53] G. Wahlström, *Life Sci.*, 5, 1781 (1966).
[54] W. Rummel, U. Brandenburger, and H. Büch, *Med. Pharmacol. Exp.*, 16, 496 (1967).
[55] E. Degkwitz, V. Ullrich, and H. Staudinger, *Hoppe-Seyler's Zeit. Physiol. Chem.*, 350, 547 (1969).
[56] R. L. Furner, J. S. McCarthy, R. E. Stitzel, and M. W. Anders, *J. Pharmacol. Exp. Ther.*, 169, 153 (1969).
[57] J. S. McCarthy and R. E. Stitzel, *J. Pharmacol. Exp. Ther.*, 176, 772 (1971).
[58] H. Büch, J. Knabe, W. Buzello, and W. Rummel, *J. Pharmacol. Exp. Ther.*, 175, 709 (1970).
[59] M. T. Bush, *J. Pharmacol. Exp. Ther.*, 61, 134 (1937).
[60] T. C. Butler, J. M. Ruth, and G. F. Tucker, *J. Am. Chem. Soc.*, 77, 1486 (1955).
[61] G. V. R. Born, *Biochem. J.*, 44, 501 (1949).
[62] M. T. Bush, *Microchem. J.*, 5, 73 (1961).
[63] B. B. Brodie, S. Udenfriend, and J. E. Baer, *J. Biol. Chem.*, 168, 299 (1947).
[64] M. T. Bush in L. C. Craig, *J. Biol. Chem.*, 150, 34 (1943).
[65] J. Cochin and J. W. Daly, *J. Pharmacol. Exp. Ther.*, 139, 154 (1963).
[66] M. W. Anders, *Anal. Chem.*, 38, 1945 (1966).
[67] M. W. Anders and J. P. Latorre, *Anal. Chem.*, 42, 1430 (1970).
[68] L. C. Craig, *J. Biol. Chem.*, 155, 519 (1944).
[69] M. T. Bush and O. W. Post, *Anal. Biochem.*, 32, 145 (1969).
[70] O. W. Post Scientific Instrument Co., Middle Village, N.Y.
[71] H. Tsukamoto, H. Yoshimura, and S. Toki, *Pharm. Bull. (Tokyo)*, 4, 364 (1956).

Accepted for publication November 18, 1971.

Benzodiazepine Metabolism in Vitro

S. GARATTINI, F. MARCUCCI, and E. MUSSINI
Istituto di Ricerche Farmacolgiche "Mario Negri",
Milano, Italy

I. INTRODUCTION

The benzodiazepines represent a group of powerful drugs particularly known for their tranquilizing and anticonvulsant activities. Their extensive use in therapeutic practice justifies a continued interest in

the metabolism of these compounds. Of further importance is the
fact that several metabolites of the benzodiazepines also show pharmacological activity and the metabolism of these compounds is also
discussed below. This review endeavors to summarize our present
knowledge on the metabolism of benzodiazepines in vitro in the hope
that such a synthesis may not only be useful to workers in the field
but that it will stimulate further study.

II. DIAZEPAM

Diazepam is 7-chloro-1,3-dihydro-1-methyl-5-phenyl-2H-1,4
benzodiazepin-2-one (I); chemical structures related to roman nu-
merals are reported in Fig. 1 and Fig. 7. The major routes of
diazepam metabolism studied in vitro are represented by N_1-demeth-
ylation and C_3-hydroxylation according to the scheme presented in
Fig. 2. These pathways were first postulated by Schwartz et al. [1]
and Ruelius et al. [2] on the basis of studies carried out in vivo and
later demonstrated by perfusing isolated rat livers [3]. In this in
vitro preparation, diazepam was metabolized to form three metabolites: N-desmethyldiazepam (II), N-methyloxazepam (IV). Oxazepam
was also formed when either N-desmethyldiazepam or N-methyloxazepam was added to the perfusing blood.

However, when 9,000 × g liver homogenate [4] or liver microsomal preparations [5] of rats were used, only traces of oxazepam
were formed, whereas N-desmethyldiazepam and N-methyloxazepam
were present in measureable amounts.

The relative rate of N_1-demethylation or C_3-hydroxylation shows
a characteristic pattern for different animal species. Table 1 indicates the percentage of diazepam metabolized by utilizing liver microsomal enzymes. It is evident that rats show more hydroxylation than
N-demethylation [5], whereas the opposite picture is evident for
guinea pigs [6]. In mice the two metabolic pathways are similar,
whereas in rabbits and cats the results (unpublished) are more difficult to interpret because of the formation of unknown metabolites
that may represent the further metabolism of N-methyloxazepam
or N-desmethyldiazepam. Schwartz and Postma [4] have investigated
the metabolism of diazepam by 9000 × g liver homogenate of dogs.
Their data, although not quantitative, indicate that both N-desmethyldiazepam and N-methyloxazepam are formed in about equal concentrations, whereas oxazepam is formed only in trace amounts. Precise
kinetic constants are not available because the metabolism of diazepam under the utilized experimental conditions does not follow the
Michaelis-Menten equations. When mouse liver microsomes were

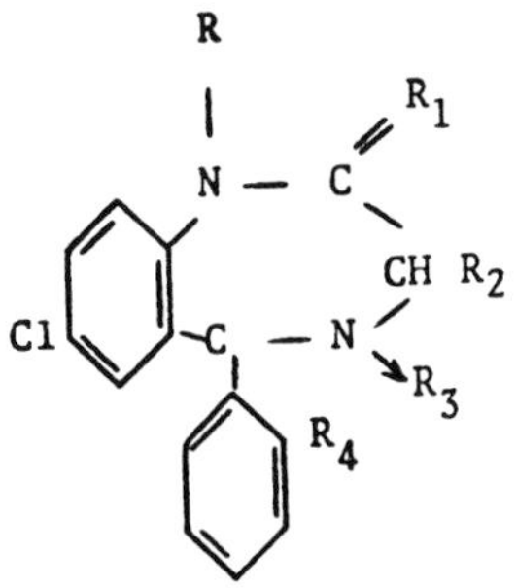

	R	R_1	R_2	R_3	R_4
(I) Diazepam	CH_3	O	H	–	H
(II) N-Desmethyldiazepam	H	O	H	–	H
(III) N-Methyloxazepam	CH_3	O	OH	–	H
(IV) Oxazepam	H	O	OH	–	H
(V) o-Cl-Desmethyldiazepam	H	O	H	–	Cl
(VI) o-Cl-Oxazepam (lorazepam)	H	O	OH	–	Cl
(VII) N_4-Oxide diazepam	CH_3	O	H	→ O	H
(VIII) N_4-Oxide-N desmethyl-diazepam	H	O	H	→ O	H
(IX) Medazepam	CH_3	H_2	H	–	H
(X) N-Desmethylmedazepam	H	H_2	H	–	H
(XI) Flurazepam	—$C_2H_4N(C_2H_5)_2$	O	H	–	F
(XII) N-Desethyl flurazepam	—$C_2H_4NHC_2H_5$	O	H	–	F
(XIII) o-F-N-Desmethyl-diazepam	H	O	H	–	F
(XIV) Prazepam	—CH_2—◁	O	H	–	H
(XV) Chlordiazepoxide	–	$NHCH_3$	H	→ O	H
(XVI) N-Desmethylchlor-diazepoxide	–	NH_2	H	→ O	H

FIG. 1. Chemical structure of some benzodiazepines. Roman numbers refer to the text.

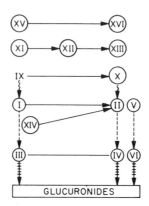

FIG. 2. Pathways of benzodiazepine metabolism demonstrated in vitro. ⟶ N-Dealkylation; ⟿ oxidation; -----▶ hydroxylation; ⊶⊶⊶▶ conjugation. (I) Diazepam;
(II) N-desmethyldiazepam; (III) N-methyl oxazepam; (IV) oxazepam; (V) o-Cl-desmethyl-
diazepam; (VI) o-Cl-oxazepam; (IX) medazepam; (X) N-desmethylmedazepam; (XI) flurazepam; (XII) N-desethylflurazepam; (XIII) o-F-N-desmethyldiazepam; (XIV) prazepam;
(XV) chlordiazepoxide; (XVI) N-desmethyl chlordiazepoxide.

TABLE 1

Metabolism of Diazepam by Liver Microsomal Enzymes

| Species | Percent of diazepam converted to: | |
	N-Desmethyldiazepam	N-Methyloxazepam
Mouse	22	15
Rat	2	14
Guinea Pig	60	n.m.
Rabbit[a]	3	5
Cat[b]	0.5	10
Dog	15	13
Dog[c] [4]	16	14

[a]Unknown metabolites: 20%. n.m. = not measurable.
[b]Unknown metabolites: 16%.
[c]Unknown metabolites: 13% (9000 X g liver homogenate).

utilized, it was established that the apparent Michaelis constant (K_m) was 1.21×10^{-5} M and the estimated V_{max} was 3.35 nM/mg protein/10 min [5]. Typical plots for diazepam biotransformation in relation to drug concentration, duration of incubation, and amount of liver microsomes are presented in Fig. 3.

The activity of liver microsomal enzymes of newborn and adult rats and guinea pigs are shown in Fig. 4 and Fig. 5, respectively. In newborn rats there is relatively more C_3-hydroxylation than N_1-demethylation relative to adult rats, whereas in newborn guinea pigs the N_1-demethylation is reduced in comparison with adult guinea pigs. It is remarkable that newborn guinea pigs show the capacity to hydroxylate diazepam because N-methyloxazepam was never found in adults. These findings are important because the metabolism of diazepam in vivo is quite different in newborn and adult guinea pigs or rats. These data were obtained at equal concentrations of microsomal proteins. However, when the same data are expressed per gram of liver, the liver of newborn rats and guinea pigs metabolized diazepam less extensively than did adult liver (unpublished results).

It is well known that liver microsomal enzymes may be activated by the administration of several drugs; this effect is known as induction. When phenobarbital was administered as a typical inducer, the hydroxylation of diazepam was enhanced in mice and rats but not in guinea pigs, whereas the N-demethylation was increased in guinea pigs and rats but not in mice (see Table 2) [7]. In mice, but not in rats or guinea pigs, there was formation of oxazepam usually not present in noninduced animals. However, there were two limitations to this study. First, phenobarbital was given to the three animal species at the same dose level and this may not have been optimal for enzyme induction in all of the species considered. Second, the relative increase of hydroxylation or N-demethylation induced by phenobarbital was assessed only by the formation of these metabolites. In control animals the disappearance of diazepam was completely accounted for by the formation of metabolites, whereas in phenobarbital treated animals the metabolites assayed represented only a fraction of the diazepam metabolized. We considered the possibility that diazepam metabolites might have been bound to constituents of the endoplasmic reticulum, which was proliferating under phenobarbital treatment [8-10], but this hypothesis was not supported by our attempts to recover more diazepam by changing the conditions of the extraction. It may be, instead, that minor routes of diazepam metabolism become important under the action of phenobarbital. It may also be that in induced animals the diazepam metabolites are

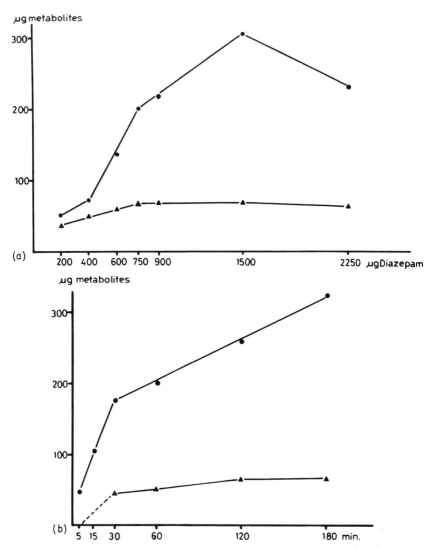

FIG. 3. (a) Effect of substrate concentration on diazepam metabolism by mouse liver microsomes. Incubation time, 3 h; amount of microsomes used, 24 mg of protein corresponding to 1 g of fresh liver. (●) N-Methyloxazepam; (▲) N-desmethyldiazepam.
(b) Time course of diazepam metabolism by mouse liver microsomes. Substrate concentration, 1500 μg; amount of microsomes used, 24 mg of protein corresponding to 1 g of fresh liver. (●) N-Methyloxazepam; (▲) N-desmethyldiazepam. (c) Effect of increasing amount of mouse liver microsomes on diazepam metabolism. Incubation time, 3 h; substrate concentration, 750 μg. (●) N-Methyloxazepam; (▲) N-desmethyldiazepam.

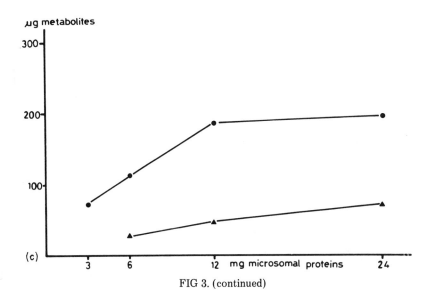

FIG 3. (continued)

further metabolized to form compounds not measured by our assay conditions. In this respect, it is interesting that Schwartz and Postma [4] recently observed that phenobarbital treatment in rats caused an increase of more polar non-ether-extractable diazepam metabolites. These investigators [4] also studied the effect of phenobarbital in dogs (9000 × g liver fraction) and concluded that the formation of N-desmethyldiazepam and oxazepam were increased about 1- and 3.6-fold, respectively, without any change in the formation of N-methyloxazepam.

The hydroxylation of the phenyl group at C-5 of the benzodiazepine ring, reported in vivo [11, 12], was not observed in vitro either in normal or in phenobarbital-induced rats [4].

Although diazepam, as well as other benzodiazepines, is frequently combined in therapy with a large number of drugs, very little is known about the effect of other drugs on the metabolism of diazepam. The classical inhibitor SKF 525-A completely blocked the mouse liver microsomal metabolism of diazepam. Preliminary work indicates that some tricyclic antidepressant drugs, such as amitriptyline and nortriptyline, must be considered inhibitors of diazepam metabolism in vitro when mouse liver microsomes are utilized (unpublished results).

It is important to emphasize that the presence of diazepam may inhibit the further biotransformation of diazepam metabolites. In

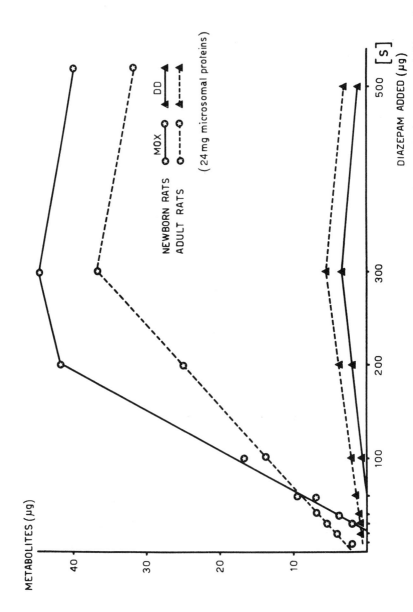

FIG. 4. Diazepam metabolism by liver microsomes of newborn (——) and adult (--) rats. Amount of microsomes used, 24 mg of protein; incubation time, 10 min. N-Methyloxazepam (MOX) formed; N-desmethyldiazepam (DD) formed.

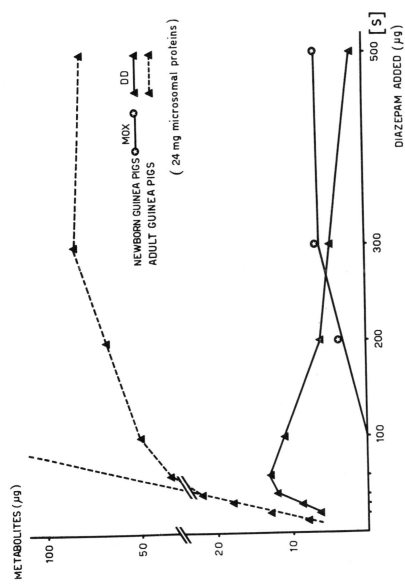

FIG. 5. Diazepam metabolism by liver microsomes of newborn (——) and adult (---) guinea pigs. Amount of microsomes used, 24 mg of protein; incubation time, 10 min. N-Methyloxazepam (MOX) formed; N-desmethyldiazepam (DD) formed.

TABLE 2

Effect of Phenobarbital on the Formation of Diazepam Metabolites
in Various Animal Species[a]

Benzodiazepine added in vitro	Species	N-demethylated metabolite		C_3-hydroxylated metabolite	
		N	I	N	I
Diazepam	mouse	22	18	16	26
	rat	2.2	8	14	34
	guinea pig	51	75	0	0
N-Desmethyldiazepam	mouse	–	–	3	7
	rat	–	–	4	12
	guinea pig	–	–	0	0
N-Methyloxazepam	mouse	37	15	–	–
	rat	4	5	–	–
	guinea pig	7	46	–	–

[a]Values are expressed as percent of the measured metabolite relative to the concentration of the added benzodiazepine (100 μg). It should be noted that under normal conditions (N) the metabolites accounted almost entirely for the disappearance of the benzodiazepine, whereas in phenobarbital-induced animals (I) a large part of the benzodiazepine was metabolized through pathways different from those considered here.

fact, the conversion of N-methyloxazepam to oxazepam by mouse liver microsomes is competitively inhibited by the presence of diazepam (5).

III. N-DESMETHYLDIAZEPAM

N-Desmethyldiazepam is 7-chloro-1,3-dihydro-5-phenyl-2H-1, 4-benzodiazepin-2-one) (II). This metabolite of diazepam, which shares the pharmacological properties of the parent compound [13, 14], undergoes in vitro a process of hydroxylation at position 3 to form oxazepam (IV). This step was shown to occur in isolated perfused rat liver [3], dog liver homogenate (9000 × g) [4], and dog liver microsomes [5]. The extent of hydroxylation varied with the animal species, as summarized in Table 3. Rat and mouse liver microsomes can hydroxylate at C-3, whereas the microsomes of guinea pigs, rabbits, and cats are unable to do so. It should be added, however, that in the case of rabbits and cats 20% and 16% of N-desmethyldiazepam, respectively, was metabolized to form unknown compounds. This was not the case with the guinea pigs, where N-desmethyldiazepam added to liver microsomes was recovered quan-

TABLE 3

C_3-Hydroxylation of N-Desmethyldiazepam and N_1-Demethylation
of N-Methyloxazepam by Liver Microsomal Enzymes

Species	Percent hydroxylation of N-desmethyldiazepam	Percent N-demethylation of N-methyloxazepam
Mouse	2.6	37
Rat	4.5	4
Guinea pig	n.m.	7
Rabbit	trace	2
Cat	trace	1.5
Dog	trace	trace

titatively [6]. It should be emphasized, however, that the in vivo
administration of N-desmethyldiazepam to guinea pigs results in the
excretion of oxazepam glucuronide in the bile [15].

The formation of oxazepam from N-desmethyldiazepam was not
evident when liver microsomes were obtained from newborn rats or
guinea pigs (unpublished results). When liver microsomes were obtained from animals pretreated with phenobarbital, the hydroxylation
of N-desmethyldiazepam was enhanced about 3-fold in rats and in
mice but it was not detectable in guinea pigs (see Table 2). Again,
as for diazepam, the metabolism of N-desmethyldiazepam by liver
microsomes of phenobarbital-induced rats and mice yielded unknown
metabolites in addition to oxazepam, indicating the operation of other
metabolic pathways. Liver homogenates (9000 × g) obtained from
dogs treated with phenobarbital converted N-desmethyldiazepam to
oxazepam to the extent of about 15% (4).

IV. N-METHYLOXAZEPAM

N-Methyloxazepam is 7-chloro-1,3-dihydro-3-hydroxy-1-methyl-
5-phenyl-2H-1,4-benzodiazepin-2-one (III). This pharmacologically
active metabolite [14, 16, 17] is transformed in vitro by N_1-demethyl-
ation to oxazepam. This step was shown with isolated perfused liver
[3], liver homogenates [4], and liver microsomes [5]. Table 3 summarizes the quantitative differences observed with various animal
species. Mouse liver microsomes showed the highest capacity to
demethylate N-methyloxazepam, followed by guinea pigs, rats, rabbits, and cats. In the case of guinea pigs and cats, N-methyloxazepam was also metabolized by an unknown pathway. The demethylation
of N-methyloxazepam in mice followed the Michaelis-Menten equation,
giving an apparent K_m of 3.92×10^{-5} M and a V_{max} of 8.10 nM/mg

liver microsomal protein per 10 min [5]. The demethylation of N-methyloxazepam occurred to the extent of only 1% in newborn rats and guinea pigs (unpublished results).

After phenobarbital treatment, N-demethylation was increased severalfold in rat and guinea pig liver microsomes, whereas in mice it was considerably decreased as judged from the formation of oxazepam (see Table 2). However, it should be emphasized that the disappearance of N-methyloxazepam in these three animal species was only partly accounted for by the formation of oxazepam. Liver homogenates of dogs pretreated with phenobarbital converted N-methyloxazepam to the extent of about 14% [4].

V. OXAZEPAM

Oxazepam is 7-chloro-1,3-dihydro-3-hydroxy-5-phenyl-2H-1,4-benzodiazepin-2-one (IV). This metabolite of diazepam was not metabolized further in vitro by liver microsomal enzymes obtained from rats, mice [5], guinea pigs [6], rabbits, and cats. Also, the liver microsomal enzymes from newborn rats and guinea pigs and from adult rats, guinea pigs, and mice pretreated with phenobarbital were unable to metabolize oxazepam. However, oxazepam glucuronide was produced by incubating the drug with added UDPGA plus suitable liver homogenate preparations, guinea pig microsomes, or dog liver microsomes [18]. The conjugate was separated by column chromatography on DEAE-52 [19]. Studies on the kinetics of the enzyme reaction are in progress. The formation of oxazepam glucuronide was evident when enzymes were prepared from livers and kidneys of pregnant rats and guinea pigs but the reaction proceeded to a lesser extent when enzymes were prepared from the same tissues of the fetuses [18]. This metabolic pathway was observed also with isolated dog liver in situ and oxazepam glucuronide was found in the liver and in the bile [20]. The rabbit placenta is apparently able to form oxazepam glucuronide in vitro, a conversion that is increased by a previous treatment with phenobarbital but not with oxazepam [21]. However, it should be noted that the technique employed to study oxazepam glucuronide formation [22] should not be regarded as a specific method, because it utilized a strong acid hydrolysis and measurement of the aminobenzophenone resulting from this hydrolysis. Although it is established that oxazepam glucuronide is formed in vivo [22], a more critical experimental approach must be devised in order to study the problem in vitro on a quantitative basis.

VI. o-CHLORO DERIVATIVES OF DIAZEPAM METABOLITES

o-Chloro-N-desmethyldiazepam (V) is converted by liver micro-somes of mice into o-chlorooxazepam (VI) (lorazepam) at about the same rate as N-desmethyldiazepam. As oxazepam, o-chlorooxazepam is not metabolized by rat or mouse liver microsomal enzymes in vitro.

VII. N-OXIDE DERIVATIVES OF DIAZEPAM (VII) AND N-DESMETHYLDIAZEPAM (VIII)

Diazepam N_4-oxide (VII) and N_1-desmethyldiazepam N_4-oxide (VIII) did not yield either N-methyloxazepam or oxazepam upon incubation with mouse liver microsomes. Sadèe et al. [23] also evaluated the possibility that diazepam N_4-oxide may be an intermediate in the con-version of diazepam to 3-hydroxydiazepam. However, they were un-able to detect the N_4-oxide in incubation mixtures of diazepam and rat liver microsomes and their enzyme preparation failed to con-vert diazepam N_4-oxide to N-methyloxazepam. Therefore, the mech-anism for the 3-hydroxylation of benzodiazepines remains unknown.

VIII. MEDAZEPAM

Medazepam is 7-chloro-1,3-dihydro-1-methyl-5-phenyl-1H-benzo-diazepine (IX). This compound is metabolized by a relatively com-plex pattern according to Fig. 2. The work in vitro is relatively scanty. Schwartz and Carbone [24], using rat liver homogenate (9000 × g), found that 12-14% of the substrate was present as diaze-pam after 30-60 min of incubation. Other metabolites identified were N-demethyl medazepam (X), N-desmethyldiazepam, and N-methyl-oxazepam.

In dog liver homogenate, the metabolism of medazepam involves the formation of N-desmethyl medazepam and an intermediate, which is transformed nonenzymically into 2-amino-5-chlorobenzophenone (see Fig. 6). There was the formation of about 4% N-desmethyldiaze-pam but of only traces of diazepam and oxazepam (24).

IX. FLURAZEPAM

Flurazepam is 7-chloro-1-(2-diethylaminoethyl)-5-(2-fluorophenyl)-1,3-dihydro-2H-1,4-benzodiazepin-2-one (XI). This compound was

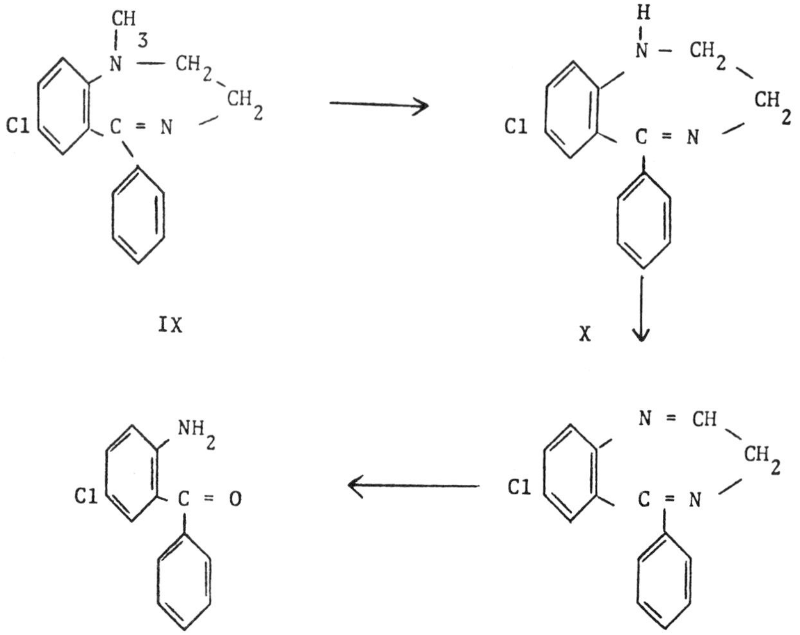

FIG. 6. Metabolism of medazepam to form 2-amino-5-chlorobenzophenone. Other routes of medazepam metabolism are shown in Fig. 2.

extensively metabolized in vitro by rat and dog liver homogenates (9000 × g). The major metabolite produced was identified as the N-deethylated derivative (XII) but small amounts of N-dealkyl derivative (XIII) were also found (M.A. Schwartz, personal communication).

X. PRAZEPAM

Prazepam is 7-chloro-1(cyclopropylmethyl)-1,3-dihydro-5-phenyl-2H-1,4-benzodiazepin-2-one (XIV). This benzodiazepine was studied in vitro by Viau et al. [25], using liver supernatant fractions (9000 × g) obtained from mice, rats and dogs. Table 4 summarizes the findings obtained. It is evident that prazepam is mostly dealkylated to form N-desmethyldiazepam. Presumably, this compound was then hydroxylated by rat and dog microsomes, but not by mouse microsomes, to form oxazepam. Prazepam metabolism was also investigated with liver homogenates obtained from humans at different times postmortem. The results were quite variable but the only metabolic pathway observed was N-dealkylation. When animals were pretreated with phenobarbital, dealkylation increased twofold for mice but not for rats. In both species, there was a marked increase in the formation of oxazepam. It is a difficult to establish whether the oxazepam was formed from an increased hydroxylation of N-desalkylprazepam (N-desmethyldiazepam) or from the dealkylation of 3-hydroxypraze-pam. However, the first hypothesis seems more probable. Oddly, the opposite sequence, namely C_3-hydroxylation followed by dealkylation, is clearly favored in vivo, at least in man [26, 27]. As noted for diazepam, prazepam is not hydroxylated in vitro at C-4', although the reaction proceeds in the intact dog [28].

TABLE 4

Percentage of Metabolites Formed from Prazepam
Incubated in Vitro with Liver Homogenates

Metabolite formed	Mouse	Rat	Dog
Hydroxyprazepam	n.m.[a]	n.m.	n.m.
N-desalkylprazepam[b]	38	79	72
Oxazepam	n.m.	10	10
Unknown	–	8	8

[a]n.m.-not measurable.
[b]Synonymous with N-desmethyldiazepam.

XI. CHLORDIAZEPOXIDE

Chlordiazepoxide is 7-chloro-2-methylamino-5-phenyl-3H-1,4-benzodiazepin-4-oxide (XV). Figure 7 represents the known metabolic pathway of chlordiazepoxide, the prototype of the benzodiazepines utilized in therapy. According to the work of Schwartz and Postma [29], rat liver slices, rat liver homogenates, and the 9000 × g supernatant fraction of liver from a dog pretreated with phenobarbital were able to N-demethylate chlordiazepoxide with the formation of N-demethyl chlordiazepoxide (XVI). This step, representing about 20% of the added chlordiazepoxide, was increased by about threefold when the rats were pretreated with phenobarbital. Livers from these animals also metabolized chlordiazepoxide to form unknown polar metabolites that are not ether extractable. Also, the administration of DDT (dichlorodiphenyl trichloroethane) at a daily intake of 0.04-0.10 mg in the food resulted in a significant increase of the metabolism of chlordiazepoxide by rat liver homogenates (9000 × g). This increased metabolism of chlordiazepoxide lasted for at least 12 weeks after withdrawal of DDT. This study also indicated sex differences;

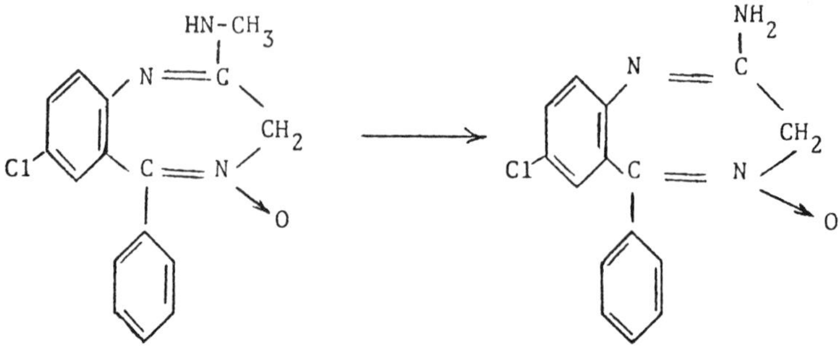

(XV)   (XVI)

FIG. 7. In vitro metabolic pathway of chlordiazepoxide.

livers obtained from male rats metabolized chlordiazepoxide at a
faster rate than those of females [30].

XII. NITRAZEPAM

Nitrazepam is 1,3-dihydro-7-nitro-5-phenyl-2H-1,4-benzodiazepin-
2-one (XVII). The metabolic products identified after the administration of nitrazepam to mammals are presented in Fig. 8. Particular
attention was devoted to the reduction of the nitro group in vitro to
produce the 7-amino derivative (XVIII). When rat liver enzymes
were used under anaerobic conditions, it was found that this metabolite was formed either by purified microsomal preparations or by
the 9000 × g supernatant fractions. Phenobarbital treatment enhanced
the reduction of nitrazepam by only about 20% [31].

Nitrazepam reduction also occurs to a minor extent in other tissues. The activity calculated per milligram of protein was 100 for
liver, 12 for kidney, 11 for heart, 7 for lung, 6 for skeletal muscle,
3 for spleen, and 0 for brain [31]. The kinetic constants of nitrazepam reduction by liver of various animal species indicated a similar
affinity of nitrazepam for mammalian nitro reductase (see Table 5).

Reduction of nitrazepam by rat liver (9000 × g supernatant fraction) was inhibited noncompetitively, as expected, by SKF 525-A [29]
and by KCN [31]. With the last compound, the K_i was calculated to
be 3.3×10^{-4} M. At 10^{-3} M, imipramine and diazepam inhibited the
reduction by 50%, whereas ascorbic acid, chlorpromazine, cysteine,
and EDTA were ineffective [32]. The formation of the 7-amino derivative of nitrazepam was also demonstrated by utilizing the iso-

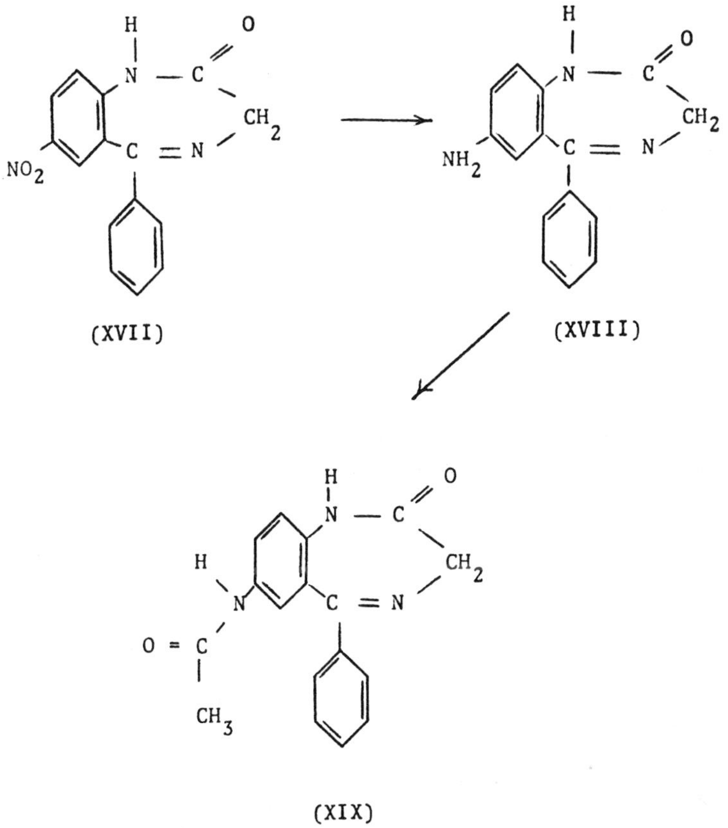

(XVII)   (XVIII)

(XIX)

FIG. 8. Pathway of nitrazepam metabolism in vitro.

TABLE 5

Kinetic Constants for the Reduction of Nitrazepam by the
Liver of Various Animal Species under Anaerobic Conditions

Animal species	K_m $(10^{-4} M)$	V_{max} (μmoles/hr/g/liver)
Mouse	1.88	1.58
Rat	2.30	1.32
Guinea pig	1.74	1.41
Rabbit	3.54	1.22

lated perfused livers of mice, rats, guinea pigs, and rabbits. Furthermore, the 7-amino derivative was acetylated under similar experimental conditions by rats, guinea pigs, and rabbits but not by mice. The two metabolites represented only a minor fraction of the converted nitrazepam, however.

The 7-acetylamino derivative (XIX) remained unchanged when perfused through isolated rat liver. Similar perfusion through mouse liver resulted in the rapid deacetylation of (XIX). The latter observation may well explain the lack of 7-acetylamino derivative accumulation in isolated perfused mouse liver [33].

Acknowledgments

The experimental work performed by the authors was supported by the NIH (contract No. PH 43-67-83 and grant No. 1 P01 GMI 8376-01 PTR). The authors are grateful for the editorial assistance provided by Dr. Jean-Paul Viau, Department of Drug Metabolism, Warner-Lambert Research Institute.

REFERENCES

[1] M. A. Schwartz, B. A. Koechlin, E. Postma, S. Palmer and G. Krol, *J. Pharmacol. Exp. Ther.*, 149, 423 (1965).

[2] H. W. Ruelius, J. M. Lee, and H. E. Alburn, *Arch. Biochem. Biophys.*, 111, 376 (1965).

[3] J. Květina, F. Marcucci, and R. Fanelli, *J. Pharm. Pharmacol.*, 20, 807 (1968).

[4] M. A. Schwartz and E. Postma, *Biochem. Pharmacol*, 17, 2443 (1968).

[5] F. Marcucci, R. Fanelli, E. Mussini, and S. Garattini, *Eu. J. Pharmacol.*, 7, 307 (1969).

[6] E. Mussini, F. Marcucci, R. Fanelli, and S. Garattini, *Biochem. Pharmacol.*, 20, 2529 (1971).

[7] F. Marcucci, R. Fanelli, E. Mussini, and S. Garattini, *Biochem. Pharmacol.*, 19, 1771 (1970).

[8] H. Remmer and H. J. Merker, *Ann. N. Y. Acad. Sci.*, 123, 79 (1965).

[9] L. Shuster and H. Jick, *J. Biol. Chem.*, 241, 5361 (1966).

[10] J. L. Holtzman and J. R. Gillette, *J. Biol. Chem.*, 243, 3020 (1968).

[11] G. Jommi, P. Manitto, and M. A. Silanos, *Arch. Biochem. Biophys.*, 108, 334 (1964).

[12] M. A. Schwartz, P. Bommer, and F. M. Vane, *Arch. Biochem. Biophys.*, 121, 508 (1967).

[13] L. O. Randall, C. L. Scheckel, and R. F. Banziger, *Curr. Ther. Res.*, 7, 590 (1965).

[14] F. Marcucci, A. Guaitani, J. Květina, E. Mussini, and S. Garattini, *Eu. J. Pharmacol.*, 4, 467 (1968).

[15] P. Bertagni, F. Marcucci, E. Mussini, and S. Garattini, *J. Pharm. Sci.*, in press.

[16] S. C. Bell, R. J. McCaully, C. Gochman, S. J. Childress and M. I. Gluckman, *J. Med. Chem.*, 11, 457 (1968).

[17] L. H. Sternbach, L. O. Randall, R. Banziger and H. Lehr, in *Drugs affecting the Central Nervous System* (A. Burger, ed.), M. Dekker, New York, 1968, p. 237.

[18] F. Berté, G. Benzi, L. Manzo, and S. Hokari, *Arch. Intern. Pharmacodyn.*, 173, 377 (1968).

[19] E. Mussini, F. Marcucci, L. Airoldi, R. Fanelli, P. L. Morselli, and S. Garattini, to be published.

[20] E. Arrigoni, L. Manzo, and P. Sarti, *Boll. Soc. Ital. Biol. Sper.*, 43, 859 (1967).

[21] F. Berté, L. Manzo, M. De Bernardi, and G. Banzi, *Arch. Intern. Pharmacodyn.*, 182, 182 (1969).

[22] S. S. Walkenstein, R. Wiser, C. H. Gudmundsen, H. B. Kimmel, and R. A. Corradino, *J. Pharm. Sci.*, 53, 1181 (1964).

[23] W. Sadèe, W. Garland, and N. Castagnoli, Jr., *J. Med. Chem.*, 14, 643 (1971).

[24] M. A. Schwartz and J. J. Carbone, *Biochem. Pharmacol.*, 19, 343 (1970).

[25] J. P. Viau, J. E. Epps and F. J. Di Carlo, *Biochem. Pharmacol.*, 21, 563 (1972).

[26] F. J. Di Carlo, J.-P. Viau, and J. E. Epps, *Clin. Pharmacol. Ther.*, 11, 890 (1970).

[27] F. J. Di Carlo, J.-P. Viau, J. E. Epps, and L. J. Haynes, *Ann. N.Y. Acad. Sci.*, 179, 487 (1971).

[28] F. J. Di Carlo and J.-P. Viau, *J. Pharm. Sci.*, 59, 322 (1970).

[29] M. A. Schwartz and E. Postma, *J. Pharm. Sci.*, 55, 1358 (1966).

[30] P. R. Datta and M. J. Nelson, *Toxicol. Appl. Pharmacol.*, 13, 346 (1968).

[31] I. Bartosěk, E. Mussini, and S. Garattini, *Biochem. Pharmacol.*, 18, 2263 (1969).

[32] I. Bartosěk, E. Mussini, C. Saronio, and S. Garattini, *Eu. J. Pharmacol.*, 11, 249 (1970).

[33] I. Bartosěk, J. Květina, A. Guaitani, and S. Garattini, *Eu. J. Pharmacol.*, 11, 378 (1970).

Author Index

Numbers in parentheses are reference numbers and indicate that an author's work is referred to although his name is not cited in the text. Underlined numbers give the page on which the complete reference is listed.

L

Subject Index

A